D1068274

Individuality

SUNY Series in Philosophy
Robert Cummings Neville, Editor

Individuality

An Essay on the Foundations of Metaphysics

Jorge J. E. Gracia

State University of New York Press

Published by
State University of New York Press, Albany

© 1988 State University of New York

For information, address State University of New York
Press, State University Plaza, Albany, N.Y., 12246

Library of Congress Cataloging-in-Publication Data

Gracia, Jorge J. E.
　Individuality: an essay on the foundations of
metaphysics.

　(SUNY series in philosophy)
　Bibliography: p.
　Includes indexes.
　1. Individuality.　2. Individuation.　I. Title.
II. Series.
BD450.G677　　1988　　　　111　　　87-10766
ISBN 0-88706-626-7
ISBN 0-88706-627-5 (pbk.)

10 9 8 7 6 5 4 3 2 1

To Leticia and Clarisa, the best examples of
individuals I know

"... true learning must not be content with ideas ... but must discover things in their individual truth."

Umberto Eco, *The Name of the Rose,* 4th day.

"Sólo los individuos existen, si es que existe alguien."

Jorge Luis Borges, "El otro."

Contents

2. Extension of 'Individuality'

3. Ontological Status of Individuality

4. Principle of Individuation

5. Discernibility of Individuals

6. Reference to Individuals: Proper Names, Definite Descriptions, and Indexicals

Assessment: A Metaphysics of Individuality

Preface

From the very beginning, practitioners of philosophy have been concerned with what are usually known as "universals," notions such as "whiteness," "justice," and "beauty." One has only to recall Plato and Aristotle to understand the depth to which Western thinkers have gone to investigate these notions. In the Middle Ages, in particular, the so called "problem of universals" occupied not only a very central position in theological discussions, but actually consumed a substantial portion of the efforts of medieval authors directed toward philosophical inquiry. In our century, also, there has been a well-marked interest in issues of this sort, especially within what is generally referred to as "the analytic tradition," although in other traditions similar issues have also been raised and discussed. Indeed, it seems as if almost every major philosopher has had something to say about universals, and studies on the subject abound. On the other hand, in contrast with all this philosophical interest in and activity related to universals, discussions of the correlative notion of individuality are not abundant and, by comparison with the number and depth of treatments on universals, may even be considered scarce. There are very few works not just in contemporary thought but in the history of philosophy as a whole, that attempt a systematic account of this notion. One of the most important is Francisco Suárez's *Metaphysical Disputation* V, where he raises several of the major problems involved in individuality. Another is P. F. Strawson's *Individuals,* which takes a markedly post-Kantian approach to it and, in spite of many brilliant insights, leaves much ground to be covered. There are, of course, many partial, and often fragmentary, studies of individuality, but very few attempt to present, let alone succeed in presenting, an overall view of it. As a result of the absence of a systematic, yet clear, propaedeutic, and comprehensive approach to individuality, terminological and conceptual imprecisions and confusions, sometimes of an elementary sort, abound in the literature.

The relative neglect of individuality in the philosophical literature is surprising, for surely individuality seems to be one of the most fundamental and brute facts of our experience. No ordinary person doubts that she sees, touches, tastes, and experiences individuals. I see Leticia and Clarisa; I touch this or that rough surface; I taste the artichoke from the large jar or the piece of candy you gave me; and I experience my memories. It is true that there are some debatable cases. The question of whether I experience the black color of my hair and other qualities and features of things as individual is not as clear as the experience I have of the individuality of the things mentioned earlier. But that is a matter to be discussed later. For the moment, it is sufficient to draw attention to the ubiquity of individuality in our experience and that seems clear from the examples cited and from the many others that could be added.

Under these conditions, then, what could be the reason for the relative neglect of individuality in the philosophical literature? The answer to this question is not easy and, moreover, it is beyond the purpose and boundaries of this essay. My primary concern here is with individuality and not with the reasons why philosophers have neglected it; an inquiry into that problem would have a historical rather than a systematic character, and the present investigation aims to be systematic. All the same, I would like to suggest briefly two reasons which may have had something to do with this strange phenomenon. The first is historical: the enormous influence that Greek thought, and particularly Platonic philosophy, has exerted over Western philosophy. That Greek philosophy in general and Plato's thought in particular have been at the basis of most Western philosophical speculation is generally acknowledged. Gilson went so far as to point out that behind every flowering of philosophy in the West, there is always a return to the Greeks. And it is not less true that the Greeks, and especially Plato, were concerned primarily with the universal and not the individual. In their search for universal laws, rules, and concepts that would ground values and take morality and knowledge out of the realm of subjectivity and relativism, they tended to neglect the individual, relegating it often to the realm of appearance. Unfortunately, along with most of their discoveries, the West also inherited this disregard for individuality.

The second reason is methodological. For in contrast with the universal, which adjusts easily to our mode of knowing, the individual seems to defy analysis. Knowledge of every sort is expressed in universal terms and concepts, and as such it can be easily grasped. But the individual seems always to be beyond our grasp insofar as it cannot be reduced to the universal notions in terms of which we understand the world. To deal, then, with the individual and to try to explain the nature of individuality, its status and causes, is indeed a difficult task that some philosophers have explicitly regarded as impossible. In short, it is difficult for philosophers, who generally see as their aim the understanding of the world, to deal with something that seems to defy understanding.

Both history and the nature of the subject matter, then, have worked against the investigation of individuality, but the need to undertake the task should be quite evident. First, there is the scarcity of materials, and, second, there is individuality's fundamental presence in our experience, two facts already mentioned. In this study, therefore, I propose to take the first step toward remedying this situation. My primary intention is to present a systematic overview of the main philosophical issues connected with individuality and to erase some of the most common terminological and conceptual confusions associated with it that pervade the philosophical literature. I do not claim, therefore, to provide a complete and definitive treatment of this difficult subject, whence the use of the term 'essay' in the title. Anyone who knows anything about philosophy should realize that there are few, if indeed there are any, definitive treatments of any subject in it. As to completeness, the issues discussed here are too complex and numerous to be able to deal with all of them during a lifetime, let alone in the limited amount of time and space I can devote to them. My attempt, then, is only propaedeutic, provisional, and of limited scope, although the approach is systematic and aims at an overview. This approach will hopefully result in a general understanding of problems and possibly in some insight into their solutions. At no time do I try to provide an account of the development of the issues as they appear in the history of philosophy as a whole or in any of its periods in particular, even though I provide frequent references to historical figures who have proposed opinions relevant to the subject matter of this study, and I hope my efforts will contribute to the understanding of such development. Most references to historical and contemporary figures have been consigned to footnotes, however, where interested readers can find the pertinent information and that those readers with an exclusively systematic interest may ignore. Readers who know my historical work will be surprised at the methodology I have followed in this book, but they should not be; for the value I place on the study of the history of philosophy is only that it helps in the understanding of philosophy itself, not in the mere gathering of historical facts. Indeed, I believe that no philosopher *qua* philosopher can think otherwise, unless he or she is confused about the nature of the discipline.

Apart from this primary intention, however, the book also serves a secondary aim. I hope to shake the philosophical community a bit and make it realize that most of the accepted wisdom concerning individuality is challengeable and rests in many cases on dubious arguments and contestable intuitions. The reader should expect the view I present here to depart in fundamental ways from the most accepted current philosophical opinions concerning individuality. In some cases, I do accept and defend the current wisdom, but in most instances I have found that my sympathies and arguments take me to old rejected views and, in a few cases, even to positions that do not seem to have had any clear defenders in the history of philosophy.

In addition to many specific views presented at the appropriate places, there is one general thesis that I defend in this study. According to this thesis, many of the confusions present in the philosophical literature which deals with individuality are the result of more basic confusions among the various metaphysical, epistemic, semantic, and logical dimensions of the problems they involve, and particularly among six fundamental questions that I distinguish in the book. These questions have to do with the intension of 'individuality', its extension, the ontological status of individuality, the principle of individuation, and the discernibility of and reference to individuals. I try to show that when the distinctions among the various dimensions of the problem and among the six fundamental questions are acknowledged and preserved, many of the traditional difficulties associated with individuality disappear and/or can be solved.

Some of these questions and their solutions are, as stated, epistemic, logical, and semantic and would normally be excluded from a purely metaphysical discussion. However, since one of my claims is that failure to distinguish epistemic, logical, metaphysical, and semantic issues is precisely the source of much confusion and difficulty in philosophical discussions of individuality, and many of the semantic, epistemic, and logical issues are closely tied to purely metaphysical ones, I see no alternative but to discuss some semantic, epistemic, and logical questions in what is intended primarily as a book of metaphysics. For similar reasons I have generally preferred the use of the term 'metaphysics' to the now common 'ontology'. The latter seems too restrictive, while the former has been used traditionally to cover a wide range of issues. As we shall see, only Chapters 2 and 3 of this book deal with purely ontological subject matter.

One more point about the nature of this book and what it purports to do. A quarter of a century ago, P. F. Strawson published the volume to which reference has already been made and which has since then become a contemporary philosophical classic. In its Introduction, he made a distinction between what he called "descriptive" and "revisionary" metaphysics. Descriptive metaphysics, in his own words, "is content to describe the actual structure of our thought about the world, [while] revisionary metaphysics is concerned to produce a better structure."[1] Examples of descriptive metaphysicians, according to Strawson, are Aristotle and Kant; examples of revisionary metaphysicians are Descartes, Leibniz, and Berkeley. In both cases, as is clear from Strawson's characterization, the task involves our thought structures, the way we think about the world rather than the way the world is. This approach to metaphysics is the result of a long process of change, which may have begun as early as Suárez, or perhaps even earlier, and which had its foremost defender in Kant. It was Kant who did most to do away with traditional metaphysics. What I mean by "traditional metaphysics" is what, contrary to Strawson's belief, philosophers like Aristotle practiced. They did not for a moment believe that they were describing the way we think about the world; in their view, they were attempting to describe the way the world is. And this may or may not involve revision of the way we think about it. Whether revision is required or not is immaterial to the main task, which is to find out the way the world is. For this reason, I like to call this brand of metaphysics "realistic," and I like to oppose it to "phenomenalistic" metaphysics.[2] The latter, being concerned only with conceptual frameworks, includes both descriptive and revisionary metaphysics. It is a mistake, I believe, to do away with either the realistic or phenomenalistic approaches to metaphysics. Both have advantages and disadvantages and in many ways complement each other, as the history of the discipline amply illustrates. Those who object to the practice of realistic metaphysics usually do so because they are doubtful about our ability to get at the "thing in itself," that is, at the way things are independently of the way they are given or appear in experience. How can we know, so the argument goes, what things are in themselves, since they are always presented to us in an experiential context which seems itself to have certain structural coordinates? It would seem, then, that the only task we can effectively carry out is to describe that experience and its content without bothering with the way things are outside of it and, therefore, that we should be concerned only with them as objects actually or potentially given in experience.

The appeal of this Kantian argument has been so great that the initial steps of the two major philosophical methodologies introduced in the twentieth century, phenomenology and the analysis of language, have been guided by it to a large extent. Thus, phenomenology has devoted a considerable part of its efforts to the description of experience, and analysis has had as its principal aim the investigation of the language we use in expressing it. In both cases, they have been engaged, in a way, "in the description and investigation of the way we think about the world," rather than in the investigation of the world, thinking that the latter still is best left to science.

What practitoners of these methodologies do not seem to realize, however, is that experience or thought (depending on the way one wishes to refer to it), and the language used to express it are also part of the world. Therefore, if we were to take seriously the above objection concerning the indescribability and/or unknowability of chairs and colors, or, to put it more precisely, of chairs and colors in themselves, independently of experience and/or language, we would have to conclude that the difficulty applies also to our thoughts, experiences, and language. For there is really no fundamental difference, insofar as they are considered objects of knowledge, between a chair in itself and a thought in itself, or between a color in itself and a linguistic expression in itself. Of course, those who disagree with this assessment will no doubt point out that, indeed, there is a difference between things-in-themselves and phenomena, since we have privileged access to phenomena. One's thought has a special status with respect to oneself, quite different from the status of a chair, for example. But again this objection misses the point that in order to consider phenomena, as we in fact do with things themselves, such phenomena must be objectified and, therefore, acquire, if not all, at least some of the more fundamental characteristics of things in themselves. As objects of thought, they cease to have the privileged status required to differentiate them from so called "things in themselves."

Naturally, if the point made is sound, then those who find fault with realistic metaphysics will have to find fault as well with phenomenalistic metaphysics, since clearly phenomenalistic metaphysics is nothing but a part of realistic metaphysics, concerned with thought, experience, and language. And they must, if they wish to be consistent, reject it and remain silent—as any good skeptic ought to do—or give up their fight against realistic metaphysics and embrace it. Those metaphysicians who understand this situation, on the other hand, will try to exploit the advantages and avoid the disadvantages of both realistic and phenomenalistic metaphysics. I have followed the latter procedure in this book. Rather than choosing *a priori* between one of these two approaches, I have tried to keep both in mind, although taking care to distinguish them as I proceed.

This does not mean that I believe that I have said here the last word on the topic of this book or even that I have grasped some immutable and absolute truths about the world and about the way we think and speak about it. No, philosophy has not proven to be a discipline that easily achieves such results. Its conclusions, as its history clearly indicates, are always subject to revision, clarification, and change. When writing a book of philosophy, then, the most one can hope for is to produce a tentative theoretical model which will contribute to further discussion of the issues. And that is how the present book should be interpreted: as a provisional model intended to contribute to the development of the discussion of philosophical issues of some importance. If the book succeeds in calling attention to the issues it discusses and opens new areas of philosophical exploration, and even controversy, I shall be satisfied, for it will have achieved its fundamental aim. That does not mean, of course, that I am not convinced that what I say and propose here is true. It only means that I know quite well the limitations of the human mind and particularly of my own.

Now, apart from these considerations, it should become clear in the pages that follow that, regardless of the approach one adopts with respect to individuality, whether one favors a realistic approach, a phenomenalistic one, or a combination of both, individuality presents the philosopher with various problems that require clarification and explanation.[3] The approach one uses will no doubt affect their analysis and solution, but it certainly does not remove the need to address them systematically.

Before we leave the distinction between "realistic" and "phenomenalistic" metaphysics, I should add that the use of the term 'revisionary' by Strawson has recently come under fire from another quarter. One of Strawson's critics has suggested that it is unfortunate because it suggests that what is sought to be revised in metaphysics is "our ordinary ways of thinking about the world," and that of course is not what is being revised at all.[4] What is under revision, if anything, are other philosophical views.

I must say that I am generally sympathetic with this sort of Moorean objection—what puzzled Moore was not ordinary language, but rather what philosophers had to say.[5] After all, the technical talk about "bare particulars" we shall discuss later is meant to replace the equally technical terminology of "bundles of qualities" and not the ordinary talk about "individuals" and "things." In this, therefore, I am in agreement with this criticism. But one can go too far in this direction, for philosophy surely should not be banned to a dusty corner of the academic edifice. Philosophy should and does have something to add to the ordinary view of the world. And if this is the case, then one must be willing to accept that it may perhaps lead to changes (i.e., revisions) of that view. This does not mean, of course, that we will ever abandon ordinary language in favor of technical jargon. Indeed, it is unlikely that we will cease to speak about individuals and begin to use the terms 'bare particular' or 'perfect particular' to refer to them. But philosophical views do have consequences in the ordinary world by changing the way people think about certain things, their values, and their goals. There are clear cases in the history of the world where ideas have had a substantial impact not only in the thinking of people but in their actions. Hence, although it is good to view the revisions that may come out of philosophical speculation and dialogue as primarily affecting philosophical views, it may also apply in more general and subtle ways to the more ordinary ways of thinking about the world.

As far as the methodology used in the book is concerned, I believe it will become quite evident to the readers as they go along, and, therefore, I need not dwell on it at length at this point. I would like to add two sets of observations, however: one about the general approach I have followed and the other about the way I have gone about substantiating my views. Concerning the general approach I have followed, I should mention three points: First, this book is not just an exposition of a view; it contains arguments in support of the views it proposes and against those it opposes. Not all the arguments have the same weight, and some are even rejected. I have selected some arguments because they seem to me to be sound, others because they seem to be persuasive within the parameters I use, and still others because they are frequently found in the literature. In some cases, the last ones have been found to be weak and/or inconclusive, but nonetheless helpful in the dialectical progression of the book. Second, I have tried to avoid technical jargon in order to make the book accessible to a wider audience of philosophers and intellectuals than those narrowly interested in individuality and/or metaphysics. In particular, I have tried to keep my observations close to ordinary experience by providing ample examples as we proceed. Many philosophers have the opinion that for philosophical writing to be profound, it must be obscure. I do not share that view. Philosophy can be clear and easy to understand and still be enlightening. Obscurity, mystery, unresolved ambiguity, and the mystical insight are the prerogatives of religion and perhaps literature, not philosophy. Finally, I hope it is clear to the reader that this book does not fall into any philosophical tradition narrowly understood. I have no manifesto to defend and, therefore, engage in no partisan or ideological controversy. I have no interest in being identified with analytic or continental philosophy, neo-scholasticism, or any contemporary or traditional school of thought. This book is rooted solely in the dialectic of the problems it discusses and the authors who seem to me have had something worthwhile to say about it.

With respect to the way I have sought to substantiate my views and reject those that I oppose, one thing needs to be made clear, namely, that I have given consideration to a variety of factors. Some of these are experiential. True, philosophy consists to a large extent in analyses rather than in descriptions of experiences and, therefore, one should not expect to be able to verify philosophical statements as one would verify many ordinary language statements. Nonetheless, since all philosophy arises from and begins with experience, experience needs to play an important role in the development and control of philosophy. No philosophical view should be allowed to contradict our most basic intuitions unless there is overwhelming evidence to the contrary. Science generally seems to follow this procedure, and there is no reason why philosophy should be permitted to do otherwise. The function of philosophy is to relate the elements presented in experience and to give a cogent interpretation of them, not to reject and/or contradict them. Hence, when arguing against other views and in favor of my own, I have frequently referred to ordinary experience, pointing out how it seems to confirm or undermine a particular philosophical statement. In addition to experience, I have also taken into account the need for consistency. Although some philosophers show a rather scandalous disregard for consistency, I take seriously any contradiction, whether in my own views or those of others. Finally, following the Principle of Parsimony, I have always favored positions that are economical as long as they are effective. The arguments that I propose, then, both against certain views and in favor of others, involve experience, consistency, and economy, and it is the interplay of those three that leads me to the dialectical adoption of the views I propose here.

The book is divided into an introductory section, six chapters, and a conclusion. The introductory section, entitled "Prolegomena," distinguishes the problems to be discussed and clarifies and establishes the terminology which will be used throughout. The conclusion, entitled "Assessment," summarizes the basic theses defended in the book and briefly identifies some areas that need further work. The six chapters found between the Prolegomena and the Assessment constitute the core of the study and discuss substantive issues. Each addresses a different problem involved in the questions mentioned earlier: the intension of 'individuality', its extension, the ontological status of individuality, the principle of individuation, the discernibility of individuals, and the problem of reference. Following the Assessment, I have added an index of authors and another of subjects and terms for the convenience of the reader. The bibliography includes the works used in the preparation of this book or read as background materials; it has no claim to completeness in the subject matter. Its purpose is primarily to facilitate the location of references made in footnotes and to encourage further study of the literature.

Most of the material and views defended in this book are being presented for the first time here. However, in some instances I have used material which has already appeared in print, although in every case substantial modifications have been introduced. The distinction among the six issues presented in this book was first introduced in a rough and abbreviated form in the first chapter of *Introduction to the Problem of Individuation in the Early Middle Ages* (Philosophia Verlag and The Catholic University of America, 1984) and in an even more incipient form in the Introduction to *Suárez on Individuation* (Marquette University Press, 1982). I have also used other materials from these books and in some instances have borrowed entire paragraphs, although in most cases they have been substantially modified. Moreover, part of Chapter 1 of this book appeared as an article entitled "Individual as Instances" in *Review of Metaphysics* (1983) (a Spanish version appeared simultaneously in *Revista Latinoamericana de Filosofía*); a Spanish version of part of the Prolegomena appeared in *Revista Latinoamericana de Filosofía* (1985) with the title "Problemas filosóficos de la individualidad," and an early version of Chapter 3 was published in *Manuscrito* (1986) with the title "The Ontological Status of Individuality." I am grateful to the following for their permission to use the mentioned materials: Hans Burkhardt, editor-in-chief of the Analytica Series of Philosophia Verlag; James Robb, editor of the Series of Medieval Studies and Texts in Translation of Marquette University Press; as well as Jude Dougherty, Ezequiel de Olaso, and Marcelo Dascal, respective editors of the cited journals.

Finally, I would like to close by expressing my appreciation to those of my colleagues, students, and friends who encouraged me to take on this task and to many others who read drafts of the manuscript and made many valuable suggestions and corrections. To mention all of them would be a formidable task, but I must make special note of at least five of my colleagues who devoted considerable time to reading all or parts of the manuscript and who made numerous suggestions for improvements and brought to my attention many errors in historical judgments, weaknesses in the arguments, and infelicities of style. To Kenneth Barber, Peter Hare, John Kearns, Zeno Swijtink, and William Rapaport I will be forever indebted. And I am also grateful to Kah-Kyung Cho for bringing to my attention several relevant bibliographical sources with which I was unacquainted. Finally, I would also like to thank Marie Fleischauer for typing and correcting the many drafts of the manuscript of this book. Without her expert help and good-natured cooperation, the production of the manuscript would have been very difficult.

Jorge J. E. Gracia
1986

Prolegomena:
Nomenclature and Problems

Perhaps the most immediate intuition that human beings have about the world is that it is composed of individuals. Cats, dogs, Socrates, Leticia, the two-by-four-inch white card I have in front of me, and my own self and memories seem to be clearly individual. Yet, when we reflect about this intuition and try to analyze its various aspects, we run into serious conceptual difficulties. Some of these arise because of the variety of questions that come up. How can we explain, for example, what individuality is? What are its causes or principles? What are the criteria of identification of individuals? Is individuality a feature of things, such as their color and length, or is it to be interpreted as something else? Which things are individual and which are not? Indeed, are there any things that are not individual? How do and can we refer to individuals? Do the linguistic terms that we use to refer to individuals have meaning in addition to reference, and how is their reference related to their meaning? If these questions were not enough, some of their answers also produce difficulties and raise further questions. For example, if one were to accept that individuality is to be interpreted basically as some kind of difference or distinction among things, how does one then explain the sameness among them? If to be an individual is to be different, how is it that Leticia is like Clarisa in so many ways, even though both of them are individual? On the other hand, if one adopts the view that to be individual, one must have a determinate and unique set of characteristics, how can the philosopher explain the individual's capacity to endure through time and change? And, if to

1

be individual is to have something unique that nothing else has, what kind of thing is it?

Considering the puzzling nature of these questions, it is not surprising that philosophers have been attracted to the philosophical issues surrounding individuality. In the Middle Ages, in particular, for reasons that I have discussed elsewhere, individuality was regarded as a fundamental subject of philosophical discussion.[1] Most major thinkers of the age and even many minor ones devoted questions, disputations, and entire treatises to the discussion of individuality.[2] And in our century, there has been likewise some interest in problems related to individuality, although the contemporary understanding both of the problems and of the debate that took place among medieval authors has not been by any means satisfactory.[3] A cursory reading of the literature is sufficient to find discussions filled with elementary misunderstandings of a historical as well as a conceptual nature.

These misunderstandings are most often the result of two factors. The first is the terminological confusion prevailing in the literature. Terms such as 'nature', 'individual', 'individuation', 'individuality', 'singularity', 'particularity', ' numerical unity', 'individual unity', and a score of others are frequently used, but their meanings seldom clearly explained. A second and no less important source of misunderstanding is the mistaken assumption that there is only one important philosophical problem related to individuality. For some this is the problem of finding the cause or principle of individuation; for others it is the problem of finding acceptable criteria to discern individuals. In either case, they omit consideration of some of the most basic issues involved in individuality.

It is appropriate, then, that a systematic investigation of individuality should begin by clarifying some of the terminology used in connection with it and by identifying what are to be regarded as the most basic philosophical questions surrounding it. This is the purpose of these brief introductory remarks. Accordingly, we shall begin with a section on nomenclature to be followed by one devoted to problems.

Nomenclature

It is common experience that when we reflect about an individual, concrete thing such as a man, or a tree,[4] one may consider what the thing has or seems to have in common with other things, or alternatively, what is peculiar or unique to the thing under consideration. What is common to the thing and other actual or possible things is usually referred to by philosophers who use traditional terminology as the thing's "nature." In turn, the nature can be specific, generic, or accidental. A specific nature, for example "human being," consists of what is called the "specific difference" and the "genus." The specific difference in turn consists of the common features that are part of what distinguishes the thing from a larger group of actual or possible things and at the same time makes it part of a smaller group of things, the members of which can be distinguished only as individuals. One such specific feature frequently cited, for example, may be the capacity to reason in human beings. The features that all members of several species have in common and that make them part of a larger group, which is in turn distinct from other larger groups, constitute the genus or generic nature. Both generic and specific features are said to be "essential" to the thing; that is, it is thought that they are necessary conditions of its kind and existence. Human beings, for example, are not human and cannot exist as human beings if they do not have the capacity to reason (specific feature) and a body (generic feature). The features that a thing may or may not have, and thus are not necessary conditions for its kind or existence, are usually called "accidental." The brown color of a person's hair, for example, is said to be an accidental nature to her.[5]

On the other hand, what sets a thing apart from all others, including those things that belong to the same group, is generally regarded as constituting the thing's "individuality." In both the case of the nature and of the individuality, the mental content involved when one thinks about them seems to be different. Take, for example, the case of Clarisa. A consideration of her specific nature focuses on her humanity, that is, the group of features, such as the capacity to reason, the capacity to laugh, etc., that make her human and that render her both indistinguishable from other human beings and distinguishable from nonhuman beings such as dogs, trees, and rocks. A consideration of Clarisa's individuality, on the other hand, will focus only on what separates Clarisa from Leticia and any other individual being, whether human or not. In the first case, we think of how and in what respects Clarisa is the same as others, in the second of how and in what respects Clarisa is unique. The cluster of philosophical issues concerned with natures go by the generic name, "the problem of universals"; those concerned with individuality are usually gathered under the term "the problem of individuation." The latter group of issues is the subject of our inquiry. Before we turn to the discussion of the various issues involved in individuality, two points need to be made. First, we need to point out that the standard way of understanding the nature and individuality of things described above has its limitations. The understanding of "nature" as what is common, in fact or in principle, to many and thus as explaining similarity or sameness among things is standard in the literature and will serve the purpose of getting the discusison started, but later we will discover that this way of interpreting this term is not appropriate. More importantly, the understanding of "individuality" as what explains a thing's distinction or difference from other things is likewise common in

3

philosophical discourse and will serve us for the moment, although, as it will become clear in Chapter 1, it will have to be discarded or at least modified if one wishes to maintain a certain conceptual precision.

Second, some further terminological clarifications are in order. We may begin with the term 'individuation'. This term is used in the literature for two things: (1) the process by which something becomes individual, and (2) individuality itself, that is, the character of being individual. In terms of the morphology and etymology of the term, 'individuation' should be used only in sense (1). 'Individuation' like ' universalization', 'externalization', and many other substantives related to verbs, refers primarily to the process that is carried out by the action expressed by the verb. The universalization of a principle, such as the moral imperative "Do unto others as you would have them do unto you," is the process by which the principle is extended beyond a particular case to all pertinent cases.

It is true, however, that in some cases, such as "coloration" and "restoration," both the process and the feature brought about by the action designated by the verb are called by the same name. This may be the result of morphological analogy. In cases like that of "restoration," the language has no term by which to refer to the feature; in cases like that of "coloration," the term is used to designate the feature in question in spite of the fact that the language has a term for it (i.e., 'color'). These cases can be considered exceptions to what is a fairly general rule. Therefore, 'individuation' can be taken to refer primarily to the process whereby something universal (say human being) becomes individual (for example, Leticia or Clarisa) and that is how we shall use the term here. To fail to use it in this restricted way carries with it the danger of confusion. Thus, if one were searching, for example, for the principle of individuation without distinguishing clearly between individuality and individuation, the answer would be in doubt, since in one case one would be searching for the principles or causes of what is, let us say for the same of simplicity, a feature of a thing, and in another for the principle or cause of a process. This may seem a rather pedestrian and obvious distinction difficult to miss, but there are many examples in the history of philosophy of those who failed to make it and/or maintain it.

The confusion between individuality and individuation is often the result of the fact that, as with 'restoration' in English, in some languages there is only one term for both individuality and individuation. In English the most frequently used term to refer to the character of an individual as such (that is (2)) is 'individuality', although there are also other terms in use to which reference shall be made shortly. It should be noted, however, that the ambiguity between meanings (1) and (2) of 'individuation' is already present in Latin, where the medieval term *'individuatio'* took on both meanings, even though there was also a separate Latin term for individuality: *'individualitas'*.

'*Individualitas*', however, is not frequently encountered, and its use is recorded primarily in later Medieval Latin. Neither '*individuatio*' nor '*individualitas*' are recorded in Classical Latin, but '*individuitas*' is used by Tertullian in the *Monogamia*.[6]

Closely related to the terms 'individuation' and 'individuality' is the term 'individual' (from the Latin, *individuum*). In the Middle Ages, this term acquired a peculiar meaning that still lingers in some contemporary discussions. In addition to its standard reference to individual things, such as a man (e.g., Socrates) or a quality (e.g., the particular black color of Socrates' beard, for those who hold that qualities are individual), 'individual' was also used interchangeably with 'individuality' to refer to what individuates a thing. It is in this sense that one finds the term used in late scholastic expressions such as "the cause of the individual is matter" or "an individual is really distinct from the nature";[7] for strictly speaking, the causes of an individual according to medieval scholastics were the four Aristotelian causes and not just matter or form or, as Thomas Aquinas would put it, matter designated by quantity.[8] What is meant by 'individual' in this context is individuality: "The cause of the individuality [of an individual] is matter." Similarly, one cannot properly speak of the nature of an individual as really distinct from it. For the specific nature of an individual, for example, is presumably the group of characteristics that the individual has in common with other members of the species to which the individual belongs, and, therefore, the individual cannot be considered to be really distinct from it. If it were, the individual would not really be a member of the species: A human being (for example, Leticia) would not be human.

This use of 'individual', therefore, is confusing, although frequently found in medieval and even in some contemporary sources, as already mentioned. In order to avoid confusion, individuality should be distinguished from the individual. The former is that whereby an individual is considered to be such. The individual is contrasted to the universal, while individuality is contrasted to universality.[9] Universality, on the other hand, is that whereby a nature (specific, generic, or accidental) has its special character as universal. How these terms are explained or defined (using 'definition' here in a nominal sense) is a separate problem, which shall be discussed shortly. At present, my concern is only to explain how they are related. 'Individual', therefore, has at least two uses in this context, although in order to avoid confusion I shall use it primarily to refer to individuals themselves rather than to their character as individuals. Again, as in the case of individuality versus individuation, a lack of clarification between individual and individuality can be unfortunate. For the causes or principles of an individual, say Peter, can be very different from the causes or principles of Peter's individuality. In one case, the question concerns everything involved in the individual considered as a whole, while in

5

the other, it concerns only what brings about the individual's individuality.

Going back to what characterizes an individual as such, it is clear from the literature that there are several terms used for this purpose in addition to 'individuality'. One of the most common is the term 'individual unity'. It was introduced by scholastics in the Middle Ages because they thought, following Aristotle, that to be an individual was to be *one* and, consequently, that individuality was a kind of unity.[10]

Often individual unity is also called "numerical" and contrasted with "specific" unity. The latter is the unity that a species has in spite of the potential or actual plurality of its members. Those who use this terminology say that the members of a species may be said to be one in the sense that they are of the same kind or belong to the same type; for example, both Leticia and Clarisa are one specifically in that both of them are human in the same sense. Numerical unity, on the contrary, is the separate unity of each individual within the species. It is called "numerical" because to be an individual is to be *one* thing, that is, to be a unit or, as it is frequently but somewhat awkwardly put in medieval discussions of this issue, to be *a number*.[11] Each individual is "a number" in the sense that it is "one" in the group, "one" among many. For example, Paul is *one* man, Peter is another *one*, and Socrates is still another *one*. Each is *one*, and all together they form the total collection of men, which is composed of all these units or numbers: the first one, the second one, the third one, and so on. And this contrasts with being *a kind* of thing, such as a *man* or a *dog*. Strictly speaking, however, one may distinguish *intensionally* between numerical and individual unity even though the adjectives 'individual' and 'numerical' can be, and in fact are, interchanged since they have the same extension, namely, they both refer to the unity proper to individuals. Thus, the unity of the individual is called "numerical," as already stated, because the individual is one. It is called "individual," because the individual is not divisible; that is, according to a traditional point of view that will be discussed in Chapter 2, it is not divisible into individual units of its own specific kind.

From all of this, it should be obvious that the use of this kind of terminology takes for granted some very definite views about individuality, which may or may not be correct. Indeed, the contrast between being "one in number" and being "one in kind" suggests that individuality involves no differences of kind, and this is a view not universally accepted by those who deal with individuality, as we shall see below. Therefore, since the more neutral the language, the better we will be able to determine the value of conflicting theories concerning individuality later on, I shall ignore this terminology, and unless otherwise stated I shall refer to what characterizes an individual as such with the term 'individuality'. One last proviso: As already stated earlier, the use of this terminology should not be taken as implying a commitment to a particular view of the ontological status of individuality, but as a convenient, ordinary way of speaking about individuality that leaves open ontological questions about its ultimate status. This will be discussed in Chapter 3.

Also in use are the terms 'singularity' and 'particularity'. But there is widespread disagreement as to whether their intensions and/or extensions coincide with each other and with that of 'individuality'. Some ancient and medieval authors seem to have regarded these terms as coextensional, but not necessarily as cointensional with 'individuality'. Some thought particularity had to do with an individual's "participation in" or "partaking of" an idea, nature, or universal. In this sense, the individual was considered to be a part of something else, or to partake of it. Thus, Socrates, for example, is particular in that he participates in man, which itself is not particular.[12] The case with singularity is similar. An individual was called "singular," or was said to have singularity, because it is not many ('plural' or 'multiple' are also used). A singular tree, unlike the species "tree," is not a plurality or collection but a "single" thing. Boethius seems to have been one of the first to have made an explicit distinction between particularity and individuality.[13] Individuality, for him, appears to be a metaphysical feature that he interpreted as an individual quality belonging to things (Socrateity in Socrates, for example), while particularity was a logical feature of terms used to refer only to one thing ('Socrates', for example). In the latter part of the early Middle Ages, there was an attempt to interpret singularity as something more basic than individuality. Gilbert of Poitiers claimed, for example, that singularity extends to everything, interpreting it as a kind of unity, with universal extension, while he regarded individuality as having only limited extension.[14] More recently, there have also been attempts to draw distinctions among some of these notions. The best known case is Strawson's various distinctions in *Individuals*.[15] But most authors from the modern period onwards seem to regard the distinction between singularity, particularity, and individuality as a verbal matter.[16] Given present purposes, however, it is not necessary for us to dwell on these distinctions. Our aim is the clarification of the general terminology related to individuality and the most immediate philosophical problems related to it, and in order to do that we do not need to discuss the notions of singularity and/or particularity at this point. For the moment, then, I shall regard the terms 'singularity', 'particularity', and 'individuality' as coextensive and cointensive until further is said about them at the end of Chapter 1.

Apart from the terms already mentioned, there are several others that are commonly used and are in need of clarification. Particularly important are the terms and expressions 'diversity', 'distinction', 'difference' (and their compounds when 'numerical' is added to them), 'identity', and 'indiscernibility', among others. But I shall leave consideration of these until later, since the discussion of their meanings fits well in subsequent chapters.

Having given a brief discussion of the philosophical terminology used in the discussions of individuality in the philosophical literature, and having identified some of the most basic terms that shall be put to use in the pages that follow, it is time to turn to the second source of misunderstanding concerning individuality: the lack of proper distinction among the various philosophical problems connected with it.

Problems

Contrary to a widespread misconception according to which there are only one or two legitimate philosophical problems involved in individuality, there are at least six different basic problems involved in it. These have to do with the intension of 'individuality', its extension, the ontological status of individuality in the individual and its relation to the individual's nature, the cause or principle of individuation, the discernibility of individuals, and finally, the linguistic means of reference to individuals.

The first of these issues is logical, since it is concerned with the intension of 'individuality' and its distinction from other notions; it involves defining and conceptually clarifying the notion of individual. The second, third and fourth issues are metaphysical. They concern the description of reality—how far individuality extends and its status and foundation in things. The fifth issue is epistemological, for it has to do with determining criteria for the discernibility of individuals. Finally, the sixth issue is semantic, since it deals with the linguistic ways by which we refer to individuals. From this it should be obvious that one's views about the nature of philosophy will determine to a large extent the sorts of issues that one will address with respect to individuality. The logical positivist, for example, will find little to say about the metaphysical issues surrounding individuality and will concentrate on the logical, epistemological, and semantic issues. On the other hand, the traditional metaphysician will pay little attention to the first, fifth, and sixth issues and will concentrate on the second, third, and fourth, which are metaphysical in character and, to his mind, at the basis of all other matters.

Most of these six issues have attracted the attention at one time or another of those philosophers who have been concerned with individuality, but, as should be expected, they seldom deal with all of them and most frequently discuss one to the exclusion of the others. Indeed, it is the fourth and fifth that are most often regarded as fundamental. For example, of these two, the fourth is the favorite choice of scholars concerned with the philosophical history of individuality in the Middle Ages. And in fact, there is some reason for this attitude, for it is true that, up to the fourteenth century, one seldom finds a careful and clear distinction between these six different issues, and much more effort is put into the solution of the fourth than into the solution of all the others taken together. Yet, it is also evident that, as the age progresses, they become more and more defined until we find late scholastics, such as Suárez, carefully separating some of them in their discussions. Some of the issues never became quite independent in treatment. For example, the first one, concerned with the intension of 'individuality', was usually discussed in the context of the second, the extension of 'individuality'. And even this last one does not become the subject of separate investigation until late in the Middle Ages. Only the ontological status of individuality, its principle, and the discernibility of the individual were generally discussed separately in the latter part of the period.[17] In nonhistorical contemporary treatments of the problem, it is the last two issues, concerned with the discernibility of individuals and with reference, that are discussed most often. This is no doubt the result of the predominantly epistemic and semantic approach that characterizes modern philosophy.

Let us turn, then, to the six basic philosophical issues involved in individuality and briefly formulate them one by one.

Intension of 'Individuality'

Above I gave a very general description of individuality as what characterizes an individual as individual, leaving open the determination both of the reference of the 'what' and the meaning of the verb 'to characterize' in this context. This was done in order not to prejudge the issue of the ontological status of individuality. We should leave open, therefore, the possibility that individuality may be characterized ontologically as a feature, a relation, a substance, or something else, until this matter is discussed in Chapter 3. Now, the question involved in the intension of 'individuality' is quite a different issue, since it asks about what it is to be individual as opposed to something else. Some philosophers have referred to this problem as the problem concerned with "the nature of individuality." But this nomenclature is confusing, for, if a nature is considered, as is generally taken in traditional circles, as a feature, simple or complex, which is or may be common to several things, then individuality cannot be a nature since the individuality of something should not be shared by anything else. This pen's individuality is not and cannot be the individuality of this paper on which I am writing, and vice versa, at least not *prima facie*. There have been philosophers, like Duns Scotus, for example, who have maintained that individuality is indeed a nature of sorts;[18] but that is a position for which arguments have to be provided. As already stated at the starting point of any investigation, we must try to avoid language that prejudges the issue. Moreover, there are other problems with

9

the term 'nature', since it is frequently reserved for the features that natural kinds (for example, human being, dog) as opposed to artificial ones (for example, table, painting) share, and individuality, whatever it may be, does not seem to be a natural kind, as "dog" and "human being" are. Therefore, instead of speaking of "the nature of individuality," I shall speak of its "intension," in order to avoid unnecessary complications. The use of the term 'intension' with an abstract noun such as 'individuality' is, of course, unorthodox, but I believe it best brings out the kind of issue with which I am concerned at this point without making some undesirable *prima facie* ontological commitments involved in the use of other terminology.

Now, to determine the intension of 'individuality' is nothing other than to determine the necessary and sufficient conditions of individuality or, in still another way, to determine the necessary and sufficient conditions for something to be individual. The intension of 'human being', to use a standard analysis of this term is "rational animal," where 'rational' stands for "capacity to reason." This means that anything that is a human being is an animal capable of reasoning and that any animal capable of reasoning is a human being. To look for necessary and sufficient conditions is, of course, a very traditional sort of investigation and one that most philosophers have considered fundamental to the philosophical enterprise. Therefore, there should be nothing puzzling about trying to apply this procedure to individuality. In contemporary philosophy, however, two fundamental challenges have been made to this procedure. One comes from the theory of language developed by Wittgenstein and his disciples; the other is based on the recent theories of reference proposed by Kripke and others.[19]

The first challenge goes something like this: Common terms, such as 'human being', 'game', and 'red', do not function as traditionally thought. In the past, it was believed that one could identify features common to all and only those things which were called by the same term. But that does not seem to be so, since in most cases no single feature or collection of features can be identified which is common to those things referred to by the same term, except for the fact that we refer to them with that term. The term 'game' for example, is used to refer to such things as baseball, basketball, chess, canasta, poker, etc.; but it does not seem to be possible to identify one or more features common to all these. There are features common to canasta and poker (both are played with cards) and to baseball and basketball (both are played with a ball), but no feature can be found that is common to all things called "games" except that they are called "games."[20] If this analysis were correct in general, the search for the list of necessary and sufficient conditions of games would be futile, as would the search for the necessary and sufficient conditions of individuality; for, although all things that are called "individual" would have some kind of family resemblance, not every one of them would share even one feature that could be identified as both the necessary and sufficient condition of all of them.

There are various answers that one may give to this objection. One would be to accept the conclusion at which it arrives, but nonetheless argue that it is always useful to engage in the search for necessary and sufficient conditions. Indeed, although one may not, or could not, find any, the enterprise helps to clarify concepts and establish relations which would otherwise escape us. This kind of analysis, therefore, has a therapeutic effect, beneficial to those who engage in it, even if it does not serve the function that traditionally it was thought to serve.

One may also want to respond that even if one cannot identify a single necessary and sufficient condition of individuality, it may still be possible to establish ranges of conditions. That is, although it may not be possible to say that all games share the use of a ball, or some such feature, one could say that all games share "the use of a ball, and/or the use of cards, and/or . . . and so on," and that the range of these possibilities is not unlimited. Moreover, one could add that it is these, always limited, common ranges that constitute necessary and sufficient conditions of games, rather than particular features.[21]

On the other hand, one may want to argue further that, although there may not be identifiable features which are both necessary and sufficient conditions of things called by the same name, there are some features whose absence is at least necessary, even though not a sufficient condition for something to be called such and such. For example, the absence of extreme pain could be regarded as a precondition of happiness. Indeed, it would be hard to believe that anyone could argue that one could be happy under extreme pain. One may perhaps be content and resigned to suffering, but extreme pain, like extreme misery as Aristotle noted well, prevents us from being happy.

All these strategies accept to some extent the premise on which the objection is based: that no necessary and sufficient conditions of things called by the same term are to be found. But there are also other alternatives which challenge this premise. For example, one could argue that the theory of family resemblance is based on the wrong paradigm—the example of games. The paradigm is wrong because games are human creations and, therefore, artificial, rather than natural kinds; and this is what originates problems for the identification of their necessary and sufficient conditions, something which may not be necessarily the case with natural kinds. The particular definitional problems of artificial kinds to which natural kinds are not subject arise from the fact that they are human creations, and human creations tend to be subject to historical and social pressures and changes that make reflection about them difficult and generally imprecise. While the notion of "female cat" can be easily determined by criteria such as capacity (in principle) to become pregnant, the case of "chair," for example, is not easily determined. Of course,

11

ultimately the validity of this argument rests not only on being able to show how natural kinds are different from artificial ones, but also on how one can come up with necessary and sufficient conditions for natural kinds. I am not going to argue in the present context that this is so. I shall let stand the examples I have given as illustrations that this argument seems to go in the right direction. But I shall show in Chapter 1 that, indeed, one can come up with at least one such necessary and sufficient condition of individuality, and that seems sufficient to answer the objection based on the Wittgensteinian theory of language.

The second objection is based, as already stated, on a more recent theory of reference developed by various philosophers.[22] According to this theory, it does not seem possible to identify the necessary and sufficient conditions of the application of common terms because in these terms, as in the case of proper names, the reference determines the meaning, rather than the other way around, as the classical theory of reference derived from Frege maintained. That 'game' is used to refer to chess, basketball, baseball, etc., determines the features associated with the things to which the term refers, and not vice versa. Things are, as it were, baptized or given their name at a determined time, and it is because they are called what they are called that 'game' means what it does. Accordingly, intensional analyses may be useful, but cannot be taken to be complete and/or strict, if by that one means that they identify all the necessary and sufficient conditions for the application of a term. A tiger will still be a tiger if it loses its stripes, its teeth, or if it changes color, since "possession of most of these properties [usually associated with tigers] need not be a necessary condition for membership in the kind, nor need it be a sufficient condition."[23] And thus, even having those features will not insure that we do have a tiger. It is true that certain features may serve to fix the referent of a term in some circumstances, but the fact that those features are always contingent and, therefore, could possibly not be associated with the things with which they are usually associated means that they cannot be regarded as both necessary and sufficient conditions of the application of the term. Cats might turn out not to be animals at all, but something else.[24] Likewise, 'individual' will refer to individuals, not because there is a set of identifiable criteria, on the basis of which the term is applied, which may reflect a complete and strict set of characteristics common to all things we call "individuals," but because its reference has been fixed from the start by a baptismal ceremony. And we cannot be sure that the features we associate with individuality, whatever they may be, are the necessary and sufficient conditions that something be individual. Something having those features could turn out not to be individual at all, and something not having them could turn out to be so.[25]

The answer to this objection could proceed in three ways: (1) It could assail the new theory of reference on which it rests, a task which would be marginal to the intensional issue, but one that will be discussed in Chapter 6; (2) it could show that the theory of reference in question does not imply the objection, but, whether this is the case or not, we would nonetheless have to answer the objection and, therefore, to proceed in this way would unnecessarily complicate matters; and (3) it could try to show that indeed necessary and sufficient conditions of individuality can be identified. The most sensible and economical procedure is (3) and, therefore, the issue can be allowed to rest until we get to Chapter 1, where a solution to it is offered.

Extension of 'Individuality'

Next to the intension of 'individuality', one of the most basic philosophical issues involved in individuality is extensional. For even if it is granted that individuality is a viable concept, the question as to whether there are any entities that are individual and, if there are any, which are and which are not are still questions that must be answered. Again, as with 'intension', the use of 'extension' in connection with 'individuality' is unorthodox, but I hope it will not be confusing and its advantages will become clear as we proceed.

Now, if it is true that intension determines extension, as most philosophers used to believe and some still do, then our analysis of the intension of 'individuality' will play a major role in solving the extensional issue.[26] On the other hand, if extension determines intension, as the recent theory of reference discussed above suggests, then it is what we say in the chapter on the extension of 'individuality' that will determine to a large extent what is said in the chapter on the intension of 'individuality'.

Apart from whether, strictly speaking, the relation of the intension and extension of terms is one or the other, it would seem that an intensional analysis is always important and useful for finding a solution to the extensional problem. Indeed, it is a matter of common sense that often before one tries to determine whether a term applies to an object, one attempts to establish what the term means; for, how do I find out if something is a human being, for example, if I do not know what it is to be a human being? Of course, one could argue that no scientific and/or complete notion of human being is necessary to identify and recognize human beings. But certainly having *some* notion of what human being is can be very useful, even if not necessary, for identification and particularly for determining the sorts of things that are human.

Moreover, it may be argued that, even if intension does not determine extension completely, an intensional analysis does determine to some extent the extensional one. If the capacity to reason is regarded as a necessary feature of being human, for example, then it is clear that snails, air, and light cannot be classified as human. Likewise, if one were to accept the view that spatio-temporal duration is a necessary condition of individuality, as many philosophers seem to do, then one would have to rule out the existence of atemporal individuals. Under those conditions, God would have to be regarded as lacking individuality, something very puzzling if one were to hold also that individuality and universality are mutually exclusive and exhaustive notions and that God exists. Similarly, if one were to adopt a view of individuality as difference or distinction, it would be difficult to hold also that simple features are individual. It would not make much sense to say, for example, that the white color of this two-by-five inch card is individual (i.e., different from) and that the white color of that two-by-five-inch card is individual (i.e., different from) when there is no determinable difference between them. Finally, in many philosophies the view of individuality that determines the extension of the notion is tacit rather than explicit, and, therefore, it would seem useful for any extensional analysis of individuality to take into account the exact conception of individuality presupposed by the philosophy in question.

These brief remarks are not intended, of course, as a demonstration that, indeed, a clarification of the intension of 'individuality' is a necessary condition of any discussion of its extension. These remarks are meant rather to show that it seems reasonable to hold that it is at least useful to give an intensional analysis of individuality in order to settle and/or understand the extensional issues related to individuals. The admission of a relation between intension and extension, or at least between intensional and extensional analyses, and of the benefit of beginning with the intensional analysis is all that is needed to proceed with our discussion. A refutation of the recent theory of reference already alluded to is by no means required by our procedure.

One more point needs to be noted, however: If the procedure we have outlined is correct, then the determination of the extension of 'individuality' should be rather straightforward, close in some ways to an empirical study. For what needs to be determined is what things fulfill the criteria identified in the intensional analysis and that would seem to involve matching the criteria with the objects of our experience.

Ontological Status of Individuality

A third important philosophical issue concerning individuality has to do with its ontological status in the individual and its relation to what was called earlier the individual's "nature." This issue has not been explicitly discussed to any serious extent in the contemporary literature, or even in the Middle Ages, where individuality was a topic of considerable controversy, it was only in the thirteenth century and after that serious attempts were made to settle this matter.[27] Part of the early medieval neglect of this issue can be attributed to two factors: first and foremost is that individuality never became the object of separate philosophical investigation, thus precluding any systematic effort to deal with all the philosophical problems it might pose. And, second, in turn a partial result of the first, is the rather superficial treatment of individuality given by most authors at this early time. They were often too concerned with universals and theological disputes to give to individuality the attention it required.[28]

The neglect in contemporary philosophical circles, on the other hand, has to be attributed to other factors, since neither of the two mentioned in connection with the medieval period would apply. My conjecture is that the reason for the neglect of this problem is the suspicion that most contemporary philosophers share of metaphysics in general and metaphysical entities in particular. The distrust of metaphysics characterizes not only the analytic movement, with its roots in British empiricism and the Vienna Circle's positivism, but also the type of continental philosophy that springs from Husserl. But this is a historical matter that need not concern us at the moment.

The issue of the ontological status of individuality has been framed in various ways, but, in any way in which it is formulated, it must address two issues. First, it should present an ontological characterization of individuality. This entails its categorization and requires giving answers to questions such as the following: Is individuality a feature of things, as red and rough are, or is it a relation, like fatherhood? Is it real or a mere construct of the mind? If a feature, can it be regarded as a quality? These questions give an idea of the sort of problem involved and explain my prior search for neutral language that would not entail a particular ontological commitment before having had the opportunity to discuss individuality's ontological status. There is also another type of question, however, that must be answered, and this has to do not with the ontological type to which individuality belongs but rather with its relation to the other constituents of an individual. How is individuality to be distinguished from the features (such as color, size, height, etc.) that characterize an individual? As the medievals would ask: Is individuality something really distinct from these features or is it only conceptually distinct from them? And, in either case, how are they related? Are they separable or inseparable?

Clearly, these questions involve a highly metaphysical level of speculation that would normally not appeal to those who adopt a strictly empirical methodology and/or are from the start suspicious of metaphysics. All the same, it seems that a systematic discussion of individuality would do well to take up these questions, even if it ended up by dismissing them as illegitimate. Therefore, I shall deal with them in a separate chapter.

Before I turn to the next issue, one more point needs to be made clear: although related, there are important differences between the intensional issue discussed earlier and an ontological characterization of individuality.

The intensional issue involves a definition and the specification of necessary and sufficient conditions. Take the case of human being, for example. Its traditional definition, "rational animal," specifies the necessary and sufficient conditions of something being human. But that leaves open the question as to the ultimate ontological analysis of human being. Are human beings to be considered substances in the Aristotelian sense of primary substance, or are they to be interpreted as bundles of features, for example? The answer to the intensional question, then, although related to the ontological issue, does not always determine it, nor does an answer to an ontological issue always determine the answer to the intensional issue. G. E. Moore, for example, interpreted the good as a simple quality and yet not for that reason did he think that he had provided a definition of it. Indeed, to the contrary, he thought the good was indefinable.

Principle of Individuation

In addition to the three issues raised thus far, anyone who wishes to present a systematic philosophical discussion of individuality must also deal with another important issue, the so called "problem of individuation." There are two questions which are usually taken up in this context: (1) the identification of the principle or cause of individuation, and (2) the determination of whether this principle, or cause, is the same for all entities. These two questions are exclusively regarded as the fundamental problem of individuation by many, particularly scholars of medieval scholasticism, as already mentioned above. And not without reason, for Aristotelians regard as the fundamental function of science the identification of principles or causes, and, thus, a scientific investigation of individuality within the tradition that follows Aristotle would seem to have to be primarily directed to that end.

The use of the term 'principle' in this context is widespread, and it is particularly understandable in contemporary contexts where the approach is epistemological, as we shall see shortly.[29] But, all the same, it stands in need of some explanation, since it is not always clear. The term 'principle' dates back to the medieval schoolmen who used it to translate Aristotle's *archê*. The Latin term '*principium*' for them meant not only principle but also beginning, source, element, and foundation, as well as cause. Its extension, therefore, was much wider than that of the term 'cause'. Some causes could be regarded as principles, but not all principles were causes. 'Cause' was used by scholastics to refer specifically to physical causes, that is, one of the four types of causes identified by Aristotle as the sources of change (form, matter, the agent, and the end). But principles need not be physical. For example, logical rules, such as the principle of noncontradiction, the rules of inference, and in many cases just the premises of particular demonstrations, were called principles because

16

they were considered the starting points of knowledge. Moreover, scholastics spoke of metaphysical principles as well. Like logical principles, these are not generally separable from the things of which they are principles, but, unlike them and like physical principles, they are really distinct from that of which they are principles. As such, they are neither physical things nor mental concepts, but, nevertheless, they are to be considered as real constituents of things. Among the most commonly accepted metaphysical principles accepted by scholastics were form and matter, essence and existence, and substance and accident.

Those philosophers who reject metaphysics as a proper science, or who at least reject metaphysical principles as constitutive of things, prefer to speak of the "cause" or "causes" of individuation, although often they will use the words 'principle' and 'cause' as synonymous. The reason for their preference is that they reject the possibility of identifying "metaphysical" principles, but they accept without difficulty physical causes. Thus, while it may be legitimate to speak of the causes of individuation for them, it is illegitimate to speak of the metaphysical principles of individuation.

Before we go any further, however, it should be noted that the positions adopted with respect to the issue of the principle or cause of individuation will depend to a large extent on the intensional interpretation of individuality adopted. If, for example, individuality is understood primarily as noninstantiability, as we shall indeed do later, the principle or cause of it must have to do with rendering a thing such that it cannot be instantiated. On the other hand, if individuality is understood as distinction or difference, then it would have to do with a principle or cause that distinguishes a thing from all others. And so on with the other ways of understanding individuality. Moreover, the principles or causes identified in each case may not be the same. One could hold, for example, that the principle of individuation, when individuality is understood as distinction, is the bundle of features which characterize a thing and at the same time hold that the principle of division (i.e., the principle responsible for causing plurality within the species) is one of those features, such as materiality. So it is not by any means clear that when authors speak of "determining the principle of individuation" they are speaking of the same issue and, therefore, that their theories are comparable. Often, however, difficulties arise because they themselves do not clearly understand the notion of individuality and as a result muddle related issues. Most authors, either because they do not distinguish among diversity, division, distinction, and the like, or because they aim to develop parsimonious theories, or, further, because they think all these features are closely related, try to offer theories that would be sufficient to account for several of them at once.

It should be rather obvious that not all ontologies confront the issue of determining the principle or cause of individuation. A view that holds that everything that exists is essentially or *per se* individual faces no such problem. Indeed, if there are no universals or natures, no realities that in some way must undergo a process in order to become individual, the issue of determining the principle or cause of such a process does not arise. It is only within a context where universals or natures are given some status that this question surfaces.

This does not mean, however, that those who take the first approach do not raise the issue. They do. But their purpose is usually to provide a platform for attacks against those who adopt the second approach, where universals are given some status. The two questions involved in individuation, therefore, are germane to what are usually called "realist" or "moderately realist" ontologies. Other types of ontologies have to worry about other matters.

To frame this issue in terms of "principles," or "causes," and "individuation," therefore, introduces certain conceptual parameters that may not be desirable at this point in the inquiry. For it would be preferable to leave open the possibility that even in so called "nominalist ontologies" one could give an account of individuality even though in those ontologies there is no "individuation" as such, since according to them there is no process whereby the universal becomes individual. Moreover, there are problems with the terminology of "principle" and "cause," which spring from the fact that both of these notions have been subjects of much discussion, and yet no clear understanding of them has become generally accepted. For these reasons, it would be advisable to drop the nomenclature of "causes and principles of individuation" and speak instead of "the necessary and sufficient conditions of individuation." This would leave open the question of whether there has or has not been a process of individuation whereby something universal has become individual. It would make room for the view which holds, as we shall see later, that there are no special causes of the individual's individuality beyond the causes of the individual, removing the problems associated with the terms 'principle' and 'cause'; the resulting language would be neutral and thus more appropriate for the investigation.

Note, however, that the use of the newly proposed terminology of necessary and sufficient conditions should not blur the differences between this issue and the first issue discussed, concerned with the intension of 'individuality'. As pointed out earlier, the intensional issue involved the determination of the necessary and sufficient conditions *for something to be individual*, while the issue presently under consideration concerns the necessary and sufficient conditions *for something to become individual*.[30] In the first case, we are looking for the logical conditions of individuality; in the second, for the metaphysical conditions required to bring about individuality. We want to know, to put it differently, what it takes for a universal to become individual. Perhaps an example will clarify this matter. Take the universal "human being."

The necessary and sufficient conditions for something to be human are, following the traditional definition, the capacity to reason and animality and whatever is implied by these. But the necessary and sufficient conditions for "human being" to become an individual human being, say Plato or Socrates, is certainly more than that. Capacity to reason and animality by themselves do not change human being into Plato, since there is more to Plato than the capacity to reason and animality. Likewise, it is one thing to ask for the necessary and sufficient conditions for something to be individual and another to ask for the necessary and sufficient conditions for something to become individual. One way of distinguishing these issues is to refer back to the distinction between individuality and individuation and point out that the necessary and sufficient conditions of one need not be the necessary and sufficient conditions of the other. Now, this does not mean that the necessary and sufficient conditions of individuality and individuation may not be related. After all, the capacity to reason and animality are necessary conditions not only of something being human but also of something becoming a human being, even if some of the necessary conditions of something becoming a human being are not necessary conditions of something being human. Likewise, whatever is a necessary condition of individuality will be a necessary condition of individuation, but not every necessary condition of individuation will be a necessary condition of individuality.

But, then, does this mean that the answer to the question of individuation must coincide with the answer provided by a scientific causal analysis of a thing? In the earlier example, would the principle of individuation of a human being include his parents? No, and the reason is that the parents of a human being are not both necessary and sufficient conditions for the human being to exist. There is no contradiction in the notion of a human being who has no natural parents but was produced in a lab, for example.

We must, therefore, resist the temptation to identify the problem involved in the principle of individuation with the intensional problem discussed earlier and/or with the purely scientific search for causes. The first is a logical issue, the second is an empirical enterprise, and what we are discussing here is a metaphysical problem.

Even with these changes in the formulation of the problem and the stated clarifications, someone may still want to object that this inquiry is too metaphysical and that, in order to bring it in line with contemporary thinking, one would have to frame it differently. The question would have to concern not the necessary and sufficient conditions for something becoming individual, but the necessary and sufficient conditions for our determination of something as individual (an epistemic inquiry). A stronger version of this objection, which I like to call the Epistemic Objection, and versions of which are used frequently when a metaphysical issue surfaces, argues that this metaphysical issue is spurious, dealing as it does with the "thing-in-itself" rather than with things as objects of knowledge and, therefore, this inquiry makes sense only if framed epistemically. For, it objects, how can we expect to discuss individuality when we do not know if we can discern it? Indeed, so the objection goes, the problem of individuation reduces to the problem of individual discernibility, since to solve the problem of individuation is nothing other than to solve the problem of how we are able to discern individuality. In short, individuality and what individuates individuals can be known only as they are related to us as knowers. To ask what individuates something is nothing but to ask what makes us know something as individual. Hence, the principle of individuation is in fact the principle of individual discernibility and turns out to be a criterion for the determination of such discernibility. To ask for more than that is to ask for the impossible and to fall back into the confusions that predated the publication of the *Critique of Pure Reason*.

This is a standard objection against all attempts at raising and solving metaphysical problems, and it is responsible to a great extent for the predominantly epistemological character of most contemporary philosophy. Yet, the objection and the philosophical perspective from which it arises are quite mistaken in trying to reduce metaphysics to epistemology. For questions about things (such as "What is the nature of X?") are reduced in the perspective from which this objection is raised to questions about our knowledge of things (such as "What criteria do we use to identify X?"). But if this reduction were to be allowed, then it would have to be extended also to other sciences besides metaphysics, and we would have to object to the conclusions of physics, chemistry, medicine, and any other discipline of learning. And this does not make sense, not only because these sciences have independent spheres of operation, but also because they are generally effective; that is, in spite of the Epistemic Objection, many of the conclusions reached by these sciences can be confirmed by experience and help to predict future events. To say that we do not know why and how they do is not a failure of those sciences or of the scientists who practice them, but of the epistemologist who has not been able to explain it. For it is not the task of the physicist, for example, to come up with a theory of knowledge that explains the epistemic bases of his conclusions; that is the job of the epistemologist. Likewise, it is not the task of the metaphysician to explain the epistemic principles behind his procedures and theories. The failure to come up with satisfactory epistemological explanations is not a failure of the metaphysician, but of the epistemologist. Under those conditions, the epistemologist has no right to demand that the metaphysician cease investigating metaphysical problems, or to suggest that the problems he investigates are spurious simply because the epistemologist has not been able to come up with a satisfactory explanation, just as it would be absurd for the epistemologist to ask the physicist to stop his research until the epistemologist could come up with an adequate theory of knowledge that would explain it. In short, to reject the question of individuation on the grounds of the Epistemic Objection is unacceptable; it is very much like what Parmenides did with change: Since he was unable to explain it, he rejected it.

But one can also answer the Epistemic Objection by showing that the issue of individuation is different from the issue of discernibility. For if we should succeed in doing so, then it seems that a systematic discussion of individuality must address both, regardless of its success in providing answers to them. Indeed, to rule one out in favor of the other would require substantial argumentation on the part of those who wish to do so, and until that is provided it would seem better to explore them both. Now, since the distinction in question involves both the present issue and the next one on my list, I shall turn to the next issue and discuss this matter in that context.

Discernibility of Individuals

In contrast to the logical and metaphysical issues discussed thus far, the issue of the discernibility of individuals is epistemological. It concerns the way we discern individuals *qua* individual. How do I discern Socrates, for example, as an individual? In traditional terminology, we could ask, What is the cause or principle that allows me to know him as individual? Or, put in a different way, What are the criteria that serve to identify individuals as such?

As in the case of individuation, the answer to these questions will depend to a large extent on how one interprets individuality. For example, if to be an individual has primarily to do with distinction, the issue will concern how we discern the differences between Socrates and some other individual(s). Other conceptions of individuality yield different formulations of the issue and, as a result, different answers. But this matter should be discussed only after an interpretation of individuality has been presented, so I shall leave its examination for Chapter 5. What is pertinent to us at present is that, while the ontological approach to individuation attempts to determine the necessary and sufficient conditions *for something to become individual,* this approach seeks the necessary and sufficient conditions *on the bases of which minds may know something as individual.*[31] That these two problems are different seems obvious for the following reasons. The proposition 'X is an individual because Y' is quite different from the proposition 'I know that X is an individual because Y'. Indeed, 'Y' in the second proposition could easily be substituted by the expression 'Peter told me that it was individual', for example, and still the proposition would make perfectly good sense: 'I know that X is an individual because Peter told me that it was individual'. It is altogether possible to know the individuality of something on the basis of hearsay or authority and, therefore, those could constitute perfectly good reasons, at

21

least sufficient ones, to know that X is individual. But the same substitution in the first proposition yields an absurdity: 'X is an individual because Peter told me that it was individual'. What would this mean? Suppose X is an ape; what causal relation could Peter's statement have with the individuality of an ape? For the ape's existence, individuality, and other ontological features are without a doubt independent of Peter's statement. Peter's statement may be important and relevant, but not to the ape's individuality—rather it is relevant to my understanding of the ape's individuality. Therefore, it could never constitute a sufficient condition of the individuality of X, even if, as noted earlier, it can be a sufficient condition of the knowledge someone has of it.

Similarly, we could point out some factors which, at least in principle, could be taken as sufficient conditions of individuality, but that could under no circumstances be taken as sufficient conditions of individual discernibility. Take, for example, matter. This is a favorite individuator for many philosophers.[32] After all, the stuff out of which something is made seems to be what causes it to be this rather than that—the marble in the two identical statues of Apollo appears to be the cause that there be two and not one. But matter cannot be the reason of our discerning an individual, since matter, considered in itself and apart from the particular circumstances and features that accompany it, has no perceptual characteristics. It must be remembered that within the Aristotelian framework accepted by most of those who adopt this view, matter in itself has no qualities, quantity, relations, and so forth; it has no features that fall within the Aristotelian categories. Under these conditions, then, how could matter be the source of individual discernibility? Indeed, the example of the two statues of Apollo is misleading, for marble may have perceptual characteristics while matter does not. So if it is marble that is considered an individuator, this is a theory of "characterized matter," not of matter as such. Matter, however, as mentioned before, has been defended as a principle of individuation by many philosophers. To say that "X is an individual because of matter" makes some sense, but to say that "I know X to be an individual because of matter" is at the least odd and possibly absurd.

Not all philosophers, however, have distinguished between these two issues, namely, between the problem of individuation and the problem of individual discernibility, or, as I have put it, between the search for the necessary and sufficient conditions for something to become individual and the search for the necessary and sufficient conditions for something to be known as individual.[33] Moreover, many have attempted to identify or at least relate them or their solutions.[34] Perhaps the best known of these attempts is the one proposed by those who accept the so called "Identity of Indiscernibles."[35] This view, to which further reference shall be made in Chapter 5, can be formulated as a principle in a number of ways. One of these is as follows: If

22

X is indistinguishable from Y, X and Y are the same entity. But the identity of X and Y does not necessarily follow from their indistinguishability. For one may want to argue that individuality and distinction, on the one hand, and discernibility, on the other, are two different things. The first two could be interpreted as absolute features of individuals, while the last could be understood as a relation of the individual to a mind, actual or potential, who plays the role of knower of individuals. Interpreted thus, a lack of discernibility does not necessarily entail the nonexistence of distinct individuals.

Of course, the matter may not be as simple as that. Someone may wish to argue, for example, that the distinction which has been drawn is not as clear as it may seem. For one thing, one could draw a distinction between discernment and discernibility and argue that, while lack of discernment does not entail lack of distinction, lack of discernibility does. And the reason is that whether two things are discerned as two is a matter of fact, contingent on particular circumstances surrounding the case and involving both what is to be discerned and a discerner. But discernibility is not a contingent matter; it has to do with the conditions which in principle would render something capable of being discerned. In this, discernibility is like perceivability, for example. That something is perceivable does not entail that it is perceived, but that something is not perceivable entails not only that it cannot be perceived on a particular occasion, but also that it is such that it cannot, under any circumstances whatsoever, be perceived.

I shall discuss this matter further in Chapter 5, but for the moment let me say that this objection is misguided. Although it is true that indiscernibility entails the impossibility of discerning the thing to which it applies, and discernibility implies only the possibility of discernment, not its actuality, this does not mean that indiscernibility entails lack of difference or that difference entails discernibility. The point I want to emphasize is that discernibility is a relational feature and as such depends not only on the thing to which it applies but also on a knower, whether actual or potential. This is where the difference lies between the problem of individual discernibility and the problem of individuation.

That these two issues are different, however, does not imply that their solutions must be different. In fact, most theories of individual discernibility resemble closely the theories of individuation. The most common exceptions to this are those theories which, because they involve nonobservable entities, such as matter, bare particulars, and the like, do not readily lend themselves to account for discernment.

One last point: some of those who prefer a metaphysical approach to individuality object to the attempt to deal with the epistemic issue just described. After all, they argue, this epistemic approach does not deal with the way things are, but only with the way they are perceived, and thus contributes nothing to the understanding of individuality itself.

But this objection, which I like to call "the Metaphysical Objection," and which is used not only in this context but elsewhere as well, is misguided on two counts. First, it must be accepted that to determine necessary and sufficient conditions of knowing something as individual is, of course, not to know the necessary and sufficient conditions of something becoming individual or even the necessary and sufficient conditions of something being individual. But even then it is in a sense to know something about the way things are; for knowing about something and the conditions of that knowledge are indeed part of the way things are related to each other, even if one of the relata is a knower. Second, the objection has no power against those who distinguish the issues mentioned and attempt to deal with both; it affects only those who either reduce the metaphysical issues to epistemic ones or who reject the metaphysical issues altogether, considering them spurious.

Reference to Individuals

If, instead of using an ontological or epistemic approach to individuality, one adopts a semantic perspective, one ends up with an entirely different issue. While the ontologist is concerned with individuals themselves, their principles and nature, and the epistemologist is concerned with the way we know them, the semanticist is interested among other things in the nature and function of terms and expressions used to refer to individuals. He wants to know, for example, how terms such as 'Socrates', 'Leticia', 'this', 'that', 'I', and the like, and expressions such as 'the owner of the calico cat' function; he wants to know how they are used, how they are instituted, and the differences between them and terms and expressions which are used to refer to many individuals, that is, class or generic terms such as 'woman' or 'tree', or expressions like 'a beautiful sunset'. That this is a separate issue or set of issues from those raised above seems quite evident even from a superficial inspection of the question. It is one thing to ask, for example, about the necessary and sufficient conditions of Socrates' individuality or of what allows us to distinguish him as such, and another to ask how the term 'Socrates' functions, its reference and sense. True, it is altogether possible to give accounts of the usage and meaning of 'Socrates' which will take into consideration both what Socrates is and what we know about him; we could say, for example, that the function of 'Socrates' is to refer to Socrates and no other individual. But even in such cases the semantic, as opposed to ontological and epistemic, nature of the answer is evident.

The linguistic expressions which are more commonly used to refer to individuals are proper names, indexicals, and definite descriptions, expressions that are, of course, quite different.[36] Ever since Peirce, the term 'indexi-

24

cal' has been used in connection with demonstratives, pronouns, and tenses. None of these are names. Proper names, on the other hand, are names that apply to one and only one individual. The main difference between proper names and indexicals is usually thought to be that the referent of indexicals changes according to circumstances. When I say "I am a man," the pronoun 'I' refers to me. But if you say "I am a man," it refers to you. This is why Russell called them "egocentric particulars."[37] Proper names are unlike indexicals in that they refer to one and the same individual regardless of circumstances. 'Socrates' refers to Socrates and no one else. Of course, this difference may not be as strong as has been suggested, since several individuals can and in fact often have the same proper name. For example, my friend's cat is also named Socrates. All of this goes to show that the distinction is not as clear as it is often thought to be. But that is immaterial to our present purposes, and so we shall leave it for the moment.

Definite descriptions seem to be quite different from indexical terms and proper names. While proper names are conventional linguistic signs and indexicals are usually pronouns or terms which indicate time, definite descriptions are compound expressions which are made up of names and terms of multiple references. But, again, it is not necessary that we detain ourselves at this point. For the present propaedeutic purposes, it is sufficient to point out an initial difference. We shall take the matter up again later, in Chapter 6.

In addition to the mentioned questions, there are many other philosophical issues related to the notions of proper name, indexical, and definite description. Perhaps the most pressing of these concerns the issue of whether proper names have meaning and sense as common names have, or whether they do not. The often called "classical" answer is that they do not; proper names have only reference.[38] The problem with this answer is that if that were the case, then all identity statements in which the subject and predicate are proper names referring to the same individual would become noninformative, as, for example, in the proposition, 'Cicero is Tully'.[39] But it seems that some of those propositions, such as the one given as an example, do convey information, since the interlocutor can learn something through them that he did not know before. This is what led Frege among others to reject this view and suggest that proper names have sense or meaning, even if this sense or meaning is somewhat different from the one common names have.[40] Their interpretation of proper names is that they are in fact disguised definite descriptions. But this view also has problems which stem from the fact that our common-sense intuitions seem to be contrary to it. Proper names do not seem to be definite descriptions. When I say "Socrates," I do not intend to describe, or do in fact describe, Socrates; I am only naming or singling him out.[41] In fact, if I had wished to describe him, I would have used a description instead.

From all of this, it is clear that any systematic discussion of individuality would do well to address these issues. Since we use language to refer to individuals, and the language in question ranges from proper names and indexicals to descriptions, it is necessary to establish how the language of reference functions in relation to individuals.

In contemporary philosophy, the set of questions involved in the semantic issues mentioned have had enormous impact in analyses of individuality, often dominating the discussion to the detriment of the other, more traditional, issues. This is a consequence of the general contemporary emphasis on language and the prevalent linguistic approach in the discipline. To reduce the philosophical discussion of individuality to this issue is, of course, a mistake, but to ignore it is no less misguided.

Concluding Remarks

The purpose of this chapter was twofold. First, to discuss and clarify some of the general terminology in use in the literature about individuality and, second, to distinguish six philosophical issues surrounding this notion. It was my contention at the beginning that to achieve both of these tasks is essential if any clarity in the study of individuality is to be maintained, and I trust the chapters that follow will bear witness to this claim. It was also my contention that many of the difficulties surrounding the notion of individuality are the result of terminological confusions and/or the confusion of issues that should be kept separate. Again, it is for the rest of the book to substantiate this claim. What I hope has been demonstrated at this stage is that indeed there are differences in the terminology used and that the issues which have been discussed are distinguishable and important. With this in mind we can turn to the first chapter of the study proper, which deals with the first of the issues mentioned, the intension of 'individuality'.

1

Intension of 'Individuality'

The purpose of this chapter is to provide an intensional analysis and elucidation of individuality. The chapter is divided into two parts. The first discusses five erroneous interpretations of individuality, and the second deals with what I propose as the correct way of interpreting it.

The main thesis of the chapter is that individuality is to be understood in terms of the primitive notion of noninstantiability.[1] This means that noninstantiability is both a necessary and sufficient condition of individuality. Accordingly, individuals are viewed as instances that are themselves noninstantiable. The term 'individual' does not convey this understanding and must be used carefully in learned discourse about these matters; otherwise, unfortunate confusions and misunderstandings may follow. Once this view of individuality is adopted, various difficulties traditionally associated with this notion can be avoided. This will become evident in subsequent chapters.

What Individuality Is Not

Individuality has given philosophers considerable trouble. There are conflicting views as to how to understand it and even as to its intelligibility in spite of what appears to be its fundamental character in our experience. For, on the one hand, we seem to experience the world in terms of individuals. Cats, dogs, trees, human beings, tables, and our own minds and memories are all individuals. This does not mean that our experience is of individuals *per se;*

that is, we do not experience pure individuals. What we perceive, in what Kearns has called "first level experience," are individuals of a type or, put in another way, characterized individuals.[2] But when we try to explain the individuality of the individuals present in experience, we run into difficulties. Indeed, even a view which at first glance appears innocuous, defining individuality formally as a feature that characterizes individuals *qua* individuals is strongly rejected by many. They argue that individuality cannot be a feature at all in the strict sense of the word, since its being a feature would presuppose that something else could share it or have it, and that seems to contradict the very notion of individuality as something *sui generis* to an individual.[3] At any rate, this is of no concern to us at present, since it is an issue that pertains to the ontological status of individuality rather than its intension and with which I shall deal in Chapter 3. It suffices for the moment to point out that there is ample disagreement concerning the proper understanding of individuality.

Traditionally, individuality has been analyzed in terms of five features that correspond to what seem to be immediate metaphysical intuitions that we have about the world as given in experience. The world appears to be composed of entities that (a) lose their fundamental character if they are divided into parts; (b) are distinct from all other entities, even from those that share some features with them; (c) are part of a group-type or class which has or can have several members; (d) can remain fundamentally the same through time and various changes; and (e) are the subject of predication but are not predicated of other things.

The first point is quite obvious in the case of natural beings. If divided into parts, a man (e.g., Socrates) ceases to be a man, and the particular man he is (namely, Socrates), and becomes a collection of inert limbs. But even in the case of artifacts, it is also quite evident, for a table broken into pieces is no table at all in any ordinary sense of the word. The second point seems also a basic *datum* of our experience, for each of the particular entities that compose the world with which we are acquainted seems unique and distinct in some way from everything else. True, Socrates is, like Aristotle, a man and a philosopher to boot; but they are distinct, separate beings, whose differences seem quite obvious. The same can be said about the table at which I am sitting while writing these words or even, some philosophers have argued, about the color and other characteristics of this table. A similar case can be made for the third, fourth, and fifth points. Socrates is one among a group, in this case a group of all men, and the same could be said about the table or its brown color. Indeed, even if all tables but one were destroyed, the remaining table would be one among the group of all possible tables, and that group would include the real table and all other tables, past and future. Also intuitively obvious is that Socrates endures while undergoing some change and that he is not predicable of other beings. It cannot be said of Aristotle that he is

Socrates—unless, of course, Socrates and Aristotle are two different names for the same person, in which case there is no real predication when one says, "Aristotle is Socrates," but rather the statement of an identity between the terms of the proposition.

Although philosophers frequently disagree about these intuited features and how to interpret them, and some have gone so far as to say that individuality is "ineffable,"[4] the general tendency among those concerned with this subject matter has been to regard one of them as basic and some or all of the rest as secondary but somehow related to individuality. Four of these features may be classified as metaphysical, since they are supposed to characterize the things that are said to be individual; these are indivisibility, distinction or difference, division, and identity. On the other hand, the fifth feature, impredicability, can be interpreted as metaphysical or logical, depending on the approach used, for it may be regarded as characterizing individual things themselves and/or the words (or alternatively, signs or concepts) used to refer to them. According to my thesis, none of these features, taken by itself or together with others, provides an appropriate understanding of individuality, since none is both a necessary and sufficient condition of it; only noninstantiability provides it.

Individuality and Indivisibility

The understanding of individuality as some kind of indivisibility has been perhaps the most widespread view of individuality in the history of philosophy. In the medieval period in particular, for example, this seems to have been the prevalent view, although in the early part of the age the situation is somewhat different, as I have pointed out elsewhere.[5] In our time, there are also adherents to this view, and not all of them are neo-scholastics.[6] Those who uphold this view find support for it, among other things, in the very etymology of the term 'individuality', which suggests that the intension of 'individuality' has to do with indivisibility. Most often, this has meant that indivisibility is to be understood both as a necessary and sufficient condition of individuality: Whatever is individual is indivisible and whatever is indivisible is also individual. Consequently, to counter this view, it suffices to point out something indivisible which is not individual or vice versa, something that would not seem *prima facie* very difficult. Not every author who holds this view, however, interprets indivisibility in the same way, and thus we must take account of at least the most basic of these differences of opinion if a determination on this matter should claim any credibility.

Absolute Indivisibility. The understanding of indivisibility has varied from author to author, depending on many factors, not the least of which are the difficulties of which they became aware as they constructed their views. These various views can be gathered into two basic positions. The first is the most uncritical and as a result is the weakest. It understands indivisibility simply as the inability to become or to be divided: Whatever is individual cannot under any circumstances be divided, and whatever is divided or is divisible in principle cannot under any circumstances be individual.[7]

Understood in this way, this view of individuality is clearly false. A single counterexample is sufficient to prove the point. Most obvious is the case of any individual physical object, such as a man or a table. These can be easily divided and broken up into parts, and yet they are not less individual for that reason. One might wish to argue that absolute indivisibility could be considered to be only a sufficient condition of individuality and not also a necessary condition, since if something is indivisible, it would seem to be individual. But this is not enough to establish the view: If indivisibility is not a necessary condition of individuality, something may be individual and not indivisible, and this is all that is required to reject this position.

On the other hand, it may even be possible to find fault with the view that holds absolute indivisibility to be just a sufficient condition of individuality, in the following way. "Man," for example, is universal and yet, considered *qua* man, does not seem to be divisible. True, there are and can be many men, but that does not seem to be a division at all for two reasons: First, in a true division the original ceases to be the whole it formerly was, and man does not change by virtue of the existence of many men; and second, in a true division the divided are parts of the original, but human beings do not seem to be parts of man in any ordinary sense of the terms.

I must confess that I am not very impressed with this objection, but I do believe it underscores one of the key problems with the view of individuality as absolute indivisibility; namely, the notion of indivisibility considered by itself is too imprecise. There are many types of indivisibility so that in order for it to serve as a defining feature, a *differentia* must be added to it. This is precisely what is attempted in the view that will be examined next.

Relative Indivisibility. The difficulties that the Absolute Indivisibility View encounters lead to its modification by the introduction of a further condition of individuality. Of the modified versions of the view, the most important and cogent appears clearly stated in the latter part of the Middle Ages, and Francisco Suárez was one of its most articulate exponents, as I have shown elsewhere.[8] According to it, individuality is to be understood as "indivisibility into entities of the same specific kind as the original."[9] In this respect, for example, Socrates is an individual even though he is divisible, since the parts into which Socrates could be divided would not be of the same specific kind as Socrates; that is, they would not be human beings. In contrast, universals are divisible into units specifically the same as themselves: man is divisible into men, and cat into cats. Both the universal and the individuals into which the universal is divided belong to the same specific kind. The indivisibility that is both a necessary and sufficient condition of individuality is not just indivisibility of any sort (the thesis of the Absolute Indivisibility View) but a very particular kind of indivisibility.

This version of the view renders it immune to the counterexamples brought out against the first version and, therefore, makes it both stronger and more appealing. Nevertheless, there are still several objections that can be brought against it, and although some of these difficulties are ineffective, they are nonetheless sufficiently interesting to be taken up and discussed. The most interesting ones are based on counterexamples of two types: homogeneous substances and collections.[10] One may want to argue, for example, that a quantity of water is individual and at the same time divisible into other quantities of water; and a pile of stones is likewise divisible into other piles of stones and cannot be considered less individual because of it. These examples purport to show that individuality cannot be understood primarily as indivisibility into individuals of the same species as the original individual, since various quantities of water are all the same specifically (i.e., water) and likewise piles of stones.

The type of answer that is most frequently given to this objection runs something like this: This objection is not effective, for those who view individuality as indivisibility into individuals of the same specific kind as the original hold also (1) that what is individual is a *particular* quantity of water or a *particular* number of stones (for example, one gallon of water or ten stones), not just any quantity of water or any number of stones; and (2) that the quantity in homogeneous substances and the number in collections function as specific differences.[11] Consequently, a particular quantity of water cannot be said to be divisible into particular quantities of water equal to the original one. To make the example more clear, a gallon of water is not divisible into gallons of water, even if it is divisible into smaller quantities of water. The original quantity (a gallon of water), therefore, is not divisible into quantities specifically similar to itself. Likewise, a group of ten stones is not divisible into groups of ten stones each, although it is divisible into two groups of five, five groups of two, and so forth. That (1) is true seems quite obvious: It is not quantity that is individual but "this quantity," (i.e., one gallon or two). Moreover, although (2) is not as obvious as (1), it is certainly not an unusual position. Aristotle, for example, treated quantity as a category, and all categories for him were groups of kinds.

This sort of answer appears at first quite plausible, but upon reflection it is not convincing. For one might want to point out, for example, that an infinite collection of things is individual and at the same time divisible into other infinite collections.[12] This brings to the fore the inadequacy of the conception of individuality given above if left unchanged. Those who adopt that view, however, explicitly add, or implicitly assume, a further condition, namely, that the original individual must not disappear or change as a result of division. Since an infinite collection, when divided into other infinite collections, would no doubt change or disappear altogether, the fact that it is divisible into individuals similar in kind to itself would not militate against this view. By itself, indivisibility into individuals specifically similar to the original, then, does not seem to be a sufficient condition of individuality, although with the added condition it seems to be so.

But even if the appropriate changes in the view are made so as to meet this last objection, there is a further consideration which creates problems. This has to do with the assumptions on which this view rests, namely, that both the universals and the individuals under it are of "the same specific" kind. This seems to be a serious mistake of the categorical sort. It makes good sense to classify men together into one species, but to say that both the species "man" and the men who belong to it are "specifically the same" is odd to say the least and downright false upon closer examination. Let us take a closer look at this from an Aristotelian point of view, which is in fact the point of view of most of those who defend this approach.

For Aristotelians, men belong to the same species because they have the same essence. That essence is expressed by the definition, whose *definiens* can be predicated of each of the individuals who belong to the species. If we take the *definiens* to be "rational animal," Socrates can be said to be a rational animal and so can Peter and Paul. It is because the *definiens* can also be predicated of man, that is, of the species, that both men and man are said to be specifically the same, according to those who adhere to this view. The fact is, however, that "specifically the same" does not mean here more than that the same predicate can be predicated of man and men. Yet when one looks closer at the predicate, it is clear that there is an important difference. In the case of a man, the predicate expresses either an identity between two descriptions of the same individual or a class inclusion reference in which the particular man is said to belong to a class. When the case of the species "man" is examined, the situation is different, for in this case there is never the possibility of class inclusion. Man cannot be a member of a class that is identical with itself. In "man is a rational animal," the relation between "man" and "rational animal" is always one of identity and not of predication. And this goes to show that, although in a narrow sense man and men may be said to be specifically the same, this is misleading if extended beyond that.

Of course, if the universal and the individuals which belong to it are not specifically the same in a stronger sense than the one mentioned, then this view of individuality will not do. And indeed it does not. Its main difficulties spring from the unclarity with which it conceives the notion of indivisibility, which is in turn the result of the very wide and variegated uses of the term 'indivisible'. These uses spring primarily from a physical metaphor that obscures, rather than helps to clarify, the notion of individuality.

Individuality and Distinction

A second condition that is regarded by many, particularly in contemporary literature, as fundamental to individuality is the distinciton of each and every individual from all other individuals, whether actual or possible.[13] I do not mean to endorse by this the view that there are possible individuals at this point, but only to make clear that if individuality is understood as distinction, and if there are possible individuals, the distinction will hold between each and every individual, including possible ones if there were such. If there are no possible individuals, then the distinction will hold only among actual ones.[14] Those who favor the interpretation of individuality as difference argue that it is a matter of experience that individuals are distinct from each other. Socrates is a distinct being from the dog he owns, for example: Socrates may move, change position, become senile, and even die, yet nothing of the kind may happen to his dog. This distinction of the individual from other individuals, which seems to accompany all individuals, is called by different names in the literature. Some call it "individual distinction," in order to separate it from other types of distinctions, such as the distinction that exists between two different concepts (conceptual distinction), say "featherless biped" and "rational animal." Others, however, prefer the term 'numerical distinction', in order to emphasize the contrast between this distinction and the specific and generic distinctions. The specific distinction is the distinction there is among species, for example, between man and dog. The generic distinction holds among genera, say animal and plant. In this context, then, the distinction between Socrates and Aristotle is not regarded as specific or generic but numerical, for each of them is, as it were, a different unit within the species. But between Socrates and his dog there is not only this sort of individual distinction, but also a distinction of kind (species in this case).

Other terms used in this connection are 'numerical diversity' and 'numerical difference'. Strictly speaking, these are not synonymous terms. Traditionally, two things are said to be "diverse" if they differ by themselves. For example, in Aristotelian metaphysics, the categories (substance, quantity, quality, relation, and so on) are said to be diverse because they have no features in common. Substance is wholly diverse from quantity and vice versa. They do not differ in just something or other but, we might say, in everything. On the other hand, two things are said to be "different" because in spite of some common features, they have one or more features that are not common to them; using the same example of Socrates and his dog, they differ, among other things, in rationality. Both are members of one generic class, but within it there are one or more features that set them apart. A necessary condition of difference, then, is some common feature, while there is no such necessary condition for diversity.

Another term also used in this context is 'otherness'. The philosophical origin of this term goes back to Boethius.[15] It is rarely used today,[16] and even in the medieval period it is not encountered frequently except in commentaries on Boethius. However, its opposite, 'sameness', is frequently found both in the Middle Ages and in contemporary discussions. The sense of 'otherness' in this context should not be confused with the contemporary phenomenological usage of the term, in which it is supposed to underscore the foreign and alienating barriers between a person and the world.

Finally, one occasionally finds the term 'unique' in this context. But the use of this term is rather unfortunate, for what is unique is "one *and no more* of a kind," while the individual certainly can, but need not, be such, so that the individual may be "one *among many* of a kind." When a precious stone is said to be unique, this means that it is one of a kind, such that there can be no others like it. And indeed, that would seem to entail that the stone would also be individual, since if it were not, there could be other stones similar to it. But that a precious stone is individual does not entail that it be unique. The emerald my daughter has on her ring I believe everyone would agree is individual, but it is not unique—there were several stones of the same kind which fit the same description at Stern's, where I bought it. And the same can be said of more pedestrian things, like a loaf of Wonder bread. Thus, if the view of individuality as distinction is to have any merit, it should not be identified with uniqueness, and the term 'unique' should be reserved for something else.

The view which regards distinction as both a necessary and sufficient condition of individuality encounters serious difficulties. Two merit particular attention. The first, (I), is that distinction does not seem at all a necessary condition of individuality, *let alone a sufficient condition,* since there seems to be no logical connection between the concept of individuality and the concept of distinction. That distinction is not a sufficient condition of individuality is clear from the fact that it seems to be a general notion that applies not only to individuals but also to nonindividuals. Indeed, universals, like "human being" and "ape," are clearly distinct, since they are defined differently, and yet in spite of that they are not individual. Consequently, distinction does not seem to be a sufficient condition of individuality.[17]

Those who favor the understanding of individuality as distinction will want to respond to this by arguing that the distinction existing among universals is not the same as the distinction among individuals. "Human being" and "ape" are distinct in a different way than "Leticia" and "Clarisa." Consequently, according to them it would still be possible to hold that distinction is a sufficient condition of individuality even when universals are also distinct form each other.

But this retort clearly begs the question, for to say that the distinction implied by individuality is different from other types of distinction would require either the identification of what makes it different or the claim that the difference is *sui generis*. To say that it is *sui generis* is nothing more than to say that individuality is individuality and, therefore, quite ineffective as a response to the objection. Thus, we need something more, if we are to accept that distinction is a sufficient condition of individuality. We need an analysis that will show, first, the relation between individuality and distinction and, second, the differences between the distinction proper to individuals and that proper to universals. But that, I am afraid, cannot be easily done, since most distinctions drawn among things are made in terms of universal features.

On the other hand, (II), it would also seem that distinction does not qualify as a necessary condition of individuality, for one can, indeed, think of a universe in which there can be only one individual. In such a universe, the individual would not be different from anything else, since there would be nothing from which it could be distinguished, either actually or potentially. Yet in spite of that it could not be said that the sole being of that peculiar universe would be universal.[18]

There are three ways of answering this objection, none of which are effective, although all of them have been used at one time or another for various purposes by segments of the philosophical community.[19] For that reason, they merit discussion. The first answer, (A), points out that arguments based on imaginary examples do not prove anything, because we tacitly introduce in them the features they set out to prove.[20]

Against (A) it can be replied that these examples are not meant "to prove" anything. Rather, these examples are meant "to show" logical possibility.[21] In the present case, they illustrate that it is logically possible for something to be individual without being distinct. If they prove anything, it is that the contradictory of that, namely, that it is not logically possible for something to be individual without being distinct, is false. In order for the objector to succeed, he would have to prove that the example of the one individual universe is contradictory. But that does not seem possible.

The second answer, (B), is that, although the example is supposed to operate under a condition that prescribes the nonexistence of other entities in the universe, it functions under the tacit assumption of the possible existence of other entities.

But this answer is not convincing, for there seems to be nothing wrong with establishing, as conditions of this imaginary universe, that it not only have but necessarily have a solitary entity in it. This answer seems to confuse logical necessity with psychological necessity.

The third answer, (C), points out that the introduction of an observer in the universe with only one entity violates the conditions of the example and that, therefore, if such a universe existed, we could not know or speak of it.

This answer, I believe, rests on a logical mistake which confuses "being in a universe" with "thinking about a universe." There is no reason why "thinking about a universe" should imply "being in a universe," just as there is no reason why thinking about the ancient world implies existing in it.

A third objection, (III), against the view that conceives distinction as a necessary and sufficient condition of individuality, points out that it is distinction that seems to presuppose individuality, rather than the reverse. Take, for example, the case in which A is distinct from B. Doesn't the distinction of A from B presuppose that A is not B and, therefore, that they are individual? Indeed, so the argument goes, in the proposition 'A is distinct from B', the assignment of the predicate 'distinct from B' to A already presupposes that A is not B. Therefore, there seems to be no way in which one can truthfully predicate distinction without assuming the individuality of the very thing which is supposed to be distinct. And this fact undermines the claim that distinction is a necessary and sufficient condition of individuality.[22]

Unfortunately, this argument seems to me to beg the question. For what needs to be established in order for it to work is precisely that distinction presupposes individuality, and this argument does not establish that, but rather assumes it. Thus, this objection against the view that interprets individuality as distinction, unlike the previous two objections, is ineffective. Our case, therefore, must rest on the previous arguments. But they seem enough to establish that distinction is not both a necessary and sufficient condition of individuality and, therefore, they make evident the untenability of the interpretation of individuality as distinction.

The problems with the view that regards individuality as distinction stem from a basic source, namely, that distinction is an extrinsic relation and as such cannot be used in the analysis of something like individuality, which is intrinsic to those things that have it. This sort of consideration is in part what scholastics had in mind when they argued against relational principles of individuation.[23] The only way to avoid this criticism would be to make distinction a nonrelational feature, but that seems quite impossible. There is no sense in saying that X is distinct unless what one has in mind is that X is distinct from Y. Expressions of the sort 'X is distinct' and 'X is different' are elliptical for 'X is distinct from Y' and 'X is different from Y'. When things are distinct or different, they are always distinct or different *from something else.* From all this we may conclude, then, that the understanding of individuality as distinction is not appropriate.

Individuality and Division

A third feature that is often associated with individuals is the capacity to divide a species or specific kind into many or, to put it differently, the capacity to belong to a specific set comprised of more than one individual. Supporters of this view point out that it is a fact of our experience that within each specific kind of thing there are many individuals. Indeed, even if we have experience of only one, there seems to be nothing to prevent the multiplication of such individuals. There are many human beings, but even if there were only one, there would be nothing illogical in thinking that perhaps there could be more, although the way to bring about this multiplication could present serious practical difficulties.

The terminology used in connection with this feature of individuals varies considerably. Boethius, following Porphyry, introduced the term 'divisive' *(divisivum)*.[24] This term has the advantage that it points to a feature of the individual, for it is the individual that "divides" the species. Its main disadvantage, however, is that it has the connotation of creating dissension or of separating what ought to be kept whole. In the Middle Ages, the terms most commonly used in this connection were 'multiplicity' and 'plurality'. But these terms are even less satisfactory, first, because multiplicity and plurality are the result of the dividing effect of individuals within the species, rather than the cause of it, and, second, because they, unlike the capacity to divide the species, are not features of the individual but of the group or type: What is multiple or plural is the group of individuals within the species considered as a whole, and what is subject to multiplication and plurality is the type involved. In neither case is the individual involved.[25]

This position is seldom explicitly stated in contemporary literature, but it had some adherents during the early part of the medieval period, when the problems associated with individuality had not been examined in detail. Moreover, the corresponding view of universals has adherents among contemporary authors, and frequently one finds language that implicitly suggests an identification, or confusion as I would like to say, between individuality and division.[26]

The lack of explicit supporters indicates the quality of the theory. Indeed, it would seem hard to hold a view which made division of the species or membership in a group a necessary and sufficient condition of individuality. For it is quite clear that there is no compelling reason why individuals necessarily should have to divide the species or form part of a group. There is nothing wrong with the conception of an individual who comprises an entire species, for example, just as there is nothing wrong with the notion of a universal that can have only one instance, as we shall see later, although there are quite a few philosophers who object to this point. In fact, some scholastics thought that each angel comprises an entire species.[27] Whether we talk about angels or other things is, of course, quite irrelevant. But the example illustrates well that there does not seem to be anything logically wrong with the conception of an individual that does not divide the species, that is, forms part of a group. Whether individuals divide the species or not does not seem to depend on the individual and its individuality, but rather on the nature of the species in question. For all we know, and as the medievals believed, there may be angelic species that do not admit of division and have only one member. And even if that were not the case, we can always think of classes, such as "the first male born" or "that than which nothing greater can be thought," which show the logical possibility of classes that can admit only one member. I shall return to this issue later on.

Moreover, the division of a class or the participation in a group is not a sufficient condition of individuality. Monkey, whale, cow, and human being form a group (with other things) that divide mammal, but we cannot conclude for this reason that they are individual, as indeed they are not. Thus, division of a class or participation in a group-type cannot be considered a sufficient condition of individuality. Since division considered by itself cannot be either a necessary or sufficient condition of individuality, we must reject it as a proper understanding of it. The fundamental character of individuality must be found elsewhere.

Individuality and Identity

Another condition that is frequently regarded as important for an understanding of individuality is identity. By this is usually meant the capacity of some individual things to endure through time and partial change. A tree, for example, will go through the four seasons, lose and add leaves and branches, change color, and yet remain the same tree it was before the changes occurred.

Something similar is often claimed about properties and accidental characteristics insofar as they characterize a changing substance. Socrates' hair color, for example, changes location with Socrates but seems to remain the same black hair color. Another case is that of accidental characteristics subject to change of intensity or degree, such as heat.

Various terms are used in the medieval and contemporary literature to refer to this feature of individuals. Among the most common terms are 'identity', 'sameness', 'duration', 'permanence', 'continuity', and 'persistence'. None of these is sufficiently neutral to be regarded as completely satisfactory; all of them have connotations that carry with them unfortunate consequences for the understanding of this feature, either apart from or within a determinate historical context.

'Identity' and 'sameness', although used often, normally carry a mental, epistemic connotation that is foreign to many discussions of this feature. For example, what medieval authors generally called *'identitas'* (identity, sameness) was not primarily a feature of things but of the observer, who "identified" a particular thing as being the same. As such, they conceived identity as a mental phenomenon based on the conceptual distinction necessary for a thing to be regarded as the same, and not as a real feature or unity present in individuals.[28]

The term 'duration' has the disadvantage of an earthly temporal connotation. Things that endure are generally taken to be "in Earth's time," that is, "to be the same through time on Earth." But this temporal-terrestrial aspect introduces an unnecessary limitation in the concept, at least for some authors who desire to extend identity to beings not subject to earthly time, as medieval authors did with angels.

The term 'permanence', which literally means "remaining through," has the undesirable connotation of a complete lack of change, a fact that would exclude material individuals from its extension.

The term 'persistence', although appropriate in many ways, is not entirely suitable, for it means "to exist through," and not every author holds that individuals must necessarily exist. This is the case, for example, with merely possible individuals: a possible Socrates seems to be as much a Socrates as an existing one. That is, there is nothing in the concept of an existing Socrates that is not also part of the concept of a possible Socrates.[29]

Finally, 'continuity', like 'duration', seems to involve the notion of "being one *through something*" (change, time), a point that would offhand exclude God from the category, even though he must certainly be regarded as individual. Moreover, scholastics generally associated this term primarily with physical change. As they put it, "continuity pertains to the essence of motion."[30] And this could create confusion.

In short, then, none of the terms in use is completely satisfactory, since they all lack sufficient neutrality, but among them the least harmful are 'identity' and 'sameness'. If it is kept in mind that the feature in question is not a conceptual phenomenon in some mind, but a feature of individuals themselves, their main undesirable connotation is removed.[31]

The view which makes identity, understood in this way, a necessary and sufficient condition of individuality is seldom explicitly defended, although it is occasionally attacked.[32] What is commonly found are implicit confusions between identity and individuality. The reasons for these confusions have to do with the close relation between individuality and identity. But, upon reflection, it is clear that they should not be confused and that identity is not a sufficient condition of individuality; for example, something may be said to be formally the same through time and partial change and yet it may not be individually the same. Some would argue that a man's humanity would still be the same in spite of changes in spatio-temporal location, and so forth. One can, of course, speak of "numerical" or "individual" identity, but that itself is enough to show that the intension of 'individuality' adds something to the intension of 'identity' and, therefore, that the latter does not imply the former.

One can argue in another way that the intension of 'individuality' does not imply the intension of 'identity', because the concept of an instantaneous individual is quite possible and implies no contradiction. An instantaneous individual is one that is not subject to duration and/or partial change. A being of this sort would come and go out of existence in an instant. Another example would be a nontemporal and unchanging being of the divine sort.[33]

Both of the arguments given rely on at least some debatable assumptions and, therefore, are weakened by them. However, there is a third sort of consideration that proves much more effective. It argues against the interpretation of individuality as identity from the fact that the problem concerned with finding the principle of individuality is not the same as the problem concerned with the principle of identity. This can be done by pointing out that some solutions to the first problem are clearly impossible for the second, or at least that the reasons for rejecting some solutions to the first problem are different from the reasons why they are rejected as solutions to the second, and vice versa.[34]

Take, for example, spatio-temporal relations, a favorite individuator for contemporary philosophers. According to this view, an individual being is said to be individual because its spatio-temporal relations are unique and cannot be shared by anything else in the universe. The fact that I am here at this time is what ultimately individualizes me, since no one and no thing could be here occupying the same space at the same time I am. Although this view forwards some good reasons in its support as a solution to the problem concerning the principle of individuation, as we shall see in Chapter 4, neither those reasons nor any others could surmount the obstacles it encounters if interpreted as a view on the principle of identity. It would be absurd to say that Socrates, for example, is the same individual throughout his life because of his spatio-temporal location, since such location is precisely one of the things that is constantly changing. Indeed, the changes involved do not even depend on Socrates. Any movement in the universe, whether far from or near Socrates would seem to change (if this view is to be taken seriously) his spatio-temporal location, since it would change the relation of Socrates not only to some other individual but ultimately to every individual.

Alternatively, the type of answer that may be possible in the case of individuation is not always possible in the case of identity. It is altogether possible to answer the question, "What makes S to be the same S through time?" by saying that S has not changed or has not changed much. But certainly that answer is not sufficient or even appropriate to answer the question, "What makes S to be the individual it is?" After all, one could very well argue that universals, such as "human being" or "good," do not change and yet are not individual because of that. True, if something has not changed, it must be the same, and if an individual (for example, this human being) has not changed, that means it is the same individual (this human being). But that does not mean that what does not change must be individual; it means only that if it is individual, it will be the same individual. Hence, the reason or explanation of its individuality is still wanting, in spite of the apparent explanation we have of its identity.

The problem concerning the principle of identity, therefore, is quite different from the problem that concerns the principle of individuation, and, although related to it, it should not be expected that whoever deals with one should also deal with the other or that the solution to one should be the solution to the other. All of this points to the need for distinguishing individuality from identity and also to the fact that identity is not a necessary and sufficient condition of individuality.[35]

Individuality and Impredicability

In very general terms, to predicate is to say something of something else. Some philosophers hold predication to be a mental act expressing a relation between concepts (or words). As such, predicability is a feature of concepts (or words), not of the things for which those concepts (or words) stand. It is, for example, the concept "man" or the term 'man' that is predicable of Socrates. For this reason scholastics called it "formal predication." On the other hand, other philosophers also like to speak of "things" being predicated or being predicable of other things. In that case, predication refers to the conjunction or union of what is predicated with the subject of which it is predicated. For example, the quality "white" is said to be predicated of a piece of paper and not just the concept (or term) 'white' of another concept (or term). This is what scholastics called "material predication." Understood in this way, predicability becomes a feature of things and not just of concepts (or words).

A common understanding of individuality is that it consists in impredicability; that is, the individual is what cannot be predicated. This definition of the individual is generally contrasted with that of the universal, which is interpreted, in turn, as what is predicable. 'Socrates', for example, is not predicable, for if it should be found in third place in a sentence of the form 'X is Y' (X is Socrates), the copula in that case would not be the 'is' of predication but rather the 'is' of identity. The sentence 'X is Socrates' can only mean that X and Socrates are the same thing and not that Socrates belongs to X or

41

characterizes X, as would be the case with some property or accidental feature. On the other hand, 'tall' is predicable, since it can occupy the third place in a sentence of the type 'X is Y', when the sentence is not an identity sentence.[36]

Since the distinction between the 'is' of predication and the 'is' of identity was not widely used by ancients and medievals, they were forced to talk about the individual as "being predicable of only one."[37] For example, 'Socrates', they pointed out, is predicable of Socrates and only Socrates. By contrast, they defined the universal as "that which is predicable of many." For instance, 'man' is predicable of Peter, Paul, and any other man. Both of these definitions are based on texts of Aristotle and were passed down to the Middle Ages by Boethius.[38] The view that individuals are paradigm logical subjects that cannot serve as predicates has been defended among others by Strawson.[39]

Apart from the fact that this interpretation of individuality, in Ayer's words, "is not illuminating,"[40] if impredicability is considered to be a feature of words or concepts, then it should be clear that it cannot be considered a necessary and sufficient condition of individuality. It may perhaps function as such in the case of individual words such as proper names and indexicals, for it might make sense to say that it is an essential feature of terms, such as 'Socrates', not to be predicable. But it would not make much sense to speak of impredicability understood in this way in relation to things. Indeed, no one could seriously hold that the impredicability of 'Socrates' is a necessary and sufficient condition of Socrates' individuality, since 'Socrates' is really a conventional sign devised by speakers to refer to Socrates and has no causal relation to him. To make impredicability, then, a necessary and sufficient condition of individuality in this way would be like mixing apples and oranges or, to put it in Ryle's nomenclature, to commit a category mistake.

But, of course, if impredicability is interpreted as a feature of things and not of words or concepts, then the situation may be quite different. Indeed, many of those who have argued for the interpretation of individuality as impredicability followed this path, making impredicability and predicability something more than purely logical relations among words and/or concepts.[41] More recently, however, the most favored view among those who implicitly or explicitly interpret individuality as impredicability identifies the world of things with the world of concepts and/or words.[42] This identification is a direct outcome of Kant's distinction between phenomena and noumena, and his identification of reality with the first, coupled with the linguistic emphasis of contemporary philosophy. If either of these two alternatives is adopted, the distinction between logic and ontology collapses. This collapse seems to me to be undeniable, even if there may be some who disagree with this assessment. To convince them, however, would require the kind of effort that cannot be made here; therefore, it will have to wait for a more auspicious occasion.

Before leaving this section, one more observation needs to be made. The interpretation of individuality as impredicability implies that individuals are either metaphysical substances of the sort Aristotle called primary, or logical subjects, or both: primary substances if impredicability is interpreted metaphysically, and subjects if it is interpreted logically. Indeed, one may want to argue that it is precisely the confusion between substance and individual and between subject and individual, or among all three, that gives rise to the interpretation of individuality as impredicability.[43] A common statement of this view, for example, which is in fact a modification of the well-known Aristotelian definition of substance found in *Categories*,[44] defines an individual as "a possessor of properties and itself not a property."[45] Another statement of the view also dependent on Aristotle says that individuals are things subject to changes and/or things which can possess contrary features.[46] But, of course, if individuals are defined in this way, then they are necessarily substances and/or subjects, and two important consequences follow. First, the individual must be other than its properties. The individual Socrates must be something other than the features that characterize him. This leads to the view called nowadays the Bare Particular View, which will be discussed and rejected later on in this work. Second, simples such as colors, for example, cannot be individual, for they cannot have properties, and having properties is a necessary condition of individuality according to this view. The particular black color of Leticia's hair cannot be individual, since it has no feature other than what it is. If one were to take away the blackness of the color, we would have no feature left.[47]

Naturally, most of those who identify individuality with impredicability and/or substantiality accept and defend the corollaries of their view. But if we should find that the features of things can or should be regarded as individual, and that the notion of a bare substratum is unacceptable, as we shall argue in the following chapters, then this view becomes untenable.

Individuality as Noninstantiability

All five of the conditions mentioned above have been regarded at one time or another in the history of philosophy as fundamental to individuality. Therefore, the first and foremost task confronting the philosopher concerned with the analysis and elucidation of individuality is to determine to what extent these claims are correct, and what is the relation between these five conditions. However, not all philosophers who have addressed this problem have actually distinguished these five conditions, let alone explained their interrelations. Often one finds that even if they do distinguish some of them, they confuse others. Indeed, only very few philosophers have isolated some of these notions and attempted, although not always with success, to develop a coherent framework in which to fit them. In the foregoing, I have tried to distinguish them clearly, within the parameters of a study of this sort, and to show the applicability of each of them to the understanding of individuality. But none of them by themselves seem adequate to account for individuality, since none of them constitute both a necessary and sufficient condition of it. Indivisibility was discarded because there seem to be clear counterexamples of individuals that are divisible and universals that are not, and this fact forces the view that interprets individuality as indivisibility to adopt various modifications, which nevertheless proved futile as attempts to save it. The position that held that individuality is to be understood as distinction also runs into trouble, for, as we saw earlier, something may be individual and yet not be distinct from anything else, as illustrated by the example of the universe containing only one entity, and something can be distinct and not be individual, as is clear from the examples of various universals. In short, the relational character of distinction undermines this view. The capacity to divide the species, in turn, was considered even less adequate to account for individuality, since this condition seems to be dependent more on the nature of the species to which individuals belong than on the individuality of individuals. And something similar can be said about identity; for that an individual be subject to change and duration depends more on the kind of universe of which it is a part than on the fact that it is an individual. Finally, if impredicability is a relation between words or concepts, it would appear to be a feature resulting from the reflection about the world and not a feature of the world itself, while individuality is without a doubt something in the world. And even if impredicability were interpreted metaphysically, this view leads to a confusion between the distinctions substance/feature and individual/universal.

Of all these conditions, only indivisibility seems to be logically independent of and prior to the other four. Distinction is a necessary condition only in a universe where there is more than one, real or possible, individual, but even there it is not a sufficient condition if taken by itself (more on this in Chatper 5). The division of the species into many is a condition operative only within species capable of multiple instantiation. Identity is a feature of individuals that are part of a universe subject to time and change. And impredicability is a feature of individuals considered as objects of reflection and is, therefore, logical. Identity and the capacity to divide the species into many are in fact features of individuals that depend on the kind of individual the individuals are rather than on their individuality. Distinction, on the other hand, is a relational feature that depends on the kind of universe to which the individual belongs. All of this goes to show that indivisibility is the best candidate of the five conditions examined to account for individuality. Unfortunately, for the reasons stated earlier, it seems hardly adequate to play this role.

What is, then, the proper understanding of individuality? The clue is to be found in scholastic discussions after all, something which should not surprise us given the energy medieval thinkers put into this problem. In Boethius we find the first use of the term 'incommunicability' to describe what is fundamental to individuals.[48] This term is later dropped or largely ignored for several centuries, but it is picked up by thirteenth century scholastics.[49] Although there are several senses in which the term 'communicable' was used by scholastics, the most central and pertinent to the present issue is that in which the universal, for example, tree, is said to be communicable to its instances, trees. To be communicable, therefore, means to be able to be made or to become common to many. This relation is exactly the converse of the relation of participability of which Plato spoke so frequently. That which is capable of participation is simply what is able to take part in or be a part of something else, which by that very fact of participation is made or becomes common to those things that participate in it. An individual, therefore, is said to be incommunicable because, unlike the universal, it cannot be made common to many or, as some followers of Plato prefer to put it, it cannot become "participated by many."

Unfortunately, the term 'communicable' or its negation 'incommunicable' are too imprecise, for they have too many connotations and equivocal uses that preclude their employment in technical philosophical discourse. Indeed, Boethius himself was aware of some of these difficulties and tried to pin down the various ways in which the terms are used. In his *Commentary on Porphyry's "Isagoge,"* he pointed out three ways in which something can be common: by parts, in the way a pie is common to all those who eat a piece of it; successively, in the way a baseball is common to all those who hold it; and extrinsically, in the way an event is common to all those who observe or participate in it.[50] Universals, of course, are not common in any of these ways, and individuals are not non-common in any of the ways directly opposed to them. What is meant by saying that individuals are incommunicable is something else: the impossibility that they be instantiated. Socrates, for example, cannot become instantiated in the way "human being" can. It is, then, noninstantiability that provides us with a precise understanding of individuality, since it is both a necessary and sufficient condition of it. Individuals cannot be instantiated, as universals can. They are instances of instantiables and noninstantiable themselves. Individuals, properly speaking, are instances, while universals are instantiables. Note another advantage of the term 'noninstantiable' and its counterpart 'instantiable' over 'incommunicable' and 'communicable': communicability is tied to the notion of being made common, and to be made common implies that there are several things involved, while the notion of instantiable does not imply multiple instantiation. I shall return to this point in a moment.

Etymology itself indicates further advantages of using the term 'noninstantiability' to refer to the fundamental feature of individuals and of the term 'instance' to refer to individuals themselves.[51] For the English term 'instance' comes from the Latin *instantia*, which means "presence." *Instantia* in turn is a substantive derived from the verb *insto*, "to stand in." And that which "stands in" or, to put it differently, "is present," constitutes one case, an example or instance of a type.[52] *Instantia* has also given in English the term 'instant', which clearly points to the atemporal character of instances. This, as we saw earlier, is one of the conditions necessary for individuality. The other conditions, which surfaced when discussing the various inadequate views of individuality discussed above, involved the independence of individuality from particular specific kinds, the kind of universe in which individuals were to be found, and the ontological character of individuality. Noninstantiability fulfills all of these: It is ontological and independent both of the specific kind of thing the individual is as well as of the kind of universe to which the individual belongs. Whether the universe in which the individual is found has one or more individuals in it is immaterial if noninstantiability is considered to be fundamental to the individual, since noninstantiability, unlike distinction, is not an extrinsic relation. Similarly, noninstantiability seems independent of duration and change, as well as of the specific kind of individual involved, whether material or spiritual.

As stated, the view of individuality as noninstantiability seems quite attractive, but at least two counterexamples to this position suggest themselves at the outset. First, contradictions such as "round-squareness" and, second, clones.[53] Round-squareness seems to fit the criterion of noninstantiability, and yet, in spite of it, it cannot be considered individual. And cloned organisms seem to be instantiable and yet individual. Consequently, it would not seem possible that noninstantiability can be interpreted as both a necessary and sufficient condition of individuality.

But neither of these counterexamples affects the Noninstantiability View of Individuality, although they provide an opportunity to clarify it. The first counterexample makes explicit that the Noninstantiability View does not apply to contradictions, but that is not a failure of the theory. The fact is that neither universality nor individuality apply to contradictions for the following reasons: An analysis of round-squareness would lead one to think that it is a universal, since it is composed of the universals "round" and "square" and nothing else. Yet, it is not really universal because universals must be instantiable, and an instance of round-squareness is impossible. On the other hand, although round-squareness is noninstantiable, it cannot be individual, since, being composed of two universals, there is nothing in it that can account for its individuality. So what is it? Obviously, what we have here is a puzzle generated by the attempt to apply to contradictions categories that do not apply to them. Contradictory notions are neither universal nor individual and to try to classify them as one or the other is to fall into a category mistake.

The counterexample of cloned organisms provides an opportunity to bring out the differences between noninstantiability and noncloneability on the one hand, and cloneability and universality on the other. Cloning is not a case of instantiation but rather a case of reproduction. The original cloned individual does not cease to be the individual that it is in order to become a universal by virtue of being cloned. For example, a cloned frog does not become a universal type by the fact that many other frogs identical to it are created.[54] Nor are the various frogs resulting from the cloning process instances of the original frog. Both the cloned frog and its copies are all instances of a type of which the original frog is as much an instance as the other frogs. I would like to offer two considerations in support of this. First, the original frog is, by the process of cloning, exactly like all the other frogs and, consequently, genetically indistinguishable from them. This fact illustrates the point made, for one could very well clone the clones and produce frogs exactly like the original. Second, if cloneability were the same as instantiability and cloning the same as instantiation, then the cloned frogs would be as universal as the original, since they themselves can be cloned. And this is absurd, for it would imply that the same frog would be both an instance of a universal and the universal itself, an open contradiction. Consequently, the cloned original cannot be considered a type, but only a noninstantiable instance of a type. This should be sufficient to establish that cloning is not the same thing as instantiation and, therefore, noncloneability is not the same as noninstantiability.

While speaking about clones, I specified that individuals are noninstantiable instances. I did this because the term 'instance' is frequently used to refer to subclasses that can be instantiated themselves. For example, one can say that "human being" is an instance of animal, or "rose bush" an instance of plant. In these cases, both "human being" and "rose bush" are called instances of more encompassing types, yet at the same time they can be instantiated: "human being" into Clarisa, Leticia, and other individual human beings; and "rose bush," into mine, my neighbor's, and so forth. It should be kept clear, then, that being an instance does not seem to be, without further qualification, a sufficient condition of individuality, unless of course the use of the term 'instance' is reserved for noninstantiables. But this, of course, is more a matter of terminology than substance and, therefore, needs no further elaboration. Indeed, most contemporary philosophers distinguish between class inclusion—human being is included in "animal"—and instantiation—Leticia is an instance of "human being." At any rate, the point that must be kept in mind is that individuality consists in noninstantiability and that individuals must be understood accordingly, whether they are called noninstantiables, noninstantiable instances, or simply instances.

It should also be noted that noninstantiability is not to be confused with "multiple noninstantiability." Multiple noninstantiability precludes multiple instantiation but not single instantiation. If we were to accept, for example, that there can exist one and only one God, then, whether he exists or not, he would necessarily be both multiply noninstantiable and noninstantiable, being as he is the one and only noninstantiable instance of divinity. On the other hand, divinity itself would be multiply noninstantiable, since it could be instantiated only once, but it would not be simply noninstantiable, since it could be instantiated by the one God. Individuality, then, should not be analyzed in terms of the negation of multiple instantiation, but rather in terms of the negation of instantiation.[55] Nor should universality be analyzed in terms of multiple instantiability.[56] The notions of "instantiability" and "multiple instantiability" should not be confused. That they are not equivalent should be quite evident, since the second implies the first, but not vice versa. Indeed, apart from divinity as understood in the Judaeo-Christian context, there are many universals that cannot be multiply instantiated even though as universals they are, as should be expected, instantiable. "The first man born," "the last man on Earth," and "the last Dodo bird" are all cases of universals that, if instantiated at all, must necessarily be instantiated only once: The classes have one and can only have one member. Unfortunately, the view that it is in the nature of universals to be capable of multiple instantiation and that, if they are not, this is a contingent fact, is widespread in the literature.[57]

Of course, those who support the view that universality involves multiple instantiability could argue that the examples I have given in support of the view that universality does not necessarily involve multiple instantiability but only instantiability ("the first man born," "the last man on Earth," and "the last Dodo bird") are expressed by definite descriptions referring to one and only one individual and therefore cannot be, as I claim they are, universal.

To this one could answer in turn that this objection begs the question. For, indeed, if one assumes that universality implies multiple instantiability, then clearly "the last Dodo bird," for example, cannot be a universal. So the objection rests on a particular assumption about the nature of universality.

But this is not sufficient to do away with the objection, for the objector could still point out that if the objection begs the question, so does the answer, since in order to classify "the last Dodo bird" as universal, one would have to assume that universality does not imply multiple instantiability, which is likewise a particular assumption about the nature of universality, in this case contrary to the objector's own assumption.

Obviously, we have reached an impasse, and this shows that the way we have gone about this matter is not the way to proceed if we wish to defend the view that "the last Dodo bird" is a universal and, therefore, to substantiate the view that universality does not necessarily involve multiple instantiability. What needs to be done is to show that there is a fundamental sense in which "the last Dodo bird" is like "Dodo bird" or, to put it generically, that definite descriptions, like indefinite ones, are fundamentally universal even if they differ from some other universals in important respects. And this is what I shall try to do now.

That definite descriptions are universal should be obvious from the fact that, after all, definite descriptions *are* descriptions, even if only "of a sort." But, we may ask, what is it that definite descriptions have in common with all descriptions? They have in common the fact that they specify certain features. But features considered in themselves are instantiable, as we shall see in Chapter 2 and is clear from examples such as "white," "human being," and "tree." Consequently, both descriptions and definite descriptions are composed of instantiables and as a result must be themselves instantiable, since they have no noninstantiable components. Therefore, there is a fundamental difference between themselves as instantiable on one hand and their instances on the other. The case with accepted universals, such as "Dodo bird" is clear both because "Dodo bird" is instantiable and also different from its various possible and/or actual instances: "Dodo bird" is one thing, actual and possible Dodo birds are something else. But the case with "the last Dodo bird" and the like should not be any different, since one can easily see that there are fundamental differences between the instantiable "the last Dodo bird" and its instance. That the instantiable "the last Dodo bird" and its instance are not the same can be seen from the fact that the instantiable "the last Dodo bird" could have turned out not to have any reference—it not having reference is a purely contingent matter—and therefore it should be clear that it cannot be identified with the both possibly and actually existing last Dodo bird, or just the possibly existing but not actually existing last Dodo bird, even if, as in this case, there can only be one last Dodo bird. There is then a common feature to the descriptions "Dodo bird" and "the last Dodo bird." This feature is fundamental because it is generic to them and because the differences between the two descriptions—single versus multiple instantiability—arise not from them *qua* descriptions, or as I would like to say, *qua* universals, but from the specific content of the descriptions. The possible number of instances depends not on the nature of the descriptions, but rather on whether the features that the description includes preclude more than one instance.[58]

In conclusion, then, it seems that it is only noninstantiability that can properly be regarded as a fundamental condition of individuals *qua* individuals; for it seems to be both necessary and sufficient for individuality. Distinction is a necessary condition of individuals in a universe where there are more individuals than one. Division is a necessary condition of individuals that belong to a species where more than one individual is possible. Identity is a necessary condition of individuals that endure in a world of time and change. Impredicability is a necessary condition of terms that refer to individuals and, therefore, presupposes both a language and a language user. Finally, relative indivisibility is a necessary condition of material individuals. But none of these is both a necessary and a sufficient condition of individuality. Only noninstantiability seems to function this way. But that this is the case should not obscure the fact that we do live in a world of multiplicity, in which not only are there many beings but in which species, at least most of them, are capable of multiple membership. Moreover, at least the beings that are part of the spatio-temporal world of our experience endure and are subject to change and to reflection. And, finally, most of the beings we experience are material or have a material dimension. All of this naturally complicates things. For, although individuality by itself has noninstantiability as its only necessary and sufficient condition, most of the beings with which we come in contact are conditionally related to distinction, division, identity, impredicability, and some kind of indivisibility. Indeed, it is precisely because of these close connections that individuality has so frequently been confused with these other notions.[59] How this affects the various other problems surrounding individuality will become clear later, in the course of this study. But before we proceed in that direction, there are two more issues related to the present discussion that need to be mentioned. The first is the question of whether noninstantiability is itself subject to further analysis or whether it should be regarded as primitive. The second has to do with the relation of individuality to singularity and particularity. I shall deal with these in the order given.

In general, to say that a concept or notion is primitive is to claim that the concept or notion is such that it cannot be further divided and analyzed into simpler concepts or notions.[60] A notion such as "bachelor" is not primitive because it can be analyzed into the notions of "unmarried" and "man." But not all notions are like "bachelor." Some are such that they cannot be further separated into other, more simple, components. Indeed, some philosophers have argued that even some composite notions such as "person" and "characterized particular" are, or should be considered, unanalyzable and, therefore, must be regarded as primitive.[61] Most frequently, philosophers regard as primitive the most fundamental notions in their metaphysics, analyzing all the rest in terms of these basic conceptual building blocks. The notion of "being" in Thomas or of "thisness" in Scotus are good examples of notions that function as primitive notions.

There are at least two reasons why one may want to regard a notion as primitive. The first is that, indeed, the notion is such that its analysis into other notions is not possible. If this is the case, it would be unavoidable to use the notion in any definition or analysis of it. This use can be explicit or implicit. It is explicit when the analysis includes the same term that is being analyzed or a synonym of it, as in the definition "'teacher' means a person who teaches." And it is implicit when the complementary notion is used. For example, when one defines "whole" in terms of parts, and the notion of part is not taken as primitive, the definition is circular, since a part is itself definable in terms of a whole. Now, that the analysis or definition of a term or notion be circular, of course, does not indicate that the term or notion is primitive. I can define "teacher" as a person who teaches and yet the notion of "teacher" is certainly analyzable into other notions. A notion is primitive in the sense under consideration only if any kind of definition or analysis that may be given of it is necessarily circular. In the case at hand, noninstantiability could be regarded as primitive if any definition or analysis that can be given of it would have to be circular either (a) because it used the notion of noninstantiability itself; (b) because it used its complement, instantiability; or (c) because it used derivative notions, such as instance or instantiable, which imply them. And, indeed, it does seem that this notion is primitive in this sense, for any definition or analysis of it would, in order to be complete, have to make reference to instantiation, instances, and/or instantiables, that is, to the relation between the universal and the individual, to the individual, and/or to the universal.

The second reason why one may want to regard a particular notion as primitive is that by doing so one is able to organize one's theory in such a way that all or at least many notions within the theory are explained in terms of the original one(s). In this way, as mentioned earlier, one can argue, for example, that notions such as "person" or "characterized particular" should be treated as primitive even though they are composite notions. For, although they may in principle be analyzed into more simple notions, to do so creates serious problems, while not doing so helps considerably in the organization of the theory. Thus, some philosophers argue that, although the notion of "characterized particular" can in principle be analyzed into the notions of a particular and its characters (or features in our terminology), such analysis is misguided because of the consequences it has. Others, however, argue that it is not because of the consequences that a notion should be regarded as unanalyzable but because indeed it is unanalyzable. This is Strawson's point, for example, when he argues that the notion of person needs to be regarded as primitive even though it involves both corporeal and noncorporeal elements.[62]

If these are the reasons one uses to substantiate the primitive character of a notion, in order to justify it one would have to show how treating the

51

notion in this way is more helpful in an overall explanatory metaphysical scheme than giving an analysis of it. Thus, in order to justify the primitive character of noninstantiability, it would have to be shown that to do so produces a coherent and intelligible metaphysical account of individuality. This is one of the things that I intend to do in the rest of this book, and, therefore, I need not elaborate this matter further at this time.

There is, however, one further point that needs to be clarified in connection with the primitive character of individuality. It is frequently the case that philosophers who use the notion of primitiveness are accused of obscurity and that the notions they regard as primitive are cited as examples of mysterious metaphysical entities resulting from a superactive imagination and/or a disregard for the Principle of Parsimony, which, as generally agreed, should guide all philosophical and scientific inquiries. Usually there are one or two things that are meant by this criticism. One is that the metaphysical notions in question are not derived from ordinary views. The other is that the entities to which they refer are not present in experience. Thus, Bergmann's bare particulars are often given as an example of mysterious entities that have no counterparts in an ordinary view of the world, but are rather elements in a technical analysis of that view. Likewise, Duns Scotus' notorious thisness *(haecceitas)* is frequently cited as a good example of an entity not present in our experience. It is true, so the objection goes, that we perceive this or that chair, but there is no evidence that the thisness of the chair is something found in experience. Indeed, as with many other metaphysical notions, it is in the philosophical analysis of that experience that these entities appear. Now, apart from whether these criticisms are correct or incorrect, I would like to claim that the primitive notion of noninstantiability is not unrelated to our ordinary view of the world and that the noninstantiable instances to which it refers are an everyday occurrence in experience. This is the case not only with noninstantiability but can also be illustrated with many other primitive notions. The notion of person proposed by Strawson, for example, is not mysterious. One may want to dispute whether it is in fact primitive given its complexity, but certainly it is taken from ordinary discourse and persons are present in our experience of the world. The notion of noninstantiability, like that of person, is not only clear but also quite unmysterious.[63] Indeed, it seems intuitively obvious to anyone who reflects on the relation between, say, "human being" and "this human being." And our experience seems full of noninstantiable instances: this human being, that cat, Clarisa, and so forth. True, it may not be possible to point to thisnesses and bare particulars, but it is certainly possible to point to cats and chairs, and these are noninstantiable instances. In short, then, we need not hold the primitiveness of noninstantiability as a serious difficulty for the intensional theory of individuality proposed here.

The second question that needs to be discussed before we move to the next chapter is the relation of individuality to singularity and particularity. In the Prolegomena, I pointed out that most authors regard the terms 'individual', 'singular', and 'particular' as intensionally equivalent, but that a few do not. The most common view among those who do not is that they are coextensive but not cointensive terms, that is, that whatever is individual is also singular and particular and vice versa, but that 'individuality', 'singularity', and 'particularity' mean different things. Those who hold this view usually identify singularity with the opposite of plurality and individuality with the opposite of universality. That they are not cointensional seems quite clear, unless one holds also that universality implies plurality, as some authors indeed maintain. But if one does not hold that universality implies plurality, then it is obvious that their opposites, 'singularity' and 'individuality', are not coextensive. Indeed, if a universal need not be multiply instantiable and therefore actually or potentially plural in order to be universal, it can very well be singular. And this means that there can be singulars that are not individual, and that 'singularity' and 'individuality' do not necessarily have the same extension.

The relation between singularity and individuality can be described like this: Whatever is individual is singular, because individuality is incompatible with plurality (we discussed above how this is applied to the case of groups and collections), but not everything that is singular is individual, since even universals are singular in that they are not aggregates. "This human being" (e.g., Socrates) is, therefore, both individual and singular, while "human being" is singular but not individual. What is not possible is to have something individual that is not singular. "Human being" is singular because it is not equivalent to many human beings, but it is not individual because it can be instantiated. And this human being (e.g., Socrates) is both singular and individual because he is neither many nor instantiable.

But what about the relation between particularity and individuality? In contrast with the notion of singularity, where there are some advantages in making a distinction both intensional and extensional between it and individuality, there is no great advantage in making a distinction between particularity and individuality. The language of particularity is a remnant of the Platonic language of participation, in which the individual was conceived as being a part of or as taking part in the universal. In this sense, 'particular' was contrasted with 'general', which has to do with what pertains to the whole. But, of course, this is not what is involved in the usage of the term here. Thus, unlike singularity, which has plurality as its own opposite, particularity has no appropriate opposite of its own in this context, allowing us to use it as a synonym of 'individuality', and to oppose it to universality. To make a distinction between particularity and individuality would require reviving the

Ciceronian language of "dividuality," to which reference was made in the Prolegomena. But there seems to be no need for that. For the sake of economy we might as well use 'particular' to mean just what is meant by 'individual', except in nontechnical contexts, where it can be used to single out any thing, including universals, or as the opposite of 'general'.

The view presented here, then, is that individuality needs to be understood primarily in terms of the primitive notion of noninstantiability. As such, it is to be distinguished from singularity even if there is no great advantage in distinguishing it from particularity. There is, however, one last possible difficulty that must be raised before finishing the discussion of the intension of 'individuality'. It has to do with what some might consider the rather negative way in which individuality has been analyzed. We may raise the objection with the following question: Isn't the understanding of individuality too negative? After all, if individuality is *non*instantiability, it becomes a kind of negation; one might even call it a "privation." And, indeed, some medieval writers used that very term, '*privatio*', to refer to it.[64] But if individuality is a privation, then we must contend with two things: first, privations, as the medievals noted, seem to presuppose something in which they are found, and, second, they seem to be lacks of what a thing ought to have.[65] The first point would seem to create problems because it makes individuality secondary in some sense and not as ontologically fundamental as is claimed throughout this book. And the second point creates problems because it implies either some kind of ontological defect or at least that individuality plays second fiddle to universality: Whatever is individual is something less than what it ought to be, namely, universal and therefore instantiable.

The answer to the first point is that, although the notion of "noninstantiability" presupposes the notion of "instantiability," since it is clearly its negation, this is a logical presupposition that does not necessarily have to have an ontological counterpart. That is, it is not necessary to hold that in order for there to be an individual there needs to be some other thing preceeding it which is ontologically more basic. Whether there is or not will depend not on the logic of the concept, but on the ontological commitments that one wishes to make in order to preserve the overall coherence of the theory and its concordance with experience. This matter will have to be discussed separately and is in fact raised in later chapters of this book. Note also that the logical priority of instantiability over noninstantiability does not militate against the primitive character of the latter, for the simple reason that the two notions are complementary.

The second point raised the possibility that individuality would imply some kind of defect or at least subservience to universality, since privations seem to be lacks of what something ought to have. But this difficulty can be easily avoided. In the first place, leaving undisputed the understanding of privations as lacks of what something ought to have, there is nothing in what has been said in this chapter that would imply that individuality is a privation. True, individuality has been characterized in rather negative terms as noninstantiability, but negation and privation are quite different. The negation of something does not imply that what is being negated is somehow valuable or necessary. As the traditional example points out, there is nothing wrong with the fact that human beings *do not* have wings. It is only when one speaks of privations that there is some implication of lacking what is valuable or necessary. If I am "deprived" of something, we are probably right in assuming that I should have it, as when I am deprived of my rights or my health. But simply "not having something" does not imply the same. Indeed, I am quite pleased that I do not have a cold at the moment. Of course, there are cases where not to have something is actually to be deprived of it. Thus, when I do not have health I lack something that I ought to have. But this is not always the case. Therefore, the characterization of individuality in negative terms as noninstantiability does not imply that it is something lacking or defective, or even that ontologically it plays second fiddle to universality. Whether it does or not depends, as already stated, on the sort of ontological commitments that one makes based on other considerations.

Another way of bringing out the same point is by noting that the account of individuality given here is not inconsistent with the interpretation of individuality as a special kind of unity. Indeed, this is the way some late scholastics regarded it, even though they also conceived it in negative terms as incommunicability. Suárez, for example, speaks of individuality as "individual unity."[66] And some contemporary authors like Popper, also speak of individuality as unity.[67] The problem with using the term 'unity' at this stage is that it does not tell us much, since unity is a very wide notion. Philosophers frequently speak, for example, about conceptual, mathematical, formal, structural, substantial, spatial, temporal, organic and class unities, and many more. So in order to capture the essence of individuality, we must go beyond that very general term and say that this individual unity consists in noninstantiability, and this noninstantiability is in fact what distinguishes it from other notions.

One final point: If we were to characterize individuality as a kind of unity, would this mean that we must characterize universality as another kind of unity also? Not necessarily. In fact, we could deny such unity to universality and end up with universality as the negative concept (the lack of individual unity) and individuality as the positive concept. This underlines an important point of the theory presented here, namely, that although the theory understands individuality negatively, it makes room for an ontological characterization of individuality as something positive. (This shall become clear in Chapter 3.) Epistemically we approach individuality negatively, but ontologically it is something positive. And this is in accordance with our experience, for generally we think of what is individual as *one* thing, but the way we become aware of it is negatively—through the fact that it is not and cannot be other. There is then a negativity, a resistance, if I may be permitted the metaphor, in individuality, that is very evident in experience and surfaces in "phenomenological descriptions" of it. And the theory presented here captures that quality of it.

With these considerations in mind, then, let us turn to our next topic, the extension of 'individuality'.

2

Extension of 'Individuality'

Next to the intension of 'individuality', the most basic of the issues that may be raised concerning this notion involves its extension. For even if it is granted that individuality is a viable concept and we are able, as we have claimed in Chatper 1, to identify what it is, the questions as to whether there are any entities that have it, and, if there are any, which do and which do not have it, are still questions that must be answered. In this chapter, I am going to deal with this issue in two stages. First, I shall discuss various standard theories that I consider incorrect, although some of them approach in many ways what I consider to be the correct, or at least the most viable, view on this matter. I shall deal in particular with two forms of Realism, seven forms of Nominalism, and three forms of Eclecticism. This will be followed in the second stage with the presentation and defense of the position I adopt. Its main theses are as follows: (1) 'individuality' has universal extension, that is to say, all that exists or can exist, including both things and their features, is individual; and (2) universals are "neutral" with respect to existence. The discussion as a whole, however, will be preceded by some remarks concerning the relation between individuality and universality.

In the past, the issue of the extension of 'individuality' has in many ways monopolized the attention not only of those who have concerned themselves with individuals, but also of those who have explored the so called "problem of universals." The reason for this is that, generally speaking, individuality and universality have been regarded as mutually exclusive and exhaustive notions. This means that everything in the universe is either individual or universal, but not both. This position has not gone without challenge, however. Although it is not my business here to settle this issue, since my present concern is only with individuality and not with universality, and nothing that will be claimed here will be defended only on the basis of a particular view of this relation. However, I believe it is appropriate to say something about this matter at least in passing.

The first thing that needs to be said is that it is by no means universally accepted that the distinction between individuality and universality is exhaustive. In the Middle Ages, for example, there were some authors who disputed the point, arguing that God was neither universal nor individual. Of course, few of those understood individuality as noninstantiability, as we do here, for then they could not but have granted, given their belief in God's uniqueness and oneness, that God could under no circumstances be subject to instantiation: God cannot be a genus or species. But some thought that individuality primarily involved being a member of a divisible class and, since they believed God belonged to no divisible class, they were compelled to deny his individuality. Others, however, went further than this. Even though they may have understood individuality correctly as noninstantiability, or, as they preferred to put it, incommunicability, and individuals as noninstantiable instances, they argued that God is not an instance of any class even if he is noninstantiable, because there is no such class as that of the divine.[1]

None of these views are very convincing, relying as most of them do on theological assumptions, the sense of which is very much a matter of dispute not only among philosophers but also among theologians. For present purposes, it is sufficient to point out that none of these authors would argue that God could be instantiated and that therefore, regardless of other factors, they must concede that God, if he exists at all, is not universal. Moreover, if the distinction between universals and individuals is exclusive, as is more generally accepted, God must be individual.

More recently, however, the exhaustive character of the distinction between individuality and universality has again come into question in the context of examples such as the liberal tradition, the Declaration of Independence, the theory of relativity, works of art, and the like, which do not seem to fit easily into either one of these categories.[2] Indeed, they seem to share features that belong to both categories. The Declaration of Independence, for example, seems to have been drafted at a particular time and place and to be different from other declarations and things. And these features, it must be remembered, are often associated with individuals. But, on the other hand, many copies of the Declaration of Independence have been and can be made, and so it looks as if it were a sort of universal which can be instantiated in various spatio-temporal coordinates.

When one reflects more carefully on the example, however, it becomes clear that the fact that the Declaration of Independence seems to have characteristics proper to both universals and individuals and, therefore, does not fall squarely into either one of these categories arises from an ambiguity in the example. The expression 'the Declaration of Independence' can refer to various things depending on the context. It can refer to the actual piece of paper with ink marks, used by the forefathers of the United States of America in Philadelphia in 1776. Or it may refer to any copy of that document. Or it may refer to the meaning of those marks on the paper. Or it may refer to what children and historians think when they learn and discuss the Declaration of Independence. But, of course, all these things are ontologically different and may have different *status*. The piece of paper with writing on it dating to 1776 is obviously an individual, as are the reproductions one can buy in any bookstore around Philadelphia and elsewhere. All of these, including the 1776 document, are noninstantiable instances of a universal type. On the other hand, the meaning of the writing on the document is a complex set of ideas, subject to multiple instantiation, and therefore universal. That it is a complex set of ideas does not alter its character as universal any more than the complexity of the idea of man makes it individual. Complexity is not a necessary and/or sufficient condition of universality, for there are complex universals and individuals. Nor does there seem to be anything wrong with the notion of a simple individual. The instances of this complex universal, which is the meaning of the symbols written on the 1776 document (and its reproductions) and, therefore, a complex set of conceptual relations, are the thoughts in the mind of each thinking being who reflects about those ideas. And those are individual.

The example of the Declaration of Independence poses no serious problem, therefore, for the view that the distinction between universality and individuality is exhaustive. And since similar analyses can be given of the other examples cited, these do not constitute obstacles to the mentioned view. We omit discussion of them for the sake of brevity, although I shall get back to the example of a work of art later on in the chapter, since it has been the focus of particular attention in recent philosophy.

That the distinction between universals and individuals be exclusive is. not as easily doubted as that it may be exhaustive.[3] Indeed, it is generally taken for granted that if something is universal, it cannot be individual and vice versa. Most philosophers, going back to Plato, have considered these two notions antithetical and have often opposed and contrasted the features associated with them. Moreover, if, as we saw above, noninstantiability is both a necessary and sufficient condition of individuality and universality is understood as instantiability, it should be clear that universality and individuality must be considered exclusive categories.

Our conclusion, then, is that there is strong support for the view that the distinction between individual and universal is both exhaustive and mutually exclusive: Everything in the universe is either one or the other, and if it is one, it cannot be the other.

Now, if the stated relation between universality and individuality is accepted, then much of what will be said about the extension of 'individuality' will have direct relevance for the extension of 'universality' and, therefore, for the solution to the problem of universals. But this is only an unintended consequence of the discussion. The thesis that I propose to defend in this chapter, apart from a substantive thesis concerning the extension of 'individuality', is more formal. I shall try to show that the impasse which has developed concerning this issue is to a large extent the result of two factors: First, the lack of a proper understanding of individuality and, second, a lack of clarity in the formulation of the problem. Consequently, if the issue is formulated clearly and if the appropriate view of individuals as noninstantiable instances presented in the first chapter is accepted, this problem can be resolved.

Traditionally, there have been three basic positions that philosophers have adopted with respect to this issue. The first, inspired by Aristotle, holds that everything that exists is individual.[4] A second view, following Plato, proposes the contrary, namely, that nothing that exists is individual. The third view, attempting a compromise between these two extremes, holds that some things that exist are individual and some are not. The existence to which all three positions refer is real existence and opposed to imaginary, mental, possible, or apparent existence. How this is unpacked further varies considerably from author to author. Since this is not a historical study, I shall not in general present and/or explain historical versions of the various positions but rather what I take to be standard formulations. On occasion, however, I shall make some exceptions and refer to historical figures, although again the aim will not be historical accuracy and/or information. That is the task of scholars working on those figures.

Realism: Nothing that Exists Is Individual[5]

This view has taken two different forms in the past, both of which have important advantages and serious disadvantages. The most extreme form of this position is what I like to call "Transcendental Realism" for reasons which shall become clear immediately. The other form I shall call "Immanent Realism," to differentiate it from the first.

Transcendental Realism

There has yet to be a more eloquent defender of Transcendental Realism than Plato. Throughout his *Dialogues,* one finds a host of arguments which purport to show that the world we are acquainted with through our senses, and where individuality is to be found, is a world of appearance. The real world is the world of abstract, absolute, immutable entities capable of instantiation on which the world of individuals depends for its characteristics. Much has been argued about the correct interpretation of what Plato called "forms" or "ideas," but that is immaterial at present. The exact nature of the historical Plato's view should be left for scholarly rather than purely philosophical investigations.[6] What is pertinent at present is the general extensional thesis proposed by this sort of view, namely, that individuals, or noninstantiable instances in our terminology, are not part of reality; they do not truly exist.

This view, then, divides the world into two realms: the realm of the real, composed of universal entities; and the realm of the unreal, composed of individual entities. Individuality is relegated to the world that is not real; it is turned into an illusory feature of reality. What is real is not Socrates or his act of justice but humanity and justice. The individual Socrates and his act are mere appearances and, as it were, reflections of real natures. Accordingly, what many philosophers call substances, such as a human being or a tree, and what they call features of those substances, such as the capacity to laugh or the black color of the hair of an individual human being, may be individual, but they are not real; they do not truly exist. It is only the features of individual things considered as abstract and separate entities, such as humanity, justice, blackness, and so on, that are considered real, but by the same token are not individual. For these reasons, this view is generally regarded as a most extreme form of Realism. I have decided to call it "Transcendental Realism" to underline the fact that, according to it, what is real *transcends* the world of experience. This view should not be considered, as some of its critics do, a naive form of Realism, since it is far from being naive. Indeed, it is a very sophisticated position, which rejects the ordinary or commonsensical view of the world in favor of one that seems to contradict it, based on very profound philosophical reasons.

This position, then, holds that no individuals exist in the true sense of the word, while universals do. In order to substantiate this thesis, it identifies individuals with objects of sense perception and universals with the objects of thought, through which we think about the objects of sense perception. Having done this, it proceeds to show that the objects of sense perception do not fulfill any of the necessary conditions of existence, while the objects of thought do. These conditions are variously specified as immutability, absolute unity, necessity, and independence. These are the same sort of conditions that Parmenides and his disciples read into the formula "what is, is, and what is not, is not."[7] Of course, once these conditions have been accepted, the remaining task is easy, for it suffices to point out through examples taken from experience that none of the objects of sense perception fulfill them. Socrates, for example, is always in a process of change and therefore cannot be considered immutable in any true sense of that word. Moreover, Socrates, just like any object of sense perception, has many different parts and, therefore, can hardly be said to be one absolutely. Nor is Socrates necessary in any strict sense; human beings come and go out of what, in sense perception, is taken as existence. Finally, what Socrates is seems to depend on what human being is rather than vice versa, since in order for something to be a human being it must fulfill certain necessary conditions imposed on it as it were from outside, from the nature or idea of human being, and not the reverse. Socrates, therefore, cannot be said truly to exist, and the same can likewise be said concerning any other object of sense perception.

The case with the objects of thought, on the other hand, is different, for ideas do not seem to change at all. The idea of triangle is what it is and does not undergo change. Moreover, it is one, not a collection of separable parts, and independent of its instances. Whether there are or are not triangles in the world of sense perception, and whether there are or are not thoughts about triangles, does not seem to affect the idea of triangle; for it would still be true, for example, that one of the necessary conditions of triangularity would be to have three sides. And the same can be said about other universals.[8]

Transcendental Realism, therefore, provides a useful basis for our knowledge by securing its object. And it does the same with moral principles. Moral principles become transcendental realities not contingent on the changing opinions of human beings. Apart from this, Transcendental Realism also supplies a foundation for the meaning of tautologies and mathematical truths, which do not seem to be based in the world of experience, and in addition it provides criteria of perfection that can serve as measures of judgment. The truth of tautologies and mathematical propositions is grounded transcendentally, apart from the contingencies of changing experience. Likewise, absolute perfections, such as absolute goodness, absolute compassion, and so on, find a foundation outside a world in which clearly they are not to be found.

In spite of this favorable presentation, it does not take much to doubt the adequacy of this view. In the first place, from a commonsensical standpoint, the realist's commitment to the real existence of universals and the only apparent existence of individuals seems to contradict our most basic experiences. Indeed, it is the existence of my cat, Minina, that is most real to me; the existence of "catness," on the other hand, is something vague, outside of my experience, and based only on dialectical considerations quite distant from my most basic perceptions. It would seem at least odd and possibly absurd to discard what seems basic evidence for what looks like pure speculation, a point that common-sense philosophers like G. E. Moore never tired of making.

Of course, one may want to argue that this sort of reasoning begs the question. One cannot reject offhand the basis on which Transcendental Realism is constructed without having examined the reasons given for it. After all, this position is developed only because what is normally regarded as a commonsensical view of the world is incapable of solving various conceptual difficulties that arise in the understanding of the world. For example, the problem of sameness: how Plato's hair color can be the same as Aristotle's. Or the problem of the constancy and necessity of certain truths: triangles always have three sides. Still the analysis of individuals into universals, whether they transcend the world of sense perception or are part of it, is puzzling and difficult to accept. And the reduction of experience to appearance does violence to some of our most basic intuitions. My cat Minina is still more real to me than triangularity.

Note that this argument does not try to ridicule Transcendental Realism by ridiculing the claim that tables and chairs do not exist. For, although some transcendental realists have gone so far as to make similar claims, most claim only that universals have ontological priority over individuals and not that individuals do not have ontological status at all. The claim is that "tableness" and "chairness" have priority over tables and chairs. Naturally, the talk about "appearance" and "reality" initiated by Plato tends to lead to the most extreme claim, but most sober transcendental realists manage to avoid it. At any rate, the argument given is directed against the more reasonable claim by questioning the priority of universals; it points to the paradox created by those who try to describe the nature of reality by denying the most basic intuitions of experience.

But one can proceed to undermine this view in other ways as well; that is, a Moorean type of attack based on common sense, or on experience, is not necessary. One can question what this view identifies as necessary conditions of existence. Why, for example, must we conceive real existence as requiring immutability and necessity? Perhaps, as Heraclitus said a long time ago and process philosophers have repeated in this century, change is part of the very nature of existence. And why, moreover, do we have to conceive being as necessary? Couldn't there be a whole universe composed of contingents and be itself contingent, as Hume suggested? These questions do not, of course, prove that Transcendental Realism is false; they only point to some serious difficulties it must solve or assumptions it must justify before it can be accepted as a viable theory.

There are, moreover, arguments that question in more detail both the theory and its implications. Most of these have to do with the various relations, such as participation, imitation, sharing, resemblance, exemplification, and so on, which upholders of the theory claim exist between universals and individuals. Plato himself raised some of these in the *Parmenides,* and Aristotle built them up considerably in the *Metaphysics.*[9] As a result, there have not been many adherents of Transcendental Realism in the subsequent history of philosophy; today, one finds only traces of this theory in some contemporary views.[10] For this reason and because other authors have already provided convincing accounts of the difficulties of Transcendental Realism, I do not see the need to discuss them in any serious detail here.[11]

One thing that should be mentioned, however, is that most versions of this view assume that the problem of universals is fundamentally the problem of explaining sameness among several things, and the problem of individuality is that of explaining their differences. Thus, the issue is usually formulated in terms of why two or more things resemble each other, and the answers given are that they participate or share in the same thing (form or idea), or imitate or resemble it, for example. But, as we concluded earlier, universality does not have to do primarily with sameness but rather with instantiability, and individuality does not consist in difference but rather in noninstantiability.

Immanent Realism

The second version of Realism is more moderate in its stance and as a result has been considerably more popular. It holds, like Transcendental Realism, that everything that exists is universal and, therefore, there are no such things as individuals, but it does not posit the world of universals in a realm separate from the world of experience. The world of experience, according to this view, is composed of universals and not individuals. It is for this reason that I have called this view "Immanent Realism"; it is a realism of this world, as it were.

This position avoids some of the most obvious difficulties associated with Transcendental Realism, but nonetheless it has problems of its own. Its proponents defend it by pointing out that anything we can say or think about what are thought to be individual things is said or thought in terms of universals. Indeed, even the features of things we see, such as colors and the like, are perceived, so they claim, as universals even though they seem to belong to clusters and be capable of differentiation by association. When I perceive the color of this paper, for example, I do not perceive "this white color," but "white color." The white color of this paper is not different in any way from the color white except insofar as it is associated with this paper and not something else.[12] Moreover, if one were to proceed with the analysis of the paper into its features, it would soon be clear that all the features of the paper appear to be universal and, therefore, that the paper is nothing but a cluster or bundle of universal features—a complex universal. Accordingly, individuals are not ontologically different from universals; they are simply more complex. It is this analysis that gives rise to the name "Bundle View," for individuals become equivalent to bundles of universals.

However, it must be added that most supporters of the Bundle View do not consider individuals mere appearances. They insist that there are both universals and individuals, although the latter are analyzable into the former.[13] Since according to this version of Immanent Realism both universals and individuals exist, we must leave its discussion for the section devoted to eclectic views and concentrate at this point on the version that grants only apparent existence to individuals. Note, however, that some of the objections given below against Immanent Realism will also apply to the eclectic version.

At the basis of this position, as with Transcendental Realism, lies the conception of universality as sameness and of individuality as difference: A and B are the same insofar as they share a common feature, but they are different insofar as they do not share all their features. To be an individual, therefore, is simply to have or to lack some feature or features which other individuals lack or have, respectively. Individuality is interpreted as difference, and difference is explained in terms of the presence or absence of a feature or features.

An objection that some have brought up against Immanent Realism has to do with the various degrees of perfection with which members of a class seem to exemplify the universal feature they share.[14] For, indeed, since they are supposed to have the feature in common, it is not clear why some are better at it than others. Transcendental Realism may not have this problem, since according to that view the possession of features by things is always mediated by the relation to the universal and that relation presumably could be affected by other factors. Thus, the imitation of a transcendental form by two different things may be different owing to the circumstances in which each of them finds itself. Peter may not be as good as Paul, for example, because his participation in goodness is affected by his situation; there is a "logical" or "metaphysical" distance, if we may use such metaphors, between goodness and Peter and Paul, and that distance and the obstacles in it may explain the differences in degree of goodness which Peter and Paul have. But if, as immanent realists must hold, there is no distance between the universal and the individual, and the universal is in things whole and complete, then how can we explain that in Peter there is more goodness than in Paul?

This argument, of course, is not conclusive. Immanent Realism can always answer that degrees of perfection in things are possible because the very features or universals in question are by nature subject to degrees and that in those cases the degree in question depends on the relation of the feature to other features of the individual. For example, one could say that certain metals can get hotter than other types of material because of the very nature of the metals in question. Thus, although iron and water can both get hot, and therefore both can have heat, iron can be hotter than water. And something similar could be said about degrees of heat in the same thing at various times.

Another standard argument that is brought to bear against all sorts of Immanent Realism, but which does not affect Transcendental Realism, consists in pointing out that when features of things undergo changes the same features in other things do not.[15] Consider, for example, the color of this paper on which I am writing. I can take the paper and put it in the fire, and with the burning of the paper, its color also will be destroyed. Yet, the supposedly same color that is also present in a similar paper on my desk would not have been changed at all. From this it is usually concluded that the color of the two papers, even though indistinguishable, must be two and not one. Since Immanent Realism holds that they are one and the same, the implication is that it must be wrong.[16]

One way in which proponents of this position can answer this objection is by giving a reinterpretation of the notion of the unity or sameness of universals. So that, for example, to say that X and Y are one and the same with respect to M does not imply that M is one and the same in the way X is one and the same as itself, or Y is one and the same as itself, so that the termination of X or Y does not imply the termination of M. Armstrong makes this point by saying that "Properties [i.e., universals] are not the sort of thing which can be destroyed (or created)."[17] In other words, the identity of universals cannot be destroyed because, by definition, this language does not apply to them. Indeed, so the argument goes, to claim that the color of a table burns when the table burns is to confuse the issue and to beg the question. It is to confuse the issue because features such as colors are neither like their subjects nor part of them; they are not tables or parts of tables.[18] And it begs the question because it treats features as individuals and that claim is precisely what is at stake.

Well that may in fact be the case, but in arguing in this fashion the immanent realist has compromised his position. He has done so because he has introduced a distinction between individuals and their features such that it becomes impossible to reduce the first to the second, as the pure form of Immanent Realism claims. For there is the individual "this table," on the one hand, and the features of the table on the other. And all of this means, of course, that the objection is quite effective against the pure form of Immanent Realism we are discussing at this point, since it forces it to abandon its most fundamental claim. Whether the objection is also effective against the more eclectic version of this position to which reference was made earlier is of no concern at this point; we shall return to this issue later.

Note that the response to the objection indicates also that Immanent Realism is a result of the conception of individuality as difference. If, contrary to this, one were to hold that individuality is to be conceived fundamentally as noninstantiability, then it would not be necessary to reduce individuals to complex bundles of universals and hold that they do not, as it were, have an existence of their own.

There are other problems with the view as well, some of which will become evident in Chapter 4. Let me just mention another one in passing, however. It is that a view such as this fails to differentiate effectively between complex universals of the individual type, such as Socrates, and complex universals of the nonindividual type, such as human being.[19] Yet, Socrates and human being seem to be quite different. We shall return to this point later.

Appeal and Weakness of Realism

The great appeal of Realism, whether Transcendental or Immanent, is based largely on the fact that it serves as a theoretical foundation for knowledge and morality. One of the fundamental concerns that philosophers have is that what is generally called "knowledge," or more specifically, "scientific knowledge," is expressed in general terms that do not have individual objects of sense perception as referents. This not only includes scientific concepts, such as "matter" and "mass," which do not seem to be exemplified in sense perception, but also concepts that we use in connection with objects of sense perceptions, such as "human being," "water," "triangle." When the scientist says, for example, that water boils at 100 degrees C at sea level under normal atmospheric conditions, there is no such thing as an individual object of sense perception to which 'water' discretely refers. "Water" is universal and is not this or that quantity of water in particular. But if this is so, we may ask, what does 'water' refer to, then? What accounts for the indistinguishability of two objects, both of which are called "water"? If 'water' does not have an object of reference, as 'John' has, doesn't that mean that the term stands only for a mentally constructed concept, and not for something real? The desire to find an object of reference for the universal concepts and terms used in science, and thus to dispel the suspicion that science may not after all be about real things but about humanly created concepts, is what has made some philosophers posit the existence of a world of scientific objects, that is, a world which corresponds exactly to our universal concepts and grounds the similarities we find among things.[20] Once this is understood, it is also easy to see how Transcendental Realism has transferred the characteristics of scientific propositions (immutability, absolute unity, necessity, and independence) to the world they are supposed to describe. For if the world is not as we think it is, then how did we develop our thought? Where did we get these ideas, and why do they serve us so well? This sort of reasoning assumes that science loses something, perhaps its "objectivity," if the concepts it uses do not have referents in the way proper names do. And, regardless of whether this is correct or not, the assumption has had and still has wide appeal.

Similarly, moral principles and notions would seem to require a firm ontological foundation, otherwise morality could degenerate into the sort of relativism in which moral concepts are defined in terms of expedience. To echo Thrasymacus in the *Republic*, justice would become the interest of the stronger. But if goodness, justice, beauty, and such other value notions do indeed exist immutably, necessarily, and eternally, then the disagreement about and relativity of human values can be attributed not to the notions themselves, but rather to our poor understanding of them. And this gives both hope and a goal to the moralist.

On the other hand, Realism has also some serious weaknesses. In the first place, the realist commitment to the real existence of universals and to only apparent existence for individuals seems to contradict our most basic experiences, as already pointed out. For it is the existence of my cat Minina that is real to me; the existence of "catness" is something vague, outside of my experience, and based only on what seem to be dialectical considerations quite distant from my most basic perceptions. It would seem at least odd and possibly absurd to discard what seems basic evidence in favor of what looks like speculation. The analysis of individuals into universals, whether they transcend the world of sense perception or are part of it, is puzzling and difficult to accept. My cat Minina still appears more real to me than "catness." And so also does my own individual existence. Indeed, my existence is presupposed by my very knowledge of "catness" even if it is not presupposed by "catness," for the proposition 'I understand catness' certainly implies its subject. This is not to say that I exist because I think. It is more like saying that 'I doubt X' implies 'I'.

There are also problems involved in the relation between individual and universal, as mentioned earlier. And these difficulties do not beg the question since they do not reject Realism's arguments offhand. They simply point out that Realism never succeeds in explaining how individuals, whose ontological features are incompatible with those of universals, can in fact be analyzed in terms of universals. Taking what this view holds to be features of individuals, for example, how can what is mutable and contingent participate in and/or be related to what is immutable and necessary? How can the triangle that I have drawn on the blackboard participate in and/or be related to triangularity, when to be a triangle drawn on the board implies mutability and contingency and to be triangularity implies immutability and necessity?

Before we move to the examination of the next view, it should be pointed out that most realists are rationalists. And, indeed, it makes sense that rationalists should favor this view. For, as the examples and arguments just presented show, there is no direct empirical or experiential support for Realism. Its support is fundamentally dialectical, coming from arguments based on the analysis of various problems that the rationalists think can be solved by positing the existence of universals. The empiricist, on the other hand, wary of speculative constructions, usually rejects Realism, since he cannot find universals in experience. We turn now to the positions he favors.

Nominalism: Everything that Exists Is Individual

The contrary view to Realism holds that everything that exists is individual.[21] Like Transcendental Realism, it divides the world into two realms: one is regarded as real, the other as unreal. But this time the terms are shifted, for it is universals that are regarded as unreal in some sense. They are called concepts, words, or tokens, and believed to be the product of mental operations,[22] or alternatively they are regarded as collections or similarities among things. Humanity, justice, and so on are either concepts, words, or tokens abstracted or derived in some way from a world composed of individuals, a collection of some of those individuals, or the similarity among them. It is the individuals that are real, both things and their features, while universals have only the reality appropriate to concepts, words, tokens, collections, or similarities. From this it should be clear that there are several varieties of Nominalism, depending on what precisely is identified as universal—words, tokens, concepts, collections, similarities. But often these possibilities are mixed with each other in the theory, for what seems most important to the nominalist is not what universals are ultimately, but rather that they are not real, as individual things are. In this sense, much of the import of Nominalism is negative and in many instances the position reduces to a criticism of Realism.

Most supporters of Nominalism regard their view as almost self-evident, even though evidence from ordinary language and thought has been interpreted quite differently by supporters of Realism, and some authors have argued that on those bases no decision can be reached concerning the dispute between these antagonistic positions.[23] Nonetheless, nominalists argue that it is obvious that the things we perceive are individual and that, unless we want to deny reality to the whole realm of experience as the transcendental realist does, we must view the world as composed of individual entities. Individuality, they hold, extends not only to such things as my cat Minina or the tree I planted in my backyard last year, but also to their features, such as their color and size. This attitude, which regards the basic nominalist thesis as practically self-evident, is well exemplified in the medieval period where it was quite

69

predominant, but it is also present in contemporary circles. The arguments normally given in support of it are aimed to show that alternative views are incorrect. The position, then, like Realism, is proven by default, as it were, indirectly.

Those nominalist authors who, contrary to the practice of most nominalists, have attempted to give some sort of positive argumentation for it have done so by pointing out that all entities we experience, including the features of things, are distinct and therefore must be individual. Distinction, as we saw, is often regarded as both a necessary and sufficient condition of individuality, and it is through this understanding of individuality that this position has found some positive support in the past.

Those who favor Nominalism have developed several versions of it, which can all be understood as alternative interpretations of the formula given above. I shall discuss the most important of these next.

Essential Nominalism

The most extreme interpretation of the general nominalist formulation holds that everything that exists is *essentially* individual or, as others prefer to put it, individual by itself. It is in the nature of both things and their features to be individual, and even concepts themselves are no more than individual acts of understanding of individual minds, although their denotation may be multiple. "Human being," for example, is and can be nothing but this very act in my mind or in the reader's mind, here and now by which I, or the reader, understand what a particular human being is. This position is generally called "nominalism" in the literature, although other terms, such as 'conceptualism', are frequently used to describe various versions of it, putting different emphases on the nature and reality of concepts. I shall call it Essential Nominalism to underscore the fact that, according to it, things are individual essentially; their individuality is not derived or accidental in any way but is rather part of the nature of things: It is a necessary condition for them.

The five versions of Essential Nominalism that I would like to discuss here develop their respective positions from the manner in which they understand universals, rather than from the way in which they understand individuals. I call these five versions Tokenism, Wordism, Conceptualism, Similarism, and Collectionism.[24]

Tokenism. "Tokenism" is the view that understands universals to be tokens. What this means exactly is not clear to me and perhaps it has never been clear to anyone, since only one author in the history of Western philosophy is credited with having upheld this position. He was Roscelin of Compiègne, teacher of Abailard. Unfortunately, we know very little about Roscelin's view, and what we know came to us largely through his critics, who, as critics,

70

should not be trusted. At any rate, Roscelin is reported to have said that a universal is nothing but the emission of sound uttered *(flatus vocis)* when one says, for example, "man."[25] Note that in this view the universal is not a type of sound, but simply a token; the same universal cannot, therefore, be repeated.

Obviously, this view is highly inadequate and cannot be taken very seriously. In it the distinction between universal and individual collapses completely. Indeed, it is not that there are no universal things or features of things; there are not even universal concepts and words. Consequently, we cannot be given any sort of explanation as to why something is such and such. In fact, if the universal is a token, then it is not clear at all what things are. Take, for example, these two sentences written on this paper: 'X is red' and 'X is red'. (To adhere strictly to Roscelin's view as reported by Anselm, we would have to use utterances as examples, but for convenience's sake I hope I may be allowed to use the stated example.) According to this view, the first sentence does not assert the same thing as the second, for the token predicate in the first is not the token predicate of the second. Even the subjects are different, since they are different tokens. But where does this lead us? We need not investigate further. What is relevant for us here is that this theory as it stands completely lacks explanatory power; it fails miserably in what it is supposed to do and, therefore, need not be given serious consideration.

This unusual position may have developed as a reaction to the excessive Realism of some early medieval authors who openly turned universals into substances.[26] How this extreme position was reconciled with notions such as meaning is not clear, and since no significant texts from Roscelin have survived, we must remain in the dark as to how he, or his followers if he had any, addressed these issues.[27] It should be noted, moreover, that this position has very little to say about individuality except for the point that its extension is absolutely universal.

Wordism. 'Wordism' is another term I have devised for the more traditional term 'nominalism', which in this book is given a more general meaning, as pointed out earlier. 'Nominalism' was derived from the Latin *'nomen'* (name) and seems to have been introduced in philosophical and theological discourse in the twelfth century, when medieval authors were trying to distinguish realists (those who held universals to be *res*—things, realities) from those who held them to be merely words *(sermones, nomina, voces)*. Apart from Roscelin, who, as we saw, seems to have regarded universals as utterances *(voces;* the term *'vox'* can mean both word and utterance in Latin), most medieval nominalists held that universals were either words, that is, logical or grammatical type-terms, or alternatively concepts (mental terms). The latter position I shall discuss separately under "Conceptualism" and the position of Roscelin we have already discussed under "Tokenism." We are left, therefore, with the middle position. Perhaps the most famous of medieval authors who

71

adhered to it was Peter Abailard.[28] According to him, universals are significant words. They differ from utterances in that utterances may or may not be significant, while all words, considered as such, are significant; that is, they are capable of causing the understanding of something.[29] Another way in which this position has been expressed is by saying that universals are predicates.[30]

This is primarily a "logical" theory of universals that depends on the understanding of universality as predicability and of individuality as impredicability. Its roots go back to Aristotle.[31] Its advantages over Tokenism should be obvious: The use of meaningful language is possible, and communication becomes viable. If I say "X is red" and you say "X is red" under this view we can say further that we have said the same thing. Moreover, the position economizes on ontological entities, doing away with the crowded ontological world of realists.

Still, Wordism faces serious difficulties that have often led its defenders to create ontological entities of their own in response to standard objections raised against the view. This, of course, is an indication of the intrinsic weakness of the position, but it is no decisive objection against it. I do believe, however, that there is at least one consideration that brings out clearly the untenability of this perspective, at least in its simplest form: Wordism cannot explain the nonarbitrary character of predication. That the predication of terms is generally nonarbitrary—only madmen and liars do otherwise—is clear from the fact that we do judge whether they are truly or falsely applied. If I say that trains are flying machines, I am quickly corrected and told that they are not, rather it is *airplanes* that fly. But, if it is the case that predicates are nonarbitrarily applied to things, then there must be bases for their nonarbitrary predication. Take the following example: If 'white' is predicated of X nonarbitrarily, then either 'X is white' is true or it is false, and that entails that either X is white or it is not. But if universals are mere words and nothing else, first, X could not possibly be white since 'white' is nothing more than a word; second, 'X is white' could neither be true or false; and third, the nonarbitrary predication of 'white' would remain unexplained. The problem with Wordism, then, is that it can point to no basis of nonarbitrary predication if it wishes to maintain the purity of the position. Of course, as already stated, some proponents of this view go on to say that the basis of the nonarbitrary predication of universal terms is the *status* of things,[32] and other proponents of the view find other bases for it. But once these other entities are added, we do not have the original, clear, and economical position but rather something else, often not very clear and certainly more cumbersome and complicated. There are other serious problems with this view, but since other authors have already dealt with them to a considerable extent, I do not see the need to repeat them here.[33]

Conceptualism. The third version of Essential Nominalism, which I have chosen to call Conceptualism, is quite common in the history of philosophy. It identifies universals with concepts, which are in turn said to be expressed by linguistic signs. "Human being" is a concept in someone's mind. When we speak of it, we use the term 'human being' or any other conventional (spoken, written, and so on) sign to refer to it. The concept is individual and present in an individual mind, although as a mental sign it is used to denote many things. By denotation it is meant that the term used to express the concept can be predicated of various subjects in true propositions. For example, 'Aristotle is a human being', 'Socrates is a human being', and so on, where 'human being' is predicated of Aristotle and Socrates. What the mental reality is (i.e., the ontological status of the concept and its nature) is a matter of debate and a point that has often led to the rejection of this view or at least to its criticism.[34] Apart from Behaviorists, who reject their existence altogether, some philosophers identify concepts with images, while others conceive of them as qualities, and still others regard them as acts.[35] Empiricists, like Hume, tend to think of a concept as an impression that has lost some of its distinguishing features and has therefore become a somewhat vague image.[36] It is this vagueness or indistinction that makes possible its application to many particular things. When I first perceive an apple, for example, I have a very strong and particularized impression of it, since all its peculiarities, or at least most of them, are present in my perception. But with time I forget some of these, making possible the association of this vague image, sometimes called "idea," with other similarly vague ideas of other apples.

Those who interpret universals as qualities of the mind argue that a concept is like a qualifying feature. Just as red qualifies a red flag, so they say, the concept "apple" qualifies the mind and changes its character. This approach is frequent among Aristotelians. They view concepts as accidental qualities that inform the intellect. Using the metaphor of the wax and the seal, they explain that the concept "apple" is like a seal which imprints a certain shape in the mind; the mind is likened to the wax.

Finally, there are some that interpret concepts as mental acts. The concept "apple" is nothing more than the mental act whereby one understands what it is to be an apple. There is no quality or image involved, but only the act of understanding. Just as running is nothing but an act of a runner, the concept "apple" is nothing other than the act of the mind when it understands what an apple is.[37]

All of these views about concepts have problems of one sort or another. The image view of concepts explains how we come to have vague ideas, but does not explain the similarity among the objects from which those ideas derive; that is, the fact that the ideas of various things, and not of others, can be associated seems to imply that those ideas and the things for which they stand have some similarities that other things and ideas do not have. For not even contiguity, something that does not always operate since, for example, our perceptions of apples are not always spatio-temporally contiguous, could explain this association and ultimate assimilation.

The view that holds concepts to be qualities must likewise account for their origin as well as for their generality. But the fact that they must arise, according to this view, from the perception of particular things creates difficulties. How can "red" be a quality informing the mind and be universal, denoting as it does any red thing, when (1) it is a quality of this mind and therefore particular, and (2) it arose from the consideration of particular things?

Finally, the interpretation of concepts as acts must explain how concepts are stored and memorized, while it is not clear that acts can be stored and memorized after they have ceased to be in operation. Just as my act of writing these words stops, so the corresponding mental act also ceases. One could, of course, argue that universals are not acts in just this way, but rather dispositions to act in a certain way or dispositions toward certain acts. But then the position boils down to the quality view, for in that case acts become more like features of the mind that predispose the mind to do certain things.

These, of course, are important difficulties that must be resolved if the stated views of concepts are to be maintained. There are, however, difficulties that arise not in connection with the interpretation of concepts as images, qualities and acts but with the interpretation of universals as concepts. In the first place, Conceptualism seems to fall into a serious categorical confusion. It holds that universals are concepts and, therefore, that things like "human being" and "cat" need to be conceived as "the concept human being" and "the concept cat." But this creates a problem, for the instances of "human being" and "cat" are human beings and cats, while the instances of "the concept human being" and "the concept cat" are the concepts I, the reader, and other thinking beings have of human being and cat, and, certainly, that is not what human beings and cats are.[38] Universals, then, cannot be identified with concepts, since the notion of "concept" itself is but one particular kind of universal.

Another difficulty arises when one considers the case of a universe with only one being that is not itself a knower. In such a case, the universe could not contain concepts since there would be no knowers to have them, and thus, presumably, the universe would also lack universals. But it makes no sense to say that the universe would have no universals, since the single individual in that universe would certainly have some features and as such would be an instance of them. Indeed, we need not go so far as to stipulate a case such as the one mentioned. In our own natural world, it is generally acknowledged that there was a time when no thinking beings existed (I am not speaking of supernatural beings, of course), and yet the world was full of instances of instantiables—there were plenty of sticks and stones. And even now, we lack many concepts of things and their features and relations that exist. The part of the universe known to us is infinitesimal, and yet it would be completely absurd to say that only what we know exists. Conceptualism, then, makes no sense unless the notion of "concept" is reinterpreted to mean something other than what is usually meant, and made completely independent from knowers.

But these are not the only difficulties with the view of universals as concepts. Indeed, we may ask, if universals are concepts, and there are no other universals, then where do our concepts come from, and what is their value in dealing with things, being as they are different from them? The realist, as we saw, does not encounter this problem, since he also accepts the extraconceptual reality of universals. But the nominalist must look for another answer, and yet none suggests itself easily. Traditionally, a way out frequently used tries to explain how we form our concepts in terms of some epistemic process whereby individual perceptions are transformed into universal concepts. It was already suggested above that Hume followed this path. Earlier nominalists, like Ockham, although puzzled by this problem, simply did not give any clear and satisfactory answer to it. It is only with modern philosophy and particularly the British empiricists that this issue is explored to any depth by supporters of Nominalism. But even here, no matter the answer given, it is still true and acknowledged by those who proceed this way that (1) we think about things in terms different than they are, and therefore, (2) human science and knowledge is not an exact representation of reality. The fact is that, so the argument goes, there is no such thing as "human being," or "water"; there are only individual human beings and individual quantities of water. Thus, when we think in terms of "human beings" or "water," our thought does not adjust completely to reality.

This is the most basic objection not only to Conceptualism but also to all forms of Essential Nominalism. It is repeated frequently in the history of philosophy, and it is one of the main reasons why philosophers move to the realist camp. They find it difficult to preserve the objectivity of human knowledge within a nominalist ontology, and so they give it up and adopt a realist position. Others, weary of Realism, modify Essential Nominalism in order to maintain the position while avoiding its undesirable consequences. There are various versions of this alternative, which I have gathered under the name "Derivative Nominalism" and which will be examined later.

Similarism. This view, sometimes called Resemblance Nominalism and frequently found in the history of philosophy, holds that universals are nothing other than the similarities that exist among individuals.[39] There are two important versions of it. The first maintains that the similarities in question are dependent on knowers and therefore are mental phenomena of some sort.

75

Understood in this way, this position is not different from the position I have called Conceptualism and therefore need not be discussed separately; as should be expected, it has the same advantages and disadvantages as that view. The second version, on the other hand, is quite different and marks a shift from subject-dependent views of universals to subject-independent views. In the cases of Tokenism, Wordism, and Conceptualism, the universal, whether an utterance, a word, or a concept, depended on some utterer, speaker (or writer), or conceptualizer. But those who hold that universals are similarities among things and that those similarities are not mental have liberated the universal from the subject. This yields certain advantages. As we saw above, one of the problems encountered by Conceptualism and the other forms of Essential Nominalism examined thus far was that it made no sense to hold that the features of things were dependent on something like a subject, external to the thing. But by making similarity independent of subjects, Similarism has done away with this objection. Still some difficulties remain.

Many of the best known difficulties encountered by Similarism stem from the interpretation of similarity as a relation. Indeed, it is difficult to see what else but a relation similarity could be. But, apart from whether similarity is a relation or not, a subject to which we shall return later, there are other questions that Similarism must answer. One source of these difficulties has to do with the fact that, regardless of what similarity is, if it is not a mental, subject-dependent phenomenon of some kind, it must be either something in the things that are similar or something outside the things that are similar. But, of course, to say that it is something, whether in those things or outside them, is in fact to open the door to Realism. For, what was the realist's contention but that the universal was something other than individuals, found either in things (Immanent Realism) or outside them (Transcendental Realism)? The realist holds that "cat" is a universal common to all cats (Immanent version) or in which cats participate (Transcendental version). And the similarist says that "cat" is either something in cats or something outside cats in virtue of which cats are such or are called or thought to be so. But this is not significantly different from what the realist says; consequently, Similarism becomes open to the same attacks to which Realism is open. These attacks are discussed in the appropriate sections of this chapter.

Unfortunately, this is not the only difficulty with Similarism. Another difficulty has to do with degrees of similarity, for it seems that the similarities among things are infinite. Does this mean, then, that the number of universals is infinite? This is not an insurmountable objection, of course, but it is certainly an irritant to a theory that purports to be in search of parsimony.

We can also raise here a difficulty that resembles one which will be raised in connection with Collectionism: the coextensivity of some similarities. How can one justify Similarism when the same things can be similar in various respects? What this question tries to point out is, first, that if things are similar, they must be so in virtue of something and, second, that similarity must be reduced to that. Hence, contrary to what similarists hold and must hold if their view is to have credibility, similarity is not primitive. But if it is not primitive, then similarity is not a good candidate as the source of universality.

The problems of Similarism go even deeper than these objections suggest. In Chapter 1, it was pointed out that the case of a universe with only one individual is certainly within the realm of possibility. In such a case, we would have to concede not only the individual but also the universal or universals that it instantiated, since the individual would necessarily have to be of a certain kind. But what this indicates is that no similarity of any sort is necesary for universality, since there not being more than one individual in the universe would preclude the similarity of that individual to something else. Granted, this is a rather unusual example, but more common examples are perfectly conceivable. Indeed, there is nothing contradictory in the notion of only one thing in the world having a feature, such as a particular shade of color.[40]

To this one may wish to retort that, in the two examples cited, there would be possible individuals of the same kind and that, as such, similarity would still be in the game. The answer to this is twofold: First, it is not clear that potential similarity, which is what we would have in this case, could do the job. It could perhaps do it ontologically, but it is hard to see how it could do it epistemically, since we could not know about this similarity until it became actual in individuals. Second, possible individuals are such only in the case of individuals that belong to types subject to multiple instantiation. Individuals such as "God," "the first human conceived in a test tube," and the like, that are not subject to multiple instantiation, cannot involve similarity, for similarity requires at least two things. Similarity is fundamentally a relational notion and universality, just as individuality, is not. This is part of what I tried to establish in Chapter 1.

Some have answered that even if there is only one individual, the individual would have parts, and therefore there would still be similarity, in this case among the parts.[41] But this answer assumes that the individual in question is physical and/or complex and so likewise with its features. And this is not necessarily the case. In fact, I am not even sure one can justify Similarism on the basis of similarity of parts, but even if one could, it cannot be done with features, such as rationality, which lack physical extension.

Collectionism. Collectionism is as old as Tokenism and Wordism and, as with them, its adherents have not been many.[42] The view can be simply stated as holding that universals are collections. 'Collection' is a traditional term that goes back to the Middle Ages.[43] The more contemporary versions of this view identify universals with sets or classes.[44] Another but rare version of it goes back to Plato and identifies the universal with wholes of which the individuals are parts.[45] There are, therefore, three different versions of Collectionism, depending on whether the universal is identified with aggregates, classes, or wholes. Except for the class view, all forms of Collectionism reduce the universal to a group of individuals. Cat, for example, is the same as the group of individual cats. What the group includes varies from author to author. Some include past, present, and future cats, while others include only past and present. Still others speak of all cats, whether real or possible, and so on. These distinctions are immaterial at present. What is relevant is the point that the universal is nothing more than a collection of individuals. For those who identify universals with classes or sets, however, the situation is different; they usually make a distinction between a mere aggregate or collection and a class or set. If the distinction is not made, then the position is reducible to one of the other two versions of Collectionism mentioned. But if it is, those who maintain this position have to contend with the explanation of the notion of class and how that is to be distinguished from the notions of aggregate and whole.

Supporters of Collectionism have found it attractive because among other things it avoids positing universals as empirically unverifiable entities. By identifying the universal with a set or collection of individuals, it avoids the problems that plague most forms of Realism. If one takes for granted that the objects of experience are or at least are perceived to be individual, it would be impossible for the realist to establish the reality of universals on empirical grounds. But, of course, the collection nominalist does not have that problem, since it is individuals gathered in groups that are regarded as universals.

Unfortunately, the disadvantages of this view outweigh this initial advantage. Some of these are quite obvious and have been frequently noticed throughout the history of philosophy. In a number of cases, they have to do with particular formulations of the view. The version of the view that identifies the universal with a whole fails miserably, as both ancient and medieval authors pointed out. The problems arise from the fact that each individual instance of a universal seems to instantiate the universal completely.[46] Thus, a man is fully man. But it is not clear at all that parts have all the features of wholes. A piece of pie, for example, does not have the same weight and size of a whole pie.

The version of Collectionism that identifies universals with classes or sets and then goes on to distinguish these from aggregates encounters difficulties, as already suggested, related to the nature of sets and classes and to the proliferation of entities. For after all, if classes and sets are something other than the collection of their members, what has the collection nominalist gained over his opponent, the realist? He still has an entity that is other than individuals. To call this entity a universal, as realists do, or a class, as this version of Nominalism does, makes no great difference. In short, this version of Nominalism has not gained anything in terms of economy over Realism by identifying universals with classes or sets.

Apart from these specific objections to the different versions of Collectionism, there are also more general objections that tend to apply to all of its versions.[47] One of them is related to predication.[48] For it is generally accepted that one of the fundamental features of the universal, or at least of the terms that stand for it, is to be predicable of many individuals. 'Human being' is predicable of all human beings, and 'red' of all red things. However, if the universal is interpreted as a collection, how can it be predicated of individuals? If "human being" is equivalent to "the collection of all human beings," what sense can we make of the sentence 'Socrates was a human being', which would, according to this view, be equivalent to 'Socrates was the collection of all human beings'. Clearly, universal terms do not stand for collections since they are predicable of many and collections are not.

To this the collection nominalist may wish to answer that, according to his view, 'Socrates was a human being' is not translated into 'Socrates was the collection of all human beings', but into 'Socrates is a member of the collection of all human beings'. In this way the difficulty seems to be avoided.[49] Yet, it is not entirely avoided, for it is one thing to say that something belongs to a group and another to say that it is of this or that sort. The propositions 'Minina is a cat' and 'Minina belongs to the collection of all cats' are not equivalent. The first one tells us something about what Minina is; that is, it specifies some property or feature that Minina has, while the second only identifies Minina as a member of a group. Moreover, if the collection nominalist were to rejoin by saying that it is not just any group that is in question and, therefore, that 'belonging to the group of all cats' implies having some property or feature, then, of course, the original point of the objection is granted, namely, that what is important and determining is not that Minina *belongs* to a group but that after all she *is* a cat. Hence, we cannot conclude that 'Minina is a cat' is analyzable into 'Minina belongs to the group of all cats', but rather the other way around.

This same point can be put in a different way. If Collectionism were to be taken seriously, it would have to hold that the features of things which constitute the bases of their being of a certain type are the result of grouping. But this seems contrary to experience, logic and metaphysics. Taking experience first, it seems that things are grouped into collections because they have certain features which are similar to or, depending on one's interpretation, the same as the features of the other things that constitute the collection, not vice versa. A human being, for example, is part of mankind or the collection of all human beings because the individual in question is a human being. It would be odd to say that someone is a human being because that person is part of mankind. Individuals, as it were, come first in experience, since it is individuals that are first perceived in sensation and only later understood in terms of general concepts. And they also seem to come first in logic, for meeting the conditions necessary for belonging to a collection precedes the actual belonging. (I do not believe the Causal Theory of common names interferes with this view, as will become clear in Chapter 6.) Metaphysically also there seems to be a priority of individual over collection, since it is not clear that a collection can exist without members (the case of the so called "null set" is peculiar), while the existence of a unique individual is certainly not contradictory.

Another common objection is quite related to the one just mentioned. It points out that if Collectionism is correct, then one would have to expect changes in universals with changes in membership.[50] Anytime the population of mankind increases or decreases due to births and deaths, "human being" would have to change, and so would the corresponding characteristics of individuals. But, of course, experience tells us that that is nonsense.

One way of answering this objection is to identify collections only with the group of all possible individuals rather than with groups of actual individuals.[51] But this will not help much, for how can possible individuals be distinguished except by reference to some feature or other? The point I am making is that with possible individuals it is even more difficult to argue for this view. Even if one were to accept this as an answer to this particular objection, the upholder of Collectionism would still have to answer the questions already raised. This means that this objection cannot stand alone, of course.

The explanatory power of Collectionism, then, is not great. If collections are seen as arbitrary, then the view clearly does not explain how the nonarbitrary character of universals can be derived from them. But if collections are not seen as arbitrary, then their nonarbitrary character must be due to a condition that the members of the collection meet, and it is the latter that should be regarded as the universal, not the collection, which is after all only one of its results.[52]

Another difficulty that is sometimes brought up against Collectionism points out that this position has a problem in accounting for noninstantiated universals.[53] Let us assume, with Collectionism, that 'red' names the set of red things, but what does 'unicorn' name, since there are no such things as unicorns?

There are two ways of answering this objection. One simply says that there are no noninstantiated instantiables.[54] Thus, notions such as "unicorn," which are uninstantiated, either have no sense or, if they do, when they are predicated of something they yield a false proposition. 'Socrates is a unicorn' is either nonsensical or false. This way of answering this objection does not appear to me to be convincing. The reason is that there are many instantiables that are neither contradictory nor instantiated and therefore could at some time be instantiated even if in fact they never are. A notion such as "unicorn" could in fact become instantiated through special breeding, even if it has not happened yet.[55] Thus, there can be noninstantiated instantiables.

The second answer to the objection fairs much better. It argues that uninstantiated notions such as "unicorn" are instantiated in members of the set of possible unicorns, and therefore they are not empty terms. This defense, of course, relies on the notion of "possible individuals," but apart from the questions which that may entail, I believe it is successful in answering the original objection. This means that the objection is not sufficient to undermine Collectionism; we must rely then on a different argument to do so.

A way of bringing out the objectionable character of Collectionism is by pointing out the actual and possible coextension of different universals. For, if Collectionism were correct and the universal were simply a collection, the same collection of things could not possibly be regarded as two different universals. Take the class of "daughters of Norma Gracia" and the class of "daughters of Jorge Gracia." It turns out that these two classes have the same members, Leticia and Clarisa. How then can we justify the two ways of conceiving them? Of course, this may seem a somewhat contrived example, but what of "earthling capable of laughter" and "earthling capable of reasoning"?

Armstrong suggests that one could answer this objection by adopting an ontology of possible worlds, which he finds quite disagreeable.[56] However, I do not see that even that could help the view. It might in some cases, but it certainly does not seem to do so in cases of necessarily coextensive properties like "capacity to reason" and "capacity to laugh."

Finally, it should be pointed out that Collectionism depends on a view of individuality which was found objectionable in Chapter 1 and which, to a large extent, may be responsible for the basic tenets of the view. The view holds that individuality implies somehow being a member of a group or collection, and it is this view, coupled with the view that universality and individuality are mutually exclusive categories, that leads to the position that universals must be collections of individuals. But there can be individuals that are not part of any collection of actual or possible individuals, and therefore universals need not be collections of individuals. Examples of these individuals would be God, the first male born, and the satellite of the Earth, all of which belong to classes that have only one member.

Before we move on to the discussion of Derivative Nominalism, one last general point must be made, namely, that none of the versions of Essential Nominalism examined here discuss individuality to any extent. We saw that Collectionism seems to presuppose a definite view of individuality that involves being part of a group. But the other versions add very little to this. In the case of Conceptualism, it would appear that the fundamental character of individuals presupposed is their difference and discreteness; hence, the efforts to explain how the universal concept in the mind can be derived from the perception of things that are "different" and "discrete." But this is seldom explicitly explored to any extent, in spite of the important role it plays in the view. Since essential nominalists hold that everything that exists is individual essentially, one would expect a more developed notion of individuality in this view. But, on the other hand, these versions of Essential Nominalism could regard individuality as primitive, that is, as one of the basic ontological categories of reality and, therefore, argue that no further analysis is necessary. The only analysis necessary would be of universality, which is derivative.

Still, the unexamined assumption by conceptualists and collectionists that individuality has to do primarily with difference and discreteness militates against Conceptualism and Collectionism, rather than helps them.

Derivative Nominalism

A second understanding of the formula "everything that exists is individual" is possible if one interprets it to mean that all existing things are individual, but their individuality is derived or, as the scholastics put it, *per aliud*. In this sense, both things and their features are considered individual, but they are so as a result of some action or process arising from a principle or factor other than the thing itself or its nature. A man's nature, for example, his humanity, is individual, and therefore it exists as his and only his humanity. It is not shared with or common to any other man. And the same may be said about the color of his hair or the size of his waist. But the individuality of his humanity and of his hair color and waist size is due to something other than the man's humanity. What this "other" is depends on the theory of individuation proposed and will be discussed later, in Chapter 4.

There are at least two versions of this position that merit attention. I shall term them Weak Derivative Nominalism and Strong Derivative Nominalism, respectively.

Weak Derivative Nominalism. This view has also been called "Moderate Realism," a name that is not quite appropriate for it, as we shall see immediately. It holds strictly to the notion that, although individuated, things like natures do have some unity and being (not existence, but nevertheless some ontological status) in addition to the unity and being they have as individuals.[57] "Horseness," for example, in addition to being "this horseness" (i.e., the horseness of this horse and of none other), has in some sense some being and unity. And this being and unity are not the being and unity of this horse, even when, strictly speaking, it does not exist except as "this horseness" or "that horseness" in this or that horse, or as "this concept of horse" or "that concept of horse" in someone's mind. It is the interpretation of this "some sense" that measures the degree of Realism or Nominalism of this view. Certainly it is a sort of Realism in that it posits some reality in natures, but it is a form of Nominalism in that it does not accept their existence and/or independent ontological status. It is for the latter reasons that I regard this view as a weak form of Derivative Nominalism, although it could also be classified as a form of Realism.

Criticisms of this view have centered around the being and unity attributed to the nature: (1) it does not seem clear what this sort of being and unity peculiar to natures is, and (2) if it were clear what it is, it is not clear that it is necessary to posit it. Indeed, the whole notion of "degrees of being" is one that always has been regarded with suspicion by philosophers, particularly by those who belong in the empiricist tradition, and I tend to sympathize with their attitude. There is no difficulty with the existence of cats, chairs, or even centaurs. The first two exist in the way members of the spatio-temporal world perceived by our senses exist. And the last is a case of conceptual or mental existence. We speak of something or other existing as "figments of someone's imagination," and this is the way in which centaurs exist.[58] But to speak of natures as having some sort of being is certainly odd, for we are told by those who accept this view that this sort of being is not to be identified with the types of existence that chairs and centaurs may have. Indeed, one of the best known exponents of this view, John Duns Scotus, specifically pointed out that the being of natures was peculiarly their own. And this seems to preclude its comparison with that of anything else, whence the difficulties one finds in accepting it. For it would seem reasonable to expect that a concept used to explain something else should be clear and have some basis in experience. And, yet, the peculiar ontological status that this view attaches to natures is neither clear nor grounded in experience. For this reason, this view appears confusing and uneconomical, facts that have not escaped its critics. Indeed, it seems to combine some of the disadvantages of Nominalism with some of the problems associated with Realism, and, when one tries to explain it, it turns into a stronger form of Nominalism or into an Immanent Realism.

Moreover, it also complicates matters with respect to individuality, for if natures have some being and unity peculiar to themselves, then one must explain how that being and unity is related to the being and unity proper to individuals. But more on this later.

Strong Derivative Nominalism. The second version of Derivative Nominalism borders on Essential Nominalism. It holds that the natures that exist as individuated have no unity and being except for the unity and being they have as individual things or as concepts in the mind of some individual knower. "Horseness," for example, has no ontological status in itself—no being and unity—except for the unity and being of an individual horse or of a concept of horse in some individual mind.[59]

Even though this position has been quite favored in the history of philosophy, it faces some difficulties. There are two that need to be mentioned at this time. First, there seems to be an incompatibility between the notion of derived individuality and the view that natures have no being and unity apart from the being and unity they have as individuals. For, one may want to ask, doesn't the process of individuation entailed by the derivative character of individuality according to this position (i.e., the process whereby a non-individual nature, or universal, as we have been calling them here, becomes individual) presuppose some ontological status in the nature prior to individuation? The process of individuation seems to presuppose some entity. The second difficulty arises from this, since it is not clear what the ontological status of that entity could be. In short, Strong Derivative Nominalism would seem to face a dilemma: either (a) to become weakened by positing some ontological status in natures, turning as a result into Weak Derivative Nominalism; or (b) to abandon the whole notion of derivative individuation, and then, of course, to turn into Essential Nominalism. By itself Strong Derivative Nominalism would seem to have difficulty standing up.

Appeal and Weakness of Nominalism

The appeal and weakness of Nominalism are precisely the reverse of the appeal and weakness of Realism. The main appeal of Realism is that it grounds knowledge and morality, giving science and ethics the ontological foundations they need in order to maintain objectivity. Its primary weakness is that it posits as reality a world without individuals and, therefore, different from the world of experience. The fundamental weakness of Nominalism is that it conceives science and ethics as products of the mind rather than reflections of what is real. Since the world is composed of individual entities, the general concepts and principles that constitute the elements of science and morals must be mental constructs of one sort or another. But if this is so, then how do they arise, and why do they not seem arbitrary? If there is nothing universal in things that determines and/or controls conceptualization, how can a universal concept be but arbitrary? And yet experience seems to suggest it is not; we cannot at will change species and regroup the elements of our experience. We can, of course, decide that from now on we will group human beings and rocks together and give the new group a name, but still that would not change the facts that human beings would be human beings and rocks would be rocks and that it is human beings and rocks that we have arbitrarily decided to place in the same class.

The great advantage of Nominalism is that it is an economical view that seems to take into account some of the most basic ontological features of the world as revealed in experience. Unlike Realism, it does not claim to rely solely on dialectical argumentation for its support but on a kind of basic intuition of common sense. For it seems a fact, for example, that Leticia is an individual and Realism's denial of it is quite contrived, to say the least. Yet, experience is not completely unambiguous, and therefore Nominalism cannot claim complete proof of its fundamental tenets from experience. For this and the other reasons already alluded to, philosophers have sought other perspectives that would combine the advantages of both Nominalism and Realism without their respective disadvantages.

Eclecticism: Some Things that Exist Are Individual and Some Are Not

Eclecticism holds a middle ground between Realism and Nominalism: Some things that exist are individual and some are not.[60] The nonindividual things in question are generally interpreted to be the features of things. Things themselves, such as Socrates or the tree I planted last summer in my garden, are considered to be individual, but their features are not.[61] Socrates is individual but his height, weight, and hair color, for example, are not, since some other man, such as Aristotle, may be as tall as he is, and as heavy, and he may have the same hair color. This position, then, differs from the ones outlined above in significant ways. It does hold to the same notion that there are two fundamental realms of things, but, contrary to Realism and Nominalism, it holds that these two realms are both real and not separate. Universal entities, such as whiteness, beauty, and the like, are as real as individual things, such as Socrates or my cat Minina, although different ontologically. Thus, the position could be described as holding in fact that there is just one world, but composed of both universal and individual entities.

Most authors refer to this sort of position as a form of Realism, since it is committed to the existence of some universal entities. But to do so tends to create confusion, since many of those who favor this position have strong nominalistic tendencies. Indeed, the position could also be regarded as a form of Nominalism, given that the universal entities it accepts are often thought to exist only in their instances, which makes them dependent for their existence on individual entities. In short, it is misleading to interpret this position as a form of Realism or Nominalism, and for this reason I prefer to keep the name Eclecticism for this middle-of-the-road view. The use of the term 'eclecticism', however, should not be taken to imply some kind of historical and/or logical priority of Realism and/or Nominalism over this position. Eclectic positions have often arisen as ways of dealing with the conflict between

Realism and Nominalism, but there are examples that show that in some cases they have preceded versions of the other views. Thus, historically there is no reason to regard Eclecticism as derivative. Nor is there reason to think of it as logically derivative, since its common sense and comprehensiveness give it a kind of preanalytical quality that puts it ahead, at least in these respects, of Realism and Nominalism.

There are three positions that may be considered versions of this view. All three have received considerable attention both in the history of philosophy and in more recent times and, therefore, merit separate discussion. Two are clearly eclectic, but the third may be classified differently, depending on the way it is interpreted. I shall refer to these three positions by their contemporary names: the Bare Particular View, the Characterized Particular View, and the Bundle View.

Bare Particular View

According to those who hold the Bare Particular View there are two types of entities. One type consists of what are variously called properties or qualities, in other words, features of things. These are considered to be universal, since they are the same in all their instances. Leticia's black hair color, for example, and Clarisa's black hair color are the same black hair color. In addition to these universal entities they also posit other entities, which, unlike them, are not universal but particular (the difference between the use of 'particular' and 'individual' in this context is not significant). They call these entities "bare particulars," to indicate that they cannot be analyzed or described in terms of features and characteristics, whence their bareness or decharacterized nature.[62] Yet, their existence is established on the basis of a dialectical need to account for differences among such beings as Leticia and Clarisa, or this sheet of paper and that one.[63] For, if all features were universal, and as such the same, how could individual differences among things be established? Indeed, herein lies the strength of this view, namely, that it neatly accounts for both the difference and sameness intuitively evident in the world of experience. The sameness among things is based on common features, the difference on the presence of a noncharacterized entity. Leticia and Clarisa, then, can be said to be the same with respect to hair color and other features, but they are said to be different in that each of them has a particular entity that renders them different from the other and from all other things as well.

This view is not a newcomer in the history of philosophy.[64] For example, John Duns Scotus, in the late Middle Ages, held a similar position, but he called bare particulars "thisnesses" (*haecceitates*). The features that substances had in common he called "common natures." The difference between his view and that of most holders of the contemporary Bare Particular View is that for

Scotus the common natures are individualized in the individual, while it is not clear that such is the case for those who propose the Bare Particular View.[65] It is for this reason that I classified Scotus' view as a form of Nominalism.

Other notions that are sometimes identified as direct ancestors of bare particulars are the Aristotelian notion of matter as ultimate substratum and the Lockean notion of substance. And indeed there is some sense in which Aristotle's view of matter as an ultimate substratum, bare of all features, resembles bare particulars. On the other hand, he is quite clear to note that this ultimate substratum "is of itself not a particular thing."[66] Since the cornerstone of the Bare Particular View is the substratum's particularity, we must avoid drawing too strong a parallel between the two views. Likewise, it has been pointed out that Locke's notion of substance as "something I know not what" is also an appeal to bare substrata.[67] But one must also be careful here, for again there are significant differences between the two notions. First, Locke's substance, in accordance with his empiricist—I would like to say "phenomenalistic"—approach is an idea, not really a metaphysical entity, as is the case of bare substrata. And, second, Locke's notion arises as a response to the need to account for a support for features. As such, it is indeed a notion of substance, if by substance one means, as he meant, what stands under and upholds features.[68] But the notion of bare substratum arises not primarily in response to the need to account for the support of features, but rather in response to the need to account for difference; bare substrata, if I understand this view correctly, are not primarily substances, even if in fact they turn out to have some of the functions that some authors have associated with substances.

In spite of the obvious advantages of the Bare Particular View, there are at least two serious objections to it.[69] The first is that it violates the Principle of Acquaintance; the second objection is that it does not solve the problem it sets out to solve, namely, to account for individuality. I shall take up the first here, leaving the second for Chapter 4, where I shall deal with it in detail. Concerning the first, it seems quite clear that the existence of these bare particulars is established dialectically and not empirically; it is because there is a need to explain numerical differences among things that appear otherwise to be the same that bare particulars are posited and not because we can point to bare particulars in experience. But this seems to violate the Principle of Acquaintance, a basic tenet of empiricism accepted by most of those who adhere to the Bare Particular View. This principle stipulates that "the indefinable terms of ontological descriptions must refer to entities with which one is directly acquainted."[70] And the term 'bare particular' does not seem to refer to any such entity.

Those who adhere to this view could and do reply to this objection in various ways. First, they can simply accept that their view violates the Principle of Acquaintance but reject the validity of the principle. They could argue, indeed, that ontological descriptions are not directly based on experience, but rather are the sorts of structural commitments which are used to make sense of experience. As such, they are only mediately and indirectly related to experience. Experience grounds the first level of discourse—sentences of the sort 'Leticia has black hair'—but not a second order, which attempts to explicate the elements given in experience, such as the ontological status of "Leticia" or "black."

This is, indeed, the road that many metaphysicians have followed in the past, but it is full of pitfalls and often leads to extraordinary violations of the Principle of Parsimony, multiplying entities beyond necessity. The Principle of Acquaintance, although controversial in itself, functions as a controlling device, which both discourages the multiplication of entities in an ontology and limits their number. Most proponents of the Bare Particular View recognize that once the principle is rejected, there seems to be little one can do to control their proliferation, for it becomes easy to solve problems by simply positing more and more entities. Of course, even the most notorious violators of the principle maintain that they adhere to it, so often arguments about metaphysical entities revolve not around whether the principle is violated or not, but around whether the entities posited are required or not.

It is these dangers that make a second response to the objection more acceptable to those who adhere to the Bare Particular View. Unlike the first response, it fully accepts the Principle of Acquaintance and consequently tries to show that we are in fact acquainted with bare particulars. Edwin B. Allaire made a gallant effort in this direction years back, and there have been others.[71] Unfortunately, this effort does not seem to be fruitful. Allaire, for example, argues that although individuals (i.e., bare particulars for him) are unknowable in the sense that they are not recognizable or reidentifiable, yet they are known in the sense that we are acquainted with them. Two discs that have all features in common could not be reidentified precisely because "they are the same in all (nonrelational) respects." Nevertheless, the fact that they are two, and we know them as such, shows, according to Allaire, that we are acquainted with them.[72]

This is an interesting analysis, but fails to establish its thesis. For it neglects to take into account the fact that the numerical difference of the two discs could be grounded in their relational differences and thus in fact it is the relational differences that, as some realists have argued, distinguish this bundle from another. In other words, by abstracting from relational features, Allaire's position is weakened and leaves us no closer than before to a solution of the difficulty.[73] It is this sort of consideration that leads Allaire both to attack the relational view and to present a different argument in favor of bare particulars in a subsequent article. We need not be concerned with his attack

88

on the relational view at this point, but his argument in favor of bare particulars requires attention.

He argues that to be presented with a thing is to be presented with all its constituents and therefore that, since bare particulars are constituents of things, we are in fact presented with them when we are presented with things.[74]

But this argument rests on a confusion between "being presented with something" and "being aware of something." That we may be presented with all the constituents of a thing when we are presented with the thing does not entail that we are aware of all the constituents of the thing even if we are aware of the thing. For, although "being presented with a thing" may entail—in fact, I am not even sure that is the case, but I am prepared to grant the point for the sake of argument—"being presented with all its constituents," it is not the case that "being aware of a thing" entails "being aware of all its constituents." I am aware of many people when I see them, but have no idea of the size and color of their lungs, for example. Moreover, since the Bare Particular View, as defended by Allaire, depends not only on this entailment but also on what he calls "phenomenological" grounds—which I interpret to mean some kind of awareness—and he has not shown how we are aware of bare particulars, we must conclude that there is no phenomenological support for the view.

Other supporters of the view have identified bare particulars with areas and argued that just as we are acquainted with areas, we are also acquainted with bare particulars.[75]

But, of course, this is no easy way out, since this solution seems to change substantially the original position or, alternatively, leaves matters as they were. The change has to do with the fact that areas are not de-characterized, as bare particulars are supposed to be in order for them to account for individuality. Areas have dimensions, and it is precisely because they are not de-characterized that we are acquainted with them, unlike with bare particulars. Of course, if areas were to be redefined as not being subject to characterization, then they could indeed be regarded as bare particulars, but they would also be as mysterious as the latter are.

One last point concerning this view: It should be clear from what has been said that the proponents of this view seem to assume that individuality is some kind of difference and that to be individual is to be different from others. Moreover, since this difference cannot be explained in terms of features, because these are either actually or at least potentially common to many things, they infer that it must be the result of some unique entity, which they call a bare particular. There are two problems with this reasoning. First, difference or distinction, as we saw in the first chapter, is not a necessary and sufficient condition of individuality. Second, as I shall point out in Chapter 4, positing bare particulars does not explain the individuality of things and adds another kind of entity to the already crowded philosophical world.

It is because of these and other difficulties that many philosophers have rejected the Bare Particular View and have adopted instead another eclectic position, the Characterized Particular View.

Characterized Particular View

The Characterized Particular View, also called by some the Qualified Particular View, is not new by any means. The only new thing about it is its name. In many ways, the Aristotelian view of substance, what he called "primary substance" in the *Categories,* is close to it.[76] The view argues that what it calls "particulars," which we call individuals here, are not de-characterized entities as the Bare Particular View maintained, but neither are they reducible to the bundle of characteristics they possess, as immanent realists hold. D. C. Long has put the matter as clearly as it can be put, perhaps, by saying that characterized particulars "are distinct from their qualities in that they cannot be reduced to them . . . but this is not to say that they are distinct from their qualities in the sense that they contain a distinct element which somehow possesses no qualities itself yet which is, as a matter of fact, characterized by them [even though] . . . it is not necessary that a particular thing have the quality-instances that it does have."[77]

There are clear advantages to this view. It preserves some of the advantages of the Bare Particular View, since it accounts for both the sameness and difference among things, while avoiding the violation of the Principle of Acquaintance. There is no doubt that we are directly acquainted with characterized particulars, such as Plato and this sheet of paper on which I am writing. There is nothing mysterious or unempirical about the basis on which we establish their existence within our experiential field. The problems with the view arise elsewhere, namely, with its refusal to allow the analysis of the characterized particular and, more basically, with the lack of clear elucidation of the relation between the particular and its characters.

That the notion of characterized particular cannot be subject to analysis, if this view is to work in any way, is not open to doubt. The proponents of this view explicitly acknowledge that fact. What is not at all clear is why this is so. For, in the first place, if individuals contain nothing other than their qualities, then they must be reducible to them. If A has nothing other than features *m, n,* and *z,* then A is nothing but *m, n, z.* And if we must maintain, as holders of this view wish, that A is not reducible to *m, n,* and *z,* then there must be something more in A than *m, n, z.* In short, those who maintain this view want to hold what seem to be two inconsistent views, namely, that individuals, or particulars, as they call them, are nothing but composites of features,

90

but at the same time cannot be analyzed in terms of those features.

Of course, the upholders of this position might still want to argue that if A has nothing other than features *m*, *n*, and *z*, then A is nothing but *m*, *n*, and *z*, for in addition to the features or qualities, there is the structure according to which the features are arranged. Thus, it is still possible to distinguish two things (A and B) that have the same features (*m*, *n*, and *z*) in terms of their differing structures. But this is to beg the question. For, clearly, if the structures of A and B are not the same, A has something that B does not have: whether it is called a feature, a second-order feature, a structure, a tie, a relation, or something else makes no difference.

More recently, Michael Loux has defended a version of the Characterized Particular View in which he argues that "each substance falls under a substance-kind and that since substance-kinds are not reducible to universals of any other type, each substance exemplifies a universal which guarantees its numerical diversity from every other substance."[78] Examples of substance-kinds are "human being," "dog," and they are to be contrasted with regular attributes and features such as "white," "red," and the like.[79] According to Loux's view, then, individuals that fall under the same substance-kind are indiscernible in that respect. Thus, two human beings are indistinguishable insofar as they are human beings. But he also claims that by the very fact that something belongs to a substance-kind, it is also numerically different. In short, to be a substance is to be an individual and vice versa; that is why Loux calls his theory a "substance theory of substance," although it might perhaps be better to call it a substance theory of individuality.

From what has been said, we can surmise that Loux's answer to the objection we raised against the Characterized Particular View would be to say that, while other supporters of the view did not have an answer as to why characterized particulars are unanalyzable, he does: They are unanalyzable because they are substances and substances are essentially unanalyzable. But does this answer provide a satisfactory explanation of the unanalyzability of individuals? I am afraid it does not. Indeed, it does not go much further than the traditional Characterized Particular View in that direction. Let me point out some reasons. First, what Loux calls "substance-kinds" are universals—a fact that he accepts—and as such do not contain in their nature or essence any feature that would insure their individuality. True, the individuality is in their instances, not in the kinds themselves. But this does not help, for then clearly there must be something in the instances that is not the result of the kind. And if that is so, then individuals that belong to substance-kinds are not individual in virtue of that fact, but rather in virtue of some other fact that Loux has not identified. For example, clearly there is a difference between "human being" and "Socrates," but Loux's theory has not explained it.

Second, why should we accept the view that substance-kinds like "hu-

91

man being" imply individuality, while other features, like "white," do not? What is there is substance-kinds that is not present in other features? After all, substance-kinds seem to be nothing more than complex features. "Human being" involves the capacity to reason, corporeality, and so on, while "white" presumably does not. But not all nonsubstances-kind features are simple, like "white"; some are complex, like "muscular," and entail certain shapes, forms, and so on, and even "white" entails "color." Thus, it is not evident that there is a clear distinction between substance-kind universals and nonsubstance-kind universals, and yet Loux's view requires such a clear-cut distinction if it is to work at all.

Finally, as the complex universals that substance-kinds are, they should be able to be analyzed. To refuse to do that is simply to fall into a contradiction, for the very notion of complexity and/or composition entails the notion of components, and analysis is nothing but their identification. One could, perhaps argue that it is factually or epistemically impossible *for us* to analyze certain composites, but it is logically impossible to hold that they are logically unanalyzable. Therefore, to do so is to contradict oneself. The alternative is to reject the view that substance-kinds are complex universals, but, although not self-contradictory, that would seem to contradict experience and common sense.

The general problem with the various versions of the Characterized Particular View, then, is that, to use a common expression, it cannot have its cake and eat it too. It must either accept that individuals are not distinct from their features and, therefore, that they are reducible to them or, alternatively, hold that individuals are not reducible to their features because there is something in them other than those features. But to take up either of these two alternatives is in fact to abandon the Characterized Particular View in favor of Immanent Realism (individuals are nothing but bundles of universals) or the Bare Particular View (bare particulars individuate bundles).

Of course, like the Bare Particular View, most versions of the Characterized Particular View begin with the assumption that individuality has to do primarily with difference and distinction, a fact that contributes to the dilemma they face. Indeed, if individuality is fundamentally some kind of difference, it makes good sense to conceive individuals as having to be characterized in some way, for then the difference can be traced back to those characteristics.

Bundle View

Unlike the Bare Particular View and the Characterized Particular View, both of which are clearly eclectic positions in which individuals as well as universals are given a place in the world of reality, the Bundle View does not fall so clearly into the eclectic camp. Whether it does or not depends on how its claims are interpreted. The Bundle View may be interpreted as holding that only universals exist and that what are usually regarded as individuals are appearances of sorts that can be ultimately analyzed into bundles of universal features. Socrates, for example, is not in reality an individual thing, but rather a bundle of universals: snubnoseness, baldness, five-foot-five-inch tallness, and so forth. Understood thus, this view cannot be considered a form of Eclecticism, but rather a form of Realism, since it holds that only universals exist and that individuals are mere appearances.[80]

On the other hand, the Bundle View could also be interpreted as holding that both universals and individuals exist. The first are the features of individuals: Socrates' snubnoseness, baldness, and five-foot-five-inch tallness, for example. The latter are the bundles of these universals, whose individuality is clear from the fact that they differ from each other. Thus, Socrates is a bundle of features different from the bundle that Aristotle is, for instance. Clearly, if the Bundle Theory is interpreted in this way, it looks as if indeed it commits itself to the existence of both universals and individuals and, as such, can be appropriately classified as a form of Eclecticism. Because of this, I have decided to add a brief discussion of it at this point. Naturally, if the Bundle View is interpreted as a form of Realism, there is no need for further discussion, since the points made above concerning that perspective also apply to it, particularly the remarks made in connection with Immanent Realism.

The advantages of this view should be quite evident. In the first place, it avoids the problems of analysis faced by the Characterized Particular View, and likewise it sidesteps several of the difficulties encountered by the Bare Particular View. For the bundle theorist, the individual is fully analyzable into its features, and it contains nothing mysterious, unempirically verifiable, or *sui generis,* that explains its difference from other things. Individuals (that is, bundles of features) are different because they contain different features and ultimately, as some of the supporters of this position have put it, because they cannot share the same spatio-temporal coordinates.[81]

All this seems reasonable and in many ways supported by common sense. Still, the matter is not as simple as that. The Bundle View faces serious obstacles that ultimately produce its demise. Most of these will be discussed in detail in Chapters 3 and 4 and, therefore, need not be raised here. Still, there are a couple of things that should be mentioned at this point even if they are repeated and explained at greater length later. The first is that the success of the theory and its character as an eclectic position depend on its ability to maintain a distinction between universal and nonuniversal bundles of universals. If the view is going to be successful and considered eclectic, it must be able to explain the difference between universals and individuals, and, as we shall see later, this is by no means easy. Indeed, I believe it is not possible, since complex universal features, like human being, are as much bundles as Socrates or Aristotle. But more on this in the mentioned chapters.

The second point I wish to make is that the Bundle Theory is built on the erroneous conception of an individual as what is different from everything else. Now, if one accepts this erroneous conception, there seems to be some point to the view. But if, on the contrary, one rejects that view of individuality and interprets it as noninstantiability, as I have done in Chapter 1, then the Bundle View fails to account for individuality, as we shall see more clearly later. In this, it shares the same incorrect assumption about the intension of 'individuality' present in the Bare and Characterized Particular Views. Naturally, a failure to account for individuality implies that in the last analysis the Bundle View turns out to be a form of Immanent Realism disguised under some appropriate verbiage. And if this is so, then the difficulties raised earlier in connection with Immanent Realism apply to it after all. Apart from this, as already mentioned, there are other difficulties with the theory related to both its stance concerning the ontological character of individuality (to be discussed in Chapter 3) and its claims concerning the principle of individuation (to be discussed in Chapter 4).

Appeal and Weakness of Eclecticism

The appeal of the Eclectic View is that it accounts for both sameness and difference, borrowing from the strengths of both Realism and Nominalism. Like Realism, it provides ontological status for universals and thus a basis for scientific and ethical discourse. But, as Nominalism, it tries to limit the number of entities, while leaving a place for individuals in the ontology. Unfortunately, it faces a serious dilemma: either it rejects the Principle of Acquaintance, so valued by most proponents of Eclecticism, or it turns into a Realism of sorts. And both of these alternatives have difficulties, as we have already seen, and lead to puzzling results. What can be done, then? Is there a way of determining the extension of 'individuality' without falling into one of the positions described and thus adopting its undesirable consequences? Or must we declare this problem unsolvable, or perhaps spurious?

Extension of 'Individuality'

It is clear from what we have seen that an impasse has developed concerning the determination of the extension of 'individuality' and the corresponding category of universality. Each of the basic solutions discussed faces serious difficulties of which there does not seem to be a clear way out. In a sense, it appears to make as much sense to be a realist as to be a nominalist or an eclectic. All three views and their various versions have appealing advantages and what look like insurmountable difficulties. The latter function as springs that, once set in motion, force the proponents of the view to modify it in ways that often turn it back into one or another of the other unacceptable views, for which it was supposed to be an alternative; that is, the modifications introduced in each of these views to answer the objections brought against them have the effect of metamorphosing the view into one of those that had been found wanting in the first place. That there does not seem to be a clear way out of this quagmire can easily lead one to think that this problem is unsolvable or spurious. And, indeed, there are many who choose one of these paths.[82] Neither those who find the problem insoluble nor those who find it dissoluble seem to me to be right, however. I believe both that the problem is genuine and that it has a solution, although I also believe that the way the problem is usually formulated is responsible to some extent for the difficulties involved in it and leads often to insoluble and/or spurious issues. Hence, if a solution to this problem is to be found, the first thing that needs to be done is to clarify the issue that is at stake.

Preliminary Clarifications

We began this chapter by raising the question of the extensions of 'individuality' and 'universality', but all the answers we have discussed go beyond this and deal with the existence or nonexistence of individuals and universals. Thus, the original question, i.e., "To what things (using 'things' in a very broad sense without ontological implications) do individuality and universality extend?)" was transformed into the question of whether individuals and universals exist. But these two questions are quite different. And this, apart from the intuition we have about their meaning, is clear from the types of answers that the questions can take. The first requires a specific answer that gives a list of things or types of things (if there are any) that are individual and another list of things or types of things (if there are any) that are universal. But the question concerned with existence can be simply negative or affirmative: no, individuals (and/or universals) do not exist, or yes, individuals (and/or universals) do exist. So the first source of confusion concerning this issue is that it involves two separate questions that need to be distinguished.

A second difficulty has to do with the confusion of individuality with the various notions explored in Chapter 1. For, if individuality is understood as some kind of difference or as identity, for example, the extension of the category could be different from its extension if individuality were to be correctly understood as noninstantiability. And the same could be said for universality. We have already seen examples of these implications. For instance, if individuality is conceived primarily as difference or distinction, then it would become difficult to hold that the instances of simple qualities, such as

95

yellow, could be individual. For, how would one be able to distinguish between the yellow of his shirt and the yellow of her blouse if both were yellow in exactly the same way? Indeed, most views that interpret individuality as some kind of difference or distinction restrict the extension of 'individuality' to complex things, such as a human being or a cat. But that creates difficulties also, as we shall see in a moment.

The extensional problem, then, needs to be formulated in terms of two questions. The first asks properly which things are noninstantiable and, correspondingly, which are instantiable. And the second asks whether the things identified as noninstantiable exist or not and likewise with the things identified as instantiable.

To What Things Do Individuality and Universality Extend?

In order to facilitate an answer to the first question, namely, to what things do universality and individuality extend, we will try to answer direct questions about various sorts of things. We can begin, for example, by asking whether things such as Aristotle, Socrates, my cat Minina, the shrub I planted in my garden last spring, and so on, what some philosophers call "material substances," are noninstantiable.[83] And the answer seems to be quite clear: They are. Socrates, for example, does not seem capable of instantiation. As I pointed out earlier, he could be cloned or he could be used as an example or model for others, but he is not instantiable in the way that "human being" is. Socrates is a noninstantiable instance, not an instantiable. Moreover, the same can be said about the other examples cited. Neither Aristotle nor my cat Minina nor the shrub I planted in my garden last spring are subject to instantiation. There are no instances of Aristotle, Socrates, or the others as there are of "human being," "cat" or "shrub." It is true that sometimes one speaks of someone being "an Aristotle" or "a Plato," as in the proposition 'Peter is an Aristotle, but John is a Plato'. But in these cases, the expressions "an Aristotle" and "a Plato" do not refer to the individuals Aristotle or Plato, but to the characteristics that make them a type, which in turn can be instantiated. In this sense, the instantiable is not the noninstantiable Aristotle, although Aristotle, being such a perfect instance of it, has given his name to it. So that we can translate the proposition in question to something like 'Peter is like Aristotle, but John is like Plato'. Moreover, the very features of things do not seem to be instantiable. Neither Socrates' hair color nor any of the other features he possesses seems to be capable of instantiation, for his hair color appears to be rather a noninstantiable instance of a color, which is in turn instantiated in Socrates' hair and may be instantiated elsewhere as well. These examples could be multiplied to no end, since the world of experience seems to be full of noninstantiable instances.

The view that things, such as Socrates, my cat Minina, and the shrub I planted in my garden last spring, are individual is not very controversial, at least if individuality, as I have maintained, is understood as noninstantiability. But the view that the features of Socrates, my cat Minina and the shrub I planted in my garden last spring are individual is another matter. This position was very popular in the later Middle Ages,[84] and even in this century it has had its defenders, but its supporters have been less in number than the supporters of the contrary view,[85] and its attackers have been many.[86] What the view holds is very simple, as already stated: It maintains that just as Socrates is individual, so is the color of his hair. When we speak of the colors of Leticia's and of Clarisa's hair for example, even if the color in each case is exactly the same—not just that it appears the same, but that it is the same type of color—in every way, the color of Leticia's hair and the color of Clarisa's hair are two instances of the type of color of hair Leticia and Clarisa have. These individual features have been called by different names by different authors, but since they are as noninstantiable as the things in which they are present, I find no difficulty in calling them individual features.[87] Now given the opposition that this view has aroused and its disreputable state at present, something must be said in its defense.

I want to begin by stressing the point that in order for the contrary view to be sound, namely, the view that holds that the features of things are not individual while the subject of those features is (Socrates is individual, but the black color of his hair is not), it must also hold that there is a significant difference between such things as "human being" and "black color of hair" that would explain why one can be individual while the other cannot. For, if there were no such difference, then the view could not maintain that Socrates (i.e., an instance of "human being") is individual, while the black color of his hair (i.e., an instance of "black color of hair") cannot be. But the fact is that there does not seem to be any significant difference between "human being" and "black color of hair" that may explain why one can be individual while the other cannot, a fact that most surely helps those who support the Bare Particular View to maintain that "human being" does not become individual, but rather that the individual is the bare particular to which "human being," as it were, attaches or in which "human being" is instantiated or exemplified. For both "human being," for example, and "black color of hair," are predicable of Socrates, and therefore seem to be features of him.

A clear difference between "human being" and "black color of hair" is that "human being" seems to be a complex feature which includes such other features as rationality and corporeality, while "black color of hair" seems to be a simple, or at least a more simple, feature. But complexity alone cannot be given as a reason why "human being" can become individuated and "black color of hair" cannot, since there are many complex features, such as corporeality, which, as complex, could not be distinguished from features, such as "human being," and yet upholders of this view would not wish to regard them as individual. Hence, if there are such individual things as Socrates and my cat Minina, there is no reason why there should not be such individual things as an individual black color of hair; that is, there is no compelling reason why one should oppose the view that the features of things should not themselves be individual (i.e., noninstantiable).

What this argument does is put the burden of proof on those who hold that individuality does not extend to the features of things. And I believe that in fact this is as it should be. But the controversy does not end here. There are further considerations of diverse value that can be brought to bear on this issue. One tries to support the individuality of features by arguing that the features of things are locally separate from the features of other things even if they are the same type of feature (say, for example, color) and that this shows that they are individual rather than universal. If the white color of this sheet of paper is here on this sheet, and the white color of that sheet of paper is there on that sheet, then the white color of this sheet and the white color of that sheet must be two and not one. This, of course, does not prevent the two colors from being the same one *type* of color, namely, white, and as a result specifically indistinguishable. But it is the confusion between their *type* (i.e., universality) and their *number* (i.e., individuality) that gives rise to the contrary position.[88]

On the other hand, some philosophers have argued that features, at least qualities such as colors, are not locally separate except in the trivial sense of belonging to separate concrete things.[89] But that does not seem concordant with our basic intuitions and the way we talk about the world. After all, we do consider colors to extend or spread over the surfaces of bodies and, in a particular body, over only part of its surface. So how can it be argued that the colors of two bodies are not locally separate? And there are other cases of features and relations that seem even more clear, like, for example, the relation of contact between one ball and a piece of cloth and that between another ball and a different piece of cloth.[90]

Other philosophers have argued, however, on the basis of ordinary usage, that even when colors and other such features are subject to spatio-temporal coordinates, that is no evidence that they are individual. For example, when a father teaches a child about the color green, he may say, "Here's green, and here's green, and here's green again." And we do ask questions such as "Where is virtue to be found?" And all of this, so we are told, points to the fact that universals, such as "greenness" and "virtue" do appear at certain places and times even though they are not individual.[91]

But the conclusion of this argument does not follow from the premises. In the first place, at most what could follow from them is that in English we sometimes *talk* as if the universal "green" and the universal "virtue" do appear at certain times and places. But that conclusion does not carry much weight: for we can always be mistaken in what we say; or English might have a peculiar structure and grammar; or we could always point out that, regardless of the linguistic form, what the father means to say is that "the color of X is a good example of green," or, if we are really nasty, we could simply answer that the father is not a very sophisticated individual and therefore confuses "green" with "this green." Second, even if the *talk* about green, virtue, and other features reflected the way things are, namely, that green and virtue are localized, the argument gives no grounds for the conclusion that they are not in fact localized—that they are seems rather a gratuitous assumption. Thus, all of this goes to show that the argument in support of the individuality of features based on their localization is far from being conclusive. But the objections against it cannot be considered conclusive either, for they rely on intuition and ordinary language, and therefore are subject to question.[92]

Another argument in favor of the individuality of features is an old one to which we have already referred when arguing against Immanent Realism. For this reason there is no need to reproduce it in detail here. Let it suffice to say that it questions the universality of features of things based on the fact that when features undergo changes in one thing, the same features in other things do not necessarily change. When I burn the white sheet of paper on which I am writing, its color is also destroyed, but the white color of another sheet of paper is not destroyed. Therefore, so the argument goes, the white color of the two sheets cannot be considered the same and thus universal, but rather there must be two individually white colors independent from each other.

A third argument in favor of the individuality of features is effective only against those who hold that things, such as Socrates, my cat Minina, and the shrub I planted last spring in my garden, are nothing apart from their features, but since this view is very widespread in contemporary philosophy, the usefulness of the argument is considerable.[93] It is frequently found in two modes: The metaphysical version points out that if things are nothing apart from their features, they could not be individual unless the features were themselves individual; in the terminology favored here, a thing could not be noninstantiable unless its features were noninstantiable. In its epistemic version, the argument points out that if a thing is nothing apart from its features, we could not know the thing without knowing its features, and we could not know the thing as different from its features.

The only two ways to escape these conclusions and therefore the individuality of features is (1) to accept that things are something more than their features or (2) to reject the individuality of such things as Socrates. But both of these alternatives are highly undesirable. The first has controversial consequences, which we shall examine in more detail in Chapters 3 and 4, and the second clashes too obviously with our experience. For it would be very odd to say that Socrates and my cat Minina are not individual.

Finally, it should be pointed out that ordinary usage itself does not contradict the view that features are individuals. It is true that, as we shall discuss in Chapter 6, features are not given proper names, and in this they are different from such things as my father or your cat. And it is also true that English expressions such as 'his black color of hair' are ambiguous, meaning sometimes "his type of black hair color" and at other times "this individual black hair color." But the very fact of the ambiguity indicates that English is neutral with respect to this ontological issue. Indeed, in Spanish, for example, there are commonly used expressions such as '*su blanco*' (his white) or '*el blanco del ejemplo*' (the white of the example), which carry with them more clearly the implication of an individual referent, although again it is possible, depending on context, to interpret them differently.[94] Therefore, one should not be able to disprove the individuality of features merely on the basis of ordinary language. The most that could be done is to give realistic analyses of ordinary expressions, offering them as alternatives to analyses that support the individuality of features.[95]

Before we move on with the development of this view, there is one interesting objection that should be considered. It has recently been formulated by Armstrong, but it goes back to the scholastics. Suárez, for example, devoted Section VIII of *Disputation* V to it.[96] The difficulty can be formulated thus: If features are individual, it should be possible for several features of the same type to be simultaneously present in the same subject. So that, for example, a man could have more than one black color of hair at the same time or more than one blue color of eyes, and so forth. But clearly that does not make sense. Therefore, the view that features are individual is absurd.

Armstrong suggests as a way out of this problem the adoption of an *ad hoc* principle prohibiting exactly resembling individual features to be present in the same subject.[97] And Suárez simply accepts the consequence that it is possible in principle that several individual features of the same type be present simultaneously in the same subject.[98]

The reason why Armstrong sees as the only way out of this objection the introduction of an *ad hoc* rule and Suárez simply accepts the possibility of multiple similar accidents in the same subject is that neither of them considers the individuality of features to be derived. Armstrong, in fact, is not interested in the principle of individuation, and Suárez holds that things, including features, are individual of themselves, through their whole entity.[99] But authors like Thomas Aquinas, who hold that features are individuated by the subject in which they are, can point to the single subject as the source of the impossibility that several individual features of the same type be simultaneously present in the same subject.[100] And I would like to suggest something similar here. I do not want to say, as Thomas did, that features are individuated by the substance in which they are, because I will argue in Chapter 4 that the Principle of Individuation is existence, and a substance is not existence. But I would like to suggest that since in a thing and its features there is only one existence, it is that single existence that individuates and as such prevents several individual features of the same type from being simultaneously present in the same subject. This explanation is contingent on what will be argued in Chapter 4 and, therefore, the final resolution of this matter will depend on the outcome there.[101]

This answer also takes care of another potentially problematic question that may be raised at this point: If features like colors are individual, what happens when the thing they characterize is divided? For example, what happens to the individual white color of the sheet of paper on which I am writing when I tear the sheet up into two or more pieces of paper?

The answer is that just as the division of the sheet results in the destruction of one individual (the instance of eight-by-ten-inch sheet of paper) and the creation of two other individuals (two instances of eight-by-five-inch sheets), so the individual color of the original sheet ceases to exist, giving way to the two instances of the color in the newly created sheets. And this is possible both because color is a feature and, therefore, ontologically dependent on a subject and because its individuality, as we shall see in Chapter 4, is derived from the existence of the thing that it characterizes.

On the basis of what has been said, then, I would like to maintain that both things and the features of things are individual, and therefore noninstantiable. Now, so far we have been discussing physical and perceptual objects, but noninstantiability does not seem to be restricted to physical or perceptual objects and their features. Many nonphysical things and their features seem also to be noninstantiable. Socrates' mind, for example, does not seem subject to instantiation. It is possible that there be similarly acute minds, but not instances of it. Indeed, this becomes particularly evident with our own mind: It simply does not make any sense to think of our minds as universals or even as bundles of universals in spite of Hume's statements to the contrary.[102] And if we were to accept the existence of purely spiritual beings, such as angels, these again would not be instantiable. Indeed, the case of God would be one in which the very nature of the being would preclude multiplication, let alone instantiation. And the same could be said about the features of these beings. Socrates' intelligence is not physical, but neither is it subject to instantiation. And likewise with his goodness or his thoughts. Socrates' thoughts are instances of "thought," but they themselves cannot be instantiated in Aristotle, for example. When one speaks of two minds as having the same thought, this

101

can be interpreted as meaning only that they are thinking about the same thing, that is, that the thoughts are similar or similar in content, but not that one thought is an instance of the other or that they are the same instance of something else; both thoughts are instances, but different instances, of the same instantiable thought.[103] The thought Socrates has when he thinks of Pythagoras' theorem and the thought Aristotle has when he thinks of Pythagoras' theorem are both instances of the instantiable "thought about Pythagoras' theorem," and that is what makes them similar and justifies calling them "the same thought." But that does not mean that Socrates' thought is an instance of Aristotle's thought, or vice versa. They are both individual thoughts and, as such, noninstantiable instances of the same instantiable. We can find evidence that they are not the same instantiable, but rather noninstantiable instances, in that they are subject to different temporal coordinates. And they can be independently terminated, interrupted, and the like.

Not all answers to the question "Is X a noninstantiable instance?" are as intuitively obvious as some of the ones given. Art objects, for example, pose difficulties, for they seem indeed to be individual and at the same time to be instantiable. Take Velázquez's *Las Meninas*. The original painting is in El Prado, but I have several reproductions of it in my drawer, and there are countless reproductions by young aspiring painters who copy it in order to master the Velázquez technique. Let us assume, moreover, that there is at least one of these reproductions that is indistinguishable from the original. It was done by one of Velázquez's own disciples during his lifetime who used the same type of materials as were used in the original painting. Couldn't we say under these conditions that the reproduction was an instance of the original painting and therefore that Velázquez's *Las Meninas* is instantiable and therefore a universal?

The answer to this question is similar to the one given to the case of clones raised in Chapter 1: The original painting *Las Meninas* by Velázquez is not instantiable, but rather it is a noninstantiable instance of the universal painting *Las Meninas,* of which the copy of *Las Meninas* done by Velázquez's student is also an instance. That the reproduction was made after Velázquez's painting does not make it an instance of it, just as a statue of Apollo is not really an instance of the young man who served as model for the sculptor. After all, even Velázquez, with all his realism, did not have as his aim the slavish reproduction of the young maids he painted, but a certain view of them. And it is that view, that perspective, which is the instantiable of which both Velázquez and his disciples' paintings are instances. Indeed, the best forgery is not one which slavishly follows stroke by stroke the original masterpiece, for that is physically quite impossible, but the one produced by a forger who captures "the vision" of the original painter. This is in fact what, for example, Elmyr de Hory did, apparently very successfully, since he claimed that world museums were full of his forged Picasso's and Matisse's.

But what about music, for example, one of Mozart's symphonies? Again, what we have is a musical idea, an instantiable that is captured in notation by a composer, Mozart, and then instantiated every time the piece is played. The composer is no more and no less than the individual who makes this new universal accessible to many who cannot capture it because they lack inspiration, but who can perform it. There is nothing very mysterious about this, as long as one understands that individuals are noninstantiable instances. It is only when they are interpreted as something else that puzzles arise.

Another interesting case is numbers: Are one and two, for example, individual or universal? As with the Declaration of Independence, art objects, and other problematic cases, the solution to the status of numbers with respect to individuality and universality depends on a correct analysis and clarification. For the fact is that "one" and "two" stand for a variety of things. Let me mention at least four. First there are such things as unity and duality. 'X is one' means that X is an instance of unity, and 'X and Y are two' mean that X and Y taken together constitute an instance of duality. If this is the case, then clearly one and two are to be considered universals. Moreover, they are also universals if by 'one' and 'two' is meant a certain order as in "X is one on the line and Y is two." Likewise the types "1" and "2" or "one" and "two" are universal but their tokens '1', '2', or 'one' and 'two', are noninstantiable instances and therefore individual.

Similar points can be made about such things as propositions, sentences, events, and so forth. A bit of analysis on the basis of the conception of individuality proposed in Chapter 1 reveals that the difficulties involved in these examples arise generally from a misunderstanding about the formulation of the question in which the problem is framed or about the intension of 'individuality'. For example, if a proposition is conceived as a complex conceptual idea in someone's mind, then obviously it will be a noninstantiable instance of that conceptual idea, but if it is considered just as a conceptual idea, then it is an instantiable of which any mind could have an instance.

So far we have been dealing with individuality, but what can be said about universality? To what things does universality extend? The answer to this question, contrary to what one would be led to think based on the history of the problem of universals, is neither difficult nor mysterious, since those things that are instantiable seem clearly identifiable: "human being," "cat," "shrub," "mind," "thought," "thought about Pythagoras' theorem," and others. And we saw that in even the problematic cases of paintings, music, propositions, and the like, a bit of analysis rendered the examples unproblematic, clearly determining what is individual and what is universal. The answer to the question concerning what things are universal can, therefore, be found without much difficulty.

So much, then, for the first issue. Let us now address the second, presumably more difficult, question: Do individuals and/or universals exist?

Do Individuals and Universals Exist?

I believe that part of the difficulty with the question whether individuals and universals exist has to do with the fact that many philosophers try to answer it without first pausing to think about the basis on which a decision on this matter could be reached. And, yet, this is of utmost importance, because the way one goes about answering it will ultimately determine its answer. Now, this book is not meant to be a treatise on existence and/or being, and therefore I need not discuss in any detail criteria of existence and/or being and least of all decide which criteria are appropriate and which are not. But I do need to give some general idea of what is involved in existence and to point to some examples that would help to clarify this notion so that the discussion does not become muddled. Perhaps the best way to do this is to explain briefly and give some examples of various types of existence.

One standard classification of existence is into possible and impossible. When we say that something cannot exist under any circumstances because, like a square circle for example, it is contradictory, we are referring to a case of impossible existence. On the other hand, anything that, not being contradictory, could exist, no matter how improbable its existence, falls into the category of possible existence. Possible existence is also contrasted to actual existence. In this case what is meant by possible existence is that something can but does not in fact exist, while 'actual' refers to the existence of something that is not merely possible but exists in fact. Examples of possible existents are unicorns, hobbits, and my nonexisting twin brother. Examples of actual existents are the pen with which I am writing this sentence and the piece of paper on which I am writing it.

Another standard classification of existence is into real and apparent and, although this may look in some ways as the classification into possible and actual, these divisions do not coincide. For something to be a case of apparent existence, it must appear as if it were really existing while in fact it does not exist. This is the case with imaginary objects, such as hallucinations, which exist only as objects of thought in a confused, impaired, or dreaming mind rather than as things actually perceived. On the other hand, real existents are "out there" as they purport to be. The monster I saw in my nightmare last night exists only in appearance, but my body is real.

Finally, there are also classifications of existence into spatio-temporal and mental, necessary and contingent, transcendental and immanent, and many others, but these classifications refer to either very limited categories of existence or are technical in nature. For present purposes we need to take into account a broad view of existence based on ordinary experience. When I refer to existence, then, I have in mind general categories backed up by experience: actual, possible, and real. Neither impossible nor apparent existence need concern us for obvious reasons. Nor are we concerned with some of the peculiar, *sui generis* forms of existence discussed by some philosophers. This does not mean that I reject such notions; it only means that when discussing the question of the existence of individuals and universals we are restricted to the mentioned parameters.

Now, there are at least, and perhaps at most, two possible sources of information concerning the existence about which we have been speaking: experience and definition.[104] It seems to me quite obvious that we do decide on questions of existence on the basis of experience. I know, for example, that the white paper on which I am presently writing exists simply because it is present to me now. In this I must agree with Moore wholeheartedly.[105] But the situation with definition is more controversial, since I am sure many would want to dispute that definitions can give information about existence. After all, in order for definitions to give information about existence, existence would have to be some kind of feature and this is something that few philosophers, including myself, would want to grant. But, for the sake of argument, I am simply leaving open the possibility that a definition would or could give information about existence, for the moment.

Note that, also for the sake of argument, I am assuming that both simple features like "red" and things like "Socrates" can be defined. This goes contrary to a widespread view that holds that neither is definable. The first is not definable because it is simple and all definitions require analysis, and the second is not definable because the definition of an individual thing such as Socrates is no other than the definition of the universal class to which it immediately belongs. Of course, if simple features and individuals have no definitions, we cannot find anything about their existence from them, thus restricting our field of inquiry to experience. However, in order not to prejudge the issue and present a stronger case, I shall assume for the sake of argument, and contrary both to tradition and my own view, that both simple features and individuals are definable.

Having accepted that in principle it is possible to learn something about existence, both from experience and definition, and that this applies to simple and complex features as well as to individuals, what we need to ask next is the following: whether the experiences we have of individuals and universals and what we know about their definitions do in fact tell us something about their existence.

105

From experience it would seem that we know that individuals have both mental and nonmental existence. As mentioned earlier, I know the paper on which I am presently writing exists physically, out there, and I also know that its image exists also mentally, in my mind, when I picture and think about the paper. And the same can be said about the pen with which I write or about my cat Minina. The poor, sweet animal is out in the yard, now, looking for country mice, but her image is very much with me as well. On the other hand, our experience of universals is different from our experience of individuals. I do not experience "cat" in the same way I experience "Minina." And the reason is not, as Hume mistakenly thought, that "cat" is simply a more vague mental idea than the representation I have of Minina. The difference is in fact twofold. In the first place, I never experience "cat" as being out there, present to me in an extramental existence, as I do "Minina." And, in the second place, it is quite doubtful that I have any mental image at all of "cat." Indeed, if I try to picture "cat" mentally, I always come up with an image of some cat I have owned or seen somewhere. The cat in question always has a particular color of fur and a certain expression in the eyes; it is always friendly or distant, etc., while the image I have of "Minina" is always definite. Of course, that I do not have a mental image of "cat" does not mean that "cat" is not present in my mind in some sense. Obviously it is, but it is present not as an image, but as a concept; it is not pictured or imagined, but understood.

As a concept in a mind, "the concept of cat" is not the universal "cat," but the individual (i.e., noninstantiable instance) concept of cat. It is not very important whether this "concept" or "understanding" of cat is interpreted as a feature of the mind in which it is present, as one of its acts, or as something else. What is important to see is that it is not the universal "cat," just as the image of Minina in my mind is not Minina, but an individual representation of it.

But someone might argue that I find difficulty with experiencing "cat" because it is a rather complex notion and as a result might never be wholly presented in perceptual experience, while something like "red" is.[106] But in fact I find as many difficulties with experiencing "red," a simple feature, as I find with experiencing "cat," a complex one. For when I turn to experience I never find in it "just red," but always "the red of that house" or "of this brick." I can, of course, think about what it is to be red as I can think about what it is to be a cat, but that is thinking about the universal, not the individual. I can think, then, about a type of red or a type of cat, but that is not to have an experience of red or of cat. Still one might want to argue that we do have images of just red and, since images are part of perceptual experience, this proves that we perceive universals.

But it is questionable that we ever have an image of just red. For the images of red that one has are always of this or that red thing, and even when one tries to separate the color from the thing which has it, it is always presented as extended and belonging to something. But I shall have occasion to return to this issue later in Chapter 5, when we discuss discernibility.

From all this we can conclude that experience vouches for both the extramental and the mental existence of individuals (at least of some at any rate), while it gives us no definite answer as to the mental or extramental existence of universals.

Now let us turn to definition and see what it can tell us about the existence of individuals and universals. And here what we have to consider are the definitions of particular individuals and universals. If we consider, for example, the definition of "human being"—say, that we use the traditional definition "rational animal"—what we find is that it contains no reference to existence. Not that the definition stipulates nonexistence. It is in fact neutral with respect to the existential status of human being. Thus, if definitions make explicit the necessary and sufficient conditions of what they define, neither existence nor nonexistence are necessary and/or sufficient conditions of human being. And this is as it should be, for if it were in the nature of human being to exist, two undesirable consequences would follow: (1) human being would have to be considered as necessarily existing; and (2) individual human beings would have to be understood to have a double existence, one necessary insofar as they are human, and the other contingent insofar as they are individual. But neither of these two corollaries of the view make sense. The first, because the existence of human beings does not seem to be necessary in any sense. One could perfectly well imagine a universe in which human beings did not in fact exist or even were not a possibility—say a homogeneous universe composed of only one element. And, the second, because it would be contradictory for the same thing to have both a necessary and a contingent existence.[107] On the other hand, if it were in the nature of human beings not to exist, then the result would be the impossibility of human existence, something that is contradicted by experience.

In fact, it is precisely because "human being," and other universals, are neutral with respect to existence, as evidenced by their definition, that it is possible for individual human beings, cats, and so on (i.e., their instances) to exist contingently, as they do, in the world (i.e., that they may or may not exist) depending on the circumstances. For existence is something added to whatever a thing is.[108]

The definition of particular universals, if I may be permitted the generalization, does not and cannot yield knowledge about their existence or nonexistence, except insofar as they confirm that they are neutral with respect to either. But the same is true with the definition of individuals. And the reason is that the definition of an individual, as Aristotle pointed out, is the same as the definition of the universal of which it is an instance. Thus, the definition of "Socrates" is the definition of "human being." And, since the definition of "human being" yields no information about the existence of "human being" or "human beings," the definition of "Socrates" will do no better. But, of course, an individual is more than a universal, and therefore the neutrality of the universal need not be repeated in the individual. More on this later.

All of this means, then, that the definitions of particular universals do not themselves give any information about existence. And this is consistent with the widely accepted view that existence cannot be a matter of definition but of experience. However, one must be careful not to interpret experience too narrowly, as mentioned earlier, identifying it with perception. It is true that all perception is experience, but there are experiences that do not involve perception. For example, when I close my eyes and picture my cat Minina in my mind, I am certainly having an experience, but I am not "perceiving" Minina; I am only "imagining" her. It may be possible, then, to have an experience of what one does not perceive. Thus, that existence is a matter of experience should not be interpreted narrowly to mean a matter of perception.

But, then, what is the answer to the second question: Do universals and/or individuals exist? If what has been said is true, the question has to be rephrased both to take experience into consideration and to deal with particular cases. Hence, we should ask rather: Do we have any experience of such things as "human being" existing? And, for individuals, the question would be similarly phrased: Do we have any experience of the existence of such things as "Minina"? In the first case the answer is negative, but in the second it is affirmative, as we have already seen. The first answer seems to be concordant with the neutrality of universals with respect to existence stipulated in their definitions, provided that this neutrality is not interpreted as nonexistence; that is, empirical evidence seems to support, rather than contradict, what was said about universals. Existence, or nonexistence, does not seem to be something that attaches to them, while our experience of individuals vouches for their existence, actual or possible.

Finally, having pointed out that existence is something that attaches to individuals but that universals are neutral with respect to it, we must conclude two other things: (1) there is an existential priority of individual over universal;[109] and (2) an ontological account of the world must refer to both individuals and universals. It is the acknowledgment of the first that has given ammunition to the nominalist claim, and it is the realization of the truth of the second that gives credibility to Realism. For what the first asserts is that individuals exist while universals do not. And the second maintains that a philosophical explanation of the world will involve both universals and individuals without reducing them to each other. Unfortunately, both nominalists and realists have mistakenly thought that (1) and (2) are incompatible for reasons that will become clear presently. Moreover, (1) has led to the adoption of a position which seems to me to be quite absurd, but which is nevertheless frequently defended by nominalists. It maintains that universals are dependent on individuals in such a way that if there were no individuals there would be no universals.[110] Of course, the issue at stake is precisely the meaning of 'there would be' or 'there would not be'. If by 'there would not be' it were meant that universals did not exist, I would have to agree, not because universals are dependent on individuals, but rather because existence is not something that pertains to universals. Similarly, if by 'there would not be' it were meant that no mind would have universal concepts, I would again have to agree, in that minds are individual and the nonexistence of individual minds would entail the nonexistence of their content—but, of course, I do not accept the view that universals are reducible to mental concepts, as already explained. On the other hand, if by 'there would not be' it were meant that universals would be void unless they be instantiated, that seems to be nonsense.[111] Man, for example, is still a rational animal whether there are men or not and regardless of whether there are minds that think about it or not. To make universals dependent on individuals and/or minds in this way is the result of a serious logical confusion concerning the nature of universals and their capacity for existence. Indeed, if one understands clearly that existence is not applicable to universals, then one can accept both that individuals have existential priority over them to that extent, but the nonexistence of universals does not imply that they are creations of the human mind or dependent on it or on their own instances.

Still, there are those who defend the view that there are no universals when there are no individuals based on an identification of universals with features and individuals with substances.[112] If what is meant by 'universal' is "feature of a substance" and by 'substance' is "individual," then one cannot but accept the view that features depend on substances and that there are no features where there are no substances to have them. But, as I explained in Chapter 1 (I shall not repeat my reasons here), the view that identifies features with universals and individuals with substances seems to me to be quite mistaken. Indeed, there is something drastically wrong in indentifying "human being" with Peter's humanity, for example. Thus, again, the view that says that there are no universals when there are no individuals must be rejected.

Against what has been said, three important objections can be raised. The first and more general objection argues that the position I have adopted here has not really settled the existential issue concerning universals and individuals, since after all it has not told us whether universals exist or not, even though it maintains that individuals do. The second objects that by

109

refusing to say that universals exist, this view has really turned universals into nothing, destroying the objectivity of our knowledge. And the third argues that, by refusing to say that universals do not exist, this view has erected a world of things not subject to empirical verification, thus violating both the Principle of Acquaintance and the Principle of Parsimony.

These objections, as should be evident, are really against the part of the view that concerns universals and not against the part of the view that concerns individuals. The part of the theory concerned with individuals is much less controversial than the part concerned with universals. Now, although this book is about individuality and not universality and thus would not necessarily have to address issues involved primarily in universality, because of the importance of the objections raised and because of the correlative nature of universality and individuality, I shall try to answer the objections.

With respect to the first, that this view does not settle the existential issue because it treats universals as existentially neutral, the answer is that the objection is misguided on two counts: First, because it wants to apply to universality a category, namely existence, which, considering universality *qua* universality, does not apply to it. To require, therefore, an affirmative or negative answer to the question of whether universals exist or not is to miss the point; it would be like requiring an answer to the question whether diamonds are sweet or sour. The category does not apply in either case. Second, the objection is also misguided because in principle questions of existence are settled through empirical evidence or through definition. But we have no empirical evidence as to the existence of universals as such, and on the basis of definition we know that existence or nonexistence are not categories that apply to universals. Therefore, the answer to the question must remain as we have given it. All of this goes to show that the objection is misguided because it misunderstands both the nature of universals and the nature of existence.

The second objection argues that the position I propose fails in not recognizing that universals exist and that to do that has serious consequences for the way scientific knowledge has to be interpeted. But this objection, like the first, is misguided. The reason is that it interprets the neutrality of universals with respect to existence as nonexistence. But that, of course, is an error. For that universals are neutral with respect to existence does not by any means imply that they are arbitrary creations of some mind, or that our knowledge of them is knowledge of fictions. It simply recognizes the fact that universals are universals and that existence and nonexistence do not enter into their definition. Thus, that "human being" is neutral with respect to existence does not mean that to be a human being is no longer to be a rational animal or that the nature of human beings is a fictitious creation of some mind.

Of course, one might want to argue, still, with the realist that this way of considering universals, for example, "human being," does not distinguish between them and fictitious notions, such as "centaur." And, in fact, this is correct. For, as universals, "human being" and "centaur" are not different. Their only difference, apart from the features implied by their definitions, is that from experience we know "human being" has instances, while we have not found instances of "centaur."[113] This and nothing more is what 'fictitious' means in this context. But then the objection cannot really be taken seriously.

But the matter might not rest that easily. After all, realists have been arguing for centuries that if universals do not have some being, what we know when we claim to know something is a misrepresentation of reality: We know the world differently than it is.[114]

There are two answers to this objection that should be considered. First, as formulated, the objection can be directed against all nominalist and eclectic views, for only those that deny being to individuals can claim that knowledge of existing universals can reflect the nature of reality. If there were individuals, our knowledge of them would necessarily be distorted unless the basis of their knowledge were other than knowledge of universals. The problem, of course, is that many philosophers, like Duns Scotus for example, who have been impressed by this objection, accept the existence of individuals and hold that we know them through universals.

The second way to answer this objection has a broader impact. It can be articulated as follows: The objection fails to note that there are at least three different types of knowledge. When one has the first kind of knowledge one knows propositions of the form 'X exists'. Knowledge of the second kind involves knowing propositions of the form 'To be M is to be N'. And knowledge of the third kind has to do with knowledge of propositions such as 'X is an instance of M' or 'X is of the M type'. That universals are neutral with respect to existence does not affect the objectivity of the first type of knowledge, since the proposition in question has no universal term in it. (I am assuming, of course, that 'exists' is not universal.) Likewise, the knowledge of the second proposition is not affected since, although it contains universal terms, it has no terms that refer to individuals or to existence. Finally, the third type of knowledge is similarly not affected by the neutrality of universals with respect to existence, for what it specifies is that an individual is of a certain type or that it is an instance of the type, and not that it is the type. Thus, the knowledge of the individual as instance of a type does not involve any misrepresentation. From all of this, then, it should be evident that this very traditional epistemic argument in favor of Realism fails to undermine the view defended here.

Finally, the third objection, which wishes acknowledgment of the non-existence of universals, interprets the neutrality of universals as existence, arguing that to consider them neutrally is in fact to grant them a kind of quasiexistence. But, again, to say that universals are neutral with respect to existence is not to make of them existents of any kind; it is simply to recognize that existence and nonexistence do not enter into their definition and therefore do not apply to them *qua* universals. To say that they do not exist, or that they exist only as concepts, is to go beyond what we know.

Now, someone might still want to ask: But are universals real or not? And the answer to this requires clarification as to what is meant by this much abused word, 'real'. If by 'real' one refers to existence, then it is clear from what has been said that universals are neither real nor unreal, since they are neutral with respect to existence. But if by 'real' one implies that what is not real is somehow fictitious in the stated sense of not having instances, then it should also be clear that some universals are real and some are not. Of course, individuals are real in either sense, since they can exist and are not fictitious, unless of course they are the product of someone's imagination.[115]

Summary

The answers to the two questions raised in this chapter are clear. The first question asked to what things do individuality and universality extend, that is to say, which things are noninstantiable instances and which are instantiables. And the answer is that noninstantiability extends to things such as Socrates, my cat Minina, the shrub I planted in my garden last spring, the black color of Leticia's hair, and so forth, namely, it extends to things and their features, whether material or immaterial, while instantiability extends to such things as human being, cat, tree, black color of hair, and so forth (what Aristotle called secondary substances in the *Categories,* and their features.

The second question asked whether existence applied to noninstantiables only, to instantiables only, or to both. And the answer is that it applies only to noninstantiables and that instantiables are neutral with respect to it. Universals *qua* universals do not exist or not-exist. As long as this is kept in mind, most of the puzzles associated with the extension of universals and individuals disappear. Problems arise only when attempts are made to reduce universals to individuals and vice versa; when individuality is extended to universals and universality is extended to individuals, mixing these two ontologically distinct and complementary notions; or when their existential *status* are confused, thus violating the neutrality of universals. Indeed, it is the neutrality of universals that has tempted so many philosophers to engage in reductions. A quick look at the various positions examined earlier in the chapter will illustrate the point.

Realism in all its forms turns noninstantiable instances into instantiables by analyzing the first in terms of the second. Individuals, in this scheme, disappear, becoming functions of universals or complex universals. Transcendental Realism accomplishes this by separating individuals and universals but relegating the former to the realm of the unreal. Immanent Realism, for its part, does not separate them, but still holds that individuals are nothing but complex universals. In both cases, the distinction between instantiables and noninstantiable instances is blurred and/or reversed, and there is an attempt to do away with one of the categories. And this is done by apriorily negating the existence of one of them. Yet, we saw that in definition universals are neutral with respect to existence and that there is empirical evidence for the existence of individuals.

Nominalism does not fare much better, I am afraid. For, just as Realism, it tries to reduce one of these categories to the other, except that in this case the terms are reversed: Universals are analyzed in terms of individuals. As a result, the distinction between noninstantiable instances and instantiables is again blurred. Tokenism, for example, by holding that universals are tokens, paradoxically identified the universal with what might be regarded as a paradigm of individuality. Collectionism, again, by holding that the universal is a collection or set of individuals, turns instantiables into complex individuals. This is in a sense an exact reverse of Immanent Realism. Conceptualism makes the same mistake, for concepts are not instantiables. If they were, then their instances would have to have some of their ontological characteristics. Socrates would have to be considered an instance of "the concept of human being." But Socrates is not an instance of "the concept of human being," but an instance of "human being." My concept of human being is an instance of "the concept of human being," just as yours is, but Socrates is not. This position, like all the other forms of Essential Nominalism, confuses noninstantiable instances and instantiables. The same can also be said about some forms of Derivative Nominalism, since, although they are more complex, they still attempt to reduce instantiables to instances. Instantiables in some versions of Derivative Nominalism disappear from the ontological map even though they leave traces behind, such as the peculiar being and unity accorded to natures by Scotus. Yet, as we saw, universals by definition cannot be reduced to individuals and their existence denied, since their definition is neutral with respect to existence.

Eclectic views do not escape this criticism. The Bare Particular View, for example, in spite of its efforts to keep individuals (bare particulars) and universals (their features) separate, removes individuals from the realm of experience. In this it does not do much better than Realism, for it fails to recognize that such things as Socrates' black hair color are not universals, but individuals, that is, noninstantiable instances of instantiables, such as "black hair color." On the other hand, the Characterized Particular View cannot stand by itself, turning into the Bare Particular View or Immanent Realism

113

and therefore being subject to their weaknesses. Finally, the Bundle View is not really very different from Immanent Realism, where individuals are reduced to complex universals. Indeed, as in the cases of Realism and Nominalism, what Eclecticism does is to identify certain individuals, not all, with universals and certain universals, not all, with individuals. This is better than to obliterate one of the categories altogether by philosophical *apriori fiat*, but it reduces to the same type of move: attempting to determine existence and nonexistence on the basis of stipulative definition and, as a result, distorting even some of the empirical evidence we have for it.

In short, all these views confuse noninstantiable instances with instantiables, reducing one of these categories to the other, and as a result fail to develop an ontology in harmony with experience and reason. If it is true that individuality and universality are both exhaustive and mutually exclusive notions, they cannot be coextensive and least of all reducible to one another, nor can one of them be ignored. That should be the basic principle of any sound ontology and one that was accepted by such metaphysicians as Aristotle and Thomas Aquinas. Efforts to avoid it are all doomed to failure because they blur the distinction between instantiables and noninstantiables and as a result confuse the issue of extension. Thomas stated the point quite clearly in the third chapter of *On Being and Essence*. There he pointed out that what he called a "nature"—we have been using the term 'universal' here—when considered absolutely, according to itself and its proper meaning, cannot have attributed to it the ontological features characteristic of concepts (mental realities, which Thomas calls "universals") or individuals (such as Socrates).[116] The problem of the extensions of 'individuality' and 'universality' must be solved, then, by accepting individuals as what they are and universals as what they are and by preserving the empirical intuitions we have about the existence of individuals and the information about the neutrality with respect to existence of universals that we gather from their definitions.

In general, I would like to suggest that, apart from the confusions already pointed out, most incorrect views concerning the extensions of 'universality' and 'individuality' arise from two basic tendencies among philosophers. The first is the tendency to reduce categories to the minimum possible, and the second is to be suspicious of any concept that does not have reference in the world of experience. Both tendencies are related to principles that have some regulating and controlling value in philosophy. Reductionism is ultimately based on the Principle of Parsimony, according to which entities should not be multiplied beyond necessity. The other tendency is ultimately based on the Principle of Acquaintance, according to which, experience should back up knowledge. Yet, although these principles are sound, their application can be carried to extremes, which is what has happened with universality and individuality. The Principle of Parsimony has been incorrectly used to justify the reduction of universals to what they are not: substances, features of substances, concepts, collections, tokens, words, and so forth. And the Principle of Acquaintance, paradoxically as it may sound, has been the motivation behind the view that universals must exist in the same way in which other things exist, and we are acquainted with them as we are acquainted with individuals, for otherwise universals would lack objectivity.

By now it should be clear that the position I have adopted has much in common with what was called above Strong Derivative Nominalism and may in fact be described as a version of it. The objections raised against that view were precisely that the view seemed to have difficulty standing by itself and was easily turned into an Essential Nominalism or into an Immanent Realism. But I have tried to show that it is precisely the excessive tendency toward parsimony that is responsible for the transformation of this position into Essential Nominalism and the excessive emphasis on the need to find referents in experience for every concept we have that is the primary cause of the metamorphosis of this position into Immanent Realism. Since the excessive use of the Principle of Parsimony and the Principle of Acquaintance can be regarded as misguided, we need not, after all, worry about the objections raised against Strong Derivative Nominalism on their account.

Having suggested a way out of the impasse concerning the extensions of 'individuality' and 'universality', there remain still other important questions that need attention. One has to do with what the causes or principles of individuation are, another has to do with how we know individuals, and still another with how we refer to them. The first is taken up in Chapter 4, the second in Chapter 5, and the third in Chapter 6. The first is usually called "the problem of individuation"; the second involves the issue of the discernibility of individuals; and the third concerns the analysis of proper names, definite descriptions, and indexicals. Chapter 3, however, is concerned with still another problem, the ontological status of individuality, which must be settled before we deal with these.

3

Ontological Status of Individuality

Having provided intensional and extensional analyses of individuality, it is time to ascertain its exact ontological status and its relation both to the individual and its components. These issues concerned medieval authors considerably, but have not been discussed much ever since, except in scholastic circles and/or in historical contexts. For these reasons, our discussion will be more brief than that of the other issues identified in the Prolegomena, reflecting both the relative lack of interest on this matter in contemporary philosophy and the scarcity of contemporary background materials.

Perhaps the best way to approach this issue is to begin by describing the way in which medieval authors tended to frame this problem, since it is they who first formulated it with precision and concerned themselves most with resolving it. We might then be in a better position to decide how to deal with this matter and how to present it to a contemporary audience. The primary purpose of the reference to the medieval discussion, therefore, is not historical and accordingly will be kept general. No detailed references to individual authors will be made, since the aim at present is to grasp the basic issues at stake, rather than to ascertain the views of any figure in particular.

I shall begin, then, with a discussion of the medieval controversy, which will be followed by a contemporary reformulation of the problem. Four attempts to deal with this problem will be rejected: the views that interpret individuality as a substratum, a feature, a relation, and as not having any ontological status at all. In the final part of the chapter I shall propose the view that classifies individuality ontologically as a mode.

Medieval Controversy

The best way to understand the medieval formulation of the problem concerned with the ontological status of individuality is to say that medieval scholastics generally approached it in terms of two questions: (1) whether there is some distinction in reality (roughly what we would call an extensional distinction today) that corresponds to the distinction in thought (roughly the intensional distinction today) between an individual's individuality and its nature, and (2) what the basis of the distinction is. However, these two questions were usually explored together under one, more general question: "Whether in all natures [i.e., beings or entities] the individual as such adds something to the common nature,"[1] and this, as we shall see, lent itself to confusion. The term 'common nature' in this context referred to what is generally called "the nature" of the individual, that is, what the individual has or can have in common with other individuals.[2] The term 'individual', on the other hand, referred sometimes to the individual considered as a whole, Peter for example. And at other times, owing to a peculiar usage current in medieval times, to which attention was called in the Prolegomena 'individual' referred to the individuality of the individual; for example, what characterizes Peter as the individual he is.[3] For this reason, the question that they used in order to formulate the ontological issue may be interpreted in two ways. In one way it could be interpreted as asking: (a) whether it is the case for all natural beings that an individual, considered as such, is distinguished by something from its nature; (b) the character of this distinction, that is, whether it is extensional, intensional, or otherwise; and (c) the ontological status of the individual. For example, (a) whether Peter has something that man does not have and, therefore, is different from man; (b) the type of distinction holding between Peter and man; and (c) the status of Peter.

In another way, the question could be interpreted as asking: (i) whether it is the case for all natural beings that the individual's individuality is distinct from its nature; (ii) the character of this distinction, that is, whether it is extensional, intensional, or otherwise; and (iii) the ontological status of individuality. For instance, (i) whether Peter's individuality is different from man; (ii) the type of distinction holding between Peter's individuality and man; and (iii) the status of Peter's individuality. The first of these two interpretations raises a more basic set of issues than the second, since an answer to it determines to a great extent the answer to the second set, as we shall see. It is perhaps for this reason that scholastics generally chose the first interpretation in their discussions of this matter.

Basically there were three positions medieval authors adopted with respect to the ontological status of individuality. The first not only rejected the extensional distinction between the individual and its nature, but went so far as to reject as well the intensional distinction. Moreover, as a result of the rejection of the distinction between the individual and its nature, it concluded further, that there can be no distinction between the individual's nature and individuality, since the latter is nothing but what characterizes the individual *qua* individual. According to this view, then, there is no distinction, for example, between Peter and man or between what characterizes Peter as Peter (his "Petrinity," let us say) and man (or his humanity, as some preferred to put it). In short, this view held that there is no distinction of any kind, extensional or intensional, between the individual and/or its individuality on the one hand and its nature on the other, and therefore there is no need to postulate any basis for it in the individual. This is the answer to the two questions posed at the beginning of the chapter.

For various reasons there were few authors who held this view.[4] Indeed, given the pressing witness of experience, it would be difficult to reject at the outset the fact that there is at least some sort of intensional distinction between an individual and/or its individuality, on the one hand, and the individual's nature on the other. Nevertheless, although experience seems to warrant this distinction, it should be noted that when scholastics tried to clarify it even at this level, it became difficult to do so. The main problem they encountered was that intellectual consideration takes place always in terms of universal concepts and thus seems to preclude a proper determination and understanding of the individual *qua* individual.

The second position was more easily defensible and as a result more popular. It accepted the intensional distinction between common nature and individual, but argued that there is no extensional distinction that corresponds to the intensional distinction. There were two main versions of this view, quite opposed to each other. The first, which was the position usually attributed to Plato and his followers, argued that what is real is the nature, that is, the common features of things, and thus, as a result, there cannot be an extensional distinction between the nature and the individual, since there are no two real entities which may be extensionally distinguished from each other. Man, from this perspective, is real, while Peter is not, and consequently man cannot be extensionally distinguished from Peter, or vice versa. It also follows from this view that Peter's individuality is not real and, therefore, it can only be intensionally distinct from Peter's nature, in this case man. This view faces many problems, as is well known, but perhaps the most obvious one has to do with the explanation of how the intensional distinction arises at all, given the lack of extensional distinction: How is it that Peter and man can be distinguished, for example, when man is considered to be nothing at all in the world? What gave rise to the intensional distinction in the first place?

How do we come to it? These questions may have answers, but the difficulties of finding them made many scholastics and subsequent philosophers choose other views.

The second version argued that what is real is the individual and/or its individuality, and that the individual's nature is a conceptual phenomenon only.[5] As such there cannot be an extensional distinction between the individual and/or the individuality of the individual on the one hand, and the individual's nature on the other.[6] Peter and/or his "Petrinity" are real; man is not. Therefore, there is no extensional distinction between Peter and/or "Petrinity" on the one hand and man on the other. What supporters of this view generally failed to explain adequately is the cause or causes of intensional community (i.e., the causes that give rise to the intensions of terms that refer to natures). For example, what is the source of the intension of 'man'? In addition, as some made quite plain, this sort of view puts into question the objectivity of scientific concepts and thus undermines the bases of science.[7]

From what has been said, then, it is clear that the second position accepts an intensional disctinction between the individual and/or its individuality on the one hand and its nature on the other, but it is not at all clear that this view makes clear what the basis of the distinction is. Indeed, in many ways what the position proposes is precisely that one of the terms of the distinction (the individual and/or its individuality for Platonists, and the nature for the others) is not real at all. It is this fact that precludes a real distinction. But, since they still wish to maintain an intensional distinction, they run into difficulties trying to explain what gives rise to it.

The third, more eclectic position was the one that found more adherents in the medieval community. Like the second, it did not question experience, accepting the intensional distinction between the individual and its nature, but it went further by positing as well some sort of extensional distinction between them and also, in a few cases, some sort of extensional distinction between the individual's individuality and its nature. What the distinction is, however, was variously interpreted by different authors.[8]

Moreover, given the nature of this position, it is to be expected that some of those who adhere to it will at least try to suggest an ontological status for individuals and/or their individuality and for their natures. Duns Scotus, for example, speaks of natures as having being and unity, although the being and unity he accords to them is supposed to be *sui generis*. And to individuality he grants the status of a formality which he called, as we saw earlier, the "thisness" of the individual. Therefore, at least some supporters of this third position offered some bases for the intensional and extensional distinctions they said hold between the individual and/or its individuality on the one hand and its nature on the other.

Now, what can we make of all this? It certainly does not look very clear.

Can we make some sense of it that will be helpful for a contemporary discussion of individuality? I believe the part of the problem that gave rise to the prolonged medieval controversies on this issue and that gives the impression of obscurity and confusion to a contemporary reader stems from the fact that scholastics did not separate carefully the two questions posed at the beginning of this section: (1) whether there is an extensional distinction that corresponds to the intensional distinction between an individual's individuality and its nature, and (2) what the ontological basis of the distinction is. Indeed, in most cases I suspect that, because the question they asked themselves tended to merge these two issues, they omitted consideration of (2) altogether, while in fact an answer to (2) would at least be very useful and may perhaps be necessary for giving a clear answer to (1). And then, of course, they encountered the complications that arose from the terminological ambiguity of the term 'individual' to which I have already referred. Under these conditions, then, it would be wise to begin an analysis of this issue with question (2) rather than question (1) and to rephrase both questions so as to avoid the terminological obstacles encountered by the scholastics.

Contemporary Reformulation

I propose to recast the scholastic formulation into two questions as follows: (1) What is the ontological status of individuality? and (2) How is individuality related to the individual? Obviously, the answer to the second question will depend to a large extent on the answer to the first, as we shall see shortly; the matter of the distinction becomes subservient to the matter of the ontological status of individuality. Moreover, the issues presented in these two questions are clearly formulated in terms of individuality, avoiding possible confusions between it and the individual. Finally, the use of the notion of "relation" in the second question instead of the notion of "distinction" removes any possible epistemic connotation of the issue, keeping it squarely within an ontological perspective. No reference had been made in this chapter to possible epistemic overtones, but in keeping with the emphasis proposed in the Prolegomena, it would seem more appropriate to try to prevent any misunderstandings on this account.

But, we may ask, what does the expression 'ontological status' used in the first question mean, and what is involved in determining the ontological status of something? To determine the ontological status of something or, as it can also be put, to give an ontological characterization of something involves locating the thing in question in, as it were, a map of the most basic categories of reality. To ask for an ontological characterization of triangularity, for example, might involve asking for a determination of whether triangu-

121

larity is a substance, quality, relation, or collection; whether it is something mental or something extra-mental; and determining its degree of objectivity and subjectivity. For one might wish to hold with Plato, for instance, that triangularity is a real idea (perhaps a substance) that exists outside the world of sense perception and whose reflection we see when we perceive a triangle. Or, with Aristotle, we may choose to maintain that triangularity is a structural form present in triangular things, but with no status outside them. Or, we might like to identify triangularity with the collection of all triangles, just as some have done with humanity and the collection of all human beings. Or, still, we may decide to adopt, with Hume, the view that triangularity is a vague idea present in the mind, derived through a weakening process from the vivid impression of a particular triangle experienced in perception.[9] Moreover, we could examine other views or develop other theories about whiteness, or justice, and the like, just as the mentioned authors did with traingularity. Likewise, an ontological characterization of individuality would seem to involve answering questions similar to these.

Once the ontological status of individuality has been determined, we may then address the second question of the formulation given above. That is to say, we may investigate the way in which individuality is related to the individual. Naturally, as already stated, such relation will depend largely on the ontological status of individuality. For example, if individuality were to be interpreted as a quality, and the individual as its subject, then it would be related to the individual as qualities are related to subjects. But if individuality were a substance, then individuals would have to be related to it in some other way. It is, therefore, important to begin our inquiry with an answer to the first question in order better to determine the answer to both questions.

Finally, the answer to the two questions raised will help us determine another matter that has also been of concern to those who have dealt with the ontological status of individuality, namely, the composition of the individual. This is an issue that surfaces only in the context of complex individuals, for obviously, if individuals were simple, it would be absurd to talk about their composition.[10] For this reason, this issue becomes particularly important for views that consider Aristotelian primary substances as paradigms of individuals. However, even those views which hold that the features of primary substances, including simple features such as colors, are individual, must give some account of the composition of complex individuals. Consequently this question must be addressed, even though it can be addressed in the context of answers to the earlier identified questions, since its answer will be determined to a great extent by those answers.

Throughout the history of philosophy there have been four views on the ontological status of individuality that have attracted the most attention. They interpret individuality respectively as a substratum, a feature, a relation or, finally, they deny any ontological status to it. I shall begin the analysis by focussing on these views, before suggesting an alternative to them.

Wrong Ontological Interpretations

Individuality as Substratum. This view holds that individuality is a kind of de-characterized (whence the term 'bare particular' current in the literature) substratum or entity which serves as the locus for the instantiation of the features that are instantiated in it.[11] As with other philosophical positions, there are various versions of it, but most of them fall into two categories: those that interpret individuality as a subject of features, thus considering it a kind of substance, and those that interpret individuality as a tie. The second sort of view seems to be better classified as a relation among the features that constitute a thing, although some of its adherents may prefer to interpret it as an added feature of the thing whose function is to individualize it. If either of these last two alternatives is taken, the view has the same advantages of the Feature or the Relational Views of individuality, but it is also subject to their disadvantages. And if the tie is interpreted as a substratum and subject underlying the features of a thing, then the position is not easily distinguishable from the first version. We shall, then, restrict the discussion under the Substratum View to the version of the view that considers individuality the foundation for or the locus of the instantiation of the features of individual things, and indeed some proponents of this position have referred to individuality as a substance. According to this interpretation, then, an individual being, like Leticia, is composed (a) of whatever features it has—the color of eyes and hair, the size of the waist, the consistency of the muscles, and so on—and (b) of a de-characterized entity that underlies all these features, bringing them together into the individual that Leticia is. For this view, then, individuality is a kind of substratum which is related to the features of the individual as its subject, but the individual is composed of both the substratum and the features. This is obviously an analysis of a complex individual and, indeed, those who favor this view consider individuals to be always complex, since individuality is an entity in its own right, different from any features that a thing may have.

Most of those who adhere to this view hold also that individuality is intensionally and extensionally distinct from both the features of the individual and the individual itself. Leticia's individuality is distinct in both ways, from Leticia on the one hand and any or all of her features on the other. Thus, there is both an intensional and an extensional distinction, for example, between Leticia's individuality and the black color of her hair. This should not be surprising since Leticia's individuality, being as it is a part of Leticia according to this view, would have to be analyzed differently than Leticia and

123

any or all of her features. Still, there are other authors who have been impressed by the fact that Leticia's individuality can never be separated from Leticia and even perhaps that it seems not to have any ontological status apart from Leticia. So they have concluded that, although intensionally distinct, the individual's individuality is not extensionally distinct from the individual and its features. Hence, they have tried to show that, in addition to the intensional and extensional distinctions, there is also a middle ground between the two. This is what many scholastics called, following Duns Scotus, "the formal distinction."[12]

This view has several advantages. Perhaps the most important of these is that it does not reduce, intentionally or unintentionally, individuality to something else, as some of the other views do, and this is in keeping with what was concluded in Chapter 1. It also has advantages for explaining the process of individuation, as we shall see in the following chapter, and avoids the reduction of individuals to universals so characteristic of the Bundle View. The virtues of this position, therefore, should not be underestimated. But its disadvantages are no less serious. In the first place, as we already saw in Chapter 2, this view violates the Principle of Acquaintance. Since this de-characterized entity, which is at the basis of every individual, does not and cannot have any features, it does not seem that it can be subject to acquaintance. We can be directly acquainted with Leticia's hair color, or her height, or the tone of her voice, but how can we be acquainted with the de-characterized substratum that underlies those features and is postulated by this view? As the eighteenth century empiricist would have put it, individuality conceived in this way becomes a "something-I-know-not-what."

Apart from this epistemic difficulty, however, there are also ontological difficulties arising from the relation of the substratum to the features that are supposed to inhere in it. For, if this view is to work at all, the relation between substratum and features has to be metaphysical and not just logical; that is to say, it must be a relation of substance (or substratum) to features and not just of subject to predicates. If it were otherwise, the analysis would be logical rather than ontological. To say, therefore, that the individuality of something functions as a subject of which the thing's features are predicated would not do, for this would not explain the ontological relation between individuality and features, but only the logical relation between subject and predicates. Indeed, most of those who adhere to the Substratum View recognize that features are not predicated of individuality, that is, of the substratum, but rather of the whole individual, which includes both substratum and features. 'Tall' is predicated of Clarisa, for example, and not of Clarisa's individuality.

On the other hand, the more metaphysical relations denoted by the terms 'inhere' and 'adhere', used often to analyze this relation, certainly do not clarify the matter, since these terms do not add anything more significant to the discussion than rather obscure metaphors. 'To inhere' seems nothing but to be within something, that is, as the etymology of the word indicates, to be *internally* attached to something. And something similar can be said about 'to adhere', except that with this term the metaphor suggests an *external*, rather than an internal attachment. In the first case, we have a picture of features being placed inside something and, in the second, of being attached externally to something. But to say that the features of a thing "are inside the thing's individuality" or to say that they "are attached externally to it" sounds very odd indeed. For, no doubt, what we would like to say, as pointed out in the previous chapter, is that those very features *are individual;* that is, that Leticia's hair color is individual, not just that Leticia's hair color is *in* individuality or *related to* individuality in some external way.

Others try to save the theory by speaking about the bare substratum being "the locus of instantiation" of an individual's features. But that does not help us much, for what needs to be given precisely is an analysis of the substratum and its relation to features.

Moreover, even if one were not to accept that the features of things are individual, still this view could not be effectively defended, for the relation of the features to the individuality of the thing would have to be explained anyway. We must be able to answer the question: What is the relation between Leticia's hair color and her individuality? And the metaphorical language suggested does not seem to do the job properly. Thus, what was supposed to be an answer to this very question obviously does not answer it.

Finally, there are also problems with the distinction between individuality on the one hand and the individual and its features on the other. For, if individuality is a part of the individual, then its extension must be different than (a) the complete individual and (b) its features. But, does it make any sense to speak of Leticia's individuality as being extensionally distinct from her and/or from her features? It would seem reasonable to suppose that the individuality of an individual must extend as far as the individual extends, but not beyond it.

In short, the Substratum View of individuality leaves much to be desired, since it encounters several important difficulties and leaves unanswered the very question it purports to answer. Apart from the difficulties raised there are others resulting from other aspects of this view that are as serious as these, but I shall take these up in the following chapter when I discuss the Bare Particular Theory of Individuation.

Individuality as Feature. A second view that has been quite favored in the history of philosophy holds that individuality has the ontological status of a *feature* which characterizes individual things. This view, like the Substratum View, is held by those who restrict the extension of 'individuality' to Aristotelian primary substances, such as my cat Minina, Leticia, or the shrub I planted in my garden last spring. In the most general formulation of the view, the individual is composed of (a) various universal features and (b) an individualizing feature that is identified as the individual's individuality. The universal features explain how Leticia is the same as others, while the individualizing feature explains how she is different. Some authors, however, hold that the universal features become individualized through their contact or association with the individualizing feature and so do not remain universal, but even under those circumstances, the paradigm of the individual is an Aristotelian primary substance like Leticia and not its features.

There are several versions of this view, depending on how the individualizing feature is interpreted. As mentioned earlier, some of those who interpret individuality as a tie speak in a way that suggests that what they have in mind is a feature view. And if that is the case, then their position is subject to the advantages and disadvantages of the Feature View. But I do not think that the classification of a tie as a feature is appropriate, for a tie is a relation if it is anything at all.

Another version of the Feature View interprets individuality as a quality, often giving it a name derived from the proper name of the individual that it characterizes, when the individual in question has a proper name. Thus, for example, the medievals talked about Peter's Petrinity and of Socrates' Socrateity.[13] There is some disagreement, however, among those who defend this position as to whether individuality is a complex or simple feature. The view that holds that individuality is a simple feature resembles the Substratum View in some respects, but it is different insofar as it holds that individuality, along with other features, *characterizes* the individual rather than that it is some kind of entity in which other features inhere, to which they adhere, or in which they are instantiated. On the other hand, those who interpret individuality as a complex feature usually identify it with a bundle, encompassing either all or some of the features which characterize an individual substance; they are usually the same philosophers who defend the Bundle Theory, to which some attention was given in Chapter 2 and which will be discussed in greater detail in Chapter 4. This is another reason why this view is favored by those who limit individuality to Aristotelian primary substances.

According to this view, then, the individual is a kind of bundle of features, but this bundle is interpreted differently.[14] For some, all the features of the bundle are universal (or individualized universals) except for one, which is the individuality of the bundle. In this case, individuality is conceived to be intensionally distinct from the bundle considered as a whole and both intensionally and extensionally distinct from each and every one of its other components, in a way similar to how the substratum was considered distinct from them in the Substratum View. Socrates' individuality is intensionally distinct (a) from Socrates, (b) from the gray color of his beard, and so on, and

126

(c) from all of Socrates' features taken together with the exception, of course, of the individualizing feature itself, but Socrates' individuality is extensionally distinct from each of Socrates' features. For others, however, the individualizing feature is identified with the whole bundle of features that characterize the individual. In Socrates, for example, individuality is equivalent to the gray color of his beard, the shape of his nose, and so forth considered altogether. As such, individuality is regarded as intensionally and extensionally distinct from each one of these features, but not as intensionally or extensionally distinct from the whole. The gray color of Socrates' beard, for example, is defined differently than his individuality, which includes not only the gray color of his beard but other features as well. Moreover, it has a different extension than that of the features, since Socrates' individuality extends only to him, but the gray color of his beard, as the universal it is according to this view, can be shared by many things. Still, in both cases, whether individuality is interpreted as a feature, different from the bundle of features which characterize a thing, or as that very bundle of features, the relation between individuality and the other features of the thing is different from that of a substratum to its features, advocated by the previous position. This view tries to avoid the notion of a substratum, substance, or subject by making all the components of a thing similar in entitative status: They are all features.

Many of the advantages and disadvantages of this view are similar to those identified in connection with the Substratum View, but some are unique to it. Among the advantages of the Feature View of individuality, for example, is that in most of its versions it avoids violation of the Principle of Acquaintance. Indeed, the only instance where the principle is violated is when individuality is interpreted as a simple *sui generis* feature of individuals. For, if individuality is a bundle of some or all of the features which characterize my cat Minina, for example, there seems to be no reason why we could not become acquainted with them. I am certainly acquainted with her fur color, her size, and the shape of her body. And this is clearly important, for this view does away with the "mysterious" and "ineffable" aspect of the Substratum View.

But this position has also serious disadvantages. An obvious and general difficulty of the Feature View is that, in making individuality ontologically similar to the other components of a composite individual, it fails to clarify the unique relation it must have with each and every one of the features which compose the individual. In fact, if individuality is nothing other than the bundle of features belonging to a thing, then it is ontologically equivalent to them. We see here a difficulty that plagues all bundle views, namely, the difficulty of explaining how bundles of features can be something more than complex features and how other complex features need not be individual.[15] The first part of the difficulty has to do with explaining how a bundle, say A-

B-C, can be something more than just its components, A-B-C. The second part has to do with explaining how a bundle such as A-B-C, while being ontologically equivalent to another bundle, say D-E-F, which is also composed of features but is universal, can be different insofar as it is individual. For instance, why is the bundle called "Minina" (i.e., my cat) individual, while the bundle called "cat" is not?

On the other hand, if individuality is interpreted as something different from all the features of the individual taken together or separately and thus as a unique, simple, *sui generis* feature, then the view faces the difficulties of the Substratum View.

There are other difficulties as well. As a feature, one would expect that individuality would have to characterize something. But, of course, according to most of those who adopt this view, individuality cannot characterize anything; for it does not characterize the other features of the individual, since they are universal; and it cannot characterize the whole individual, because the individual is reducible to the bundle of features, according to this position. Hence, as mentioned, individuality cannot characterize anything and, consequently, cannot be a feature. The point can be put this way. Take an individual, I, which only has the three features a, b and i, and let i be its individuality. According to this view, I is equivalent to a-b-i. But a and b are universal, while I (equaling a-b-i) is individual. Now in order for the theory to work, i as a feature of I must individualize it by characterizing either it or its features. But I is nothing but a-b-i, so it cannot be characterized by i unless i characterizes a and/or b. But since a and/or b are universal, i does not characterize them. But then, how can it individualize I? Let's use another example and put the matter in another way: We have red dye and two white shirts. The two white shirts mixed with the red dye produce "a red bundle of clothes." But the bundle is red because each of the shirts is red—otherwise it would not be red. Hence, if a bundle is individual, it must be so because its components have somehow been affected. But, of course, that is not what this view holds, since for that to happen, individuality would have to be a feature of the features of an individual rather than one among those features.

Finally, many philosophers have noted that there seems to be something contradictory about the view that individuality is a feature of things. The contradiction arises if one holds that a fundamental characteristic of features is that they can be shared or had by many things. It is in the nature of white, so the argument goes, that it can extend to many objects. But individuality seems to be precisely that which is not shareable. So how can one hold, then, that individuality be a feature? Indeed, it can be done only if individuality is understood differently than it is or if the notion of feature is changed so as not to require multiple characterization.

Now, since to be a feature and to be universal are for all intents and purposes the same, and I have defended above the view that universals do not require multiple instantiation either actually or potentially, I am not impressed with this argument. The argument is effective only in ontologies where multiple instantiation is a necessary condition of universality. Thus, in our scheme the Feature View is saved from this last attack, but is in no less of a quandary because of that, since it still has to meet the objections raised earlier.

Individuality as Relation. A third possible view holds that individuality is a relation. Although some authors have been attacked on this account, and some do indeed seem to talk as if they hold that individuality is a relation, I have not found many texts which explicitly and clearly confirm and expound this position unless one is allowed to include here those views that speak of individuality as a "tie" for example.[16] At any rate, this is a logically possible alternative answer to the issue under discussion, and as such some reference to it must be made if our account is to claim any completeness.

We must begin by saying something about relations. A more detailed discussion of them will be given later, in Chapter 5, but we need some initial analysis here.[17] Among the many ways in which relations may be classified, there are two in particular that stand out. As will be pointed out later, some relations are perspectival. This means that they are established on the basis of a point of reference other than the relata and on which the relation, therefore, depends. The relation "to the left of," for example, is perspectival because whether a particular object is or is not to the left of some other object depends on the point of observation from which the relation is established. If we have a piece of transparent glass with a red dot and a black dot painted on its surface next to each other in a horizontal position, the red dot will be to the left of the black dot if looked at from one side of the glass, while from the other it will be to the right of the black dot. In contrast, nonperspectival relations do not depend on points of reference other than the relata. The relation of contradiction, for example, between the propositions 'All S is P' and 'Some S is not P' does not depend on anything other than the propositions themselves and, therefore, is not perspectival.

Both perspectival and nonperspectival relations can be further divided in many ways, but again two in particular stand out: physical and nonphysical. The logical relation of contradiction, to which reference was just made, is a good example of a nonperspectival nonphysical relation. On the other hand, the relation "next to," for example, is both nonperspectival and physical. It is nonperspectival because, in the example used earlier, the two dots are next to each other on the glass independently of the position taken by an observer. It is, moreover, physical, because it has to do with physical objects and their relative positions. It is, of course, possible to speak about nonphysical objects

129

as being "next to" each other. For example, "one" is often said to be next to "two." But it seems to me that this is a metaphorical use of 'next to' derived from the more fundamental physical meaning of the term. At any rate, regardless of whether this is or is not the case, what I have in mind here is the physical relation and not the nonphysical ones.

The example of perspectival relation mentioned earlier, "to the left of," is clearly physical, but the relation "good for" is not physical, even though it is perspectival. It is perspectival because it depends on some rule and/or set of circumstances that are outside the relata. For example, death can be both a good or an evil. It can be good in cases where extreme pain accompanies life and no relief is possible but it can be bad under different conditons. No one in his/her right mind would argue that a prisoner undergoing torture and excruciating pain without hope of relief would not be better dead than alive. Indeed, the expression "I pray for death" is common, even among those whose religious beliefs prescribe the sanctity of life. Finally, "good for" is not a physical relation because, unlike "to the left of," it does not indicate a physical dimension of the relata.

Having made these basic distinctions among relations, we must now try to see if individuality fits any of the categories identified. Is individuality a perspectival or a nonperspectival relation? And, in either case is it physical or nonphysical? If it should be found that individuality cannot be acceptably interpreted in any of these ways, then the Relation View must be discarded (which is in fact what I intend to argue), for the categories mentioned are both mutually exclusive and exhaustive when applied to relations.

At the outset there does not seem to be any serious obstacle to an interpretation of individuality as either a physical or a nonphysical relation. Indeed, both interpretations are possible, since in principle the existence of both physical and nonphysical individuals is possible. We have already referred earlier to minds, God, and posible individuals, and whether in fact there are such beings or not, there does not seem to be anything contradictory about their notions. The case of physical things, of course, need not be brought up since experience vouches for their actual existence. Therefore, no problems with the Relation View, then, do arise from this quarter. The difficulties with the position, if there should be any, would have to come up rather from other quarters. Let us see if individuality can be interpreted perspectively or nonperspectively.

If individuality were a nonperspectival relation, then it would hold among two sorts of relata: First, individuality could be interpreted as a relation between a substratum (or substance) and the features of the individual, and, second, it could be interpreted as a relation among the features of a bundle, where the individual is equivalent to the bundle. In the first case, the individual would be composed of the substratum on the one hand, its features on the other, and the relation between the two. In the second case, the individual would be composed of a bundle of features and the relation of individuality holding among them.[18]

But neither of these two ways of interpreting individuality is satisfactory. If one accepts the view that in individuals there is a substratum (or substance) in addition to the features which the thing has, then there is no need to say that individuality is a relation between the substratum and the features. This step would only complicate the theory unnecessarily. Those who accept this view can simply identify the substratum as the individuality of the thing and thus have a more parsimonious view, which nonetheless, as we already saw earlier, encounters serious difficulties of another sort.

On the other hand, if individuality is interpreted as a relation among the features of a thing, when the thing is considered equivalent to those features, there are also difficulties, for what would this relation be? When one speaks of the individuality of X, one seems to be speaking of a feature of X, not of a relation among X's features. This means, then, that we must be able to identify the relation holding among the features. But it is difficult to do so. Terms such as 'uniqueness' 'difference' etc, which suggest themselves more readily, do not seem to help. One possibility could be to interpret the relation as that of "being altogether," so that the features could be said "to be altogether." But, of course, this would imply a pure bundle view of individuation with all the difficulties entailed in that view, and would fail to relate individuality to noninstantiability. It might, of course, help to explain how to differentiate a thing, but, as mentioned earlier, individuality has to do with noninstantiability rather than with difference.

The two interpretations of the Relation View discussed thus far consider individuality a nonperspectival relation, but one could also interpret individuality as a perspectival relation. According to this view, the individuality of a thing, which again could be said to hold either among the features of a thing, or between all those features considered together on the one hand and a substratum of some kind on the other, would depend on something other than the relata such as, for example, the point of view taken by an observer.

It is difficult to conceive of any philosophy based on common sense that would favor this position. Nonetheless, if one takes the standard interpretation of Plato seriously, it could be argued that it implies a position such as the one described. Indeed, if the world of sense perception were unreal, its illusory nature, including the individuality of the things contained therein, would be the result of the point of view from which we look at it. From a certain perspective, things would appear individual, even though in reality they are universal. That this implication is possible is substantiated by the fact that it was actually held in the early Middle Ages, when the influence of neo-Platonism was very strong. At that time there also developed another position

131

that held instead that both universality and individuality depended in some way on the point of view, that is, on the way one considered things. Hence, the same thing considered in one way would be universal, but considered in another would be individual.[19]

Naturally, this view is not easy to maintain. Suffice it to say that in spite of their relative popularity, philosophical explanations that try to explain something by turning things we experience into appearances have little explanatory power. For experience is, in the final analysis, the most important and fundamental source of information we have. A philosophy that rejects it is left adrift, like a ship without an anchor. And to turn individuality into a perspectival relation does just that, it disregards the witness of experience.

Finally, there are problems involved in the distinction among individuality interpreted as a relation, the individual, and the features of the individual. These are similar to the ones raised in connection with the Substratum and Feature Views and have to do with extension. For, on the one hand, a relation seems to be extensionally distinct from its relata, but on the other hand, it is dependent on them. And, as we have already pointed out, it does not make much sense to say that individuality is extensionally distinct from the individual, even though this view, like the others discussed thus far, seems to require it or at least to point in that direction.

Individuality Without Ontological Status. All the views discussed up to this point have in common that they consider individuality to be something (a substratum, a feature, a relation) intensionally and/or extensionally distinct from both the individual and its features, and it is to a large extent as a result of it that many think they run into difficulties. They also have in common a preference for restricting individuality to Aristotelian primary substances, although some of them leave the question of the extension of 'individuality' open and others hold that the features of primary substances are individual. In those views in which features are considered individual, however, the individuality of the features is considered to be, as it were, derived and/or acquired and a result of their association with a primary substance, bundle, or what have you, a factor which also creates difficulties for the views.

In order to avoid these problems, some philosophers have simply denied any ontological status to individuality. In addition, they have concluded that the distinction between individuality and the individual and between individuality and the individual's features is only intensional. To this is added that not only are primary substances individual but also their features, and both are individual *essentially*. This position, of course, corresponds to the view called "Essential Nominalism" in Chapter 2. According to it, individuality has no ontological status apart from or even within the individual considered as a whole. It is intensionally distinct from the individual and its features because it can be conceived differently from them, but "in reality," as the

132

scholastics would say, there is nothing but the individual and its individual features. Socrates' individuality is simply the abstract way in which we consider him as individual. But there is no individuality that, as somehow a part of him, can be distinguished from him except, as already stated, intensionally. And the same goes for his features.

In this way, individuals, insofar as they are individuals, need not be composed of anything. Complex individuals, like a man, are indeed composed of their individual features, but of nothing else. And simple individuals, like the color of a person's hair, are of course simple and therefore have no components.

There is much to commend in this view. It is simple and economical, and it does away with many of the problems which plagued the other positions. Since it interprets individuality as nothing ontologically, it can dispense completely with the discussion of its ontological status and its relation to and distinction from the individual and its features. In short, it can ignore the three issues raised in this chapter, for individuality has no ontological status, it has no relation to the individual and its features, and it is not "a part" of the individual.

Still, the position is not entirely satisfactory. Some of the difficulties it encounters have to do with other aspects and corollaries of the view related to other issues involved in individuality and, therefore, are dealt with in other chapters of this book. But there is at least one important criticism that can be made here. It can be formulated as follows: If individuality is regarded in Socrates, for example, as nothing other than Socrates, then we may ask, what distinguishes "Socrates" from "man"? The traditional answer given by this position is that in reality nothing; the distinction is only conceptual, between Socrates and a vague idea or concept of Socrates that we have formed through a mental process.[20] But, first, this fails, as I have repeatedly pointed out, to account for the nonarbitrary character of univerals, as well as for the stability and objectivity of general principles and norms to which experience bears witness. Second, as noted in the previous chapter, the difference between the analysis of "man" and "Socrates" does not lie in that the first contains the notion of "concept" while the later does not. Indeed, the definition of "man," whatever it may be, certainly does not include the notion of conceptuality. The traditional definition of man, for example, is "rational animal," and that says nothing about it being a concept. It is not "man" whose analysis includes a reference to a concept, but "the concept man." Yet, if this position were right, the definition of man would have to contain that reference, otherwise "man" would not be distinguishable from "Socrates." Hence, the view of individuality under consideration fails to account for the distinction between "Socrates" and "man."

We must consider, then, from what has been said, that the view which

133

grants no ontological status to individuality is not acceptable. Moreover, since, as we saw earlier, there are also serious difficulties with the Substratum View as well as with the Feature and Relation Views, these alternatives are not available to us. In what follows, however, I shall argue that there is another alternative and that it works: I intend to present a view of individuality as a mode, which I believe solves some of the problems faced by the views we have examined, while having several advantages of its own.[21]

Individuality as Mode

The English term "mode" comes from the Latin *modus*, which meant such things as measure, bound, limit, end, manner, way, and method. In philosophy the term does not seem to have acquired any definite technical meaning in metaphysics until the latter part of the thirteenth and early part of the fourteenth centuries, although its use in logical discourse goes back much farther. Thomas Aquinas, for example, referred to modes, but had little to say about them.[22] Durandus of St. Pourçain, on the other hand, discussed them to a greater extent.[23] However, it is only in late scholasticism and the Renaissance that modes are given substantial attention, in particular by Suárez, who provided one of the first systematic interpretations of them, and from whom, no doubt, most of the modern doctrines found in Locke, Descartes, Spinoza and others, spring.[24] The term 'mode', therefore, has a long and rather distinguished history in philosophy, even though its use has been somewhat neglected more recently.[25] Nevertheless, I believe it may serve to describe the ontological status of individuality.

Since this is not a treatise on modes, I shall not dwell at length on this notion. Yet, some clarification of it will be necessary if the thesis presented here is to have some credibility. The term 'mode', as already pointed out, has various meanings, but most of them are related to the basic notion of "manner of" or "way of." In Latin the term was used in many compound expressions, such as *modus cognoscendi* (way of knowing), *modus vivendi* (way of living), *modus essendi* (way of being), and so on. And, in the English and Romance languages, there are many expressions that use the term with the meaning "way of" or "manner of." One of the important characteristics of modes is that one can speak of them in connection with almost anything. For example, one can speak about the ways in which *things*, such as Clarisa or a tree, are and also about the way in which *their features* are attached to them. As such, modes cannot be interpreted exclusively as pertaining to so called Aristotelian primary substances, since they may also modify the features of those substances. And that goes not only for qualities, like white, but also for relations, states, actions, and so on. Whence, the uses mentioned earlier: mode of knowing, mode of living, and so forth. Modes are not, then, "features," but they do

134

characterize in some sense, since a mode of knowing, for example (say, perception) is different from another mode of knowing (say, intuition). Nor are they relations or substances, although they can modify both relations and substances.

From all this it is clear that the use of the term 'mode' is very extensive and that almost any feature can be considered a mode of something. For example, it is not unusual to refer to qualities as modes of substance—thus white can be a mode of this paper, since this paper is white and is therefore "modified" by white. Indeed, taking 'mode' in this way, any determining principle or feature can be called a mode, so that in addition to qualities, such as white, we could also speak about other features as modes. For example, "rational" can be regarded as a mode of animal because it changes it in a determinate way. However, this way of understanding modes is too broad for our purposes, since to call individuality a mode in this sense would not really distinguish it from other ontological categories, such as qualities, relations, and the like. (More on the distinction between modes and qualities and relations later.) The understanding of modes that I propose, therefore, is much more restricted. Modes are positive determinations over and above the intension of what they modify, determining its state and way of being, but without adding to it a new entity. Hence, modes are not negations. A particular mode of knowing is not just the negation of other ways of knowing, but something positive. Indeed, perception is more than the negation of reasoning, for example. As such, then, the intensional analysis of a mode includes something more than the intension of what it modifies: The analysis of perception includes more than the analysis of knowing. And because modes include something more, they can determine and modify the thing in question in ways different from the ways in which other modes modify them. Nevertheless, what they add is nothing entitative. The extension of a mode does not go beyond the extension of what it modifies; that is, the mode has no greater extension than what is modified by it, although what is modifed by it may in fact have a greater extension than it. Perception, a mode of knowing, cannot extend beyond knowing, for example, even if knowing can extend beyond perception. This means that modes depend ontologically on what they modify; by themselves they cannot consititute being in any way.

Furthermore, modes seem to pose no great problem of acquaintance. It is clear, for example, that I am acquainted with the *modus operandi* of the current provost at the University of Buffalo, whether I like it or not, and so likewise with other things. There is, therefore, no "mystery" about modes and no danger of violating the Principle of Acquaintance in using them in an explanatory scheme. Modes, moreover, are not, unlike features, relations and substances, ontologically any thing other than the things they modify. They are not separate entities, and they seem to have no status other than that of the things they modify. The *modus operandi* of the provost is not some thing other than him, and the *modus cognoscendi* of human beings is not some thing other than them and the features and faculties they have and the cognitive activities in which they engage. Finally, modes seem to be immediate to the things they modify. The way my hair sticks to my head (poorly), for example, is immediate to my hair; that is, it is not mediated by something else.

My suggestion, then, is that individuality may be interpreted as one of two fundamental ontological modes, the other being universality. The advantages of this view should be clear from what has been said already. First, it avoids the problems associated with the Substratum, Feature, and Relation Views discussed earlier, and it gives a more credible account of individuality than the view which denied ontological status to it. The main problems with the Substratum View had to do with its violation of the Principle of Acquaintance and the explanation of the relation between the substratum and the features of the individual thing. But the theory of modes avoids both of these problems. It was already pointed out that we are acquainted with modes, and, since no bare substratum is required for this view, questions concerned with the relation of substratum to features are sidestepped.

Second, the difficulties of the Feature View centered around the relation of the individuality-feature to the other features of a thing and to the question of what individuality characterized. But, of course, if individuality is interpreted as a mode, then its relation to the features of a thing is not the relation of feature to feature, but of mode to feature, thus avoiding some of the problems raised in that connection. Moreover, since under these conditions individuality is not interpreted as a feature of features, it does not characterize things in the way features do; it merely modifies them. This avoids the second problem mentioned.

Third, the problems of the Relation View, when individuality was interpreted nonperspectivally, were reduced to the problems of the Substratum and Feature Views indicated already, and when interpreted perspectivally, the difficulties involved an explanation that turned the world of experience into a world of appearance. But the view of individuality as a mode avoids these difficulties, since in it individuality need not be interpreted perspectivally, and, as we saw earlier, it also avoids the problems associated with the Substratum and Feature Views to which the nonperspectival interpretation of the Relation View was reduced.

Finally, the Mode View gives a fuller account of individuality than the view that held it was nothing. Indeed, it offers an explanation of why individuality is not "separable" from the things that have it while being intensionally distinct from them, without having to reduce it to nothing.

It makes sense, then, in terms of all that has been said, to interpret individuality as a mode. But if individuality is a mode, it must be an ontologically fundamental one. Modes come in many types. There are, for example, modes of speaking or of knowing, and modes of dress, etc. as already stated. All these are considerably restricted in extension. A mode is ontologically fundamental if together with its counterpart (its mutually exclusive mode) they extend to everything. Now, since my contention is that individuality, interpreted as noninstantiability, and universality, interpreted as instantiability, are exhaustive and mutually exclusive, they must, under any conditions, be considered fundamental. For everything is either universal or individual, and what is individual is not universal and vice versa.

We have, therefore, the answer to one of the two questions we set out to investigate at the beginning of the chapter, the question concerned with the ontological status of individuality: Individuality is something, but it is not a substratum, feature, or relation, it is rather a fundamental mode. The second question concerned the relation between individuality and the individual, whether the individual in question is something like Peter or like the color of his hair. Since the answer to the first question determines to a great extent the answer to the second, we must now be ready to answer the second question, and in fact we have to a certain extent done so by pointing out that modes "modify." Still, some distinction must be made between this and the function of features and relations in order to understand what "to modify" entails.

It is generally acknowledged that the features of a thing, sometimes inappropriately called by philosophers "qualities" and "properties," characterize the things that have them. I say "inappropriately" because the terms 'quality' and 'property' are too restrictive. Among Aristotelians, for example, properties comprise only those features which always accompany the members of a particular species, such as the capacity to laugh in man.[26] And qualities and the corresponding quality predicates, such as 'white', are to be distinguished from other predicates that point to quantities, such as 'six feet tall,' or activities, such as 'running'.[27] 'Feature' is a generic term which encompasses all of these and allows us to distinguish all of them from relations, modes, and so forth. One general character of features is that they characterize things. 'Calico' characterizes my cat's fur and 'running' characterizes the cat itself when my neighbors' disgustingly brash boxer starts to bark. Another important characteristic of many features is that one can speak of the things they characterize as "having" them. My cat "has" a particular fur color, for example. It is also true, however, that although many features can be *had*, things can also *be* others (Napoleon *was* five-feet-six-inches tall), and in some cases they can *be in* or *be at* others (I *am in* this room and writing *at* this desk). In contrast with features, modes are not generally "had" and the things they modify are not usually said "to be," "to be in," or "to be at" them. For example, take a particular mode of running such as "fast." Running is not said to have, to be, to be in, or to be at it. We do say that Clarisa *is* running fast or

137

has a fast way of running, but in none of these cases are we talking about the mode (i.e., fast) in relation to what it modifies (i.e., running), but rather of the "running as modified" in relation to the runner. Thus, a mode is clearly a different kind of determinant than features.

In the case of relations, there are also clear differences between them and modes. Some relations are very much like features in that they seem to characterize things, even if differently. Fatherhood is a relation, but we talk about fathers, and we also speak of someone *being* a father, for example. So there seems to be some common ground between relations and features that separates both categories from the category of modes. Apart from this, the main element in relations is that they are multidependent; that is, a relation always holds between at least two things and, therefore, its ontological status depends directly on all of them. But modes do not function in this way, since multiple entities are not a necessary condition of modes. A particular way of talking, for example, is not dependent on anything else but the speaker's talk.

Modes, then, can be distinguished both from features and relations and thus it would seem appropriate to speak about the way they characterize their subjects with terminology different from that used for features and relations. While features "characterize" and relations "relate," we may speak of modes, then, as "modifying."

Still, there is a difficulty that must be cleared up before this view is accepted. It has to do with the intensional interpretations of individuality and universality given in Chapter 1. There I argued that individuality is to be understood in terms of noninstantiability and universality in terms of instantiability. But so the difficulty may be formulated, both instantiability and noninstantiability are relations. Instantiability involves a relation at least potential, between something, say "female," and its instances, such as Leticia and Clarisa. And noninstantiability, as the negation of the relation of instantiability, must also be considered a kind of relation even if only negatively.

The first thing that needs to be said in answer to this difficulty is that, even if instantiability were a relation, it would not be necessary to hold that noninstantiability is also a relation. Indeed, being a father is clearly a relation, but not being a father is not. This should be sufficient to answer the objection, but more than this can be said. Even though the notion of instantiability involves a relational aspect between an instantiable and its instances, it is certainly not the kind of relation holding between two things in our world, such as a father and his daughter. For the universal, as we saw in Chapter 2, is neutral with respect to existence. Indeed, it is precisely the peculiar character of universality and individuality that I have tried to capture by describing them as modes.

Two final questions: First, are modes to be considered intensionally and/or extensionally distinct from their subjects? Since they are not things by themselves and they depend on their subjects for their ontological status, modes cannot be extensionally distinct from their subjects. The mode of running of a particular person is nothing other, extensionally, than the very act of running. On the other hand, modes are intensionally distinct from their subjects. The definition of "running" is certainly different from the definition of a particular mode of running, such as "running fast," as well as from the notion of "mode" itself. From all this, we can see that if individuality is interpreted as a mode, it must be considered something other than the subject it modifies, whether that subject is a person like Leticia, a quality like white, or an activity like running, or something else. It is also clear that it must be intensionally, even though not extensionally, distinct from it.

In all fairness I should point out that this view of individuality as intensionally but not extensionally distinct from the subject it modifies is similar in some respects to the view proposed by Duns Scotus and recently defended by Armstrong.[28] As we saw earlier, according to Scotus, there is a formal distinction between the individuality of a thing, which he called "this-ness" (*haecceitas* in Latin) and the features, which he called "forms" or "common natures," of a thing. What this formal distinction is exactly is a subject of debate among scholars,[29] but I believe it may mean that the distinct things can be defined separately (intensional distinction), although they cannot be found separately (no extensional distinction). In order to illustrate the distinction, Armstrong gives the example of size and shape, which although inseparable have different definitions.[30] I am afraid this example would not have been approved by Scotus, since for him, as for most Aristotelians, size and shape would be different accidental features belonging in fact to different categories of reality and, therefore, would have to be considered really distinct rather than just formally distinct. But all the same, aside from the historical inaccuracy, the example does bring out in an analogical way what a formal distinction is: intensional distinction without extensional distinction. Thus, the individuality of Leticia is intensionally distinct not only from her but from all her features, but at the same time it is inseparable from them. This does not mean that Leticia must always have the same features, but rather that whatever features she may have are individual.

But, then, one may ask, is there any difference between the view proposed here and that proposed by Scotus when interpreted as I have done? The answer to this question is affirmative. There are several differences, but two in particular stand out. First, Scotus conceives individuality as a formality, that is, as a kind of feature superadded to all other features which characterize a thing. But, as mentioned earlier, the view of individuality as a feature creates a number of problems. This is why I have rejected it in favor of a view of individuality as a mode, thus avoiding most of those difficulties. Second, Scotus still puts too much emphasis on the reality of the features of things in themselves, considered apart from individuality. According to him these features, which he referred to as "common natures," have a being and unity of their own, even when they have no separate existence. Presumably this means that in an individual, such as Leticia, there would be not only an individual unity and existence but also the being and unity proper to her nature(s). But this I have rejected. The features of things, which I have called universals in Chapter 2, are neutral with respect to existence or any kind of being. If they exist, they exist as individual, that is in fact why they are inseparable (i.e., coextensive with individuality). It is also in this that the position I have adopted differs from the view of Armstrong, for he, as Scotus, puts too much emphasis on the reality of universals.

Second question: What is the composition of the individual according to the Mode View? Since modes are not things apart from or even within what they modify, they cannot be said "to compose" them in any way. Hence, we can hold without difficulty, like the view that interpreted individuality as nothing, that complex individuals are composed only of their individual features, and simple features can be individual even though they have no composition.

Having explored the ontological status of individuality, we must now turn to the question of what causes it: the Principle of Individuation. This issue will be discussed in the next chapter.

4

Principle of Individuation

The next problem that must be taken up in our metaphysical investigation of individuality concerns the principle of individuation. It involves (1) the identification of the said principle, and (2) the determination of whether this principle is the same for all individuals. Both issues have been discussed widely throughout the history of philosophy, although I have argued elsewhere that it is in the Middle Ages that they first became clearly formulated.[1]

Now, as was pointed out in the Prolegomena, the terminology of 'principle' and 'cause' is not sufficiently neutral to help us formulate and settle these issues. For this reason, I shall prefer in general to avoid it and instead speak of "the necessary and sufficient conditions for a universal to become individual." In other words, we shall be concerned with what an individual does and must have, that a universal does and must lack, such that the individual is noninstantiable while the universal is instantiable. In cases where the terminology of 'principle' and 'cause' are preserved, it should be taken to mean precisely what I have stated.

The chapter is divided into four parts. The first three parts are critical; they examine the various views of individuation proposed in the literature and reject them. The last part, on the other hand, presents and defends my own view, which I have called "an existential theory of individuation." All of this is preceded by a few clarificatory remarks.

The clarificatory remarks that must be added are as follows. The first is that the positions adopted with respect to individuation will depend to a large

141

extent on the interpretation of individuality adopted. If, for example, individuality is understood primarily as noninstantiability, the necessary and sufficient conditions of individuation must have to do with what renders a thing such that it cannot be instantiated. On the other hand, if individuality is understood as distinction or difference, then they would have to do with the conditions that distinguish a thing from all others. And so on with the other ways of understanding individuality that we discussed in Chapter 1: indivisibility, division, identity, and impredicability. Indeed, the conditions identified in each case may not be the same. One could hold, for example, that the necessary and sufficient conditions of distinction are given by the bundle of features that characterize a thing and at the same time hold that the necessary and sufficient conditions of division are only some of those features, such as materiality. So that it is not by any means clear that when authors speak about the principle of individuation or, even in our more precise terminology, of the necessary and sufficient conditions of individuation, they are speaking about the same issue and, therefore, that their solutions to it are comparable, since they are not always understanding the same thing by "individuality" and "individuation." Often, however, the difficulty is that they themselves do not clearly understand the notion of individuality and as a result muddle related issues. Most authors, as suggested earlier in this book, either because they do not give a proper intensional analysis of individuality or because they aim to develop parsimonious theories or, further, because they think all these features to be related, try to offer theories that purport to account for several of these features at once. In particular, they regard noninstantiability and distinction as inseparable and, therefore, as accounted for by the same conditions. Naturally, to try to answer several questions with the same answer is indeed commendable, since philosophical theories, just like scientific ones, should be as parsimonious as possible. But it is commendable only insofar as one is aware of what one is doing and no violence is done to the various questions. There is no merit in giving the same answer to several questions when one is not aware of their precise differences, or in forcing an inappropriate answer to a question for the sake of economy alone. In such cases we have no real parsimony, but rather cases of confusion and/or stubbornness.

The second point that needs to be made before we proceed is that, as we saw in the chapter dealing with the extension of 'individuality', not all ontologies confront the issue of identifying the necessary and sufficient conditions of individuation. What was called above "Essential Nominalism," namely, the view that holds that everything that exists is essentially or *per se* individual, faces no such issue. The essential nominalist has to worry about other matters, particularly as the thought of Ockham and Hume illustrates, such as how to account for universal concepts.[2] Nevertheless, those who favor this sort of position do raise the issue of individuation for the purpose of attacking

Realism, although it is in the context of realist, moderate realist, or at least moderate nominalist views that the issue is most appropriately discussed.

Likewise, what we called in Chapter 2 the "Characterized Particular View" largely avoids the issue of individuation at least in the case of substances, for it holds that substances are essentially individual. It makes no sense to look for a principle of individuation of substantial entities, but only of their features, if indeed their features are regarded as individual. In cases where they do, the individuation of those features is explained in terms of the substances whose features they are. This position may be considered a type of Essential Nominalism in this respect, but one that applies only to substances and thus falls better into the eclectic category discussed in Chapter 2.

As one would expect, to the variety of realist, moderate realist, and moderate nominalist ontologies corresponds a variety of theories of individuation. What follows is a discussion of the most important ones. Because many philosophers who address this issue accept some kind of distinction between substance on the one hand (Clarisa, my cat) and features on the other (Clarisa's knowledge, my cat's capacity to meow), the discussion is divided into three parts: the individuation of substances, the individuation of features and the individuation of other entities.[3] The third group includes all those entities that do not seem to fall easily within the other two groups. Among these are constituents or principles of substances, events, and the like.

Individuation of Substances

For our present purposes, it is not necessary to give a definition of substance or even to endorse the notion. It is sufficient to illustrate the category by examples, such as Socrates, a dog, a horse, a tree, a table, or a gallon of water.[4]

Things such as a gallon of water and a table are not regarded by many philosophers as substances in the strict sense of the term, since human action is involved in the production of both and the first is homogeneous. However, since they are certainly not features of substances, and they are generally treated as individuals of some sort in the literature, I shall regard them as substances for our present purposes. Substances are characterized by features. It is the individuation of substances, not their features, that concerns us at present.

There are at least four different kinds of theories concerning the individuation of substances: bundle theories, accidental theories, essential theories, and extrinsic theories of individuation. We shall pay particular attention to one type of bundle theory, several accidental and essential theories, and two theories of extrinsic individuation.

Bundle Theory of Individuation

One of the most widespread views of the individuation of substances is variously called the "Bundle" or "Cluster" Theory. It holds that the individuality of each individual substance is to be explained in terms of the group of features it has, since an individual substance is nothing but the bundle of its features.[5] Things are individuated by the bundle of features they possess, which constitute, therefore, the necessary and sufficient conditions of their individuation. This paper on which I am writing, for example, is an individual substance because of the set of features it has: it is white; it is twelve inches long, eight inches wide; it is smooth; it is thin; and so forth. Its features are, let us say, a, b, c, d, and e. And it is because it has this set of features and no other that it is this paper and not the one next to it on which I shall begin writing shortly. That other paper is also white (a); it has the same size (b, c); it is smooth (d); but it is thick (f) rather than thin (e), for example. Still another sheet of paper may have other features, such as a different color or a different texture, and those are the features that, taken together with all its other features, make it an individual, numerically different from the first two.

All of this seems to make considerable sense. After all, it seems quite appropriate to argue that things are what they are, including being "individual," owing to their various features. A piece of paper reflects light, for example, because it has certain features. So, why not say that it is the features of the thing that are the cause and/or principle of its individuality? Moreover, this view has the advantage, in contrast with some of the other views which have been proposed in order to account for individuality and which we shall be discussing presently, that it can extend to everything and to every possible world. It can extend to everything because it does not identify a particular feature or set of features as individuators, but rather whatever features a thing has. In this sense, the principle of individuation is always formally the same, the bundle of features, even if the features that constitute the bundle differ in each case—in a human being they might include corporeality and color, but for an angel they might involve something completely different. Moreover, it extends to every possible world for similar reasons, although in a material world, for example, the bundle will include material features, in a nonmaterial world the bundle would not include such features. This makes the Bundle Theory quite economical and simple.

Most of those who hold this view readily accept one of its consequences, namely, that no two individuals can have the same set of features. This consequence is generally known by the misnomer, "Principle of the Identity of Indiscernibles."[6] This principle is sometimes formulated as follows: If X has the same features as Y, then X is identical with Y. This consequence alone is sufficient reason to question the Bundle Theory, for there does not seem to be any compelling reason why two things may not have the same features. Indeed, if individual substances can have the same necessary attributes, why couldn't they have the same contingent ones? Two individual human beings, according to this view, share in the same humanity, so why can't they share also in their nonessential features, such as country of birth, height, hair color, etc.? True, there seems to be an incompatibility concerning certain features, for instance, place, but this is a restriction that may apply only to physical objects. In cases of nonphysical objects, for example, minds, thoughts, angels, and God (provided they are viewed as individual, of course), one would be hard put to argue for such an incompatibility. Moreover, as we shall see later, spatio-temporal theories of individuation are substantially different from purely bundle theories and furthermore have difficulties of their own.

It is considerations such as these that have led some defenders of the Bundle Theory to argue that the Principle of the Identity of Indiscernibles is not to be held as an analytic truth. It is not that two things cannot, as a matter of necessity, have all their features in common, but that the impossibility in question is empirical. As Russell put it: "Exact repetition . . . is not logically impossible, but is empirically so exceedingly improbable that we may assume its non-occurrance."[7] But certainly to grant that is to grant that the bundle of features cannot account for individuality. If the Bundle Theory is to be taken seriously, it must defend the analytic character of the Principle of the Identity of Indiscernibles, and if it turns out that the principle is not analytically true, then the Bundle theory must look for the fundaments of individuation outside the features of a thing.

Another well known objection against the Bundle Theory is closely related to the one just mentioned and goes something like this: If an individual is the same as the bundle of features it has, then any true proposition that says that any such and such individual has such and such a feature must be analytic and/or necessary and the features that it specifies are essential to the individual in question (all three terms 'necessary', 'analytic', and 'essential' have been used in the literature).[8] This creates three difficulties. The first is the fact that, based on our experience, it does not seem to be true that features, at least not all of them, necessarily belong to the things to which they belong. Is it necessary in any way, for example, that I be now in my studio writing these words? I know quite well that I am doing it because the weather is beastly outside, and it would make no sense to take a walk while a snowstorm is raging. But certainly it could have been otherwise—although it is not often that Buffalo winter weather is conducive to taking a walk. If we were not in the middle of a snowstorm, I probably would be taking a walk at this time of the day. It may be, of course, a different matter with essential features, but since there are at least some features that do not seem to be necessarily tied to things, it seems quite wrong to argue that all the features of a thing are.

145

The second difficulty that one might bring up has to do with the fact that individuals seem to have at different times in their existence contradictory and/or incompatible features. At one time Socrates' hair was black, but at another it was gray, for example. How can this be explained? But the solution to this difficulty is really not difficult to find at all, for the bundle theorist never argues that an individual must have the same bundle of features at every point in its existence. An individual is such because it has a unique bundle, but the bundle is spread out over a period of time, we might say its history, and this allows for contradictory and/or incompatible features at different times.

The third difficulty is closely related to these two. It argues that since individuals change features, their identity through time cannot be accounted for if the individual is identified with a particular bundle.[9] Individuals, such as Socrates, undergo change; they age, mature, grow, and so on. Yet, they continue to be the same individuals: Socrates at twenty and Socrates at forty is still Socrates. But, of course, if individuals are nothing but the bundle of features they have and the features change, the bundle must be different. How can the identity of Socrates at any two times of his life be maintained when at no two different times did he have the same features?[10]

There are many ways of answering this third difficulty,[11] but in keeping with what we said in Chapter 1, we can begin by responding that the objection is based on a confusion between two issues, individuation and identity. If individuation involves accounting for noninstantiability and identity requires accounting for sameness through temporal change, there is no reason why a theory meant to account for the first should also do so for the second. Of course, one may wish to argue that if it does not, then another theory would have to be found in order to account for identity, but that involves only a complication, not an unsurmountable obstacle to the theory. Second, the bundle theorist may counterargue with reason that, although the bundle changes, some features may be constant and individuality could be accounted for in terms of them.

From all this it is clear that, of the last three objections raised against the Bundle View, only the first should be taken seriously. The others, in spite of the fact that they have been favored by various philosophers, can be easily dealt with in one way or another. Still, the bundle theorist can even try to escape the first difficulty as well as the objection based on the Principle of the Identity of Indiscernibles by arguing that, apart from spatio-temporal location, there are other features of things which serve to individuate them, such as identity and relations.[12] Thus, for example, the bundle that Artistotle is differs from Plato in that Artistotle is identical with himself (identity) and/or Aristotle was a student of Plato (relation).

But under scrutiny both of these presumed ways of salvaging the Bundle Theory turn out to create more difficulties than they solve. Let us take identity first. There are at least three problems that this solution raises which cannot be easily answered. The first is that it is not clear at all that identity is a feature. It seems to be in the nature of features to belong and to be distinct from other features belonging to the thing to which the feature in question is said to belong. The relation of belonging is expressed linguistically as predication. Thus, we say that the pen with which I write is red, namely, it has that color, and this fact is expressed by the English sentence, 'The pen is red'. Moreover, the redness of the pen is quite clearly distinct from its size, its weight, and the other features associated with the pen. But identity does not seem to have these characteristics. Identity does not belong to the pen in the way its color does, a fact illustrated in the sentence, 'The pen is identical with itself', because in it the predicate is not a predicate at all or, if it is, it is a very different kind of predicate from say, 'red'. The difference between 'The pen is red' and 'The pen is identical with itself' can be seen easily because the second is equivalent to 'The pen is the pen', while the first one is not equivalent to either 'The pen is the pen' or 'The red is the red'. 'The pen is the pen' just as 'The pen is identical with itself' identifies subject and predicate, while in 'The pen is red' the predicate says something about the subject. This brings me to the second point, namely, that identity is not really different from the features of a thing but rather it includes them. To say that a pen is identical with itself means that it has all the features it has. But to say that a pen is red is only to say that it has a feature quite distinguishable from the other features it may have.

But apart from these considerations, even if we were to accept that identity were a feature, from what has been said it should be clear that it must be a very different feature from features such as color or size. And this, of course, would complicate matters considerably, for then it would be necessary to clarify what it is and establish its character before going on to use it in order to explain the impossibility of repetition. Finally, as has been often pointed out by those who have discussed this, to explain the impossibility of repetition through identity is to beg the question.[13] For it is precisely the identity of the bundles in question that is at stake. It simply will not do to say that A and B are two bundles owing to their distinct identity, when in fact what the bundle theorist needs to explain is precisely how A and B can be distinct when they have all their features in common.

But what about relational features? Couldn't we salvage the Bundle Theory by arguing that relational features do account for differences among bundles? The answer is negative for at least two reasons. In the first place, this point of view ends up by defending a spatio-temporal view of individuation and is therefore subject to the difficulties encountered by that view. Since I shall be dealing with that position separately, I would like to leave the discussion of its difficulties for later. In the second place, all relational features involve at least two entities. But if the individuality of one of the relata is to be

147

established on the basis of the relation and the relation involves at least one other relatum, we may ask whether such relatum is universal or individual. If it is universal, then the relational feature does not establish the individuality of the entity whose individuality we wish to establish. But if it is individual, then, although it does establish the individuality of the entity whose individuality we wish to establish, we must look for some other relation with an individual relatum, which in turn would establish the individuality of that individual, and so on to infinity. In short we would end up in an infinite regress and, therefore, could not claim to have established the individuality of the original entity.[14] I shall return to some aspects of this issue in the epistemic context of Chapter 5. Here I have merely discussed its ontological aspects.

But these are not the only worries bundle theorists have. They have to worry also about the obliteration of the very distinction between individual and universal that their theory aims to support, for a bundle of universals is a complex universal and cannot be regarded as an individual just by virtue of being complex. There is no way in which noninstantiability can be derived from just grouping universals. Leticia and Clarisa, according to this theory, must necessarily be complex universals and in that sense are not different in kind from other complex universals such as "human being" or "animal." The point is that if individuals are bundles of instantiables, then the whole must also be instantiable unless there is some way of accounting for its noninstantiability.[15]

At least two attempts to accomplish this have been developed that are worthy of consideration. One rejects the universality of the members of the bundle, claiming that the bundle derives its individuality from the individuality of its members.[16] This, of course, solves the issue of accounting for the individuality of the bundle, but those who adopt this view must then account for the individuality of the members of the bundle, therefore this move by itself constitutes no solution to the problem of individuation. Moreover, if what accounts for the individuality of the individual substance is not the bundle, but the individuality of the members of the bundle, this view cannot really be regarded as a bundle view of individuation at all.

Another attempt to account for the individuation of complex bundles is to derive it from the relation of the features which compose the bundle.[17] Recently this has been expressed linguistically by referring to this relation as the "tie" represented by the function of the copula, which as it were relates the various features, or alternatively as an "operator," which is applied to a set of properties.[18] But this will not do for several reasons. In the first place, the individuating relation is either something unique to the individual or it is not. If it is unique, then the theory becomes a version of the Bare Particular View, which I shall discuss later, and is subject to the difficulties connected with that view. But if it is not unique, then there is no reason why the relation in question should not be universal and, therefore, itself in need of individuation. Moreover, this relation does not explain the noninstantiability of the thing in question, for, as a universal relation, like fatherhood, it ought to be able to be instantiated. Second, even if one were to accept this view of individuation, it is clear that as a result of this modification the Bundle View has been changed substantially. For, according to the new theory, it is not the bundle that accounts for individuality, but the way the features of the bundle are related or tied. Therefore, we have a different theory, one that relies on a feature, relation, or unique element of a thing, rather than on a bundle of features for individuation.[19]

Apart from this, there are also problems arising from the logical nature of both ties and operators. If the holders of these views are willing to translate their logical language of "ties" and "operators" into the metaphysical term of relation, they face the problems mentioned. But, if they are not, we are left with individuators that are logical constructs rather than realities. No doubt such theories have a bearing on the representation of individuality,[20] but certainly not on the problem of individuation, for it would be quite odd to say that a logical tie and/or operator is a "principle or cause of individuation," using traditional terminology, or, using the terminology we have favored here, "a necessary and sufficient condition of individuality." I cannot see how the noninstantiability of my cat Minina, for example, has anything to do with logical ties or operators.

There is a further problem with the Bundle Theory, namely, that it does not account for the individuality of the features of substances. If they are regarded as individual, something must be found to individuate them and, therefore, the theory must be developed and complicated further in order to be complete. But if they are regarded as universal, as those who adhere to the more orthodox Bundle Theory hold,[21] then this contradicts the conclusions reached in the chapter on extension. In either case we face undesirable results.

In short, then, the Bundle Theory does not account appropriately for individuality. It is my contention that to a great extent this is due to the fact that those who uphold this view conceive individuality primarily in terms of difference rather than noninstantiability. And, indeed, if one does so it makes sense to talk about individuality as resulting from the bundle of features that things have. For, after all, what seems to be the difference between Socrates and Aristotle, for example, but that one is fat, bald, and has a snub-nose, while the other is thin, has all his hair, and has an aquiline nose? This is also what has led many to accept the Principle of the Identity of Indiscernibles. But, of course, these features may indeed be sufficient to account for the differences between Socrates and Aristotle and also for our discerning them as separate beings, even though they fail to account for their noninstantiability, as already noted.

Bundle theorists suffer from two errors: the confusion of the problem of individuation with the problem of discernibility and the confusion of individuality with distinction or difference. It is for this reason that their view aims to account for difference, primarily epistemically, and not for individuality understood metaphysically as noninstantiability.

Accidental Theories of Individuation

If the bundle of features a thing has does not properly account for its individuality, then, some authors reason, it must be particular features that function as individuators.

Traditionally, as mentioned earlier, the features of things have been divided into properties and accidents. Properties are features that always accompany the thing in question; accidents are features that do not necessarily do so.[22] For example, hair is an accidental feature of human beings, for any human being can lack hair and not for that reason cease to be human or the individual human being he or she is. But the capacity to laugh seems to be a property because all human beings have it, even if they never in fact laugh, and if something does not have it, it is not a human being. Of course, there are difficulties with this distinction, but my purpose is not to endorse and/or defend it here, rather I wish only to use it to present theories that rely on it.

The point relevant to our topic is that properties do not seem capable of accounting for individuation, since they are supposed to be common to all members of the species or genus. It would make no sense to say that the capacity to laugh is a sufficient condition of the individuation of Socrates, when in fact it is something all human beings have and, therefore, it is subject to multiple instantiation. Hence, if we are to argue that it is not the bundle of features, but rather specific features that account for individuation, these features must be accidents, according to this view. Let us take an example to clarify the point: If Socrates is not the individual human being he is because of all his features taken together (call them a, b, c and d), or because of features that, like properties, are shared by all members of the species (say, c and d), then perhaps the reason is to be found in some accident in particular (say, b) that is not shareable and, therefore, renders him noninstantiable. What this accident is considered to be, however, may vary since there are a number of possibilities available. Accordingly, several views of accidental individuation have been devised, but of these two are most popular: the Spatio-Temporal and the Quantitative Views.

Spatio-Temporal Theory of Individuation. The most commonly accepted view of accidental individuation is the one that holds it to be a result of spatial and/or temporal location.[23] Or, to put it differently, the view holds that spatio-temporal location is a necessary and sufficient condition of individuation. What distinguishes the universal from the individual is the spatio-temporal location of the latter. The strongest version of this view is the one that (1) combines space and time into a single principle of individuation and (2) does not identify spatio-temporal location with external relations. The version of the view that does not combine space and time together is weak, for one could always object that two or more individuals can occupy the same space at different times or, alternatively, exist at the same time in different places. Similarly, the view that makes space and/or time an external relation is also weak, for then the individual's individuality would be a result of an external relation that would change no doubt with changing circumstances outside of it.[24] Indeed, one might be tempted to say that every time something moved in the universe, the spatio-temporal location of everything else would be changed and presumably its individuality.[25] The strongest view, consequently, rejects both of these approaches. It is spatial and temporal location, considered together and as nonrelational and intrinsic, that must be used. It is because I am here, now, that I am an individual, for example, for no other individual can be in the same place I am at this very time. In order for another individual to take my place I would have to move and then at least the spatial requirement would be missing. Spatio-temporal location, in this sense, is very much like what Aristotle conceived as the inner boundary of a thing.[26] It is the sort of feature that cannot be shared and that is independent from external circumstances. I can distinguish Socrates from Aristotle because Socrates is here, in his own place now, while Aristotle is there, in his own place at the same time.

The advantages of this view are many. It is a matter of common sense and experience that spatio-temporal location cannot be shared by physical things and that often we become aware of individuals as distinct through it. (More on this in Chapter 5.) The Spatio-Temporal View, however, has many problems, but I shall mention only a few.[27] The first and foremost is that it attempts to explain what is a substantial feature of things (individuality) by reference to an accidental feature or relation—time and space. That things occupy space and are in time seems to be posterior to their constitution, that is, their individuality seems logically and metaphysically prior to their temporality and spatial location.[28] It is I who am here now, and my being here now seems somewhat dependent on me, not vice versa. This objection is particularly effective against those ontologies that in addition to holding a spatio-temporal view of individuation accept as well an essence-accident distinction, for in that case it becomes very hard to hold that something accidental, like spatio-temporal location, can determine the individuality of the substance.

151

On the one hand accidents are defined as not necessary to the substance, but on the other hand they would be claimed to be necessary for its individuality, which is in turn regarded as necessary.[29] But even in ontologies where the essence-accident distinction is not accepted, there is something odd about saying that spatio-temporal location is both a necessary and sufficient condition of individuation. Even when spatio-temporal location is interpreted as nonrelational and intrinsic, individuation seems to be a consequence of some other, more basic, feature.

A second difficulty concerns the individuation of spiritual beings, such as minds, angels, souls, and so on in ontologies where such entities are considered to be individual. For, what space and time do they occupy? [30] It is reasonable to argue that thoughts are in time, but the claim that they are in space is indeed far from being well supported and, therefore, cannot be used to support something else unless it were first well established.[31] And, at any rate, within metaphysical schemes where there are individual entities that are not bound by spatio-temporal limitations this reply is ineffective. This difficulty is not insurmountable, however, for the principle of individuation of spiritual beings need not be the same as the principle of individuation of physical beings. Consequently, the fact that spiritual beings may not be subject to spatio-temporal location does not necessarily imply that they are not individual or that their individuality cannot be accounted for, and, therefore, does not imply that the Spatio-Temporal Theory of Individuation of spatio-temporal entities is necessarily incorrect. What the objection succeeds in doing is in forcing those who accept spatio-temporal location as the individuator of physical entities to complicate their theory by having to add a different individuator for spiritural entities if they desire to preserve their individuality.[32]

Note, moreover, that those who adhere to the Spatio-Temporal Theory cannot escape the brunt of these considerations by saying either that there are no spiritual beings or that spiritual beings do not require individuation. Those who reject the existence of spiritual beings do not escape it, because the possibility of the existence of individual spiritual beings is sufficient to create the problem. And since the notion of an individual spiritual being does not seem at all contradictory, a complete theory of individuation would have to account for the individuation of such beings.

Those who argue that spiritual beings do not require individuation do so by saying that there is no context in which a problem can be generated, since I am never simultaneously presented with two spiritual beings which have all their nonrelational features in common. For example, I am never simultaneously presented with two identical thoughts.[33]

But this counterobjection is based on a confusion as to what needs to be accounted for, since the objection assumes that individuation is a matter of difference and of how to distinguish two presumably identical things. Naturally, if there is no occasion in which the need for such distinction arises, the original objection against the Spatio-Temporal View does not arise either. But, as we explained in Chapter 1, individuation does not have to do with distinction, and, as discussed in the Prolegomena, the problem of individuation and the problem of discernibility are different. Individuality has to do with noninstantiability and a theory of individuation has to account for that rather than for distinction or individual discernibility. Therefore, whether there is or there is no context in which a problem of distinction and discernibility arise, we still have to account for noninstantiability. And since there is no reason to think that spiritual individuals are contradictory, a theory of individuation must account for their individuality.

For these reasons, then, and in order to account for the individuation of spiritual beings, the theory becomes less parsimonious and has a disadvantage that the Bundle Theory, for example, did not have. By itself, without modification, the Spatio-Temporal Theory cannot account for the individuation of everything in every possible world, unlike the Bundle Theory, which can do this, at least *prima facie*. It also implies that spatio-temporal location cannot be considered a necessary and suficient condition of the individuation of all individuals even if it were so in the case of some individuals.

In addition, those views that hold that not only substances but also the features of substances are individual would be hard put to explain their individuation in terms of space and time. For, as some traditional critics of the view have it put, what individuates space and time itself?[34] This is another way of asking why it is that "this spatio-temporal location" is not subject to multiple instantiation. Or, to put it still in another way: Why couldn't there be two or more individuals sharing the same spatio-temporal location? As the medievals are reported to have asked, can more than one angel dance on the head of a pin? (More on this in a moment.) The Spatio-Temporal or, more generally, the Relational Theory of Individuation seems compatible only with a semirealist ontology in which substances are individual but their features are not. And since, as I proposed in Chapter 2, individuality extends to the features of things, this theory leaves unaccounted for the individuality of features, including that of spatio-temporality itself.

But, even apart from the mentioned difficulties, the Spatio-Temporal Theory of Individuation faces other serious obstacles. These spring to a great extent from the understanding of individuality as a kind of difference or distinction rather than as noninstantiability as I have proposed. Indeed, if one is looking to account for difference or distinction among things, spatio-temporal location may be a *prima facie* promising candidate. After all, it makes sense that the pen is different from the car because the pen is in here while the car is out there, for example. One may want to argue, with Carnap and others, that it is spatial or spatio-temporal coordinates that differentiate since these cannot be the same for two different things.

One way to argue against this is to suggest that there is no reason why two things could not occupy the same spatio-temporal location. In fact, some authors have argued that there is no contradiction in the idea of two billiard balls or two clouds coalescing into the same spatio-temporal location.[35] In certain circumstances, to put forth such a view might even be the best way of explaining certain phenomena, so they say. And it has been argued that this would not necessarily upset the accepted laws of physics provided these phenomena did not happen very often.[36] But, frankly, I do not find this argument very compelling, in part because the very examples given are inconclusive. In the case of clouds, for example, it is clear that we are speaking of rarefied bodies of particles loosely held together by forces that may not prevent the vacant spaces among particles from being occupied by particles belonging to another also rarefied body. And if this is the case, one would not be justified in saying that the two clouds occupied the same space, but only that they occupied different spaces within the same general boundary. The case of the billiard balls, also brought up in connection with this view, is more difficult to imagine, since their mass seems continuous, but I suggest that since it takes the same degree of imagination to have two billiard balls coalesce than to explain how they do so, the example should be discarded. Until those who wish to attack the Spatio-Temporal Theory of Individuation come up with a better example, I suspect the supporters of spatio-temporal individuation will ignore their views.

A more effective way of arguing against this view may be to say that even when individuality is interpreted as difference among things, spatio-temporal location cannot account ultimately for it. For we could always ask, as suggested earlier, how spatio-temporal locations (or coordinates) are distinguished. Coordinates always describe a point by reference to an origin and axes. But to identify the origin is in fact to bring in an absolute point from which all other spatio-temporal locations are established, a point not itself identifiable in terms or coordinates. Thus, spatio-temporal coordinates are not and cannot be the basis for establishing differences among individuals, since they presuppose an individual absolute point of reference that is not itself differentiated in spatio-temporal terms. Indeed, as Russell suggested while arguing against Carnap on this point, in order for spatio-temporal location to function as an individuator it must acquire the characteristics of substance,[37] which is precisely what the Spatio-Temporal Theory, according to him, was supposed to do away with. As we shall see in the following chapter, spatio-temporal location does have an epistemic role in differentiating individuals in our scheme, but it cannot be held to account for the ultimate difference or distinction among things, let alone account for the noninstantiability of individuals.[38]

Quantitative Theory. Because space and time seem too extrinsic to account for individuation, some authors have sought to explain the individuation of substances in terms of their quantitative features such as width and length. These seem, at least intuitively, to be more closely related to the substance than the time or space it occupies. After all, *prima facie* it makes some sense to say that a statue of Aphrodite cannot be instantiated owing to the dimensions it has. Its width, height, and so on appear to prevent its instantiation somewhere else.[39]

Yet, this view also faces serious objections. First, it encounters basically the same objections that work against the Spatio-Temporal View, for the quantitative features of a thing, except perhaps for its weight, are related to the space it occupies. Second, this view, like others already discussed, would encounter difficulties in explaining the individuality of substances not subject to quantification (minds, angels, souls, and so on). Third, it would also be hard pressed to explain the noninstantiability of quantity itself, which is supposed to account for individuation. For, what makes dimensions noninstantiable when we know that in fact they can and are often, separately or together, instantiated elsewhere? Finally, the quantity of a substance, as Duns Scotus stated centuries ago, changes while the individual remains the same.[40] A person may gain or lose weight and yet remain the same person. So how can we identify her weight as the reason of her individuation? Note that this argument is not meant to show that identity is a requisite of individuality. We already settled that issue in Chapter 1. It is meant to show that a particular quantity is something accidental to a thing, and therefore cannot account for one of its basic ontological characteristics.[41]

Again, as in the other cases discussed, this theory relies on an understanding of individuality as some kind of difference or distinction, for it is really when one thinks of individuality as distinction that quantity becomes appealing as a principle of individuation, although it turns out to fail even under that interpretation. But as an account for noninstantiability quantity does not have even a *prima facie* plausibility. Incidentally, the Quantity Theory of Individuation may also have its origin in the view of individuality as divisiveness rejected in Chapter 1 and not only in the confusion between difference and noninstantiability: It may be the result of interpreting division as a necessary condition of individuality.

Essential Theories of Individuation

The extrinsic nature of some accidents and the fact that particular ones are not indispensible to individual substances undermine all accidental theor-

ies of individuation, leading some philosophers to search among the fundamental constituents of substance, that is, those components essential to it, for
the necessary and sufficient conditions of individuation. Three theories of
individuation have appeared as a consequence: Material, Formal, and the
Bare Particular View.

Material Theory. The Material Theory of Individuation posits matter as the
cause or principle of individuation.[42] Socrates is an individual because of the
matter. It is in the nature of matter to be unshareable and, therefore, all
material things are rendered individual by it. The strength of this view lies in
its apparently commonsensical basis; for, indeed, at first glance it makes sense
to say that the stuff out of which a thing is made is what determines it to be
this rather than that. In the classic example of the marble statue, is it not the
pieces of marble out of which two identical statues of Apollo are carved that
make them two statues? For all their specific features are the same and even
many of their accidental ones. Their only significant difference seems to be the
marble. That is what they do not and cannot share with each other or with
anything else. Presumably, then, their noninstantiability can be traced to the
matter.

But there are problems with this view. Perhaps the most important is
that matter as such does not itself seem to be individual and, therefore, it is
difficult to see how it can be the source of the individuation of other things.
Indeed, as some have argued, matter *qua* matter is common and, therefore,
requires something extrinsic to be added to it in order to become "this
matter."[43] This is another way of saying that matter is instantiable rather than
noninstantiable, unlike the matter of a particular thing (i.e., "this matter"),
which cannot be instantiated. In the example given, marble is common to the
two statues; it is "this piece of marble" that is individual. But then the
question remains: What turns "matter" into "this matter," or "marble" into
"this marble"? It is for this reason that many philosophers have added to
matter certain features such as (1) actual particulat dimensions or (2) dimensionality, in order to allow for both its individuality and its individuating
effect.[44] It is not marble then that individuates this statue of Apollo, but this
marble, that is, marble plus certain dimensions (seven-by-two-by-one feet,
and so forth). Or, alternatively, it is marble considered as potentially dimen-
sional, that is, marble as always having to have a set of particular dimensions,
but not as actually having them, that individuates. Because it must always
have a particular set of dimensions, it must always necessarily be "a this" when
it exists, and consequently these dimensions together with matter are the
source of individuality. Indeed, according to Suárez, this is the difficulty that
led Thomas and/or Thomists to add dimensions to matter.[45] In this way a
material theory of individuation could still be preserved in the face of the
stated criticism.

156

But this modification of the view will not do, because in the first case matter is combined with an accidental feature, and as such the principle of individuation becomes partly accidental. This opens the theory to all the objections against accidental theories we saw above. And in the second case, it is difficult to see how dimensionality can help matter to individuate, for if it is understood as general, then it can belong to any individual, and, therefore, it is subject to multiple instantiation, even if this could happen only in succession. But if it is conceived as particular, there is no difference between this theory and the previous one, and, therefore, the same objections that applied to that one would apply to it. Marble considered as marble must necessarily have particular dimensions, but those dimensions could in principle be shared by many. If they are actually particular, then the dimensions (say, seven-by-two-by-one feet) are accidental and therefore dispensable, and if they are not, then they can be shared by many and cannot explain the individuality of the marble or the statue.[46]

There are also other problems with the Material Theory of Individuation. For example, it necessarily limits individuality to the physical world, an unwelcome and restricting feature as we saw above, unless, of course, one introduces multiple principles of individuation. But this, although not inconsistent, certainly complicates the theory.

In addition, in metaphysical frameworks where matter is conceived as pure potentiality, it is hard to explain how it can be a cause or a principle of individuality. This is a standard modern objection to Aristotelian metaphysics, which, in spite of its popularity with some critics, has only limited merit. It is, however, one of the reasons why some philosophers have substituted form for matter as the principle of individuation, since form, unlike matter, may be conceived as actual and as the source of a being's features. Most of those who use it argue that matter cannot be a principle of individuation because it is characterless and something characterless cannot account for the difference or even noninstantiability of individuals.

The problem with this objection is that most of those who hold matter to be the principle of individuation, including some of those who say that it is pure potentiality, do not hold it to be characterless, that is, a "bare particular," but rather they accept that matter does have characteristics of a sort even if they are not first order features like color and weight. This is rather obvious within Aristotelianism and may have been one of the reasons why this objection is rarely found even among scholastics who disputed the Material Theory of Individuation.

Another reason why form, rather than matter, is singled out as a principle of individuation is what also appears to be a powerful objection at first sight against the Material Theory of Individuation, but which upon closer inspection turns out to be ineffective. The objection argues that matter could

157

not be the principle of individuation of a thing because the matter of a thing is always changing, and this would imply that individuality would also change.[47] If what makes Socrates the individual he is is the matter he has, then when his material composition changes, as it constantly happens in material organisms that feed and excrete, Socrates should cease to be the individual he is and become some other individual. Moreover, since form seems to remain the same in spite of the material changes undergone by physical individuals, form must be the principle of individuation.

This objection, however, is not effective. The primary reason why it cannot undermine the Material Theory is that it confuses individuation with identity, that is, the process whereby a thing becomes individual and the capacity of a thing to remain the same individual through time and partial change. One can very well hold that individuation is the result of matter while identity is due to something else, for example. Of course, this would create complications, but one can always argue that they are necessary ones. So the inability of matter to account for individual continuity does not constitute the basis for a serious argument against the Material View of Individuation.

Before we turn to the formal theory of individuation let us note, furthermore, that the Material Theory of Individuation is generally a response to the need to account for distinction, separation, and plurality, not noninstantiability. The question involved in individuation, as posed by those who favor this view has to do with why "this" is not "that" and why there are "two" instead of "one." But those questions, as we saw earlier, make sense only in a certain context and not in all cases where there may be individuality. If the question is framed in terms of noninstantiability, then matter cannot account for it, since adding inches to the waist will not turn "man" into "Socrates." Matter and matter with dimensions make some sense only if the issue at stake has to do with distinction, separation, and/or multiplication, and not if it has to do with noninstantiability.

Formal Theory of Individuation. According to this view, an individual substance is individual owing to its substantial form.[48] A form is a structural principle, and a substantial form is the structural principle that determines the fundamental (i.e., necessary and sufficient) features of a substance.[49] In a human being, for example, the substantial form is the humanity, that is, those features that, like animality and capacity to reason, constitute together with others the necessary and sufficient conditions for something to be human. Since the form, therefore, is what determines what a thing is, it should also be the source of its individuality. The individuality of Leticia, according to this view, is explained in terms of her humanity.

A standard objection against this view points out that form, considered in itself and as such, is universal. In fact, the very notion of form, as opposed to matter, is the notion of what is shareable by and common to many.

158

Equinity is common to all horses, and not particular to Black Beauty alone. How can form, then, be the source of individuality? Most objections to the Formal Theory of Individuation are variations of this basic one.[50] Put in this way, however, the objection is not conclusive. For, as we saw in Chapter 1, the essential feature of universals is instantiability and not multiple instantiability. Thus, one could reply to this objection that, although not all forms could serve as individuators, some at least could. So, for example, it would be clear that forms like "man" cannot serve as individuators, since they are capable of multiple instantiation. But a form like "the first man born in space," would seem to be sufficient to function as an individuator, for, if instantiated, it can be so only once. Nor could one argue that, since the theory refers to substantial forms and substantial forms are capable of multiple instantiation, unlike the instantiable "the first man born in space," which is not a substantial form, the objection still applies. For one could bring out the example of the Judaeo-Christian God, whose substantial form (i.e., his divinity) precludes his multiple instantiation, as pointed out earlier. This way of objecting to this view, therefore, leads nowhere.

Another way of arguing against the Formal Theory of Individuation would be to point out that even if some forms, whether substantial or not, could function as individuators, most forms cannot, and, therefore, whether we want to maintain the Formal Theory of Individuation or not, such theory would have a very limited scope, leaving unexplained most cases that need to be accounted for. And, since theories that explain only few cases are notoriously inadequate, we should discard this view.

This seems to me to be a sensible objection and one that is sufficient to dispose of the Formal Theory of Individuation as a viable theory. But it really does not get to the heart of the matter, namely, the fundamental problem of the view. This problem is brought out by another objection: The difficulty of the Formal View is that it does not account for noninstantiability. Even if we were to grant that it accounts for uniqueness—something that I am not prepared to do unqualifiedly without further argument, but that I am willing to do for the sake of the present argument—uniqueness is not the same thing as individuality. To be unique, as pointed out in Chapter 1, is to be distinct from everything, but that does not imply noninstantiability. and, although individuals may be unique, their fundamental characteristic *qua* individuals is noninstantiability. The problem, then, is that forms are by nature instantiable and, therefore, cannot account for the contrary feature, namely, noninstantiability.

This position is similar in many ways to the Bundle Theory and, therefore, shares some of the same advantages and disadvantages of it. In both cases, there is an attempt to explain individuality in terms of a group of features that are in themselves universal. The difference between the views lies

159

in that the Bundle Theory does not discriminate among features, while the Formal Theory restricts the principle of individuation to a bundle of substantial features, which it terms "substantial form." But both fail to account for noninstantiability, even though both views may account for difference under certain circumstances.

These and other problems have led others to posit a different essential principle of individuation, which unfortunately is no less controversial and inadequate than the ones already discussed.

Bare Particular Theory of Individuation. The difficulties with matter and form have led philosophers who wish to restrict their search to substantial principles to formulate a bare particular theory of substantial individuation.[51] According to this view, the principle of individuation is nothing more than the principle of individuation; its only function in a substance is to individuate and as a result it cannot be identified with any other component, cause, or principle in it, nor can features of any kind be attributed to it. We know there is such a principle dialectically; we need it in order to explain the individuality of things. Its existence, therefore, is established from the requirements of reason.[52] Without it we cannot account for individuality. To ask, however, about what this principle is over and beyond being the principle of individuation is to misunderstand its role in the make-up of things, for this principle, as the basis of an individual's individuality, must be characterless. That is why it is called a "bare particular."[53] In each substance, there is, then, a bare particular which belongs to that substance and no other and which is the basis of its individuality and of its distinction from all other substances. Socrates is individual because of his Socrateity, and this Socrateity is not reducible to Socrates' various features or characteristics, considered separately or together, or to his constitutive elements; it is entirely *sui generis*.

It is this emphasis on the "bareness" of the principle of individuation that makes it possible for the view to avoid some of the complications associated with the Spatio-Temporal and Material Views of Individuation. For the characterless nature of the principle makes possible its extension to all types of things in all possible worlds. Still, although it is difficult to argue with this view insofar as it emphasizes the inadequacy of the other theories of individuation we have discussed, and there are some advantages to its identification of a principle of individuation with a bare entity, it is not too difficult to criticize the characterless nature of the principle, as pointed out in previous chapters. Indeed, as characterless, this principle cannot be described directly. What we know are its effects and the fact that it has to be posited, but nothing about the principle itself. Moreover, although this principle seems to account for the distinction between entities, it is itself not subject to distinction, since it has no feature by which it may be distinguished. Critics argue, then, that this view is not legitimate. It consists simply in giving a name to an entity that is mysterious on all accounts. As such the view does not really propose a principle of individuation but simply recognizes that substances are individual and that their individuality needs to be accounted for.[54]

This position recognizes quite well the difficulties faced by the Bundle View in accounting for individuality and it tries to make up for them by adding this bare particular, since it doesn't want to abandon the universality of the features of things. Therefore, in order to individuate the bundle it poses an individuator. But the individuator, being characterless, becomes a mysterious metaphysical entity if there ever was one. There have been recent efforts to show that the principle is not as mysterious as it was first thought. As already noted, Bergmann and his followers have claimed that we are acquainted and/or presented with bare particulars. But if we were presented with them, it would be easy to distinguish them from the other features of things. But when we try to do that the result is disappointing: Once we peel the various layers of the onion, there is no core. In other words, if we take away, mentally, all the features that a thing has, there is nothing left.

Now, some have argued that indeed there is something left—the area. But to identify bare particulars with the area occupied by something is really to interpret bare particulars with an individual's spatio-temporal dimensions. And this sort of view, as we already saw, is unsatisfactory and, moreover, does not need to be clothed in the mysterious terminology of "bare particulars." If we are to take seriously the theory of bare particulars, then let us accept that they are, indeed, mysterious and known only dialectically, as Dun Scotus did with what he called "thisness."

Finally, let me add that bare particulars, unlike many of the other individuators discussed so far, could in principle be made to function as real individuators, that is, as necessary and sufficient conditions of non-instantiability. Nonetheless, those who accept this view often fail to make them do so. They are content to use them to account for difference and distinction, because the problems that concern them are those of sameness and distinction, not the problems of instantiability and noninstantiability.[55] In that sense, their attempt to account for individuality is even more inadequate than it needs to be, since it does not account for what it is supposed to.

Extrinsic Theories of Individuation

Apart from the mentioned views, a few authors have devised other positions which, for lack of a better name, I have called Extrinsic Theories of Individuation. They are rather weak, as will become evident shortly, and they argue that individuality is the result of the action of some kind of natural agent or cause.[56] Socrates is an individual owing to the actions of his father and mother, which generated him. After all, it is one's parents who are

161

responsible for those features that make one unique. Similarly, a statue's individuality is the result of the sculptor's action, which brought it about.

The difficulties usually raised against this theory are based on the extrinsic nature of an agent's action and the intrinsic character of individuality. True, the agent is responsible for bringing about the individual substance; but that does not explain why the substance cannot be subject to instantiation. That it cannot be so must be the result of something intrinsic to the substance, not of something extrinsic to it.

An alternative to this theory, attributed to some theologians in the medieval period states that individuation is the result of a supernatural agent. It is argued that God, as creator of each individual substance, is related to it in a unique way and thus that owing to this relation the substance is rendered individual. The disadvantage of this theory springs from its reliance on religious authority. Its suitability depends not only on the existence of God, which is after all a topic of philosophical controversy, but on purely theological assumptions concerning creation and God's nature and will. For these reasons it cannot be, and indeed seldom has been, taken seriously as a viable philosophical alternative to the problem of individuation.

In both cases, whether the agent is interpreted naturally or supernaturally, the view originates from an error: It confuses a causal account of a thing with an account of its individuality. Parents and God may indeed be the causes of children, but that does not give us the list of necessary and sufficient conditions of their individuation. After all, Monica may have been the cause of Augustine's brown eyes, but that does not explain why the color and the eyes are not subject to instantiation. And what if Augustine had had other brothers with brown eyes? How could we account then for his individuality and the noninstantiability of his eyes and their color? This view does not understand that individuality is an intrinsic feature of a thing and, therefore, cannot be explained in terms of something external to it.[57]

Individuation of Features

The view that the features of things are individual is not a very popular theory these days. It was almost universally held in the Middle Ages, but in this century there have been only a few philosophers who have explicitly defended it.[58] This, as we saw in Chapter 2, is due in part to a misunderstanding about the intension of 'individuality', which, once removed, opens the way for considering features of things to be individual, that is, noninstantiable. Now, if they are individual, then we may ask for their principle of individuation. The question concerns the necessary and sufficient conditions of the individuation of such things as Plato's capacity to laugh and Socrates' black hair color.

There are two basic types of theories concerning the individuation of features: the substance and the feature views.

Substance Theory of the Individuation of Features

The most widespread theory concerning the individuation of features holds that they are individuated by the substance in which they inhere; Socrates' black hair color, for example, is individual because it belongs to Socrates.[59] It is because the black hair color of Socrates belongs to him that it is individual. There are two versions of this view. In one, (I), features are said to be individuated by a substance that is *of itself* individual. According to this view, a man for example, is always individual. What are not individual and, therefore, require individuation are his features. The substance, then, requires no individuation. In some cases, this view is subdivided further, for (a) some consider the substance to consist only of those features that are essential to the entity in question. In the example of a man, it would consist of his rationality, capacity to laugh, and so forth. But in other cases, (b) the substance is considered to consist of both essential and accidental features. According to the first subview, (a), it is only the accidental features that require individuation, since those may or may not belong to the substance. When they do, they become part of the individual and as such are individuated. But accidental features considered apart from a substance are not individual, since they are not instantiated elsewhere. According to the second subview, (b), it is both essential and accidental features that require individuation, since whether a feature is essential or accidental has nothing to do with whether it is individual or not. Sometimes this view, in which essential and/or accidental features are said to be individuated by a substance that is of itself individual, is called the "Characterized Particular Theory." The name of the theory, as we saw earlier, derives from the fact that it holds that particulars which are substances are always characterized. As presented here, according to this position, the features of a substance are individuated. In Chapter 2, however, the position was described as holding that the features of a substance are not individual. The fact is that the view has two versions, although the most commonly held today is the one described in Chapter 2. Scholastics and other traditional Aristotelians, on the other hand, favored the individuality of features in substances.[60]

The main problem with this position, as we saw above, is that it fails to explain why the complex notion of a characterized particular is unanalyzable. As a complex entity, a characterized particular is composed of the particular and its characteristics. And, if this is so, then the question of what the particular is apart from its characteristics arises. According to this view, however, the characterized particular is not capable of analysis, although the reasons for such an incapacity remain mysterious.

A second, more tradtional alternative, (II), holds that features are individuated by substances, but substances are themselves individuated by something else. A man's black hair color is individual because it is his, but the individuality of the man is based on something else. The bases of the individuation of the substance may vary, depending on the view, but that is a different issue, as we saw above.

The weakness that some authors have seen in this view springs from a general source, common to all views that rely on substance for the individuation of features; it is similar to the weakness of the Accidental Theory of Individuation of Substance. The problem with the latter was that, after making a distinction between what is essential and what is accidental, it went on to find in what is accidental to the substance the source of its individuality. The situation with the present theory is similar, for it identifies as the source of individuality in a feature something which is "external" to it. True, one may want to argue that it is essential to features to be present in substances, but it is certainly not essential to them to be present in "this" substance rather than that one. "Black hair color" must always belong to this man, or that man, and so on, but it is not necessary that it belong to this individual man, that is, that it not be instantiated elsewhere. Its individuality, then, if taken from this man, comes from a source that is external and as it were accidental to it.[61]

Feature Theory of the Individuation of Features

Another alternative for the individuation of features is to hold that they are individuated by features, either (1) by the set of features present in a substance taken together and including themselves, or (2) by some specific feature or accident such as spatio-temporal location, or (3) by the features themselves. The last view is really not a view of individuation, since saying that features are individuated by themselves is equivalent, for all intents and purposes, to saying they are individual in themselves. This is a nominalist position that is sometimes referred to as the "Perfect Particular View," because according to it each property and accident is wholly and completely, that is, perfectly, particular.[62]

The first and second views have some of the same advantages and disadvantages of the accidental theories of substantial individuation. It seems, for example, commonsensical that this black hair color is "a this" because it is in this place, at this hour, on this large head, etc., that is, together with these other features. But it is also a fact that this black hair color has no intrinsic relation to this place, this hour, or this large head. It could be somewhere else at some other time, for example. The extrinsic relation among features themselves, then, goes against the Feature Theory of Individuation of Features.

One may still want to argue, however, that in the Bundle Theory

164

features would of necessity be part of a bundle and, therefore, that it would not do to say that they "could be" part of some other bundle. In such a case, the relation of a feature to the other features of the bundle is not extrinsic but intrinsic. To argue otherwise would be to beg the question.

The answer to this is twofold: First, bundle theories do not as a rule accept the individuality of features but only of clusters or bundles. Therefore, they do not need to account for the individuality of features. Second, in cases where they do, it is clear the objection raised here does not apply, for in such a case all features are to be considered essential to the individual; that is, all members of the bundle must be taken as indispensable.

Although this view might be able to explain the "uniqueness" of a feature in terms of the uniqueness of the bundle of which it is a part, the position would be hard pressed to explain its noninstantiability in those terms. In short, bundle theories, like so many others, may do a fair job of accounting for uniqueness or difference, but they fail miserably when it comes to the foundation of individuality, (i.e., noninstantiability). For, how can noninstantiability be found in something whose components are completely instantiable? But I have referred to this point previously, so there is no need to elaborate on it further here.

This brings me to a last important point, namely, that most of the theories of individuation of features, as those of the individuation of substances, are based on the confusion of the ontological problem of individuation with the epistemic problem of discernibility and/or the confusion of individuality with some kind of distinction or difference. It is in this context that it makes sense to speak of substances as being individuators of their features, since, indeed, it would seem that we "discern" the "distinctions" among the features of various substances precisely through those substances. Likewise, it makes sense to speak of spatio-temporal location, a feature, as an individuator of other features because, again, we seem "to discern the distinctions" among the features of various substances through their spatio-temporal location. But it does not make sense to talk about either of them as "individuators" in the sense in which we use the term, that is, as principles of noninstantiability. Belonging to an individual substance and association with another feature or features do not seem to be both necessary and sufficient conditions of the noninstantiability of individual features.

Individuation of Other Entities

In addition to substances and accidents, philosophers often speak of other entities such as matter, substantial forms, modes, and so forth, which are regarded as principles and metaphysical components of things. And there are some entities that do not seem to fall into any of these categories, such as events, documents, and novels. The first problem that these entities pose is of classification within an ontology, not a problem of individuation as such. For this reason some preparatory work would have to be done before one could discuss the question of their individuality, something that does not fall within the boundaries of this study. Of course, in an ontology where these entities are considered individual, it is necessary to account for their individuality. However, since the theories concerning their individuation most likely would be similar to those concerning the individuation of substances and/or their features, it does not seem worthwhile to investigate the issue further at this point, even if we had determined their exact ontological status.

Principle of Individuation

The Problem and the Alternatives Revisited

At the beginning of this chapter, the problem of individuation was framed in terms of two issues: (1) the identification of the principle of individuation, and (2) the determination of whether this principle is the same for all individuals. In both cases, what was at stake were the necessary and sufficient conditions of individuation, that is, what an individual has that makes it noninstantiable that universals do not have. Moreover, from what has already been said in this chapter, it should be clear that there is no easy solution to the problem of individuation. Indeed, as with the problem of extension, the discussion seems to have reached an impasse in which there is only a limited number of alternatives available, all of which have already been developed and all of which have serious defects. What to do then?

Three alternatives suggest themselves: One alternative is to adopt one of the views discussed earlier and refine it to a degree that it will meet the objections brought against it; the second is to attempt to show that the problem of individuation is spurious and, therefore, that it needs to be dissolved rather than solved; and the third is to find some other view that may provide a way out of this impasse. It is difficult to see any future in the first alternative. The most basic and important views proposed earlier have been available for several hundred years, during which time philosophers have endeavored to elaborate and refine them. Yet, as shown above, they are still vulnerable to objections. Indeed, if there is anything that can be learned from the history of the controversy is that it seems to be a quagmire out of which there is no way. This brings us to the second alternative: the attempt to show that the problem of individuation is spurious and, therefore, that it needs to be dissolved instead of being solved. In short, according to this alternative, the impasse that the controversy has reached is symptomatic of the fact that the problem is apparent rather than real, and this can be detected only, as it were, from outside. Those who favor this alternative would go on to argue that the difficulty lies with the attempt to find a single condition or set of conditions necessary and sufficient for individuation. There is nothing that may be identified as the principle of individuation in all or even most cases. The reasons that would be given to substantiate this claim are similar to the objections presented in the Prolegomena against the search for the necessary and sufficient conditions of individuality.

It seems to me, however, that to adopt the second alternative is to give up too easily. We saw already that at least in one case, when discussing the necessary and sufficient conditions of individuality in Chapter 1, such procedure was not warranted. Moreover, I find the skeptical bent of this approach dangerous, for it may tend to confirm the belief that the scope of human reason is more restricted than I would like to believe and may be in fact. Before adopting this position, therefore, I would prefer to explore the third alternative and see if we can find another position whose adoption might help us with the problem of individuation while avoiding the difficulties of the two other alternatives at our disposal.

My claim is that, indeed, there is such an alternative, and thus I agree with the first view in that the problem of individuation is not spurious and as such can have a solution. But I also recognize, with the second alternative, that there is something wrong with the way in which the problem is usually approached and, therefore, that unless we are able to uncover what that is, we will make little headway toward a satisfactory solution.

Let us begin, then, by identifying the factors that distort the formulation of the problem of individuation. There are three that seem particularly important: (1) various confusions concerning the intension of 'individuality', (2) the formulation of the problem in epistemic terms, and (3) a reductionist attitude.

I have referred already to the intensional confusions which have prompted some of the standard theories of individuation. There are, I believe, two of these that are particularly important and widespread. The first is the interpretation of individuality as some kind of distinction or difference. The theories in which this conception of individuality is more evident are the Accidental, Formal, Bundle, Spatio-Temporal, and Quantitative Theories. Indeed, as noted already, it makes sense, at least *prima facie* to point to features or bundles of features, to spatio-temporal location, and/or to the thing's dimensions as sources of difference. It is a matter of common sense that Socrates is different from Aristotle because the first had a snub nose, was short and fat, had a beard, taught Plato, attended the dinner party on which the *Symposium* is based, and so on, while Aristotle had an aquiline nose was tall and thin, did not have a beard, was a student of Plato rather then his teacher, did not attend the dinner party on which the *Symposium* was based,

167

and so on. In cases where all features seem to be the same, including dimensions, there is always spatio-temporal location to account for the difference between Socrates and Aristotle and any other individuals.

But, of course, if individuality is conceived as noninstantiability, then these theories lose their commonsensical appeal and are left only with the disadvantages already pointed out earlier, for it is not easy to see how noninstantiability can be accounted for in terms of features, bundles of features, spatio-temporal location, and/or quantity.

The second intensional confusion concerns the understanding of individuality as requiring some kind of actual or potential division of a species. The three theories in which this view of individuality is more evident are the Spatio-Temporal, the Quantitative, and the Material Views. Again, if division is considered as a necessary and/or sufficient condition of individuality, it would seem to make sense to point to space-time, quantity, and/or matter as individuators. In all cases, what is needed is some element that would introduce discreteness among things, separating them. And spatio-temporal dimensions, quantity and matter appear to function in this way, since they involve dimensions, and dimensions can function as separators and dividers. This is three-by-five-by-two feet, while that is six-by-two-by-eight feet, for example. This is three feet away from the north wall and ten feet away from the south wall of the room, while that is five feet away from the north wall and eight feet away from the south wall. And the two pieces of marble are not only the reason for the fact that there are two statues of Apollo rather than one but also for the fact that they are discrete and separate from each other in distance.

On the other hand, if it is not division and discreteness that is involved but rather noninstantiability, it is not clear that these theories work, for the reasons explained already above.

Something similar can be said, moreover, about the theories concerned with the individuation of features. Both the Substance and Feature Views seem to presuppose views of individuality similar to the ones just discussed, while they fail to account for noninstantiability. But there is no need to dwell further on this matter. Let the examples given suffice to illustrate the point.

The second factor that muddles the formulation of the problem of individuation is the use of an epistemic approach in what is an ontological problem. In the Prolegomena, I have already shown how the problem of individuation needs to be distinguished from the problem of discernibility and how what appear to be good solutions to one may be absurd solutions to the other. Yet, several of the standard theories of individuation ignore this fact and treat the problem of individuation as if it were the problem of discernibility. This should have been obvious from the discussion of the Bundle and Spatio-Temporal Theories, and in general it is true of theories which interpret individuality as distinction or difference. For usually they see their aim as finding ways in which the knower can differentiate among individuals. Indeed, it makes a great deal of sense to say that we become aware of many individuals as such from their spatio-temporal location. But does it make sense to say that they are noninstantiable because of it? This confusion, then, between the epistemic and the ontic gives rise to theories that are inadequate, but on the basis of a first impression look promising.

Finally, the third factor that contributes to the difficulties in the formulation of the problem of individuation is what I have called the reductionist approach. This is not a matter of intension, or of the confusion between two separate problems; it has to do with the extension of 'individuality'. As we saw in Chapter 2, the reductionist approach is used both by realists and nominalists, who try to solve the problem of individuation by reducing universals to individuals or individuals to universals. On the one hand, Realism, as we defined this position, holds that everything that exists is universal. And under those conditions the realist has only two choices to account for individuality: He can simply deny any real ontological status to individuals, relegating individuals to the realm of appearance, or he can try to account for individuality in terms of universals. In both cases there is a reduction. In the first case, individuals are identified with appearance and, therefore, their reality is denied, thereby reducing them to nothing and keeping the world in the realm of universality. In the second case, individuals are converted into complex universals, thus again annihilating them in a complete reductive process.

On the other hand, Nominalism, as we interpreted this view, maintains that everything that exists is individual. If there are no universals, then what look like them are to be understood in terms of individuals, that is, they are to be reduced to them. The advantage of this position, of course, is that it is parsimonious, since there is no need to ask for a principle of individuation. But in order to achieve that, it sacrifices universals and thus falls into a misguided reductionism as well. Moreover, in Chapter 2 we discussed important objections to various versions of this position.

Having exposed some of the underlying confusions which contribute to the impasse concerning individuation, it would be useful to see some of the positive aspects that can be learned from the theories of individuation discussed earlier. The Material, Formal, and Bare Particular Theories teach us one lesson: Individuality is at the core of a thing, and, therefore, any principle of it must also be intrinsic to the thing. To put it in traditional terminology, the principle of individuation of a substance must be substantial and not accidental. The Bare Particular theory, moreover, recognizes an even more radical requirement, namely, that none of the features or constitutive principles of substances—features, matter, form, and soon—can function as the sole principle of individuation. Finally, the Extrinsic Theories of Individuation suggest that things and their features are fully accounted for by their causes and constituents, and therefore, that there is no need for something other than a thing, its constituents and causes to account for its individuality.

Of course, there are problems with all these views, but these points are important; any solution to the problem of individuation will have to acknowledge them. The solution I propose takes them into account and avoids the difficulties of the mentioned views. It rests on the conception of individuality as noninstantiability and on an ontological formulation of the problem, and it avoids reductionism. Moreover, profiting from the lessons learned from other theories, it identifies a substantial foundation for individuation. I call this solution the Existential Theory of Individuation, although, as we shall see, it involves a formal component as well.

The Existential Theory of Individuation

Simply put, the Existential Theory of Individuation holds that existence is the principle of individuation for all individuals. This is the answer to the two questions raised at the beginning of this chapter. In order for the theory to work, however, it must also hold another postulate, namely, that existence is not a feature of things. As such, then, one can distinguish between existence on the one hand and the features which characterize things on the other. Some medieval authors brought attention to this point by noting that, concerning any thing, such as a phoenix, for example, one may ask two different questions: What is it, and Does it exist?[63] The first question is answered by a definition or statement listing the features that pertain to the thing in question. This is what scholastics referred to as "the expression of the essence." The second question, on the other hand, is answered affirmatively or negatively, independently of any features the thing in question might have. In the example, the answer to the first will point out that a phoenix is a bird that rises from its ashes, and so on, while the second will simply point out that phoenixes do not actually exist, even though they are possible beings. (Possible being means that the concept of phoenix does not contain a contradiction.) In modern philosophy this postulate has been expressed by saying that "existence is not a predicate."[64]

The reason why it is absolutely necessary to hold that existence is not a feature if one is to hold an existential view of individuation is that features in themselves are universal. Thus, if existence were a feature, one would have to ask in turn what individuates existence. Furthermore, to hold that existence is a feature would contradict what has already been said about universals as being neutral with respect to existence. There are, of course, many other reasons why one would want to hold that existence is not a feature, but given the wide acceptance of this view, I do not see any reason to dwell on it further here.

170

At the beginning of this chapter we had discarded the terminology of "principle or cause of individuation" in favor of the more neutral nomenclature of "necessary and sufficient conditions of individuation." So we must translate what we have just said concerning existence as principle of individuation in terms of the newly adopted terminology. This is simple, for what the Existential Theory holds is that existence is the only condition that is both necessary and sufficient for individuation; that is, existence is the only necessary and sufficient condition for the instantiation of a universal. Thus, it is in virtue of it that there are noninstantiable instances of instantiables, and it is existence, then, that causes noninstantiability. Note that existence, as used here and according to what was said in Chapter 2, refers both to actual and/or possible existence. Indeed, the only alternative to possible and actual individuals would be impossible ones, which by definition could not exist.

Now, one may want to ask why, having put the answer in terms of necessary and sufficient conditions, one could not hold that form or matter, for example, could not be considered principles of individuation also, since they do seem to be conditions of it?

In the case of form, the answer is that, although form is without a doubt a necessary condition of individuality—there could be no individuals without form (or natures, as some would prefer to call it)—it is by no means a sufficient condition. Indeed, as we say in Chapter 2, forms or natures, considered as such, are instantiable rather than noninstantiable. So they could never be sufficient conditions of individuality. Moreover, form is implied by existence, since nothing exists that is not some kind of something, but not vice versa. Therefore, although form is a necessary condition of individuation, it is only existence that is both a necessary and sufficient condition of it.

The cases of other, more specific principles such as matter, spatio-temporal location, and so on are different, for their connection with the individual is through the form or nature and, therefore, dependent on it. It is true, for example, that to be material is a necessary condition of an individual man. But that is precisely a result of the fact that the individual in question is human: The form or nature (in this case human nature) determines what are the necessary conditions of the individual. But since, as we saw, the form or nature is not a proper, necessary and sufficient condition of individuation, then these secondary conditions can never fulfill that function. This leaves us, then, with existence as the only necessary and sufficient condition of individuation.

The advantages of this theory should be quite obvious when compared with the theories discussed above. In the first place, existence seems to be unshareable, for who can exist for me? My existence and yours, certainly, are distinct and unshareable and so it seems with that of everybody else. I do not exist for you, nor do you for me, and when I say that I exist this implies nothing about your existence and vice versa. Yet, existence is not unshareable owing to a process of individuation, for, not being a feature, it is not in itself universal. And this avoids an infinite regress.[65] Second, the theory avoids the fundamental difficulties encountered by accidental theories of individuation—existence is indeed a substantial principle—or by the material and formal theories—existence is not formal in any way and as nonmaterial it can extend individuality to nonmaterial beings. Nor does the theory encounter the difficulties which plagued the Bare Particular View, since the function of existence is not just to individuate, and existence seems too evident in experience to be questioned. Moreover, this view avoids the problems of the Bundle View, since existence is not a feature.

In spite of all these advantages, I have not found a single major author in the history of philosophy who explicitly and unambiguously endorses this position.[66] Indeed, it is not clear that anyone has endorsed it at all in the form I am presenting it, even though many authors have argued against it and have attributed it to various other individuals.[67] Therefore, it is with considerable trepidation that I have chosen to defend it here, particularly since elsewhere I had cast some doubts on the viability of this position.[68] Still, after giving careful thought to the objections that are usually brought to bear against this view, I have not found them convincing; no argument seems to render the view untenable. Let us look at some of these difficulties.

One may want to argue, for example, (I), that individuality extends not only to existing entities but to possible entities as well and, therefore, that as such existence cannot be the principle of individuation. Let us suppose in one case that the National Mint has been minting silver dollars and that it minted 5,000 such dollars on January 1, 1987. There is no question that each of those dollars would be an individual. Now let us suppose in another case that the Mint was supposed to mint 5,000 silver dollars but that, while the minting process was going on, the Mint broke down and had to be stopped after having minted only 4,999 silver dollars. Couldn't we speak of silver dollar 5,000 as not having been minted and as nonetheless being individual even though its existence never materialized? The point is that whether silver dollar number 5,000 was, or was not minted, there would still seem to be a difference between that silver dollar and the universal "silver dollar," as well as between that silver dollar and silver dollar number 4,999.

To this objection, one can answer in two ways. First, (A), one may argue that nonexisting objects are not individual and, therefore, that this difficulty does not constitute a serious objection against this view. After all, what would a possible individual be? Experience seems to suggest that what we refer to as possible individuals are either of two things: (1) composites of universal features that as such are instantiable; or (2) mental images of individuals that have actually existed. In the first case, the individuals turn out not to be individual at all but composite instantiables. And in the second case, the individuals in question are only those that have existed and, therefore, one could hold that their individuality is due to existence, after all. Hence, the objection against the Existential Theory of Individuation based on the individuality of possible beings is not sound.

Of course, the matter is not so simple in the case of (2). For it is not clear how actual existence can be the individuator of something that does not actually exist, even if it has existed in the past. Nor is (1) so clear, for there may be other ways of making sense of the notion of a possible individual, as we shall see later. For the moment, however, the point I wish to make is that the view which says that possible beings are individual cannot be taken for granted without question and, therefore, cannot be used to dismiss summarily the Existential View of Individuation without furhter substantiation. But I shall return to this shortly.

Second, (B), even if possible beings were individual, one could still hold an Existential View of Individuation. For, as we saw earlier, existence can be classified into actual, possible, and impossible. Impossible existence, of course, cannot be an individuator, for impossible entities are not entities at all and, therefore, cannot be classified as individual. It is inconceivable, for example, that a square circle could exist and, therefore, that it could be either an actual or a possible individual. Note that I do not wish to deny the conceptual existence of the square circle. Although there has been considerable discussion of this issue, and therefore the matter cannot be easily dismissed, I should point out that I find nothing wrong with thinking about a square circle. Indeed, in order to deny that a square circle is possible one has to consider what it is, and this is done by considering both the features of a square and the features of a circle. That the sentence 'A geometrical figure with the features of a square and the features of a circle cannot exist' is not nonsense indicates that one can not only think but also know what a square circle is even if one must also understand, if one understands at all the notions of square and circle, that it is impossible for a square circle to exist, since the features of a square and the features of a circle are incompatible. The sources of the problem are, of course, the long held belief that "to know" implies the existence of what is known—Plato's divided line is still haunting us—or the view that knowledge involves imagination—a legacy of radical empiricists. but once it is realized that knowledge of X implies neither the existence of X nor the capacity of X to be imagined, then one can perfectly well hold that we know what square circles are even if we also know that they do not exist, and we cannot picture them in our minds. In either case, however, whether we hold that knowledge of square circles is possible or not, everyone agrees that they are neither actual nor possible entities. Impossible existence, then, cannot function as the individuator of entities. But possible existence could in principle be considered as individuator, and, therefore, one must explain how this is the case.

As individual, a possible individual must be, if we adopt the understanding of individuality presented in Chapter 1, a noninstantiable instance. And as possible it must be an entity whose existence implies no contradiction but that, contrary to actual entities, does not exist. Thus, "silver dollar number 5,000 having been minted on January 1, 1987," is clearly a possible state of affairs, since it could have taken place even if in fact it did not. On the other hand, "silver dollar number 5,000 having been minted and not having been minted on January, 1987" is not a possible state of affairs, but rather an impossible one. To this, Plantinga adds another condition for possible individuals, namely, that the state of affairs in question be fully determinate. By this he means that it be a state of affairs, S, such "that for any state of affairs, S', either S *includes* S' (that is, could not have obtained unless S' had also obtained) or S *precludes* S' (that is, could not have obtained if S' had obtained)."[69] The example he gives is "Jim Whittaker's being the first American to reach the summit of Everest" because it precludes Luther Jerstad's having that accomplishment while it includes Whittaker's having climbed at least one mountain. Well, if we apply this to our silver dollar we see that it meets the criterion, since it precludes another silver dollar from being the 5,000th silver dollar minted on January 1, 1987, and it implies the minting of 4,999 silver dollars prior to it. From all this we can conclude that it does not appear that the Existential Theory of Individuation is undermined by the notion of individual possible being. In a possible individual, the principle of individuation would be possible existence, while in an actual individual it is actual existence.

However, the matter may not rest there, for one may still question the relation between a possible individual, its actualization, and its principle of individuation. Let us take the case of my only son Alexander, a possible being since I can and could have had such a son even though I do not presently have him and most likely never will. And let us call possible Alexander A. Given the specifications given above, A could become or could have become actualized anytime during my lifetime, since it involves no contradiction. And let us assume for a moment that A has become actualized—call its actualization A'. Clearly A and A' are or should be the same individual, my son Alexander. And yet the principle of individuation of A and A' according to the Existential Theory of Individuation would seem to be different in each case, since for A it is possible existence and for A' it is actual existence. Shouldn't A and A' be different individuals, then, and/or if they are the same individual have the same principle of individuation?

The answer to this is that this question implies a confusion to which we have already referred between individuation and identity. Since the principle of individuation and the principle of identity need not be the same, the identity of A with A' need not imply that the principle of individuation of A and A' be the same, nor does the fact that the individuation of A is due to possible existence and that of A' is due to actual existence imply that A and A' are not the same individual. There is one entity rendered noninstantiable by its possible existence when it was only a possible being and by its actual existence when it is an actual being.

Let me finish the discussion of objection (I) by pointing out that the possible world view is very controversial and that my discussion is intended only to show that the Existential View of Individuation cannot be easily dismissed, even if one were to accept the notion of individual possible beings. If one rejects such a notion, then objection (I) poses no threat to the Existential View, of course. In neither case should my remarks be construed as an unqualified support for the notion of possible individuals, although what I have said here together with some of the things that will be discussed in Chapter 6 clearly indicate that there are many advantages to the notion of possible individual.

Another objection, (II), against this view argues that the same individual may cease to exist at one time and begin to exist later at another time and that in this case it would have two separate existences, not one. Accordingly, existence could not be considered as its individuating principle.

This objection is particularly effective in the context of metaphysical theories that conceive existence as an act. For then it would seem that the act is not the same after an interruption. Take, for example, the case of a running man who stops running and then restarts. If the period of time between the two runnings were short, say that he had stopped for a glass of water on his way, one may perhaps be tempted to say that the running is the same. But if the time involved is fifty years, it becomes very difficult to argue that the act in one case is the same as in the other. Indeed, the type of running one does at twenty is quite different from the type of running done at seventy. But not only the type, the acts themselves seem to be two different instances of the same "type" of act. In other words, for things that occur at different times, numerical unity seems to presuppose continuity. Therefore, discontinued existence cannot be considered to be the same. And if this is correct, existence cannot be identified as the principle of individuation.

This objection is by no means unassailable. One can answer it in two ways. First, (A), one can argue that, in spite of what has been said, it is not clear at all that a temporal interruption in existence implies a difference in existence. And it does not, because in order for this to be the case, existence would have to be considered as a feature capable of multiple instantiation— existence[1] at t[1] and existence[2] at t[2]. Yet, one of the stipulations of the Existential Theory of Individuation is precisely that existence not be considered a feature and, therefore, that it not be treated as instantiable. Those views that support objection (II) rely on a feature view of existence, making it a quality or an act or some such categorical predicate.

But even if one were to accept, as I do not, that existence is to be treated as a feature and, therefore, can be subject to multiple instantiation, one can argue, (B), that objection (II) is based on the confusion between individuality and identity to which we have already referred. For what the theory proposes is that existence is a principle of individuation (i.e., noninstantiability) and not that it is a principle of identity (i.e., sameness through time and partial change). Therefore, even if one were to grant that there is not one individual, but two, before the first one ceased to exist and the second one began to exist, there is no reason why the individuals would lose their individuality. Hence, objection (II) does not count against existence being a principle of individuation but only against it being a principle of identity or continuity.

A third, (III), objection one may bring against the view could go something like this: This position postulates that existence is what instantiates a universal into a noninstantiable instance. "Man" becomes this or that man when it exists. But if existence is responsible for making "man" this *or* that man, then it cannot be the principle that makes "man" this man *rather than* that man. Something else must be required and, therefore, the view that existence is the sole principle of individuation or, as put here, the only necessary and sufficient condition of there being an individual is untenable.

But the answer to this objection is not difficult, since the objection rests on a confusion that is at the heart of many of the problems involved in individuality: the confusion between individuality and difference. To say that existence is the principle of individuation is to say that it is the only necessary and sufficient condition of there being an instance of any instantiable. It is not to say that it is the only necessary and sufficient condition of there being an instance *different from* some other instance. That existence is the principle of individuation of man explains that there be a man but not that there be Peter rather than Paul. The explanation of that, namely, of the difference beween Peter and Paul, is another issue tied to the natures and features of Peter and Paul, for sameness and difference have to do with natures and features, while noninstantiability has to do with existence. This, I believe, should have been clear from what was said in Chapter 1 about the intension of 'individuality'. Objection (III), therefore, fails to undermine the Existential View of Individuation. Naturally, those who bring up this objection would not want to give up so easily and might retort that the separation of the principle of difference from that of individuation complicates the theory. But my answer to that is that the complication is necessary for the reasons given in Chapter 2 and elsewhere in this book. Not to make a distinction between individuality and difference results in serious difficulties which are avoided if the distinction is maintained. In that sense, the complication the theory has fallen into by adopting the distinction is not only minor but necessary.

The view that is defended here, then, proposes that existence is what explains the noninstantiability of an individual in contrast to the instantiability of a universal; it is what the individual has that the universal does not have. As pointed out in Chapter 2, universals are neutral with respect to existence. What existence is and how it should be described is important philosophically, but need not concern us further here, since our task is not with existence or even being but with individuality, and already something was said about it in Chapter 2. What has been pertinent at this point to establish is that existence is both a necessary and sufficient condition of individuation. That existence is such a condition does not prevent us from recognizing that there are additional necessary conditions of individuality, but these are tied to existence in some way. So that, for example, to have a nature seems to be a necessary condition of being an individual, even if it is not a sufficient condition—universals are natures and yet are not individual. But to have a nature is in fact a requisite of existence, since only those things that are something (i.e., things which have features of some kind) can exist. Thus, the requirement of a nature is in fact contained in the requirement of existence and, therefore, need not be specified when we speak of the principle of individuation. That is why I have called the theory an Existential View, excluding any formal aspects from its name.

One of the advantages of the existential principle of individuation is that it functions universally and, therefore, applies both to substances and their features, regardless of the view of substance accepted (bundle, substratum, characterized). But, we may ask, does this mean that in cases of substances with features we have to posit several existences, separately individuating the substance and its features? The answer to this question is negative. Even if one accepts a substance-feature distinction and also accepts that both substances and their features are individual, it does not follow that one needs to accept further that a complex substance necessarily includes several existences. One need only hold that the substance is individual because it exists and that its features are individual because they exist. Since existence is not a feature, and certainly not a thing, it would be mistaken to talk about "existences" in a substance. Moreover, since features are tied to the substance and exist only vicariously in it and through it, they can be regarded as individual through the same existence through which the substance exists. This does not mean that, under those circumstances, as Suárez would put it, the individuation of features is "extraneous."[70] The individuation of features is intrinsic because they are individuated by the fact that they exist in a substance as features of it.

Finally, one might wish to object that existence has nothing to do with individuation, for after all, did not Plato hold that it was universals (the "ideas") that existed and individuals (the entities of the spatio-temporal world of experience) existed only in appearance?

The answer to this objection is that, indeed, Plato held that ideas existed, but in doing so he turned them into individuals, a fact that has not escaped his critics.[71] Indeed, that is why he found it so difficult to explain the relation between ideas and the things of this world, for his theory destroyed the distinction between instantiables and noninstantiable instances, turning both into the latter and placing them in a transcendental realm.

Before we leave this chapter, something must be said with respect to how the Existential Theory fits in with what was said in Chapter 1 concerning the primitive character of noninstantiability. For one may wish to ask: If noninstantiability is primitive, how can existence be held to account for it? Does not the Existential Theory imply that noninstantiability is not after all a primitive notion but rather is analyzable into existence? The answer to this question is negative. To say that noninstantiability is primitive is to say, as we explained earlier, that no equivalent (simple or complex) can be found for it. There is no simple or complex concept that does not include the notion of noninstantiability (or instantiability), which may be used in place of "noninstantiability." Noninstantiability is a fundamental notion, one of the building blocks in metaphysics. But to say that existence is the principle of individuation is not to say that individuality is reducible to existence or equivalent to it in any way. To exist and to be noninstantiable are two different things, even if everything that exists, actually or possibly, is noninstantiable and vice versa. To say that something is individual is not the same as to say that it is an actual or possible being, and to say that something exists is not the same as to say that it is individual. Of course, I have argued earlier that indeed only individuals exist, and this would seem to imply that existence and individuality are coextensive. But this is an ontological commitment arrived at dialectically and not an *a priori* discovery based on the relations of the concepts of individuality and existence. Although individuality and existence may be coextensive, they are not cointensive.

In order for the theory of noninstantiability as primitive to conflict with the Existential Theory of Individuation, it would be necessary to say that the notion of noninstantiability could be analyzed in terms of existence, but that is certainly not what has been claimed here. Existence does not function with respect to individuality as a conceptual component, but more like a causal principle, and this is in accordance with the distinction we made in the Prolegomena between the intensional problem of individuality and the problem concerned with the principle of individuation.

With this in mind we can turn to the problem of the discernibility of individuals.

5

Discernibility of Individuals

The issue discussed in this chapter is epistemic. As pointed out in the Prolegomena, and unlike the logical and ontological issues taken up in earlier chapters, the one we are about to raise is concerned with knowledge. It involves the determination of the conditions under which the individuality of something is known, or, to put it differently, of the conditions under which something is known as individual.[1] How do I know, for example, that Socrates is individual and, therefore, that he cannot be instantiated? Of course, not every one will agree to formulate the question in this way. Indeed, the formulation of the question will depend to a great extent on the conception of individuality one holds. For those who view individuality as identity, that is, as sameness through time and partial change, the question will be rather: How do we know that Socrates is the same individual at two different times? Or, in a more vivid example, how do I know that the three-by-five-inch card I have in front of me at this moment is the same as the one I had in front of me yesterday? Formulated in this way, the criteria sought have to do with the identification, or reidentification as it should more appropriately be called, of the same thing at two different times and under different conditions.[2] Likewise, if individuality were to be intepreted as distinction or difference, the question would have to be formulated in another way. We would have to ask how we know that something is distinct or different from something else. How do I know, for example, that the paper on which I am now writing is different from the paper on which I wrote yesterday, or from the paper on which I shall begin to write shortly? And the same could be said about the other ways of understanding individuality examined in Chapter 1. However, as we saw in that chapter, individuality properly speaking consists in noninstantiability and, therefore, the issue involved in the discernibility of individuals should be formulated in those terms. But more on this shortly.

In our inquiry into this matter we shall begin by providing a clear formulation of the problem and of the conditions under which a solution may be found. These propaedeutic remarks will be followed by a more substantive discussion concerned with the discernibility of individual substance and three theories concerning it: the Spatio-Temporal Theory, the Bundle Theory, and the *Sui Generis* Theory. Subsequently, we discuss the discernibility of features. The chapter closes with an analysis of the so called Principle of the Identity of Indiscernibles and its various formulations. The main thesis of the chapter is that the individuality of substances can be discerned in a variety of ways in context, although primarily it is discerned through spatio-temporal conditions. Spatio-temporal conditions, although not necessary for individual substance discernibility and not always sufficient conditions of it can and often do function effectively for that purpose. For features it is the substance to which they belong that primarily functions as sufficient condition of individual discernibility, although in special circumstances other specific features of the substance may also do so. Let us turn now to the issue proper.

The epistemic character of the problem of the discernibility of individuals has some important implications. One of these is that the problem has to do with the relation between a knower and an object of knowledge. This in turn suggests that any solution to it would have to depend to some extent on the nature of both knower and the object of knowledge. If we were to identify the knower as a purely spiritual being, devoid of senses and sense organs, sensation could be neither a necessary nor a sufficient condition of the discernment of individuals for these beings. Indeed, it is not easy to explain how such beings could know material objects. The medievals were aware of this problem and produced, with their typical ingenuity, theories that avoided this difficulty. But that, of course, is immaterial to the present purposes. This reference to the medievals is intended only as a historical illustration of a view that considered knowledge a relation between knower and the object of knowledge, and that as such the conditions under which it can take place depend directly on the character of the *relata*.[3]

I would like to make clear, moreover, that it is not my purpose in this chapter to deal with the conditions of individuality discernment other than in a human context. The reason for this is that the human context is the only knowledge context in which we have firsthand experience. It would be possible, of course, to discuss the conditions of individual discernment for nonhuman beings, as the medievals did with angels, for example, but such discussions would be fundamentally speculative. Since the question of human

180

discernment is closer at hand, I believe we might be able to settle it more easily, and, therefore, it should be addressed first; the others can be dealt with at some other time and in other contexts. Our question then is as follows: What are the conditions under which human beings can discern individuals *qua* individuals? That is to say, under what conditions can humans become aware of noninstantiable instances *qua* noninstantiable? This question in turn can be divided into two further questions, depending on whether the individual to be known is purely spiritual and, therefore, nonsensible, or whether it is subject to sensation (assuming, of course, that only material entities are subject to sensation). For although we are not concerned with the knowledge of individuals that nonhumans may have, we are certainly interested in the question of how humans can know individuals of whatever kind. I should add that both cases are being considered not because I wish here to endorse and defend the view that there are purely spiritual individuals—that would take considerable effort and is beyond the limitations imposed on this study—but simply because the existence of purely spiritual individuals is logically possible and, therefore, any explanation of the discernibility of individuals should cover this case whether or not there are in fact such beings.

Since the knowers with whom we are concerned are human beings, it is only their mode of knowing that should detain us. To say that this matter has not escaped philosophical scrutiny and controversy is clearly an understatement. Philosophers have disputed the way human beings know from time immemorial. Yet, at least in contemporary philosophy, the tendency is to agree that all human knowledge begins in sensation. There are disputes as to how it happens, what happens after sensation, and about the relation of knowledge to sense, but most philosophers accept sensation as a starting point of human knowledge, and I shall do the same here.[4] But if sensation is the origin of all human knowledge, then it must be a necessary condition of the human discernment of individuality. This means that whatever humans are able to discern as individual must somehow have a sensible dimension. Even purely spiritual individuals, if there were any, must appear somehow to human beings under a sensible garb. And, indeed, the commonsensical wisdom of most religious books agrees. In the Bible, for example, angels take on human form in order to converse with man, and God manifests himself through a burning bush. Even folklore confirms the point when it makes ghosts some kind of semitransparent beings, at least when they try to scare living human beings. How these spiritual individuals can take on a sensible appearance poses a problem, but not one that we need to address here.[5]

Another important implication of the way we have formulated the problem of discernibility is that it occurs only within a universe were there is multiplicity and variety. The fact that the discernment of an individual is presented as a relation between a knower and an object of knowledge introduces in the universe at least two entities (three in fact if the relation is counted as an entity).[6] But more than that, we know from experience that the world of sensation contains a multiplicity and variety of beings. In such a world, as we saw in Chapter 1, individuals are not only noninstantiable but also necessarily distinct from other things. And if distinction is a necessary feature of all individuals in the sensible world of multiplicity and variety, then it suffices to identify something as distinct in order to know that it is individual. Absolutely speaking, of course, distinction cannot be considered either a necessary or sufficient condition of individuality, as we saw in Chapter 1. That it is not a necessary condition is clear from the fact that one can conceive of an individual which is not distinct from anything else—the case of a universe containing a single individual. And it is clear that it is not a suficient condition because not all distinctions imply individuality, for example, the distinction between the universals "cat" and "dog." But not absolutely, that is, in the context of a world of multiplicity, variety, and sense, where, as we saw earlier, both things and their features are individual, distinction among its members is indeed a sufficient condition of individuality, for if something is distinct, that implies its noninstantiability. If Peter is distinct from John, they can be distinguished from each other, and since the things we experience in the world are noninstantiable, as established in earlier chapters, both Peter and John may be said to be individual. Likewise with the features of things. If I can tell the color of Peter's hair apart from the color of John's hair, or even the color of Peter's own skin, that entails, within the context we have identified, that they are two noninstantiable instances and, therefore, each of them is individual. Hence, in order to account for individual discernibility, we do not need to ask for the necessary and sufficient conditions of our knowing something as individual strictly speaking, that is, as noninstantiable, but only to ask for the sufficient conditions under which we can know something as distinct. The problem reduces, then, to finding the sensible feature or features that are sufficient for establishing something to be distinct from other things in human cognition.

This means that the answer to the epistemic problem of discernibility is contingent upon the answers to the intensional and extensional problems discussed earlier. That is to say, the view of individual discernibility being proposed here depends logically on the view of individuality as noninstantiability proposed in Chapter 1, on the view concerning the extension of 'individuality' presented in Chapter 2, and on the existential theory of individuation discussed in Chapter 4. But that is as it should be, first, because this is a book of metaphysics and not of epistemology. Thus, the epistemic issues raised here are raised in a metaphysical context and are contingent upon the metaphysical assumptions and views defended in this study. Second, because, apart from these considerations, it seems to make no sense to deal with epistemic issues without first settling the corresponding intensional and extensional issues; for, how can one determine epistemic criteria of knowability when the object of such inquiry has not been defined? Moreover, if this is the case, such criteria will necessarily be related and dependent on the definition. Third, I would like to emphasize that the problem that has been raised in this chapter is not the problem of *whether* we do or can discern individuals. The fact that we do and, therefore, that we can I believe is quite evident and, therefore, philosophically uninteresting. The problem concerns rather the conditions under which we can and do effectively carry out such discernment.[7] Hence, we can and should begin with what we have already established about individuality—the intension and extension of the term—and proceed from there to determine the conditions under which we effectively recognize it.

Now let us return to the original problem. Having formulated it in the suggested way, its solution would not seem either too difficult or extraordinarily puzzling. Indeed, if what we need to explain is how we account for distinction among the things given in our experience, and what is required is only a sufficient condition of this distinction, we need only take a close look at experience to find how we in fact distinguish things.

One last methodological point: Since the issue of discernibility concerns both substances and their features, and it is not necessary that the same condition account for the discernibility of both, it would be appropriate to divide the question and deal with each of these issues separately. We shall begin then, with the discernibility of individual substances.

Discernibility of Individual Substances

An even superficial glance at experience establishes that practically any feature of a substance is sufficient to account for its distinction from other substances, although whether in fact it does or does not depends to a great extent on a variety of circumstances present. For example, knower K may distinguish between two three-by-five-inch cards because they have different colors, or textures, or thicknesses. If the color, texture, and thickness were the same and the dimensions different, it is the dimensions that are sufficient to account for their distinction and, therefore, their individuality. Moreoever, the distinction of the cards would be verifiable even if they were not presented to K at the same time, for K would still be able to distinguish them. He would know one card as "the red one" and the other as "the white one," or, if the difference were of texture he would know one as "the rough one" and the other as "the smooth one," and so with the other features. Any sensible feature can serve as a sufficient condition of the discernibility of physical

183

substances, but not in all circumstances. Color, for example, is not and cannot always be the distinguishing feature, and the same can be said for dimensions, texture, or thickness. When K is confronted with two cards that have the same dimensions, color, texture, thickness, and similar features, the distinction needs to be made in terms of something else, and most often it is made in terms of spatio-temporal location. This has given rise to a widespread theory of individual substance discernibility.[8]

Spatio-Temporal Theory of Individual Substance Discernibility

As we saw in the preceding chapter, the Theory of Spatio-Temporal Individuation is a favorite among philosophers of all time. But, as we also showed, spatio-temporal location cannot account effectively for individuality. However, in our experience, spatio-temporal location can and does account effectively for the discernment of individual substances in most circumstances. Presented with two cards with the same dimensions, color, texture, and thickness, K may still discern them apart on the basis of their different spatio-temporal location: one is here and the other there, or one is to the left of the other, and so forth. But, we may ask, can spatio-temporal location be in *all* cases a sufficient condition of the individual discernibility of substances? The answer to this question, as with any good philosophical answer is both affirmative and negative, depending on how the question is interpreted. Let me explain by bringing up what looks like an important objection to this view.

Suppose that we have a universe composed of only two beings, two homogeneous spheres made up of the same material and having all their features in common. The spheres, therefore, are to be considered alike in all respects except for the fact that they are two. Now, if these conditions are accepted, someone might object that in such a universe spatio-temporal location is not and cannot be a sufficient condition for the distinction between the two spheres. The reason is that spatio-temporal location is relational and that under the specified conditions it would not be possible to apply any, let alone a locational, predicate to one sphere that could not be also applied to the other. I could try to distinguish one sphere from the other by saying, for example, that one is "to the left of the other" or that one is "here rather than there." But, of course, in the mentioned universe one cannot say something about the position of one sphere that could not also be said about the other. Moreover, we could also add that none of the positional descriptions of either sphere could be given without including a reference to the other. And this, of course, makes the description circular.[9] Thus, the objection runs: Spatio-temporal location does not and cannot always function as a sufficient condition of the discernibility of individual physical substances. This does not mean, of course, that it does not and cannot do so sometimes or even often or that it cannot always function as a sufficient condition in our world; it only means that it cannot do so in all possible cases and worlds, as the example of the two-sphere universe indicates. As such the objection does not try to invalidate the examples of discernibility based on spatio-temporal distinction cited earlier, since the context in question is entirely different, namely, our world. But let us look at this matter more closely.

Let me begin by making a few basic distinctions. Moreover, in order to simplify matters let us assume that the examples that will be discussed will refer to the same temporal coordinates unless otherwise specified. So let us suppose that we have three circles exactly alike drawn on a blackboard, named X, Y, and Z respectively. Each of these circles has a number of features, some of which are relational while others are nonrelational. X, for example, is "round," has "a diameter of four inches," and "is to the left of Y and Z," etc. Y is also "round," has "a diameter of four inches," is "to the left of Z," "to the right of X," and "in the middle of X and Z." Z is also "round," having "a diameter of four inches," but is "to the right of X and Y." The first two features of each circle, that is, shape and the length of the diameter, are examples of nonrelational features. We can change the order of the circles and still the features would remain in the object (i.e, could be predicated of each of the circles in exactly the same way as before); X would still be "round" and have "a four-inch diameter." Two of the circles, moreover, could be erased altogether, say Y and Z, and still X would be "round" and have "a four-inch diameter." These two features, then, are independent of the objects surrounding X. They are also independent of the knower perceiving X. Whether there is anyone looking at X or not, X's roundness and the length of its diameter do not change. The fact that it is a feature of X that prompts the judgment that "X is round" or the judgment that "X has a four-inch diameter" is a fact ontologically independent of the judgments or of the knower making such judgments. The experience of error attests sufficiently to that. Whether I am aware or not of the exact dimensions of X's diameter, or whether I regard it as three inches long rather than four, does not alter the dimensions of X's diameter; it alters only the truth-value of my own statements about X, but not X's features. X's features are the cause of my judgment and not vice versa. This is a nonreciprocal relationship, which explains precisely why error can arise in a judgment about X's features. If the knower or his judgments were in any way causes of X's features, then there could never be error in the knower's judgment about X.[10]

Features of this sort are nonrelational because they are independent of things or knowers other than the ones they characterize. There are, however, other types of features. Let us go back to our example. The last features of X and Z ("to the left of Y and Z," "to the right of X and Y") and the last three

185

features of Y ("to the left of Z," "to the right of X," "in the middle of X and Z") mentioned are examples of relational features. They are relational because they depend on objects other than the one they characterize. Although the features in question characterize one object, they are the result of that object's relation to some other subject or object. Therefore, the changes that affect them are not restricted to changes in the characterized object as is the case with non-relational features.

Let us take the example of X being "to the left of Y." If we changed the order in which X, Y, and Z are drawn on the blackboard to Y–X–Z, X would immediately lose its feature of being "to the left of Y." Now it would be "to the right of Y," although it would still be "to the left of Z." Similarly, if we erased Y and Z, X would lose all it relational features dependent on those two circles. Features such as "to the left of _," "to the right of _," and similar ones are relational in the sense that, although they are features of one object, they depend on more than one object.

A further distinction needs to be made here, however. Some relational features, such as "next to _" and "come after _" in the expressions "X is next to Y" and "Two comes after one," are dependent on two objects only. For, regardless of the position and location of everything else, it would seem that X and Y can be "next to each other," for example, and that "two comes after one." (More on this later.) Other relational features are dependent on three objects. Examples of these are the above mentioned ones (i.e., "to the left of _" and "to the right of _"). In each of the last two cases a third point, the point of reference, is necessary. In order to say that X is "to the left of Y" one has to specify in respect to what. Suppose, for example, that the alleged blackboard were transparent and the three circles in our example were thus visible from both sides of the board. Then X would be "to the left of Y" if one were looking from one side of the blackboard, but X would be "to the right of Y" if one were looking from the other side. Relational features that depend on three objects are triadic; that is to say, they are features of one object dependent on three objects. But relational features that depend on two objects are dyadic. There are also examples of tetradic relations, pentadic relations and so on.[11]

The first point I want to make here is that dyadic spatial relations cannot serve as sufficient conditions of individual discernibility in all cases. This seems to be clear with some predicates, but it may not be as obvious in the case of such spatio-temporal indicators as 'here' and 'there' or 'in front of _', or 'at the back of _'. Let us examine these cases briefly.

Let us suppose that we have a universe such as the one described above, with only two homogeneous spheres in it, but let us also assume that the two spheres are capable of thought. Couldn't it be argued that one sphere could think "I am here, and you are there?" And wouldn't this imply that 'here' and 'there' could be meaningfully used even in a case where there were only two

186

things in the universe and, therefore, that the spatial predicates which express dyadic relations are effective in accounting for individual discernibility in all cases? And the same point could be made with other spatial dyadic predicates such as "in front of _."

But a closer examination of the example shows that this objection is misguided for the following reasons. First, the proposition, 'I am here and you are there', can be thought by and can refer to either one of the two spheres, and therefore, the spatial terms it contains lack clear indexical reference. Nor would the addition of the temporal term 'now', or some other temporal indicator, like 'then', help under the specified conditions, since in a universe such as the one described, 'now' or 'then' would not be able to fix the referent of 'here' and 'there'. The fact is that in such a universe the two beings would not and could not have consciousness of themselves as distinct; that is, they could not discern their individuality *on the basis of* spatio-temporal location alone. For to say that one of the beings could be conscious of being here rather than there where the other sphere is at a particular time, is no more than to say that one of the spheres would be conscious of being itself and not the other at that time.[12] It is the consciousness, subreptitiously introduced in the example, that accounts for the apparent distinction, not the spatio-temporal predicates. The case of 'next to' brings out the same point. For in the universe that we have described, 'next to' would not be able to function as a sufficient condition of discernibility, but would in fact be meaningless. For 'next to' can convey some descriptive information only if the two spheres could also be "far from" each other. But having only two beings in the universe means that no such distinctions could be made.

But someone may want to object still that spatio-temporal dyadic predicates are after all sufficient to account for two spheres being "close to" or "far from" each other and that no other entity is required. For example, if one sphere is three feet away from the other, it would be close to it, and if it were three billion light years away, it would be far from it. Therefore, spatio-temporal location does in fact account for individual discernment.

But this objection is based on a misconception, for the introduction of space in our two-sphere universe can be interpreted in two ways. In one way, it is in fact equivalent to the introduction of an absolute point of reference in the universe. Space in this sense would be like the Newtonian absolute, a kind of receptacle or grid in which things are located. But if this is the case, then another entity is required after all beside the two involved in the example, namely, the receptacle or grid. On the other hand, if space were not understood in this way, then it could not support distinctions such as "close to" in the mentioned universe.

From all this it should be clear that spatio-temporal dyadic predicates cannot *always* be sufficient for the establishment of distinctions and, therefore, for the discernment of individual substances *qua* individuals. No further elaboration is necessary to provide an answer to the question raised earlier. Still one may want to consider another aspect of the problem, since at least *prima facie* it looks as if the failure to account for the discernment of individual substances in all cases may only apply to dyadic predicates. Supposing that the universe about which we have been speaking had three rather than two spheres, would not then some spatio-temporal predicates be effective in accounting for individual substance discernment? For, then, from the perspective of sphere X, sphere Y could be identified as being to the left of Z and Z as being to the right of Y at time t^1, and so forth.

Upon closer examination, however, we find that triadic spatio-temporal predicates are as ineffective as dyadic spatio-temporal predicates in the specified circumstances. Indeed, triadic predicates have the same problems as dyadic ones, namely: (1) the same predicates apply to the three spheres and (2) they presuppose distinction instead of establishing it.[13] Take spheres X, Y, and Z about which we have been talking and let us try to establish their distinction on the basis of the triadic relations "to the left of _" and "to the right of _." From X's perspective we could say that Z is to the left of Y and Y to the right of Z. From Y's perspective we could in turn say that X is to the left of Z and Z is to the right of X. And from Z's perspective we could say that Y is to the left of X and X is to the right of Y. At first inspection it looks as if, indeed, by doing this we have succeeded in distinguishing X, Y and Z, but in fact we have not. For if we take away the proper names 'X', 'Y' and 'Z' and substitute them for a common term, say 'sphere', which applies to all three entities, we cannot establish any distinction among the three based on the descriptions given. The reason is that the descriptions apply to all three entities and, therefore, cannot establish distinctions among them. They seemed to do so initially because the proper names 'X', 'Y', 'Z' already established the distinction among the spheres.

The inference we must draw from all this, then, is that spatio-temporal triadic predicates cannot always function as sufficient conditions of individual substance discernibility and certainly not in the universe of the example we have been discussing. And I believe the same could be said about tetradic, pentadic, and other polyadic spatio-temporal predicates, but we need not go further into this matter to make the point we are attempting to make. Still, we do know that dyadic, triadic, and other spatio-temporal predicates seem to be quite effective in establishing individual substantial distinctions in our ordinary experience. Indeed, when I tell the policeman entering the room that the murderer of the woman who lies on the floor in front of me is the man to my left, he has no difficulty identifying him. Why and how do spatio-temporal predicates work in those circumstances, then, and not in the universe about which we were speaking earlier?

188

If I am not mistaken, the answer to this question is that in all cases where they work, an absolute point of reference has been introduced. Spatio-temporal predicates, then, work as relational indicators which tie the entity which needs to be distinguished to the absolute point of reference in specific ways. Thus, the policeman is able to identify the murderer because he functions as an absolute point of reference to which both the man who identified the murderer and the murderer himself are related in determinate ways. Likewise, in the world with two or more spheres, if one of them were to be identified as an absolute point of reference, then the other sphere(s) could be identified and distinguished by establishing its (their) relation(s) to it. An absolute point of reference, then, is a necessary condition for spatio-temporal predicates to function effectively as distinguishers of individual substances.

I believe what has been said is sufficient to establish that spatio-temporal location is relational and that spatio-temporal location predicates cannot function as sufficient conditions of individual discernment unless an absolute point of reference is introduced. In this sense, the difference among dyadic, triadic, and other polyadic spatio-temporal relations is not important. There are, however, some relational features whose existence depends not only on the number of objects but also on the presence of a certain type of object. This is precisely the case with discernibility, and I believe enough has already been said about its epistemic character and what that entails. Still, even if we were to hold that discernibility is not an epistemic notion, I stipulated at the beginning that the problem to be addressed in this chapter would be consigned to the conditions under which human subjects discern individual substances and their features, and that makes further consideration of the above referred issue specious. Of course, one could ask whether discernibility would be possible in a universe that actually had no knowers, but that could in principle have knowers. And this is a perfectly valid question, but it reduces to the question we are presently dealing with. For if knowers can be part of the universe, then presumably they could make the same sort of distinctions among things based on their perceptions of their features and/or spatio-temporal locations. The case we cannot consider is one in which we had a universe in which there could be no knowers.

Still, one might want to argue that even if no knower were possible in a universe, the entities in it would still be discernible in principle when not in fact. After all, aren't we talking about them right now as distinct? But to say that or to act as we are doing now is simply to grant that it is possible for a knower to contemplate the entities in the universe and, therefore, distinguish them on the basis of his perspective. Those who argue in this way do in fact subreptitiously introduce in the universe another entity, the knower, who functions as an absolute point of reference.

But, then, someone might object, isn't this the same thing you did in

Chapter 1 when arguing about the possibility of a universe with only one individual being in it? In that case, you spoke about and raised questions concerning the single entity in the universe. So why would this not be allowed in this context? The answer to this objection is that in Chapter 1 we were discussing an ontological and nonrelational feature of a thing, not an epistemic and relational one. We may talk about a universe with one or two individual beings in it, but we cannot talk about their discernibility within that universe without introducing in it a knower, actual or potential. When we do speak about the discernibility of the entities in a universe, we are as it were, setting ourselves as part of the universe.

From all of this it seems that we can conclude that spatio-temporal location predicates can indeed function as sufficient conditions of individual substance discernment, at least in the world of human experience, where absolute points of reference are available, even if they are not sufficient conditions of it in all possible circumstances. There are, however, two other objections that need to be discussed.

The first is best introduced with an illustration. Let us suppose that we have two cards with the same dimensions, color, texture, and thickness and that the cards are presented to knower K at two different times. Under these circumstances the two cards would be, as stipulated, two, but K would not be able to discern them as two, concluding mistakenly, in the absence of other evidence, that they are one and the same. From this it can be inferred that spatio-temporal location cannot be a sufficient condition of individual discernment.

I have granted that spatio-temporal location does not function as a sufficient condition of individual substance discernibility in all cases, and, therefore, the fact that it might not do so in the specified case raised in the objection does not undermine my view; however, there are problems with the objection. Indeed, the objection rests on a confusion between the problem involved in the discernment of individual substances and the problem of their recognition or reidentification. The spatio-temporal location of each of the cards presented to K is sufficient for K to discern each of them as a distinct card at a particular time and, therefore, as individual, even when the cards may not be discernible as distinct *from each* other at a different time. And that is all that is required of spatio-temporal location. The further question of whether the cards that K perceived at t^1 and t^2 are one and the same or different is an entirely different question for which different criteria may be necessary. Here I must refer back to the Prolegomena and what was said there concerning the distinction between individuality and identity and what must also apply *mutatis mutandis* to their respective discernibilites. There has been much discussion about the issue of reidentification in contemporary philosophy, but it is one that need not be discussed in an essay on individuality, in spite of the close relations individuality and identity have.

Second, one might object that spatio-temporal location cannot be a sufficient condition of individual discernibility because to know such location would require knowing the location of everything else in the universe, and that, although not impossible in principle, seems impossible in fact.[14]

But this objection is based on the unfounded assumption that the location required for individual discernibility is absolute location; that is, that the spatio-temporal location in question involves a relation with everything else in the universe. But, of course, that is not what is required, as experience clearly indicates. The location under discussion is relative to some determinate circumstances, and in fact, as we saw above, the number of such circumstances can be quite limited, involving sometimes very few entities. The distinction to be determined is not a distinction from everything, but only a distinction from this and that within a limited experiential field. In such cases, what functions as absolute point of reference in some circumstances within the field of experience is some circumstance within the field of experience, and not absolute space.[15] Thus, this objection is not effective against the Spatio-Temporal Theory of Individual Substance Discernibility.

Before we leave the discernibility of individual substances I should like to dismiss two theories that have sometimes been suggested for this purpose. They have been used in this connection not so much because of their explicitly recognized advantages in relation to discernibility but rather because of the frequent confusion between the problems of individuation and of discernibility in which their proponents have fallen.

Bundle Theory of Individual Substance Discernibility

This theory is similar to the Bundle Theory of Individuation discussed earlier.[16] The only significant difference is that, instead of claiming that the bundle of features individuates, it claims that the bundle constitutes the basis of individual discernibility among individual substances. The advantages of the theory are clear, for it seems quite reasonable to suppose that I know Socrates is an individual distinct from Plato because the former was short, had a snub-nose and a beard, was the main speaker at a certain dinner party, and so on with the rest of his features, while the latter was taller, had an aquiline nose, was the author of the *Symposium*, and so forth. The features of things seem to be what make us aware of their distinction from other things and, therefore, of their individuality.

But there are problems with the theory. Perhaps the most important of these are that (1) we never know the complete bundle of features a thing has, and (2) for a bundle to be different, it must be composed of at least some

191

differentiating features, and most features of things do not appear to function as distinguishers, at least in principle.

The first point seems quite obvious. If it is all the features of a thing taken together that constitute the basis for discerning it as an individual, then it is doubtful that we can ever discern anything in fact, since we never know all the features a thing has. Indeed, we do not even know all the features each of us has, so how can we know all the features belonging to other things? I know, for example, that my cat Minina is female, small, calico in color, has fairly long fur, and likes to sleep on a velvet upholstered chair in our music room. And all these things distinguish her from my neighbor's Tom cat. But there are many features of my cat I don't know, for example, the color of her liver or the amount of undigested food still in her stomach at the time of writing this, or whether she killed a mouse this afternoon. To say that we discern individuals from some of their features makes sense, at least *prima facie*, but to argue that it is on the basis of all of a thing's features taken together that we distinguish it from other things makes no sense at all. Indeed, it is not just that we do not know in fact all the features things have, but that we do in fact distinguish things even though we do not know all of their features. Therefore, although knowledge of all the features of a thing could perhaps be considered a sufficient condition of its discernibility in the abstract, it is certainly neither a necessary condition nor a sufficient condition of it in our actual experience.

The second difficulty encountered by the Bundle Theory of Individual Substance Discernibility seems also quite strong, for it appears obvious that differences among bundles of features must be traced to differences among their components. This means in fact that it is the specific features and not all the features of a thing taken together (i.e., the bundle) that function as principles of individual substance discernibility. And the difficulty with this is that not all, indeed not even most, features of things do or can serve as distinguishers. Take, for example, the case of two identical bronze statues of Venus. How do I know there are two and not just one? Certainly not by the color, weight, or shape, etc. I might know there are two only if I see them at the same time in different places, but not by any of their most obvious features. Indeed, contrary to what this view proposes, most of the features of the statues, or of anything else, serve as points of similarity rather than as points of distinction. One might want to argue that if I am shown at two different times two cards with the same dimensions, thickness, and texture but different colors, it is the color that serves as the basis of distinction between the two. And, true, under those conditions, the color would certainly be a sufficient condition of the distinction. But if instead of having different colors the two cards had the same color, the color would not serve to distinguish them. The role circumstances play, then, is fundamental if features are to be considered as bases for the discernibility of the individuality of substances. These considerations have led to the formulation of other views. One is the Spatio-Temporal Theory discussed earlier; another is the *Sui Generis* Theory, which will be examined next.

Sui Generis *Theory of Individual Substance Discernibility*

The *Sui Generis* Theory proposes that individual substances have a unique feature, call it what you will, which is subject to direct intuition and which constitutes the basis of their discernibility as individuals.[17] Paul and Peter each have something unique that, when intuited, makes us discern them as individuals. But what, we may ask, is this unique feature? Proponents of this view answer that, given the radically individual character of this feature, it is impossible to explain further what it is, for all explanations are made in terms of universal and shareable features, while this feature, as radically individual, cannot be analyzed into universal terms, and therefore, may only be intuited. That there is such a feature is clear, so they argue, because we do in fact discern individuals. We know, therefore, that there is something which makes us distinguish things, even though we cannot give an analysis of it.

This account of individual discernibility, however, does not seem convincing. Its strength is deceptive, for what the theory accomplishes is only to give a name to something unknown. It mystifies individuality, and as a result it appears, like the view that made good a quality of things known only through intuition, quite doubtful.[18] The only accomplishment of the theory is to acknowledge that we in fact distinguish individual substances, but it fails to specify the basis on which such distinction takes place.[19]

Discernibility of Features

Having proposed in Chapter 2 that not only substances but also their features are individual, we must give an account of how individual features are discerned as such. There are two types of theories concerning the discernibility of the individuality of features that correspond to some extent to the theories of the individuation of features discussed in Chapter 4. One argues that individual features are discerned through the substance they characterize; the other argues that it is through other features that the discernibility of features takes place.

Discernibility of Features Through Substance

According to this theory, we become aware of the individuality of the features of substances through the individual substance in which they inhere.[20] We discern Socrates' black hair color as individual because it belongs to Socrates. Awareness of the individual substance in which the feature is

193

found and of its relation as a feature to that substance constitute the bases of the discernibility of its color as individual. Indeed, some argue that it is the substance that is first and most immediately known to be individual and features only subsequently and vicariously.

There are two ways of interpreting this view. According to one, awareness of the substance in which features are found and of the relation of those features to the substance are to be regarded as both necessary and sufficient conditions of the discernibility of the individuality of those features; according to another, they are to be regarded only as sufficient conditions of it. The first interpretation involves serious difficulties, but the second is quite plausible. Let us begin with an examination of some of the difficulties of the first interpretation.

First, it is not clear that features are posterior to substance in knowledge, although logically or even metaphysically, at least insofar as accidental features are concerned, they must be so if a substance-accident ontology is to be maintained without contradiction. It is altogether possible to hold that the first things we know about a substance are the accidental features that it has and that it is only later that we proceed to know the substance itself. For example, one could argue that it is "this red" that I first perceive when I see a red object, particularly if the object has large proportions, has been placed at a close range, and is flat. Place a person with eyes closed three feet away from a red wall and what the person sees at first when she opens her eyes is the individual color; only later does she identify the color as belonging to a wall. Experience, then, so this objection goes, militates against the view that features are posterior to substance in knowledge.

One possible attempt to answer this objection may argue that when a person opens her eyes in front of a very large flat object painted red, for example, she does not see "this red" but just "red" and that it is only later, after having realized that the color belongs to a wall that it becomes known as "this red." Therefore, it would seem after all that the Theory of Discernibility Through Substance is justified.

Nevertheless, one could counterobject by saying that it is not by all means clear that what one sees first is just "red," for red always appears as a noninstantiable instance or at least as distinct from other "reds." Thus, one could maintain that in the experiment we do become aware of "this red" independently of the awareness we may have of the individual substance. In this case, what individualizes the color red for us is not the substance— unknown to us as yet— but the spatio-temporal coordinates. If the person undergoing the experiment says to me "I see red" and I ask "What red?," the person could respond "This red, the one in front of me here and now," for example, without having to refer to the wall, still unknown by her, painted red.

Therefore, if one were to accept that one does not perceive "red" but rather "this red," then it becomes difficult to maintain that in order for one to be conscious of "this red" one must first consider its relation to a particular colored substance, since the person in the experiment would be hard put to identify the substance in question. Indeed, how can "belonging to this wall" individualize the color red in our consciousness when, according to the experiment: (1) we do not know at first that the color "belongs to a wall," and (2) we do not know that it belongs to *this individual* wall. Indeed, even if we were to know that it belonged to something, that would not be enough to individualize the feature in our knowledge, nor would it be enough for it to belong to a "type" of thing, whatever that may be. For "belonging to X," where X is substituted by a type word, does not entail by any means the individuality of what belongs. We can say, for example, that rationality belongs to humanity and that does not entail the individuality of rationality. Therefore, neither belonging to something unspecified, nor belonging to something of a certain type can be considered sufficient, let alone necessary conditions for the discernment of an individual feature considered as such.

These considerations indicate that belonging to an individual substance is not both a necessary and sufficient condition of the identification of individual features like colors, but it does not show that it may not be a sufficient condition. Indeed, if the view is interpreted as holding that awareness of (1) the substance in which features are found and of (2) their relation as features to that substance, taken together constitute a sufficient condition of the discernibility of the individuality of the features, then it makes sense. For it would seem that, although "belonging to a wall," for example, is not a sufficient condition of individual feature discernibility, "belonging to this wall" can and does function as sufficient grounds for the discernment of individual features. A reference to Socrates is sufficient to distinguish a certain individual color of hair, as in the expression "Socrates' color of hair," and likewise with other features. For such references introduce a distinction between an instance of a feature and other instances of the feature, and that difference, as we saw, is a sufficient condition of the discernment of noninstantiables.

To accept this view, in the stated form, however, does not prevent us from holding that there may also be other sufficient conditions of the discernment of the individuality of features of substances.

Discernibility of Features Through Features

Others argue that the individuality of features of substances is discerned (1) because they are part of a particular group of features; or, alternatively, (2) because of their association with some specific features, such as spatio-temporal location; or, again, (3) because of a unique feature intuited by the

195

knower. These views have advantages and disadvantages similar to those pointed out when similar theories concerning the discernibility of substance were discussed. For this reason, there is no need to give them additional detailed consideration. It should suffice to say, then, that (1) and (3) are unacceptable for the same reasons that those views were unacceptable in the cases of substances, and (2) is acceptable only if this is taken as a sufficient but not a necessary condition of discernment, and under special circumstances, again for reasons already specified.

These reasons also apply to the discernment of the individuality of entities other than substances and their features, and, therefore, there is no need for further discussion of the issue. Before we turn to the next chapter, however, it is appropriate that we give separate consideration to an issue that has received considerable attention in contemporary philosophy, the so called Principle of Identity of Indiscernibles.

Principle of Identity of Indiscernibles

The Principle of the Identity of Indiscernibles has occupied so much the attention of contemporary philosophers that something must be said about it, even though it is only marginally related to the subject of this chapter.[21] The first thing that needs to be said about it is that the expression 'Principle of Identity of Indiscernibles' is a relatively new one in the history of philosophy. Leibniz, who is generally credited with the first clear formulation of the principle, referred to it mostly as an "axiom" and not a "principle."[22] Hence, it should be clear that this terminology is of modern origin. The medievals, for example, did not make explicit references to it, although some of their statements suggest that some of them would have accepted the principle in some form.[23]

First, we must begin by making clear what the principle is, although that is not easy, since there are almost as many formulations of it as philosophers who discuss it. For our purposes, I shall introduce two formulations of the principle that I consider fundamental. One is metaphysical and the other epistemic. There is also a logical formulation, but I shall not deal with it here. I should add, however, that what I take to be metaphysical and epistemic formulations are often regarded as equivalent by many authors and as logical by others, but I disagree with those interpretations. The metaphysical formulation is as follows:

If X has the same features as Y, then X is identical with Y.

Formulated in this way, the principle does not involve indiscernibility, but just identity.[24] Therefore, the standard term applied to it (i.e., "Principle of Identity of Indiscernibles") is a misnomer if the principle is interpreted in this manner, that is, metaphysically. Hence, from now on I shall call this formulation "Principle of Identity" instead.[25]

Naturally, whether the Principle of Identity is true or not will depend to some extent on the metaphysical constitution of things. If things are reducible to their features, as bundle theorists hold, then it would seem that this principle is necessarily true. If Socrates is constituted by his features (short, fat, sub-nosed, etc.) and nothing else, then having those features is being Socrates. On the other hand, if things are not reducible to their features but are constituted in addition by substrata, principles, and/or such entities as bare particulars, then it is clear that the Principle of Identity is necessarily false. If Socrates is necessarily something more than the bundle of features he has, then not everything having those features is Socrates as long as whatever else Socrates has besides those features is not also present.

Of course, the matter is not as simple as that. Philosophers are quite divided on the issue of whether it is logically possible that there be more than one thing having the same features, as we have already discussed earlier. Russell, for example, regarded it as obvious that it is logically possible to do so,[26] although in later years he regarded this objection against the Bundle Theory as not conclusive.[27] But other authors have differed on this, and have given as one of their main reasons that in order to make a distinction between two things, some feature, even if only identity, is required.[28] Still, when "distinction" is brought in, the character of the discussion changes, becoming epistemic, as we have seen earlier. So, we may ask, Is the Principle of Identity still to be regarded as true in the face of this objection?

I must say that I am quite impressed, on the one hand, by the view that holds to the logical possibility of two or more things having the same features. But, on the other, I am also impressed with the view that to have the same features is, unless one adds some mysterious element to the composition of things, to be the same thing. How can one reconcile these two positions, then? I believe that indeed a solution can be found if some of their assumptions are rejected in favor of some of the views I have defended earlier. Although not much has been said in this book about the metaphysical constitution of things *per se*, what has been said implies the Principle of Identity in one sense. The view I have defended implies that things are composed of nothing more than their features, and, therefore, to have those features is to be the thing in question. But the features to which I refer in my view are individual or, as put earlier, noninstantiable instances, whence the impossibility that more than one thing could have the same individual features. The impossibility would not come, however, from the fact that two things could not have the same number (six or seven) and/or type (color, shape) of features, but because they could not have the same instances of them.[29] In this sense, my position differs drastically from the traditional Bundle View. The principle I accept would have to be formulated thus:

If X has the same individual features as Y,
X is the same individual as Y.

According to this principle, which I shall call the Modified Principle of Identity in order to distinguish it from the previous principle, it would be possible for two things to have the same type and number of features, but it would not be possible for them to have the same instances of those features. That is to say, the features of the two things would be individually distinct even though they could be of the same type. Thus, it is entirely possible to have a universe with two and only two identical spheres in it, since the features of each of the two spheres would be distinct instances of the same feature. Each sphere would differ only in that it would have different instances of the same features.

Given the metaphysical character of both the Principle of Identity and its modified version, and the primarily epistemic context of this chapter, we need make no further reference to this matter at this point. However, as already mentioned, in addition to the metaphysical formulation of the Principle of Identity of Indiscernibles there is an epistemic formulation, which goes something like this:

If X is indiscernible (or indistinguishable) from Y
then X is identical with Y.[30]

There are at least three interpretations of this formulation. The first is quite weak. It understands the principle as stating that if some knower cannot discern X apart from Y, then X is identical with Y.

Naturally this view can be easily rejected. Indeed, it seems a matter of common sense that inability to discern on the part of someone is not a sufficient condition of identity. That some types of animals are color blind and cannot distinguish between red and green, for example, does not entail that red and green are not two different colors. And that I cannot distinguish between two, two-by-four-inch white cards shown to me separately at different times is not a sufficient condition for inferring that they are one and the same.

A stronger interpretation understands the principle as stating that if no knower, actual or possible, can discern X apart from Y, then X is identical with Y. This is the interpretation that has drawn the most attention. It is clearly much stronger than the first interpretation, but still the truth of the principle, even

198

under these circumstances, is debatable. Consider, for example, a world composed of an infinite number of atoms, all having the same features and equidistant from each other. It is clear that the atoms would not be identical individuals, that is to say, that they would not be one and the same individual, and yet they would seem to be indiscernible for two reasons. The first is simply the fact that in such a universe there would be no knowers who could discern the atoms. But, more important than this, even if we granted the possibility of describing the atoms in some way from the outside as it were, still no description of any atom could be sufficient for distinguishing it from any other atom. The reason is that, having the same features in a universe with an infinite number of atoms, the description of every atom would apply to each of the other atoms in the universe. As such, then, one could hardly argue that any of these atoms could be individually discerned from the others.

Indeed, under the circumstances specified, it would be impossible even to begin to give a description of any individual atom, for in order to do that we would have to be able to distinguish it in some way, and that does not seem possible. We could, of course, give them names, but we would have no way of tying the name to one and only one atom. Nor could we say, for example, that a particular atom is "to the left of" another, for, as we saw earlier, predicates of location require a point of reference, which we do not have in the specified universe. Nor could we speak of this atom as being "at the fringes of the universe," or "closer to its center," or "on this side," or "on that side," for the universe, being infinite, would have no center or sides. Of course, if we introduced a point of reference in the universe, then we could establish relations of one kind or another and, therefore, discernibility. But that would mean changing the example and, therefore, giving in to the point that it is meant to illustrate. Note that I say "illustrate," rather than "prove," for examples such as the one given are used only as illustrations of the principles behind them, not as proofs of them.

The fundamental point in all of this, that is, the flaw of the principle as formulated and interpreted, is that discernibility is an epistemic notion, while identity is not. Hence, indiscernibility cannot be used as a sufficient condition for identity. To be strictly correct, the principle would have to be reformulated metaphysically, as was done earlier, or completely epistemically. One possible epistemic formulation would be as follows:

If object X is indiscernible (or indistinguishable) from object Y, then X is the same object as Y.

Of course, "object" here must be interpreted as an epistemic entity, not a thing. But understood in this way the principle is trivial, since both the antecedent and consequent assert the same thing, an epistemic identity, for to be epistemically indiscernible is to be the same thought object. Hence, the principle is true, but trivially so.

In short, then, it seems that the Principle of Identity of Indiscernibles can be interpreted in three ways: metaphysically, and then its truth depends on the constitution of things; epistemically, and then it is analytically true; and mixed, and then it is false. Since our inquiry in this chapter is epistemic, and the formulations that have epistemic dimensions are trivial or false, we can dispense with further discussion of this principle.

Still, there is an even more important reason why the discussion of the Principle of Identity of Indiscernibles is immaterial to the subject matter of this book. The principle is concerned with distinction, and specifically with the epistemic notion of discernibility.[31] But, as it has been shown in Chapter 1, individuality has to do with noninstantiability rather than with distinction; it is only related to distinction in a world of multiplicity and variety and to discernibility in a world where knowers are present. Thus, strictly speaking, the discussion of issues raised by the Principle of Identity of Indiscernibles is only marginally related to the fundamental questions of individuality, even though it acquires importance in a world such as ours, which counts with multiplicity, variety, and knowers.

Now let us turn to another issue related to the discernibility of individuals: the question of reference.

6

Reference to Individuals: Proper Names, Definite Descriptions, and Indexicals

Having discussed various logical, ontological, and epistemic issues related to individuality, it remains for us to deal with a problem which has been of major concern in recent years and which has to do with semantics. The issue involves the way in which we refer to individuals, and the purpose of the chapter will be to provide an account consistent with the views presented in the rest of this book. The chapter is divided into three parts, covering the three major linguistic types of signs used to refer to individuals: proper names, definite descriptions, and indexicals. The view that I intend to defend attributes the disputes among philosophers concerning these issues to a failure to distinguish among different questions and aims to integrate the diverse views into a consistent and more appropriate answer to the problems of reference.

Before we begin the specific discussion of proper names, definite descriptions, and indexicals, however, something must be said about reference in general and about how it can be related to the views concerning individuality proposed in the rest of this book. Reference is a complicated concept that has received considerable attention in contemporary philosophy and, therefore, the brief propaedeutic comments made here should not be taken as a theory of reference properly speaking. My comments go only as far as I believe necessary to indicate how the views concerning individuality that I have defended affect the theoretical understanding of reference.

Perhaps the best way to begin is by noting that from experience we know that we refer to individuals in various ways. Often we refer to individuals by means of proper names. I use the term 'Socrates', for example, to refer to Socrates when I say "Socrates lived more than two millenia ago," and when I say "Minina is hungry," I use 'Minina' to refer to my cat. However, in order to refer to individuals we also use demonstratives, pronouns, and other expressions that ever since Peirce have been called "indexicals" to underline the fact that they indicate or pick out things.[1] I can refer to the paper on which I am now writing as "this" and say "This is a white piece of paper." Or I can refer to myself as I just did, with the pronoun 'I'. Again, in many instances, instead of indexicals and proper names we use what have come to be called in the contemporary literature on this issue "definite descriptions." Instead of using 'Socrates', for example, in order to refer to Socrates, I can always refer to him by saying "the Greek philosopher who drank the hemlock" or "the teacher of Plato." All three of these ways of individual reference are linguistic, but not all references to individuals are made through language. Someone who is unable to speak can always use nonlinguistic signs to refer to someone else or to some individual object. It is, however, with linguistic terms that we shall be concerned in this chapter, not because other ways of referring may not be effective and/or important, but because often they function very much like language, and, therefore, the distinctions between linguistic modes of individual reference and nonlinguistic ones, insofar as reference is concerned, are not essential. This can be easily illustrated in an example. Let us suppose that there are two men standing in a room and that on the floor lies a dead woman with a stab wound. When a policeman enters the room and asks "Who stabbed this woman?," one of the men, who is dumbstricken and cannot talk, draws a picture of the murderer and writes next to it 'is the murderer'. That picture is being used by the dumbstricken man to refer to the murderer and is quite sufficient, if it is a good likeness, to answer the question posed by the policeman. But the same act of referring could have been achieved if, instead of drawing a picture of the other man, the dumbstricken fellow would have said "he," or "Peter," or "the man with the guilty look." In all cases, the dumbstricken man referred to the murderer, although the means he used were different. The linguistic or nonlinguistic character of the means of reference do not seem to matter much. It is clear, then, that the type of signs used in referring are not very important and we shall, therefore, dispense with signs other than linguistic ones. What is important to keep in mind is that, in accordance with the examples given, referring is an act in which a symbol is used to represent an individual.[2] Thus, strictly speaking, only beings capable of using symbols can refer, although often one also speaks about the symbols used in reference as themselves referring.

Having adopted the stated view of reference, we must now take note of the pertinent parts of the view of individuality presented in previous chapters. There are three aspects of that view in particular that relate to reference. First and most important is the analysis of individuality in terms of the primitive notion of noninstantiability and the resulting conception of an individual as a noninstantiable instance. Second is the theory of individuation that rejects features of any sort as individuators and singles out existence as the principle of individuation in individuals. And, finally, also relevant is the view that we discern individuals through features and most often through their spatio-temporal coordinates. So, on the one hand, the first two points make clear that reference to individuals must be reference to noninstantiables and that what is referred to when one refers to an individual, therefore, is not a type, a feature, or a bundle of features. This means that the primary function of the symbols used in referring is to represent a thing in its fundamental character as noninstantiable. It also implies that reference to individuals, strictly speaking, is nondescriptive. On the other hand, the fact that we discern individuals through their features and the spatio-temporal coordinates they occupy clearly indicates that descriptions must have an epistemic role to play in reference.

With these considerations in mind, we can turn to the most common linguistic means used for reference: proper names, indexicals, and definite descriptions. Moreover, since there are some important differences in the way these function, it will be useful to discuss them separately. We shall begin with proper names.

Proper Names

The contemporary controversy concerning proper names has centered around the question of whether they have meaning (or sense) in addition to having reference. There is really no disagreement as to the fact that proper names are used to refer to individuals and, therefore, have reference. The dispute arises with respect to whether they have meaning (or sense) in addition and whether this meaning (or sense), if they have it, is what makes possible and/or actually determines the reference. Common terms, like 'human being', and definite descriptions, like 'the Greek philosopher who drank the hemlock,' appear to have meaning; that is, we can identify certain conditions that the expressions stipulate. 'The Greek philosopher who drank the hemlock' clearly stipulates what it says, and 'human being' seems to stipulate certain conditions, such as the capacity to reason, various physical characteristics, and so on. In contemporary philosophy, some questions have been raised concerning common names and whether it is possible to identify the necessary and sufficient conditions of their use.[3] But in general the view that they have meaning is still widely accepted. At any rate, our present concerns are not with that issue, and, therefore, we shall not discuss it here. The questions that we shall discuss are, first, whether proper names have meaning, as most philosophers believe common terms and definite descriptions have, or whether they do not. And, second, how the meaning they have, if they have it, is related to their referential function. There are three basic views with respect to this issue that are taken seriously today. One view argues that proper names have only reference, and therefore, need no meaning (or sense) in order that they may be used to refer. Another argues that they have both reference and meaning (or sense) and that their reference is determined by their meaning (or sense). And a third tries to find a compromise between these two.

Reference View of Proper Names

The Reference View holds that proper names have reference but no meaning (or sense), or, to put in a slightly different way, as some of those who adhere to this position have done, that their meaning consists solely in their reference. Proponents of this view back it up with the authority of Plato, some works of Russell, statements of Wittgenstein in the *Tractatus,* and Mill, although there are substantial differences among the views of all these individuals. As Mill put it, proper names denote but they do not connote.[4] A proper name like 'Socrates' simply stands for and, therefore, may be used to refer to Socrates, in contrast with 'snub-nose', which not only stands for Socrates' nose but also connotes certain features and conditions of it. Consequently, proper names cannot be replaced by descriptions, indeed not even by definite descriptions.[5]

I should add at this point that for the sake of simplicity and economy I am assuming that a term has reference only if there exists at least one being for which it stands. This view has been challenged,[6] but whatever the outcome of that dispute, it should not affect the formulation of the issue with which we are concerned here or its solution. Having adopted the stated condition for present purposes, we can say that the Reference View of proper names holds that a proper name is meaningless unless there exists at least one thing of which it is the name. Indeed, as Russell quite clearly pointed out, if a term does not have at least one referent, it is not a proper name at all.[7] This contrasts with the case of common names, which have no such limitation. Common names and expressions, so maintains this view, are meaningful even when they have no referents, that is, existing instances of them. "Green men fifty feet tall" is a meaningful expression, and yet we know that it lacks reference.

Another difference between common names and proper names is that the first can fit one or more individuals, while the second can fit only one. Russell illustates this difference between common and proper names with the examples 'satellite of Earth' and 'Moon'.[8] The fact that both of these expressions are used to refer only to one, and the same individual does not obliterate their differences. For one can say of the first, for example, that it designates a class, while it would make no sense to say it of the second. Indeed, the fact that 'satellite of Earth' refers to one, and only one, individual is a contingent matter. It is altogether possible to conceive of other such things. It is possible that at some point in history the Earth had more than one satellite and that these satellites have subsequently collapsed into one, crashed into the Earth, or drifted into space. Or perhaps there are still some that, owing to their peculiar composition, have escaped our telescopes and other astronomical detection devices. But it does not seem possible that there be, whether in the past, present, or future, more than one Moon. Unfortunately, Russell's example does not illustrate well the distinction between common names and proper names that he intends, for we do speak of "moons," as for example when we say that Jupiter has many moons. So the word 'moon' turns out to be used as a species word or common name sometimes. At any rate, the disadvantages of Russell's example should not obscure the tenets of the theory that seem fairly clear: (a) proper names must have referents in order to be meaningful since they have no meaning other than their reference, while common names and expressions have meaning independently of whether they have referents or not; and (b) common names can have many referents, while proper names cannot.

The arguments brought forth in support of this theory are generally based on a consideration of (a) the intention of the users of proper names and/or (b) the relation between proper names and the descriptions of the objects to which they refer. Those who argue on the basis of the users' intention point out that proper names are used and serve to call, name, and indicate and not to describe. "Who spilled the milk?" intends to ask for an individual, not the individual's features. If I answer "a cat," or "a calico cat," or even if I give a more extensive description, the questioner can still be in doubt as to who spilled the milk. But if I answer, "Minina," and the questioner knows the cat for whom this is a proper name, the questioner is satisfied—he knows who spilled the milk. Indeed, even in the event that the questioner should not know the bearer of the name 'Minina' he knows we have given him a name of the individual whom we think or know spilled the milk. (We are taking for granted that the speaker is not lying to us.) The question, then, asked for an indication of the individual who committed the act, and the use of the proper name in answering it is meant to do just that. The function of proper names is to refer, that is, to be used as symbols to stand for individuals and not to give information about those individuals; it is for this reason that they do not have meaning strictly speaking. In contrast, the use of descriptive terminology is intended to do something else, namely, to describe or identify the *type* of individual in question. This is reflected in the structure of the questions themselves, which instead of being of the form 'Who did X?' ("Who spilled

205

the milk?") are usually such as, or can be translated as, 'What kind of Y did X?' ("What kind of individual spilled the milk?"). The question 'What kind of individual spilled the milk?' can be answered satisfactorily with a description such as "a playful cat" or "a reckless animal." Of course, one could still answer by saying "Minina," but in this case the proper name would be used elliptically for something like "a cat of the sort Minina is," "a cat with features such as Minina has," and the like.

The second type of argument used to support this view is based on the character of the relations holding between proper names and the descriptions of their bearers. For there seem to be only two possibilities with respect to the character of these relations: They are either necessary or contingent. But neither of these possibilities seems acceptable. If the description of the bearer of a proper name is only contingently related to the proper name, then it would be difficult to hold that the name has meaning (or sense), since no single description could be essentially tied to it. We could not very well say, for example, that the meaning of the name 'Socrates' is "the philosopher who drank the hemlock," for drinking the hemlock would not be anything necessarily associated with Socrates, and calling Socrates "Socrates" would not necessarily entail that Socrates drank the hemlock. On the other hand, if the description is necessarily related to the name, then it becomes difficult to hold that the bearer of the name may turn out not to have the features specified by the description, either because the individual in question has changed or because we were mistaken about the features he had. Yet the fact is that proper names are used and continue to be used effectively to refer to the same individuals in spite of changes in the bearer of the name or the mistakes we may make in what we believe are their features. Socrates was called "Socrates" from the time of his birth until the time of his death, in spite of the drastic changes which took place both in his body and mind throughout his life, and if, contrary to what everyone believes, he were to turn out not to have drunk the hemlock, we would still continue to use the name 'Socrates' to refer to him. From all this, it would seem that the relation between a proper name and the description of its bearer can be neither necessary nor contingent and, since these are the only possibilities available, the arguments suggest that there is indeed no relation between a proper name and the description of its bearer.

There are many variants to these arguments, but there is no need to recount all of them. Their conclusion is the same, namely, that proper names do not seem to have meaning (or sense) and, therefore, that meaning (or sense) is neither a necessary nor a sufficient condition of reference. Moreover, the assumptions of these arguments seem to be based on common sense; indeed, until Frege, most philosophers either paid little attention to this matter or seemed to take for granted the truth of the Reference View.[9]

206

Naturally, these arguments have not gone without challenge. For example, some have pointed out that temporal indicators could render the argument based on considerations of change useless. If every predicate is tied to temporal coordinates, changes would not alter the overall description of an individual and thus militate against a necessary connection between proper names and the descriptions of their bearers. Thus, we could say that wetting diapers was a characteristic of Socrates until age three and that beyond age three Socrates did not wet his diapers. The change, then, from wetting to not wetting diapers would not necessitate a change of name. But, of course, this response is not conclusive for various reasons. Let me mention the most obvious one: The answer does not account for the fact that the descriptions associated with the name are still contingently tied to the individual. So the matter cannot rest there. Indeed, although this issue cannot be settled easily, the stated arguments in support of the Reference View cannot be easily dismissed. Still, other considerations put into question the value of the Reference View.

What Frege and some subsequent philosophers noticed was that, subjected to analysis, the Reference View runs into serious difficulties. These difficulties involve primarily three types of propositions: (1) identity propositions, (2) propositions with vacuous proper names as subjects, and (3) existential propositions in which proper names occur. Let us consider identity propositions first. If the Reference View of proper names is correct, so the argument goes, true identity propositions where the subject and predicate are proper names cannot be informative. Take, for example, the proposition 'Cicero is Tully'. According to the traditional view, if this proposition is true and is taken to say something about the bearer of the name, then it conveys no information, for the function of 'Cicero' and 'Tully' is only to refer and they in fact refer to the same individual. The proposition, then, tells nothing new and can in fact be translated into a proposition of the form 'a = a'. But this seems to contradict our intuition, since propositions of the sort discussed do seem to tell us something. When I discuss in class Boethius' well known treatise *De Trinitate*, where he deals with identity and difference, I have to inform my students that Cicero is Tully, a fact that contributes to their understanding of Boethius' text, since he uses these names as examples to expound his views on numerical difference and sameness. Of course, to this one can always respond that what I am telling them is that the terms 'Cicero' and 'Tully' name the same individual, so that the information conveyed is about a linguistic and arbitrary fact, not information about the world. In order for the identity proposition to convey nonlinguistic information, it would seem that there must be more to a proper name than reference. And this is exactly what Frege concluded.

The problem with propositions that have vacuous proper names (i.e., proper names with no referent) as subjects seems likewise serious. What are we to make, for example, of propositions like: 'Don Quijote was mad'. According to the Reference View, this sentence would have to be interpreted as saying nothing. The reason is that, although its predicate is meaningful, it is asserted of a subject which is a proper name without reference and therefore meaningless. Thus, it would seem that because the subject term is meaning-less, the proposition as a whole must also be meaningless. Yet the proposition does say something, and something which is understood and about which disputes are conducted in learned discussions by literary critics. Indeed, in the case of the proposition 'Don Quijote had a horse called Rocinante' what the proposition asserts is not even disputed; it is both true and known to be true. The inference, then, is that the view according to which proper names have reference and no meaning must not be right, since it fails to account for the meaningfulness and truth value of propositions with vacuous proper names.

A similar problem arises with respect to existential propositions which have proper names as their subjects. In order to see these better and how they affect the Reference Theory, let us take two sets of propositions that affirm and deny existence and whose subjects are proper names, one of which has reference and the other does not.

(A) 1. Don Quijote exists.
2. García Márquez exists.

(B) 1. Don Quijote does not exist.
2. García Márquez does not exist.

The propositions in the first set affirm existence of the subject, while those in the second set negate it. 'Don Quijote' lacks reference and 'García Márquez' does not. Now, under these conditions, and assuming that the Reference View of proper names is correct, (A)1 is contradictory while (B)1 is necessarily true, and (A)2 is necessarily true while (B)2 is contradictory. But this is preposterous, for we know, for example, both that García Márquez exists and that his existence is a contingent fact that could have been other-wise. And we know that Don Quijote does not exist but that he could have existed and, therefore, his nonexistence is also a contingent fact.

The difficulties encountered by the Reference View led several philos-ophers like Frege, Russell, and more recently Searle to defend what has come to be called "a descriptivist" theory of proper names.[10] This theory tries to solve the mentioned difficulties by saying that proper names have meaning (or sense) in addition to reference and that their reference is determined by their meaning (or sense).[11]

Descriptivist View of Proper Names

The Descriptivist View, as already stated, holds that proper names have meaning (or sense) *in addition to* reference and that in a way they are no different from descriptions. Indeed, some of the supporters of this view conclude that there is no need, that is, theoretically speaking, for proper names since they can be converted into descriptions.[12] They hold, moreover, that the reference of the names is determined by their meaning as expressed in a description. Thus, it is because Cervantes wrote *Don Quijote* that we can identify the referent of the term 'Cervantes'.[13] The meaning of the name is the connecting link between the name and the named thing.

The support for this view comes not only from the fact that it can solve some of the problems raised against the Reference View but also from common sense. That it helps to solve some of the mentioned problems associated with the Reference View requires little elaboration. Take the problem of identity propositions whose subjects and predicates are proper names. If the proper names in question have meaning in addition to reference, then the propositions become informative. If 'Cicero' means "the Roman senator who wrote *De amicitia*" and 'Tully' means "the greatest rhetorician of the Roman empire," the proposition 'Cicero is Tully' is both informative and an identity proposition. It can be translated into: "The Roman senator who wrote *De amicitia* is the greatest rhetorician of the Roman empire," and there is little doubt that this proposition is informative.

In the case of propositions with vacuous proper names as subjects, such as 'Don Quijote was mad', again we seem to be able to solve the puzzle by giving a meaning to 'Don Quijote'. For example, we might substitute it with 'the most famous literary character created by Cervantes', hence giving meaning to the whole sentence: "The most famous literary character created by Cervantes was mad." And the same can be done with the existential propositions discussed earlier. In the case of 'Don Quijote exists', if 'Don Quijote' is understood to mean "the protagonist of a novel by Cervantes," then the existential proposition is false, but not necessarily so. Nor is it analytically true that Don Quijote does not exist.[14] And the same applies *mutatis mutandis* to the propositions about García Márquez.

But, as mentioned already, the support for this theory is not only dialectical. Common sense also seems to support the view that proper names have meaning; that is, proper names seem to be intrinsically related to descriptions. When proper names are given, for example, they are given to some determinate person, animal, or thing. In baptism, it is a particular baby, a concrete human being with all sorts of features, that is given the name, and not just a point of reference. 'Minina' is the name of my cat, a rather gentle

209

and happy animal, and not of my neighbor's scraggy and ill-tempered dog. It would seem, therefore, that a certain description is tied to the name. Moreover, when the name is used in connection with an object that does not fit the description, then we are told we have made a mistake. It is the baby with blond hair and blue eyes that is named Scott and the one with black hair and brown eyes that is named Alonzo, and not vice versa. And if I had been referring to Scott as Alonzo and to Alonzo as Scott, I could be corrected by one of their parents: "This (referring to the brown-eyed baby) is Alonzo; Scott is that one over there, with the blue eyes." And my response would be: "Oh, I'm sorry, somehow I got the names mixed up."

The relation of proper names to descriptions, once the name has been given, does not seem to be arbitrary and often constitutes sufficient basis for correction. Statements such as "You mean Plato, not the author of the *Categories*" indicate the point. Or when someone says, "Peter did it," and someone else asks, "Do you mean the man who came yesterday?," we can observe another illustration of the same point. There is some *prima facie* support in experience, then, for the view that proper names not only refer, but have meaning as well.

Finally, since bearers of proper names have features through which we identify them, it seems commonsensical to use them in order to connect the name to the bearer of the name. For if proper names have meanings, the meaning ties the name to the thing and helps us establish the connection between the two.

But the Descriptivist View faces problems. These consist precisely in the reasons brought forth in support of the view that proper names have no meaning in addition to reference. The purpose of the use of proper names seems to be different from that of descriptions. And whether descriptions that could serve as meanings of proper names are considered necessarily or contingently tied to the proper name, in either case difficulties follow. Since these difficulties have been already discussed, we need not dwell on them in detail. It should be mentioned, however, that the more recent proponents of Descriptivism try to avoid some of these problems by proposing a cluster variety of the theory. According to it, it is not a particular, definite description that is tied to a proper name, but a cluster of descriptions.[15] Thus, the description associated with Cervantes is not "the author of *Don Quijote*," but rather an indefinitely long disjunctive chain of descriptions such as "the author of *Don Quijote*, or the soldier who lost an arm at Lepanto, or the author of *Novelas ejemplares* . . . ," where the disjunction is not interpreted exclusively. Proper names, then, are logically connected with the features of the objects to which they refer, but only, as Searle puts it, "in a loose sort of way."[16] The advantage of this version of Descriptivism is that it allows for the erroneous attribution of any particular definite description to the bearer of a proper name associated with the description, while at the same time permitting identification on the basis of something else.

Clearly, this view of the meaning of proper names proves stronger than the original view. Still, it does not solve completely the difficulties mentioned earlier. It does not really deal with the intentional thrust of proper names as primarily directed to reference, for example. And even if descriptions are loosely tied to proper names in the way it prescribes, we still have to deal with the problems of contingency and necessity raised before in the following way: The disjunction can be tied to a proper name either contingently or necessarily. If it is tied contingently then the theory has the problems we discussed earlier, since no meaning can be essentially associated with the name. So the only way to defend the disjunctive descriptivist view is to interpret the connection between the disjunction and the name as being necessary. The problem with this, however, is that not all disjunctions are necessary. There are nonnecessary disjunctions such as "tall or married to Mary or the father of Esther," even if there are also necessary disjunctions such as the law of excluded middle. Whether a disjunction is necessary or not depends on the disjuncts and their relation and not on the fact that the disjunction is a disjunction. Hence, it is by no means clear how proponents of the disjunctive-descriptivist view can tie a disjunction to the name necessarily, particularly when they do not admit any necessary connection between the name and any one of the disjuncts. But, of course, those who maintain this position must find this necessity somewhere, or there is no reason to suppose that the name has any connection with the disjunction. For, if the proper name associated with the cluster of descriptions is not necessarily tied to it, then the cluster cannot be considered its meaning. This leaves us, of course, right back where we started. The Descriptive Theory, then, is no panacea.[17] This conclusion has led some recent philosophers to propose an alternative view, sometimes called "the Causal View."

Causal View of Proper Names[18]

The Causal View is meant to solve the problems faced both by the Reference Theory and the Descriptivist Theory. It is an eclectic view that combines some of the elements of each theory, discarding others it deems undesirable. It has been proposed in various garbs by Kripke, Donnellan, and others, although Kripke claims that he has not proposed a theory at all.[19]

This view may be summarized in the following way: (1) with the Reference View it holds that proper names have reference but no meaning (or sense); (2) with the Descriptivist View it maintains that the reference of a proper name may be initially fixed through a description (or alternatively by ostension), although, in contrast to Descriptivism, it holds that the name is

211

not subsequently and necessarily tied to that description or any other particular one; and (3) after the reference of the proper name has been fixed in an initial act, called by the proponents of this view "baptism," reference is fixed through a causal chain of communication in which the speakers who learn the name must intend to use it to refer to the bearer intended by the person from whom they learned it, all the way back to the original baptism.[20]

According to the theory, then, the reference of the name 'Cervantes' was fixed when Cervantes' parents took him to church and gave the baby that name in a baptismal ceremony shortly after his birth.[21] The baby that was baptized, of course, had some very definite characteristics that identified it: it wet its diapers, it was small, it had two arms, it could not write; and so on. The name, therefore, was given to it having in mind those characteristics, but the name was not tied to them, for later in life Cervantes learned not to wet his pants; he grew considerably; he lost an arm at Lepanto; and he wrote *Don Quijote*, among other things, and still retained the name 'Cervantes'. The referent of the name at any time after the baptism is not fixed in terms of a particular description, since this changed throughout Cervantes' life, but rather through a causal chain of speakers, each of whom intends the name to refer to the person to whom the speakers in the chain refer, all the way back to those who fixed the referent at the time of baptism.

Like the other theories discussed, this one appeals to common sense. Indeed, *prima facie* it seems difficult to deny that when one uses a proper name one intends the name to refer to the individual to whom users of the name refer, going all the way back to the moment when the name was first connected to a particular individual.[22] But the greatest strength of the view lies rather in the fact that it offers reasonable solutions to some of the difficulties faced by both the Reference and the Descriptivist Theories.

The difficulties of the Descriptivist Theory were related to the intention of the user of proper names and to the relation of descriptions of the bearer of the name to the name. The first sort of difficulty is formulated by Causal Theory critics of Descriptivism through a much contested distinction between *reference* and *attribution*: They say that users of proper names intend to refer to an individual when they use them rather than to attribute some feature to the bearer of the name.[23] But, of course, according to the Causal View, this poses no problem since proper names have no meaning, and, therefore, their use implies no description or attribution but only the intention to refer. The distinction between attributive and referential use allows the causal theorist to maintain that reference is possible even when descriptions associated with the proper name turn out to be false. Donnellan illustrates the distinction between the attributive and referential uses of definite descriptions with the following example:[24] We find Smith murdered and we say "Smith's murderer is insane." In this case 'Smith's murderer' is used attributively because what we intend is to say that that individual, whoever he is, is insane. Thus, whoever satisfies the description "Smith's murderer" will also be taken to be insane. On the other hand, if Smith's murderer turns out to be Jones, and based on his strange behavior during the trial in which he is convicted, we say "Smith's murderer is insane," the expression "Smith's murderer" is used referentially. For what we intend to say is that Jones is insane, even if he turns out not to have murdered Smith and his conviction was unjust.

Moreover, since according to the Causal View proper names have no meaning, descriptions of the bearers of proper names must be only contingently related to those names. This is sometimes expressed by saying that proper names are "rigid designators" while descriptions are not. For a designator to be rigid it must designate the same thing in every possible world, or to put it differently, it must refer to the same thing in any counterfactual situation.[25] Thus, when a name falls into this category it can be used to refer to a thing even if the thing does not have the features usually ascribed to it. This means that proper names do not mean the same as the description or cluster of descriptions usually associated with them and, consequently, that the bearers of proper names can continue to have those names regardless of the changes they undergo and whether they have or do not have the features ascribed to them by the descriptions associated with them. Socrates could have been called Socrates and would have continued to be called Socrates whether he drank the hemlock or not, or whether he married Xanthippe or not. And I will keep my name, although perhaps not my "good" name, whether I finish this book or not.

Likewise, the proponents of the Causal View argue that their view takes care of the puzzles faced by the Reference Theory. These puzzles, as pointed out earlier, have to do with three types of propositions: identity propositions in which the subject and predicate are proper names, propositions with vacuous proper names as subjects, and existential propositions in which proper names occur.

Those who support the Causal View seem to think that it is quite sufficient by itself to explain some of these puzzles, although some of their answers are not entirely satisfactory. Take the case of propositions with vacuous proper names as subjects. The problem with a proposition like 'Don Quijote was mad', for reference theorists, as we said above, was that it said nothing, since its subject term had no reference and proper names with no referents have no meaning, while in fact it does seem to say something and, therefore to be meaningful. Some causal theorists follow supporters of the Reference View and simply reject that sentences that contain vacuous proper names have meaning. As Donnellan puts it, in a sentence of this sort "no proposition has been expressed."[26] Another answer to this puzzle favored by those who argue for the Causal Theory, on the other hand, points out that the

213

existence of some story or fantasy is sufficient to give meaning to the proposition, for the story or fantasy takes the place of baptism.[27]

Frankly, I must say that I do not find either of these two answers convincing. The first answer simply ignores that whoever says "Don Quijote was mad" means to say something, that those who hear him understand what he says, that some think he may be right while others think the reverse, and that apart from these considerations, which cannot be easily dismissed, 'Don Quijote was mad' entails all sorts of things, including that those who think or thought he was not mad are wrong, that he may have been dangerous, and so forth.

With respect to the second answer, the problem is that it is not clear how "the story" can give meaning to the proposition, while the function of the name remains nondescriptive. For, if 'Don Quijote' has only a nondescriptive function, the proposition is vacuous in spite of the story since 'Don Quijote' has no reference, and if 'Don Quijote' has meaning also, then the Causal View must hold that there is more to proper names than reference. The introduction of a story or fantasy succeeds only in pointing out that 'Don Quijote' is after all tied to a description—"it is the name of a character in Cervantes' most famous novel, invented by Cervantes"; "it is a fiction in my mind"; and so forth. The story or fantasy is effective because it provides the meaning of the proper name and ties it to a description.

Those who maintain the Causal View give a similar response to the problem posed by existential propositions in which proper names occur. The problem with propositions like 'Don Quijote exists' and 'Don Quijote does not exist' is that, if they are true, and the Reference Theory of proper names is correct, they must be necessarily so and, if false, they are contradictory. But again, according to those who support the Causal View, this need not be so, for a story or fantasy is sufficient to explain the situation.[28] 'Don Quijote does not exist', for example, is true precisely because the character in Cervantes' novel has never had a referent, and 'Don Quijote exists' is false for the same reason. But in neither case is necessity involved.

But here also it is not clear how the fantasy or story helps the causal theorist, for what the story does is to supply a context and a description which make it possible to avoid the dilemma of the Reference Theory. Once 'Don Quijote' is substituted by 'the man who fought windmills in Cervantes' most famous novel', then it becomes clear both that he does not exist, except as a fiction, and that his nonexistence is a purely contingent matter. But if this is the case, then Descriptivism must be correct, an inference causal theorists wish to reject.

Indeed, a story or fantasy is nothing but a string of propositions and those propositions either contain proper names or they do not. If they do, an appeal to them to solve the problem of the original proposition containing a

214

vacuous proper name only postpones the problem. For now what needs to be dealt with are the other propositions with proper names in terms of which the original proposition had to be understood. And we are thus back where we started. But if the propositions of the story do not contain proper names, then they supply the meaning of the proper name of the original proposition descriptively, something the causal theorist wishes to deny.[29]

To the third problem, concerned with identity propositions in which the subject and predicate are proper names, various causal theorists give various answers. If we may be allowed to repeat what was already said earlier, the problem consisted in that propositions like 'Cicero is Tully' do not seem to be informative if one holds that proper names have only reference. And yet, the stated proposition seems to say something, and those who do not know that Cicero is Tully learn something upon hearing it uttered. For example, Kripke's answer to this problem is to say that, although the proposition is necessarily true, if true, it is not known *a priori* to be true. The proposition is necessarily true, when true, because it expresses the identity relation between a thing and itself. But this identity, which is, as it were, metaphysical, should not be confused with the epistemic issue of whether we know it *a priori* or *a posteriori*. Concerning 'Cicero is Tully', no amount of philosophical analysis will make one know *a priori* that "if such an identity statement is true it is necessarily true."[30] This answer seems to take care of objections which point out that one could know, for example, that Cicero was a Roman senator and not know that Tully wrote *De amicitia*.[31] But I am not sure it is a satisfactory answer to the problem of identity propositions with different proper names as subjects and predicates. For the point that the descriptivist is bringing out with this objection is that a purely referential theory of proper names cannot really distinguish between the meanings of the sentences 'Cicero is Cicero' and 'Cicero is Tully'. And the reason is that since 'Cicero' and 'Tully' have only reference and stand for the same thing when the proposition represented by the two sentences is true—a point readily granted by referentialists and causalists as we have seen—then there is no way to distinguish between the sentences except insofar as they are different symbols.[32] In order to distinguish them in some other way we would need some description. The distinction between necessity and apriority, although useful for other purposes, fails to deal with this objection.

Finally, defenders of the Causal Theory face another difficulty related to the way reference is determined after the initial baptism. As we have seen, this view maintains that after baptism reference "is determined by a 'causal' chain of communication" in which "the receiver of the name must . . . intend when he learns it to use it with the same reference as the man from whom he heard it."[33] And surely this seems *prima facie* to be a minimum condition of successful reference. In using a name, it appears that we must intend to use it to refer

215

to whomever it is taken to refer by the speakers of the language and members of society. But this does not seem epistemically sufficient; that is, in order to know that the name has someone for a referent, and granting that in most cases we do not have access to the chain of speakers all the way back to the baptism, we need something else to fix the reference: ostension or description.[34] This seems obvious when one teaches a name, for one does that always through ostension or description. If I use the name 'Minina' in my conversation with someone whom I just met at a party and the person asks who Minina is, the only way to enlighten that person is by giving a description of my cat or by showing it to her. Thus, the reference can and is often fixed through a description, even though the description may turn out to be misleading or even entirely mistaken (suppose I had said my cat had red rather than green eyes because I am daltonic). Of course, if the reference of 'Minina' is my cat, then the name is tied to her in virtue of the baptism, and the connection is maintained through the chain of speakers. But the actual reference at a particular moment for a new user of the name is determined through ostension or description.[35] His intention to use the name as it is used by others does not help much in fixing the reference, since what is in question is precisely how those individuals use the name. Therefore, epistemically speaking, the intention to use a name in accordance with the actual chain of communication is not sufficient. There is an important difference between "intending to use a name in accordance with a chain of communication" and "using a name in accordance with a chain of communication." For one may intend to do or be doing something and fail to do or be doing it, and one may in fact do or be doing something while failing to intend to do or be doing it. The lack of a rigorous connection between these two points to the need for something else—ostension or description.

The Causal View, therefore, does not seem to account, at least not simply and easily, for some of the problems the other theories accounted for, and this leaves the matter of the reference of proper names unresolved: We have a situation in which none of the three most common theories of proper names is completely satisfactory. What is the answer, then, to the original question? Do proper names have meaning in addition to reference?

Threefold View of Proper Names

Part of the difficulty with this issue results both from the way the problem is usually posed and from the one-sided character of the approaches used to deal with it. My claim is that if the questions involved in this issue are carefully separated and formulated and if one takes into account the various aspects of the problem, thus using a more comprehensive approach than is usually found in the literature, the answer to this problem is not elusive. Let me begin by identifying the three different questions whose distinction I believe is fundamental for a resolution of this issue: (1) What is the function of proper names? (2) How are proper names established? and (3) How do language users learn to use proper names effectively?

I believe each of the three theories we have discussed provides an answer to one of these questions, but, when they attempt to answer the others, problems arise. Therefore, all three theories have something important to contribute to a comprehensive theory of proper names, but none of them by themselves and without some modifications is sufficient to answer the three questions raised. The Reference Theory provides an appropriate answer to the first question: The function of proper names is to refer to individuals. The Causal View gives a convincing answer to the second question: Proper names are established through a kind of baptism. And the Descriptive Theory provides an answer to the third question: Language users learn to use proper names through descriptions. The Reference Theory is wrong, however, when it fails to acknowledge that descriptions do play a role in any complete account of proper names. The Causal View fails to recognize the importance of descriptions in learning to use proper names effectively. Finally, the Descriptive Theory misunderstands the role that descriptions play with respect to proper names. Let me explain.

The arguments commonly used in support of the Reference Theory may be used in support of the view that the function of proper names is to refer to individuals, but we need not repeat them since we stated them earlier. What I would like to do at this point is to call attention to a factor that accounts for the fundamentally referential character of proper names: the primitive character of individuality. I argued in Chapter 1 that individuality is to be understood properly as noninstantiability and that this notion is not subject to analysis; it is a fundamental or primitive notion that corresponds both to a basic *datum* of experience as well as to a basic building block of reality. Moreover, we have seen in subsequent chapters that an individual's individuality cannot be analyzed into a set of features expressed by a description. Moreover, we saw that referring consists of an act in which a symbol is used to stand for an individual. Therefore, the symbols used to refer to an individual do so not in virtue of any descriptive meaning they have but simply because they stand for noninstantiables. When this is applied to proper names, we can see not only that proper names need not be descriptive in any sense in order to have referents, as descriptivists believed, but also that it makes sense to consider them primarily nondescriptive and therefore as devoid of meaning and sense. Now, since the primary motive for attaching meaning to proper names had to do with explaining how they refer, and this motive is baseless, there is no need to hold that indeed proper names have meaning in addition to reference.[36]

217

The Reference Theory of proper names, therefore, captures correctly their primary function. What it does not do is explain successfully (1) how it is that proper names are established, and (2) how we learn to use them effectively. This is the contribution of the Causal and Descriptive Theories, as already pointed out. Proper names, according to the Causal View, are established in a kind of baptism where an individual is given its name. The name is given to the individual in its fundamental character as individual, and not to an individual that necessarily fulfills a particular description. This is why the individual may turn out to be different than it was originally thought to be and still retain its name. We could say, then, that the baptism ties a name to an individual in its character as noninstantiable and not necessarily to a particular description of one sort or another. This is revealed in the language used in ceremonies in which proper names are given. When the priest says, "I baptize thee _____" there is no description involved. 'Thee' is used in its referential capacity as ostensive and not as standing for a set of features that could be captured in a description. Not even relations are involved. The name is not imposed on "the son of so and so" or "the fat baby with big eyes," but rather on "thee." It is a mistake then to think, as some supporters of the Causal View have been willing to grant, that the reference of proper names at the baptism is determined by a description of the person or thing named.[37] To grant that, as some descriptivist critics of the theory have accurately pointed out, is precisely to grant that reference is related to meaning and, therefore, that the function of proper names involves more than reference.[38] For in such a case, the very imposition of the name would have to be related essentially to the description of the referent. And this makes the theory subject to the kind of objections to which descriptivist theories are liable generally. For example, the name 'Peter' would be tied to the description 'fat little baby who wet its diapers' and would be difficult to apply to the baby when it grows up, becomes thin, learns to control its bladder and does not wear diapers.

In order to avoid both the criticism of descriptivists and the difficulties associated with Descriptivism, the imposition of a proper name must not be regarded as necessarily involving description. And this goes not only for what might be called "accidental" or "extrinsic" descriptions, but also must extend to natural type or natural kind descriptions. For we must allow for the possibility, however remote that may be, that the bearer of the name is of a different natural type than we think even at the moment of baptism. Indeed, it is in the realm of possibility that the baby of our example is not a human baby at all but rather a god, a devil, an extraterrestrial, or even an automaton. And if I should find out, for example, that my daughter Leticia is not a human being at all, but rather some angel who took the place of the baby born to my wife in 1969, I should continue to call the angel Leticia, even if I did not regard her as being human any longer.

Some descriptivists object to this by saying that even ostension is somehow mediated through some kind of mentally descriptive or, as Searle puts it, "intentional" content.[39] But that is a mistake, for the intention in the imposition of a name is precisely its imposition on the individual considered as individual, not on the individual as a member of a group or type. The perception of the object and some of its characteristics are by no means the central point of the ceremony.

It is true, of course, that one may intend to give a name to an individual as belonging to a type. And I can intend to give a particular name to something only if the thing is of a certain type. But this does not mean that all naming is mediated by descriptions or that descriptions are necessarily tied to the referential function.

Another objection to the view that the imposition of proper names does not involve fundamentally descriptive elements voiced by some descriptivists is based on the supposed fact that some names seem to be introduced by descriptions. Searle, for example, brings up the case of storms.[40] These are predicted by scientists and given proper names, even though all this is done on the basis of descriptions. How can it be maintained, then, so the argument goes, that descriptions are not fundamental to the baptism of at least some things? Wouldn't we have to grant that the reference of at least some proper names is determined by a description and, therefore, tied to it?

This objection confuses the issue, for even though the scientist may know the individual only through some kind of description, when he imposes the name, he tags the individual. There are then two aspects to be considered in this process: (1) the epistemic paraphernalia through which the scientist becomes aware of the individual out there—and all of this involves description—and (2) the act of giving the individual the name—and the latter connection has no descriptive mediation. Indeed, it may turn out that the storm is not a storm at all but some artificial disturbance created by the detonation of a bomb, or perhaps that the things we call storms are not natural phenomena but rather artificially created disturbances produced by extraterrestrials, but none of this would prevent the imposition of the name or would require a change of name.

In short, the primary function of proper names is to refer, and they are established through an act of baptism. But, we may ask, how does one learn to use them effectively? This is where the Descriptive Theory plays an important role, for we learn to use proper names effectively in a variety of ways, but often we do so through descriptions. And this is particularly the case when we are not directly acquainted with the bearer of the name. When we are directly introduced to a stranger we are told something like, "Let me introduce you to Mr. Jones," or "This is Mr. Jones," or "I would like you to meet Mr. Jones," and in each case there are some bodily movements that aim to show who Mr.

Jones is. This procedure is similar to the baptismal ceremony in that a name is ostensibly related to an individual. The difference is that in the baptismal ceremony the name is given, while in the introduction the name and its relation to the individual bearer are communicated to someone. The identity of that someone to whom the name and its relation to the individual bearer are communicated is of no consequence, of course. It could even be the bearer of the name himself, although then the procedure would probably not be called an introduction. Persons who have had bouts of amnesia, for example, could be told their name by their family. And small children are likewise told that they are called such and such. But when we are not acquainted with the bearer of the name, then the way to learn the name and use it effectively is through descriptions. We learn who is called "Socrates" by learning that he is the main speaker in the *Symposium* as well as Plato's teacher, and that he was married to a scold, etc., and thanks to these descriptions we are able to use the name 'Socrates' effectively in communication.

All this is consistent with what was said in the chapter concerned with individuation. For there we pointed out that, although noninstantiability is primitive and, therefore, cannot be analyzed in descriptive terms, it is also true that belonging to a type is a necessary condition of individuation. Thus, there can be no individuals that are not instances of some universal type, and, consequently, their description in terms of those types should be possible. Indeed, it is through features as we saw in the chapter on the problem of discernibility that individual substances are often discerned and thus a theory of reference to individuals needs to incorporate a descriptive component. But no particular description specifying the features of a thing is necessarily tied to the name. We could learn, for example, that after all Socrates was not married to a scold, but that that was one of Plato's many literary inventions, and that would not change the reference of the name. Indeed, we could find out, for example, not only that Cervantes did not write *Don Quijote* after all, but that he was not even human. For it is altogether possible that Cervantes may have been a foreign intelligence or an automaton put together by a brilliant Renaissance scientist far ahead of his time, whose own name is unknown. This is possible because, although belonging to a type is a necessary condition of individuality, and we discern individual substances through their features, no specific type is required for individuality, and, therefore, no description can be necessarily tied to an individual *qua* individual. The fact that a description involving a type or sortal property may be used for fixing the reference even through ostension at the point of baptism, as Geach has pointed out,[41] does not necessarily tie the name to the description, for the description plays an epistemic role that may be effective in fixing the reference, but nevertheless may not be necessarily tied to the individual. This is, indeed, one of Kripke's most important insights into the issue of proper names.[42] This indicates that descriptions by themselves can function as sufficient conditions of effectively fixing the referent of a proper name, such as 'Socrates', only under very specific circumstances, but not that they can ever function as necessary conditions or as sufficient conditions under every set of circumstances.

Let me refer back to the example of the library where two men are standing and a murdered woman lies stabbed on the floor, but let there be three men in the room instead of two. A policeman enters and asks: "Who stabbed this woman?" One of the three men says, "Peter did it." The policeman does not know who Peter is, so he has to ask for a criterion of identification: "And who is Peter?" To which the man can give a perfectly good answer by saying, "The man with the guilty look," or by simply pointing his finger in Peter's direction. The policeman, hence, learns the use of the name 'Peter' through means which are sufficient within the circumstances but may not be sufficient under other circumstances and are certainly not necessary for identification in all circumstances. Indeed, they are not necessary in any circumstances because the description in question is not necessarily related to Peter, as we already saw. Both Peter's act of stabbing the woman and his guilty look are contingent matters which could have never happened. Moreover, the description "the man with the guilty look" would not have effectively identified Peter if more than one person with a guilty look had been present in the room.

The mistake of the descriptivist is to try to give the same answer to both the question as to how we learn to use a proper name and to the question as to what the function of a proper name is. Likewise, the reference theorist attempts to answer both questions with the same answer, although he adopts a diametrically opposed view to that of the descriptivist. Finally, the causal theorist, in spite of the fact that he is closer to the truth than the other two, tries to resolve the impasse by combining these views in a way which neglects the role descriptions play in determining reference after the baptism.

Part of the problem that gives rise to the three theories of reference of proper names and that later undermines them is, therefore, the failure to distinguish clearly among the three different questions discussed earlier, which is in turn a consequence of a more basic failure to distinguish among epistemic, logical, and metaphysical issues. But there are also other sources of the problem. The descriptivist makes the mistake of conceiving individuality primarily as a kind of distinction. Since to be an individual is to be distinct from others, so he would seem to argue, proper names and other referring expressions must be intrinsically related to the differences that make an individual distinct from other individuals. For the descriptivist, then, relation of a proper name to an individual involves not only reference, but also a description that reflects the distinct character of the individual. The descriptivist conceives individuality as distinction and reduces the individual to a cluster of features, which is appropriately represented by a cluster or family description.[43] However, if the distinction among the mentioned questions is maintained and we begin with a proper understanding of individuality as noninstantiability, regarding it as primitive, the puzzles that prompted the three theories discussed can be avoided. Let me illustrate the point.

The problems encountered by the Reference Theory had to do with identity propositions, with propositions that have vacuous proper names as subjects, and with existential propositions in which proper names occur. The problem with identity propositions with different proper names as subjects and predicates is that, contrary to our intuitions, they do not seem to be informative. But, if instead of the Reference Theory, the view proposed here is adopted, there is no reason why this problem should be regarded as unsolvable. Take 'Cicero is Tully', for example. According to the proposed theory, the answer to the question "What is the function of 'Cicero' and 'Tully' in this proposition?" is as follows: to refer to the individual called by those two names; there is no descriptive function involved. Moreover, note that the use of the expression 'the individual called by those two names' does not imply that the function of the names is in any way descriptive, although it does entail that individuals can be picked out through descriptions.

But, the descriptivist will retort, if the function of proper names is only to refer, then the proposition 'Cicero is Tully' is uninformative, and yet we do seem to regard it intuitively as informative. In other words, we still seem to have the original problem, according to the descriptivist.

There are two ways of getting out of this quagmire, however. The first, (A), is to say that what look superficially as identity propositions, often can be interpreted in other ways as well. 'Cicero is Tully' can be interpreted as an identity proposition, but it can also be translated into a proposition like 'Cicero is called Tully', which indeed gives us information, since in it 'Cicero' is being used and, therefore, functions referentially as all proper names do; but 'Tully' is being mentioned and, therefore, does not function referentially. The noninformative versus the informative character of the proposition 'Cicero is Tully', then, arises out of its two possible interpretations and does not militate against the view we have adopted.

The second way, (B), of dealing with identity propositions in this context is to bring up the distinction made above between the semantic function of proper names (reference) and the epistemic process of learning about their reference (description), a distinction often made by causal theorists. Since we learn to use proper names through descriptions, when we are presented with a proposition such as 'Cicero is Tully', the descriptions through which we learned to use these names create the false impression that the names must necessarily have meaning. But, once it is understood that this is only a result of how we learned to use the names, then the difficulty vanishes.

The second problematic area encountered by the Reference Theory has to do with propositions that have vacuous proper names as subjects, such as 'Don Quijote was mad'; for these propositions would seem to be sayng nothing under a strict referential interpretation of proper names. There are various answers to this difficulty. The most famous one comes from Wittgenstein and has been maintained by Anscombe.[44] It holds that proper names always have bearers and that expressions such as 'Don Quijote', which do not have bearers, are not proper names but definite descriptions disguised as proper names. But this view is not very credible, since it tries to solve a philosophical problem by offering an arbitrary definition which goes contrary to general practice and intuition.

A different way of answering it consistent with the position defended here is to say that so called vacuous proper names, that is, proper names without real bearers, have nonetheless "possible" bearers. In a sentence like 'Don Quijote was mad', 'Don Quijote' refers to Don Quijote, who happens to be only a possible being, but not for that reason less individual (i.e., noninstantiable).

This answer might seem absolutely preposterous at first,[45] but under closer inspection it looks commonsensical. The feasibility of the notion of a possible individual can be illustrated with reference to foreknowledge and clairvoyance, for example. Let us suppose that at t^1 a couple who wished to have a son had gone to a clairvoyant woman and she had told them that they were going to have a son at t^2 and that he would be called Jacob. And let us suppose further that between t^1 and t^2 twenty years elapsed. During those twenty years, the couple always talked about Jacob, and they planned for him, for his college career; they put aside some money for his wedding, and so on. Now, their talk about Jacob during those twenty years would certainly be meaningful and yet, during all that time Jacob did not exist. Of course, one could argue that the referent of 'Jacob' did in fact exist at t^2 even if not at t^1 and the intervening time between t^1 and t^2 and that this is why the talk from Jacob's parents was meaningful. But what if the clairvoyant woman were a false clairvoyant and Jacob was never born at t^2? Would that render the couple's talk meaningless? The point that I want to make is that we do think about nonexistent but possible individuals and that if we do that and proper names are normally used to refer to individuals, then the argument that when they do not refer to actual individuals they have no reference is not good.

But does not this entail that there is an infinite number of individuals and a potentially infinite number of proper names to refer to them? Of course it does! The only way we could limit the number of individuals, actual and possible, would be by establishing that certain classes, as some medievals did with God, can be instantiated only a determinate number of times and no more (once in the case of God).

That there is an infinite number of possible individuals does not mean, on the other hand, that we know or even can know all of them and, therefore, that we can refer to all of them effectively. We can refer to Don Quijote because Cervantes taught us through his descriptions (the learning process) about him. But, again, this does not mean that 'Don Quijote' is a disguised definite description or that its function is descriptive. Its function is to refer to Don Quijote, who, for better or for worse, has not yet existed (to our knowledge—maybe he did actually exist and Cervantes knew it, in which case Cervantes' novel might not be fiction, but history).

The introduction of the notion of possible individuals can also be used to solve the problem created by existential propositions with proper names as subjects. The problem posed by this difficulty was that in the context of the Reference Theory these propositions would have to be regarded as either contradictory or as necessarily true. 'Don Quijote exists' is contradictory and 'Don Quijote does not exist' is necessarily true. But this assumes that the bearers of proper names must be actually existing individuals. If we hold that the referent of a proper name can be a possible individual, then 'Don Quijote exists' is false but not contradictory, and 'Don Quijote does not exist' is true but not necessarily so. The truth value of these propositions is a contingent matter even though the function of 'Don Quijote' is to refer and not, as the Descriptivist Theory holds, to take the place of a description.

With respect to the problems faced by Descriptivism, again the view being proposed here avoids them. The main problem faced by the Descriptivist Theory involved the necessary and contingent character of the relation between proper names and the descriptions of the things to which the names refer. For, if the relation is contingent, then it is difficult to hold that it is the meaning of the name. And if it is regarded as necessary, then how can we account for the fact that the things to which we refer are not always the way we think they are? Of course, if, as has been proposed here, descriptions are only contingently related to individuality and serve to identify the bearer of the name only under very specific circumstances, then no problem arises by saying that proper names have no meaning and likewise for accounting for disparities of descriptions.

But, perhaps, the proponents of the Reference, Descriptivist, and Causal Theories will argue that the three questions identified above are not as fundamental as I have suggested, or at least they might say that they were not the questions they were particularly trying to answer. Their concern, presumably, has to do with a fourth question that we do not seem to have addressed at all here. It could be put like this: What are the conditions of successful reference? But this question is ambiguous. For it can be interpreted in at least two different ways. First, it may be taken to ask how a particular user of a proper name *knows* to whom the name applies. Second, it could be taken as asking what *ties* the name to its bearer. The first is clearly epistemic; it asks for conditions of knowledge, and I shall discuss it after we deal with the second. The second, on the other hand, is not epistemic but metaphysical, for it concerns the relation between the bearer of a name and the name and not the conditions for knowing that relation. Now, according to the view presented here, what ties a name to the bearer is the baptism, that is, the establishment by convention that an individual will be called by such a name. And the correct or incorrect use of the name will depend on whether the use is in accordance with that establishment. The use of 'Minina', for example, will be correct as long as whoever uses the name uses it to refer to the individual to whom that name was given.

But, one may ask, what happens when (1) a name is mistakenly believed by someone to refer to something other than what it should refer according to the baptism and (2) because of the influence of that person everyone inherits the new usage? Are all subsequent users of the name using it incorrectly? This problem has been dramatized with the so called "Madagascar example." Apparently, Madagascar was originally the name some African groups had for mainland Africa, but Marco Polo misunderstood the referent of the name and thought it referred to the island to which we refer with that name nowadays. Are we all using the name incorrectly, then? Frankly, I do not see that this example poses a great difficulty. It seems clear that since the referents of proper names are a matter of convention, correct or incorrect usage depends on the convention being adopted. Clearly, we are all using the name 'Madagascar' incorrectly according to the convention adopted by the African tribes who established the name. And if we should converse with them, we would soon find out that something was wrong. On the other hand, if we follow Marco Polo's convention, which he mistakenly thought was the accepted one, but which turned out to be his own doing, we are using the name correctly.

One more thing: convention is passed down, as causal theorists have correctly pointed out, through a chain of speakers who use the name correctly. Unfortunately, when causal theorists speak of this chain, they usually speak about the intention of the speakers in a way that suggests that the intention to use the name in accordance with the baptism is a necessary and/or sufficient condition of successful reference. But it seems to be neither.[46] For a speaker may not consciously intend to use the term that way—and thus cannot be a necessary condition—and as the Madagascar example indicates,[47] he may not in fact be using it in that way even if he did intend to do so—and thus cannot

225

be a sufficient condition. What is both a necessary and sufficient condition of the correct use of a proper name is that its referent be the referent it had in the baptism. Of course, given the fact that we are not present at the baptism of every bearer of a proper name, it is therefore necessary to account for that passage through the causal chain of speakers. But note that the necessary condition in question is a necessary condition only of the *transfer of the name in the conditions specified,* not of the successful reference of proper names *per se* or under different conditions. And in that case the intention of the speaker seems to play no role.

The first way of interpreting the question, 'What are the conditions of successful reference?', on the other hand, was epistemic. It means roughly something like: How do we know who is the bearer of a name? But the answer to this is not different from the answer to the question concerning how we learn to use proper names: We do so through descriptions, except at the moment of baptism. For it is through descriptions that we separate and distinguish one individual from others within a particular context (except when we use ostention in cases where we are present) even when the description may apply in principle to others or even when it does not apply in fact to the individual in question. If we have a room in which everything is painted white and there is a calico cat in the room, the reference of 'Minina' can be fixed simply by saying "Minina is the calico thing in the room." Now, let us suppose the room is painted red and the cat is yellow, and we are looking into the room through a blue tinted glass. Under those conditions I can fix the reference of 'Minina' for my friend, seated next to me and also looking into the room, by saying, "Minina is the green thing in the room," since everything else in the room appears purple. And yet the cat is not really green, but yellow.

The issue of successful reference, therefore, depends to a great extent on what is exactly meant by it. But in both ways we have understood it, we can provide an account consistent with the position regarding individuality presented in this book. In short, then, in accordance with the view of reference adopted earlier and the theory of individuality defended in previous chapters, proper names can be interpreted as nondescriptive symbols used to stand for individuals. They are imposed on noninstantiable instances by convention through an act of the user, but their use is learned through descriptions given in determined circumstances.

The discussion of proper names has been necessarily kept general and brief, since the main subject of discussion of this book is not this semantic issue but individuality and its metaphysics. And I shall do the same with the discussion of definite descriptions and indexicals, two other important means of referring to individuals.

Definite Descriptions

Something has already been said indirectly about descriptions in general and about definite descriptions in particular in the previous pages. Moreover, as we shall see, there is not much that needs to be added to what has already been said in the context of proper names for reasons that will become clear presently. For these same reasons the discussion of this topic will be very brief.

A description is a phrase that specifies certain features of something. An indefinite description is supposed to be as it were open-ended, without limits and thus general. As such, indefinite descriptions aim to fit many things and none in particular. Grammatically speaking (in English), they usually begin with an indefinite article, whence their name, as in 'a cat with calico fur', or 'a man wearing a red hat', although this is not a necessary condition of indefinite descriptions. On the other hand, definite descriptions are supposed to demarcate, to set limits, so that the description would fit only one thing.[48] While 'dark green, strong rye grass' is an indefinite description, because it can refer to an indefinite number of things, 'the cat that spilt milk last night' is a definite description, because it is supposed to refer to one and only one cat, the one that spilt milk last night. The trouble is that the distinction between definite and indefinite descriptions is not as clear cut as one would have expected or perhaps wished. The reason for this should be clear both from the discussion in previous chapters and from the examples just given. Take the last example, for instance, 'the cat that spilt milk last night' is supposed to refer to one and only one individual. But in fact, the conditions it stipulates are not sufficient to do that, for there may be not only one but many cats that spilt milk last night and the description as given cannot discriminate among them. The fact is that descriptions record various features and relations of things and none of these bundles, whether relational or not, can account fully for an individual. No description, therefore, seems so definite that it can sufficiently pick out an individual in all circumstances, although it is true that often they do the job within determinate circumstances. When I tell Clarisa, "Get the cat that spilt milk last night," she has no trouble identifying the cat as Minina, but that is because she knows the house has been closed all night and there was only one cat inside it. But indefinite descriptions also serve this purpose within determinate circumstances. When we are all sitting on our back porch contemplating the field behind our home and my wife exclaims, "Oh, rye grass is so green!" she is talking about the grass on the field and not some other grass, and all those present know it.[49]

The distinction between definite descriptions and proper names is less difficult to make than the distinction between definite and indefinite descriptions, although those who hold that proper names have meaning will dispute the view.[50] Be that as it may, it seems quite clear that one can talk about Socrates and about the Greek philosopher who drank the hemlock without knowing that they are the same individual, and that one may know things about one that one may not know about the other. One may know and say, for example, that Socrates was married to a scold and that the Greek philosopher who drank the hemlock was Plato's teacher and yet not know that they are one and the same person. (In fact, my daughter Clarisa does not.) All of this goes to show that definite descriptions are not equivalent to names, or vice versa, contrary to what some descriptivists have held. And the same contrast could be drawn between definite descriptions and indexicals.

It is true that often what look like definite descriptions in the language are not definite descriptions at all. Kripke mentions the well known example of the Holy Roman Empire, which was neither holy, Roman, nor an empire.[51] Clearly, in this case and similar ones, the presumed description is no description at all but a proper name that has no relation to the features of the thing presumably described by it.

Having stated a few preliminaries, we can now give an answer to the three questions identified above in the context of definite descriptions. The first question has to do with the function of definite descriptions. And the answer is that, unlike proper names, they have two basic functions. Sometimes definite descriptions function primarily as means of reference and then they resemble proper names. This can be seen in examples such as 'the Evening Star' and 'the Morning Star', which most often function referentially even though they also have descriptive content.[52] Yet, unlike proper names, definite descriptions also have meaning; that is, they specify certain features that the things they describe have. Their difference with indefinite descriptions is that they try to identify some feature which differentiates the thing in question from others, while indefinite descriptions do the opposite, identifying features which express similarities among things. It should be kept in mind, however, that there is a distinction between definite descriptions and proper names that look like definite descriptions, such as the example given above of 'the Holy Roman Empire'. The latter sort are not descriptions at all, but compound proper names. After all, most proper names also mean something in their original use ('George' means farmer, for example), although they have generally lost that function.

The second question has to do with how definite descriptions are established. Now, insofar as definite descriptions are used to refer to individuals, they share with proper names the fact that they have a process of imposition whereby they are tied to an individual. 'The cat that spilt milk last night' becomes by my act of imposition an expression that can be used in reference to my cat Minina, and only to refer to her, even though it is essentially descriptive and could apply to some other cat as well.

Finally, we may ask how we learn to use these descriptions. And the answer is that we do through their meaning and the surrounding circumstances. Clarisa knows that I am referring to Minina when I speak of "the cat that spilt milk last night," because she understands the conditions stipulated by the description and the accompanying circumstances, as mentioned earlier. Indeed, even proper names, as we saw earlier, are learned through ostension and/or description. Therefore, the case should be even more clear with descriptions, whether definite or indefinite.

Indexicals

Another type of linguistic term commonly used to refer to individuals are indexicals, terms such as 'I', 'this', 'that', 'here', 'now', and the like. As already pointed out in the Prolegomena, the term 'indexical' was first used by Peirce in connection with demonstratives, pronouns, and tenses.[53] None of these are names in the traditional understanding of the term. One of the characteristics of proper names is that they are supposed to apply to one and only one individual, but the referent of indexicals changes according to circumstances. When I say "I am a man," the term 'I' refers to me. But if someone else says "I am a man," it refers to the person who says it. This is why Russell called them "egocentric particulars" and Reichenbach referred to them as "token reflexive words."[54] Proper names are unlike indexicals in that they are used to refer to one and the same individual regardless of circumstances, while the referent of indexicals varies according to context. 'Socrates' is used to refer to Socrates and no one else. Of course, this difference is not as clear cut as has been suggested, since several individuals can have the same name. For example, the number of John Smiths in the United States seems to be practically infinite. The distinction, therefore, is not as obvious as some philosophers have believed, but, having little relevance to our present purposes, we need not dwell further on it.

There is another difference between proper names and indexicals that deserves to be mentioned. The bearers of proper names are things like a cat, a human being, a tree, a ship, what Aristotelians call primary substances or just substances. Proper names are also used in connection with aggregates of substances, such as a farm, a country, and a planet. On the other hand, they are not used, at least not in ordinary speech and circumstances, to refer to the features of things. It would sound odd to call the calico color of Minina's fur "Gretchen," for example. Indeed, if I were to talk about "Gretchen" while pointing to my cat, those present would think I was talking about Minina and not its color. True, sometimes we give proper names to parts of things,

229

particularly if the use of the common names of the parts in question creates embarrassment. Lovers, for example, sometimes refer to their private parts through proper names, as some of Igmar Bergman's movies illustrate. But, of course, parts are not features, and it is features that are not ordinarily bearers of proper names. At any rate, I am not arguing that they cannot have proper names or even that we never refer to them through proper names. For, indeed, if what was said in Chapter 2 about the extension of 'individuality' is true, namely, that features of things are individual, then it should be possible to give proper names to them. That we do not is, I believe, more a result of pragmatic considerations than of logic. To call both things and their features by proper names would create confusion in communication, just as I explained with the example of Minina's fur. This may also be the reason why even the use of proper names in connection with parts of things is not frequent.

Like proper names, indexicals are used to refer to things, but, unlike them, they also serve to refer to the features of things.[55] In the latter case, however, there is almost always an implicit or explicit specification of the type. 'I', 'he' and 'this' do not need anything but themselves to indicate a substance, but to indicate an instance of a color, for example, a term like 'color' or 'blue' is added to 'this' in order for the reference to be established. Thus, we have expressions such as 'that blue' or 'this color'. If such terms are not supplied, the context, such as a question, for example, supplies it. For a reference to this black color of hair we use 'this black color of hair', and if 'black color of hair' is missing in the referring expression, it usually appears in the context, as in the question, "Which black color of hair?" To which we answer, "This one." We need such means to determine the instance to which the reference is being made.

Naturally, the same questions that have been raised concerning the meaning and reference of proper names can be raised concerning the meaning and reference of indexicals, and practically the same answers given to the former can be found in response to the latter. The descriptivist will try to interpret indexicals descriptively,[56] the nondescriptivist will see them as nondescriptive, having only a referential function, and the causalist will offer his compromise among these two views.

The view that I propose follows the general outline presented in the context of proper names. The justification for this is that there is really no fundamental distinction between proper names and indexicals.[57] The nature and function of indexicals is the same as that of proper names. Indeed, indexicals are in fact proper names whose reference changes with circumstances. That these changes are not contrary to the nature of proper names can be seen from the fact already pointed out before, namely, that even proper

230

names, such as 'Socrates' and 'John Smith', can be used to refer to more than one individual.

My view, then, is threefold. First, the primary function of indexicals is to refer. Thus, when a term like 'this' is used in the sentence 'This is a map of Africa', its function is to refer and pick out the individual map in question. It is not to describe it, for the description is precisely what is being said about it. Likewise, when I am asked, "What did you win at the raffle yesterday?," and I answer "This," the function of 'this' is to draw attention to "whatever it is I won" and not to say anything about the type of thing I won.

Second, indexicals are established through a kind of baptism, but unlike proper names this is not a single ceremony that determines the use of the term for all times (if indeed such ceremony exists for all proper names, something rather doubtful), but rather a repeatable procedure that changes the referent of the term depending on the circumstances and the wishes of the language user. What happens, then, is that a particular person decides under certain circumstances that an individual be called "that" or "this" or any other indexical. The sound uttered or the sign made are used to refer to an individual and this relation is established entirely on the basis of the user's decision. Moreover, in establishing this relation between a term and an individual thing the user has in mind some description, even though that description is only contingently tied to the name. Thus, he has in mind something like "I give the name 'this' to the pen with which I am writing." Or, using an ostensive definition, he may hold the pen in front of himself and say "this." This brings me to the third point.

This view holds that language users learn the use of indexicals on a particular occasion, that is to say, they learn the referential relation between the term and its individual referent through ostension and description. If a student in my logic class, when doing an exercise, says "This is hard," and someone asks "What is hard?," he will answer either by pointing to the exercise in the text or by saying "Exercise number 15 on page 210." In the first case he gives an ostensive definition and in the second a description. It is through these that language users learn the connection between indexicals and referents in a particular situation.

Having given a general but brief account of how proper names, definite descriptions, and indexicals are used to refer to individuals consistent with the view of individuality presented in earlier chapters, it is time to close this chapter and begin the summary presentation of the overall position developed in this book.

Assessment:
A Metaphysics of Individuality

My aim in this essay has been twofold. First, I have tried to clarify the philosophical terminology and issues involved in the notion of individuality and, second, I have presented and defended various theses concerning this notion. The result, I would hope, may be characterized as a systematic presentation of a metaphysical interpretation of individuality. I have called this interpretation "metaphysical" because its primary aim is to provide a better understanding of what individuality is, rather than, as many post-Kantians would prefer, of what we think it is or of how we talk about it. Yet, because to know what something is involves epistemic, semantic, and logical aspects, it has been necessary to discuss issues that some past metaphysicians have ignored and/or rejected because of their epistemic, semantic, and/or logical character.

Apart from the terminological precisions made throughout the book, and particularly in the Prolegomena, to which there is no need to refer further here, the main clarificatory thesis of this study concerns the distinctions among what I believe to be six fundamental issues. It is my claim that much of the confusion and disagreement surrounding individuality is the result of a failure to distinguish among these six issues. I have tried to show, for example, how the failure to distinguish between the epistemic issue of discernibility and the metaphysical issue of individuation have resulted in disputes among theories that may be defensible as answers to one of these issues, but indefensible as answers to the other. Two good examples of this are the Material View and the Spatio-Temporal Theory of Individuation. The first, as we saw earlier,

233

has considerable merit as a theory of individuation, but is a weak prospect as a view of individual discernibility. And the second, as also pointed out before, is a satisfactory answer to the problem of the individual discernibility of spatio-temporal beings, while it is quite objectionable as a theory of individuation.

Another clear example of the importance of keeping these six issues separate, but which, at the same time, demonstrates how closely they are related to one another, so that the answer to one will often determine or at least affect the answer to the others, concerns the intensional analysis of individuality and the principle of individuation. As we saw above, if one holds a view of individuality as some kind of difference or distinction, then the principle of individuation will have to account for that difference, creating the need for a differentiating factor or feature; whence the thesis that the principle of individuation is a feature or bundle of features in individual things. But, on the other hand, if individuality is not understood as difference but as noninstantiability, as we have proposed in Chapter 1, the Bundle View of Individuation loses much of its appeal, since there is then no overriding need to account for difference.

Any theory of individuality that aims to be clear and consistent, then, must at least observe the distinctions among the six issues identified in this book. If it aims also to be systematic, then it must also address these six issues and propose answers to them.

In addition to these more formal claims, I have also made several substantive claims about the intension and extension of the term 'individuality', the ontological status of individuality, the principles of individuation and discernibility, and about the way we refer to individuals. These stand in sharp contrast, in most cases, to the generally accepted wisdom on these matters. Let me summarize them briefly.

My major claim concerning the intensional analysis of individuality is that, contrary to the standard view among present day philosophers, who interpret individuality as some kind of distinction or difference, individuality must be understood primarily as noninstantiability. Noninstantiability seems to be the only necessary and sufficient condition of individuality. It applies to all individuals, regardless of their nature and location: To be an individual is to be a noninstantiable instance and, vice versa; to be a noninstantiable instance is to be an individual. Noninstantiability is what distinguishes individuals from universals, which are in turn characterized by their capacity to be instantiated. Understood in this way, individuality must be distinguished from, although it is related to (depending on the nature of the individual and its location and circumstances), difference, identity, division, indivisibility, and impredicability. Difference is a relational feature of individuals in a universe where more than one individual is possible. Identity is a feature of individuals in a spatio-temporal universe where change and duration are

234

found. Division is a feature of individuals whose nature allows multiplicity within the species. Indivisibility, as we saw, was an inadequate way of interpreting noninstantiability, reflecting a rather physical model. And, finally, impredicability is a feature of individuals considered as subjects of thought and linguistic expression. All of these features are, therefore, contingent on factors other than the individual itself considered as such. Only noninstantiability can be regarded as the necessary and sufficient condition of individuality.

In addition to this claim concerning the intension of 'individuality' I also make the related claim that noninstantiability, just as its correlative, instantiability, are not subject to further analysis and must be regarded as primitive notions. Any analysis of them will necessarily be circular; that is, it will contain a reference, explicit or implicit, to one or the other.

The second fundamental issue involved in individuality identified above has to do with the extension of the term. Unlike the intensional issue, this one has received considerable explicit attention in the history of philosophy. The most popular contemporary views among those who address it hold that, while substances are individual, their features are not. Consequently, this view maintains, moreover, that in addition to individuals, universals also can be said to exist. My view stands in sharp contrast with this position. I make two basic claims concerning the extension of 'individuality'. First I claim that individuality and universality are exhaustive and mutually exclusive notions. Everything is either one or the other, but not both. This is the less important thesis of the two I defend. The most important thesis is that any sound metaphysical theory must include both individuals and universals, since it makes no sense to talk about noninstantiable instances without making reference to instantiables, and vice versa. This does not mean, however, that both universals and individuals "exist" in the sense in which an actual or even a possible cat exists, for example. I did commit myself to the view that not only some things that exist are noninstantiable instances (i.e., individual) but more importantly, the category of individuality extends to all existing and possibly existing things, including both physical and nonphysical substances as well as their features. This is equivalent to saying that everything that exists is individual, if one wishes to use the traditional formulation of this position. However, as far as universals are concerned, I do not maintain that they do not exist, rather I hold that they are neutral with respect to existence; existence is a category that does not apply to them. Indeed, I claim that the source of much of the controversy surrounding universals is precisely the result of the mistaken aim to reduce individuals to universals or vice versa, and thus to identify somehow their ontological status either by making universals ontologically equivalent to individuals or by making individuals ontologically equivalent to universals. Since this book is about individuals, I dispense with a detailed analysis of universals, concentrating my efforts on individuality, but I do try to show that it is a serious mistake to try to do away with one of these two categories. That is the mistake incurred by most forms of Realism (reduction of individuals to universals) and Nominalism (reduction of universals to individuals), while most forms of Eclecticism simply misunderstand the nature of individuality.

The ontological issue involves two questions. One asks for the clarification of the ontological status of individuality and the second for the explanation of the relation between individuality and the individual. This issue has been largely neglected in contemporary discussions of individuality, even though it was of much concern to scholastics. Still, while explicit discussions of this issue are not frequent, even among those who do not make explicit their ideas in this regard, there are two detectable positions. One identifies individuality with a kind of substantial substratum and the other with a feature of individual things. The first is distinguished from the other components of an individual as a substratum is to features, and the second as a feature is to other features. There are, of course, other possible views, which I have discussed in Chapter 3, but which have received less attention recently. My answer to the ontological issue is quite different. To the first question I answer that individuality is a mode. This goes contrary to the mentioned views and to those that interpret it as a relation, or simply deny any ontological status to it. My answer to the second question is that, as a mode, individuality is intensionally distinct from the individual and its features, but that it is not extensionally distinct from them, since it is not anything independently of them. Interpreted as a mode, individuality can extend to both simple and complex entities and thus be consistent with the extensional view presented in Chapter 2. Moreover, this point of view opens the way for a more economical and commonsensical answer to the problem of individuation.

The problem of individuation is, without a doubt, one of the most fundamental metaphysical issues involved in individuality, but it is also one of the most perplexing. My thesis concerning this issue is twofold; the first is rather formal, while the second is more substantive. In the first place, I claim that much of the disagreement and confusion surrounding this issue is the result of three factors: (1) various confusions concerning the intension of 'individuality', (2) the formulation of the issue in epistemic terms, and (3) a reductionist approach. Once these sources of confusion are clarified and avoided, one can answer the two basic questions involved in this issue: the identification of the principle of individuation and the determination of whether it is the same for all individuals.

My second thesis, the substantive one, is that the principle of individuation of individuals is the same for all things, and it is to be identified as existence, although it must be clear that existence in this context cannot be interpreted as a feature. In proposing an existential theory of individuation, I also reject all other current views of the individuation of substances: bundle, accidental (spatio-temporal, quantitative), essential (material, formal, bare particular), and extrinsic; and of the individuation of features: substance and feature theories. Existence is, in the last analysis, the sole ground for the noninstantiability of individuals, even if to exist, actually or potentially, also implies formal aspects.

The answer to the problem of discernibility is based on common sense and does not attempt to identify the necessary conditions of individual discernibility, but only the sufficient conditions of it in the world of our experience. These sufficient conditions vary depending on the type of individual involved and on the circumstances in which it is found, so that in fact almost any feature of things can function as a sufficient condition of individual substance discernibility. Still, it appears reasonable to hold that, at least for physical individuals, spatio-temporal location functions most often as the sufficient condition of individual substance discernibility, although not in all circumstances and certainly not in all possible worlds. The case of the discernibility of individual features is analogous—they can be discerned through their relation to substances or to other features, depending on the circumstances. On the other hand, I argue that neither Bundle nor *Sui Generis* Theories of Individual Discernibility of Substances are effective.

The last of the fundamental problems surrounding individuality discussed in this essay is the problem of reference to individuals in terms of proper names, definite descriptions, and indexicals. With respect to proper names, I have argued that most of the disagreement as to how they refer and whether they have meaning in addition to reference originates from a confusion of three issues: (1) the function of proper names, (2) the establishment of proper names, and (3) the way users learn to use proper names effectively. To the first issue my answer is that the primary function of proper names is to refer to substantial individuals, such as Peter and Paul. With respect to the second I have suggested, following the causal theorists, that proper names are established in a kind of baptism. Finally, with respect to the third, I have argued that we learn to use proper names effectively through the use of descriptions in determined circumstances. As mentioned already, one of the sources of the confusion with respect to the problem of reference is the failure to keep these three questions separate, but another important source of confusion is the understanding of individuality as some kind of distinction. Both descriptivists and causal theorists make this mistake. Having interpreted individuality as distinction, they assume that proper names and other referring expressions are intrinsically related to the differences that distinguish an individual from others. Hence, descriptivists argue, for example, that proper names and individuals are related not just through reference but also through some kind of distinguishing description. In contrast to these approaches, my view is that only if we adhere to the distinction between the mentioned issues and understand individuality as noninstantiability can an appropriate view be developed.

With respect to definite descriptions, my claim is that, unlike proper names, definite descriptions have two basic functions: description and reference. Since all definite descriptions are descriptive, they all serve that function. But, in addition, some are used also to refer. This capacity for a double function distinguishes definite descriptions from indexicals also. The latter, like proper names, have as their primary function to refer. But, unlike proper names, they are not only used to refer to Aristotelian primary substances but also to their features. In that case, however, they must be accompanied by an expression that identifies the type of feature in question.

The six problems I have identified in this book, although fundamental to any systematic account of individuality, do not exhaust by any means the metaphysical problems related to this notion. Nor do the answers I have given to them constitute a complete view of individuality. I have tried to present a systematic and fundamental account of individuality, but there are still many areas that would have to be worked out in order to claim any kind of completeness for it. I shall not try to give a list of all the gaps that need to be filled. I am sure my critics will gladly take care of that. But I shall refer to a couple of examples of problems whose investigations seems to me particularly compelling.

One of these is the problem of identity, and not just of the identity of persons but of the identity of all things belonging to natural kinds as well as of artifacts. Some philosophers have called this the problem of continuity and others have used other names. The nomenclature used is not very important. What is important is the substance of the issue. The problem in question has to do with the identification of the necessary and sufficient conditions for something to remain fundamentally the same in spite of the passage of time and of various changes. How can we explain, for example, the identity of Socrates at two different times of his life, and likewise of other things in the universe?

This issue is clearly metaphysical, since it deals with the necessary and sufficient conditions of identity, but it has often been confused with another related issue: the search for the necessary and sufficient conditions of repeated identification. This last issue is epistemic, since it involves the conditions that make possible the knowledge of individual identity. I prefer to call this latter issue "the problem of reidentification," in order to distinguish it clearly from the problem of identity.

A second set of problems that needs to be addressed has to do with universals. I have indirectly identified the intension of 'universality' as instantiability; I have said that universals are neutral with respect to existence and that universality, like individuality, is a mode. But, given my primary concern with individuality, I have provided no detailed substantiation and/or elaboration of these claims. Naturally, this is an important area that needs to be worked out, although I believe any further elaboration of it would have to take place within the parameters I have identified in this book.

Apart from the problems of identity, identification, and those related to universals, there are also a host of other problems which would have to be discussed and settled in order to claim to have provided a complete theory of individuality, but those will have to be left for another occasion or to others. In this essay I have only tried to give a systematic presentation of some basic metaphysical ideas concerning individuality which could constitute the foundations of a metaphysics of individuality. Without a doubt, my account contains many gaps and is surely in need of correction, but I hope it will contribute to the deeper understanding of individuality and, by challenging some of the dogmas and myths currently widespread in the literature, will stir others to work in this area of philosophy and perhaps succeed where I may have failed.

Notes

Preface

1. P.F. Strawson, *Individuals* (1959), p. 9.

2. Some authors prefer to talk about "phenomenological ontology," as does Héctor-Neri Castañeda in "Individuation and Non-Identity" (1975), p. 131b.

3. This point has been explicitly acknowledged by Castañeda in ibid., p. 132a.

4. D. W. Hamlyn, *Metaphysics* (1984), p. 5.

5. G. E. Moore, *The Philosophy of G. E. Moore* (1942), p. 14.

Prolegomena

1. Jorge J. E. Gracia, *Introduction to the Problem of Individuation in the Early Middle Ages* (1984), chap. V. In fact it is my view, which I have tried to substantiate both in that book and in *Suárez on Individuation* (1982), that most important philosophical issues involved in individuality become explicit for the first time only during the medieval period. There are, of course, echoes of some of these issues in Aristotle, as we shall see in texts to which reference is made later on, and even in Plato (see, for example, *Parmenides* 129 c–d, where he discusses unity and plurality), but in no cases is there an explicit formulation of a problem, and the texts are for the most part unclear with regards to individuality.

2. Among the most important texts of the period are the following: Thomas Aquinas' *Commentary to Boethius' "On the Trinity" (Expositio super librum Boethii "De Trinitate"* [1959]), q. 4; Duns Scotus' *Oxford Lectures (Ordinatio,* in *Opera omnia* [1950 ff.]), bk. II, d.3; and Francisco Suárez's *Metaphysical Disputation V,* in Gracia, *Suárez on Individuation* (1982). But there are also important texts from Ockham, Henry of Ghent, Durandus of St. Pourçain and many others, including some anonymous treatises.

3. The classic contemporary text on individuality is P. F. Strawson's *Individuals* (1959).

4. The use of these examples does not preclude the extension of 'individuality' to other things, such as events, artifacts, statements, sentences, ideas in a mind, characteristics of trees, and so on. The examples indicate that 'individuality' extends to what Aristotle called "primary substances" in the *Categories* and some have called more recently "natural kinds," but they are not intended to suggest that only primary substances or natural kinds are individual. Indeed, the issue of precisely what things are individual (substances, properties and characteristics, events, and so on) has been and still is a matter of intense debate among those who concern themselves with individuality and/or universality and will be discussed in Chapter 2. I have used Aristotelian primary substances here as examples to make easier the presentation of the problems involved in individuality, since their character as individuals is generally uncontested.

5. What in fact constitutes or does not constitute the generic, specific, and/or an accidental nature of a particular thing is of no concern or relevance in this study. Indeed, such questions have more to do with empirical science than with metaphysics.

6. Tertullian, *De monogamia* in *Corpus scriptorum ecclesiasticorum latinorum* 76 (1957), No. 5.

7. These *formulae* can be found in most scholastic literature after the thirteenth century. See, for example, Jorge J. E. Gracia, *Suárez on Individuation* (1982), pp. 78 and 41.

8. Thomas Aquinas, *On Being and Essence,* chap. 2, par. 4 (1968).

9. In the early Middle Ages, Gilbert of Poitiers, borrowing language from Cicero, used the term 'dividual' as opposite of 'individual'. See Gilbert of Poitiers, *The Commentaries on Boethius* (1966), p. 270 and elsewhere.

10. Cf. Aristotle, *Metaphysics* V, chap. 6, 1015b15 ff (1924); and Francisco Suárez in *Suárez on Individuation* (1982).

11. Note that this use of 'number' and 'numerical' needs to be distinguished from the purely quantitative uses of these terms. The medievals were well aware of this. See, for example, Godfrey of Fontaines, *Quodlibet* VI, q. 16 (1914), 3.256, and also John Wippel, *The Metaphysical Thought of Godfrey of Fontaines* (1981), pp. 25–26. What this means is that the nonquantitative use of this terminology is metaphysical and should be watched.

12. See Porphyry, *Isagoge* (1975), p. 31.

13. See Chapter II of Gracia, *Introduction to Individuation* (1984), pp. 83–87. The key texts in Boethius appear in his *Commentary on Aristotle's "Categories" (In Categorias Aristotelis); Patrologia latina* 64, 169 ff.

14. See Gracia, *Introduction to Individuation*, (1984), Chap. III.

15. These are complex and appear throughout the text. A distinction between individuality and singularity has been maintained also by José Gaos, *De la filosofía* (1982), lec. X, pp. 70 ff.; and Xavier Zubiri, *Sobre la esencia* (1962), pp. 164 ff.

16. See, for example, G. W. Leibniz, *Metaphysical Disputation on the Principle of an Individual* (1965), lines 110 ff., where he uses these terms interchangeably with each other and with 'numerical difference'. On the other hand, Hegel distinguishes them in the *Logic*, (1975), p. 163 ff. He interprets universality as "identity" (or "sameness"), particularity as "difference," and individuality as "subjectivity" (from subject, ground, and substratum).

17. See, for example, Suárez's *Metaphysical Disputation* V, where most of the text is devoted to the issue of individuation, but where he discusses separately the intensional and extensional issues (together in Sect. I) on the one hand from the ontological issue (Sect. II) on the other, and dismisses the epistemic problem of discernibility (Sect. III, par. 28).

18. John Duns Scotus, *Oxford Lectures (Ordinatio)*, bk. II, d. 3, qq. 5 and 6 (1950 ff.).

19. Some contemporary philosophers have gone so far as to reject the need for a definitional procedure. See, for example, J. Lukasiewicz "The Principle of Individuation" (1953), p. 76.

20. Cf. Renford Bambrough, "Universals and Family Resemblances" (1960–61), and D. F. Pears, "Universals" (1951). For explicit rejections of this point of view, see Alan Donagan, "Universals and Metaphysical Realism" (1963); and Michael Loux, *Substance and Attribute: A Study in Ontology* (1978), p. 22.

21. Indeed, some may want to argue that this is in fact what Wittgenstein's notion of "family resemblance" means—whether it does or not is immaterial to us at present.

22. For example, Saul A. Kripke in *Naming and Necessity* (1981), third lecture, and Hilary Putnam in "It Ain't Necessarily So" (1962). The theory was developed to deal primarily with natural kind terms, such as 'tiger' and 'tree'. Of course, if the theory applies only to natural kind terms and "individuality" is not interpreted to be one of those, this objection would dissolve. I am assuming, then, that those who would use this objection would either extend the theory to cover terms for non-natural kinds or would consider "individuality" a natural kind term. See n. 25 below.

23. Kripke, *Naming and Necessity* (1981), p. 121.

24. Putnam, "It Ain't Necessarily So" (1962).

25. One salvo: I present this objection as an extrapolation from the new theory of reference. I do not know whether any proponent of the theory (should read "theories" in fact, since there is no uniform version of it on the market) will adhere to it. I tend to think that some proponents of it would not accept it. For one thing, the term 'individual' does not seem to be a "species" or "natural kind" term, while it is the last two to which the proponents of this theory apply it, as mentioned earlier. And Kripke, for example, accepts the view that "statements representing scientific discoveries about what the [read "a"] stuff *is* are not contingent truths but necessary truths in the strictest possible sense," in *Naming and Necessity* (1981), p. 125, which I take to mean that those statements identify metaphysically necessary and sufficient conditions (i.e., essential features) of things. But all this weakens the objection, and my purpose is to present it in its strongest possible form.

26. The view that intension determines extension is still very widespread. Indeed, it is still found in standard logic textbooks; see for example, Irving M. Copi, *Introduction to Logic* (1982), pp. 155–58.

27. All later major scholastics from the Middle Ages discussed this issue in one way or another, particularly after Duns Scotus introduced the formal distinction between the nature and thisness *(haecceitas)*. See the text referred to above.

28. See last chapter of Gracia, *Introduction to Individuation* (1984).

29. Strawson formulates the issue in terms of "identification" in *Individuals* (1959), pp. 2ff. And Bertrand Russell uses a clearly epistemological approach in *Human Knowledge: Its Scope and Limits* (1948), pp. 292 ff.

30. The distinction between these issues is sometimes blurred in the literature. Cf. D. M. Armstrong, *Nominalism and Realism* 1 (1980), pp. 118, where he speaks of spatio-temporality as the nature of particularity.

31. Both of these issues are different from the problem of identity or sameness through time. The problem of sameness concerns the identification of an individual at various times. How do we know, for example, that the man who was a teacher of Plato is the same man who drank the hemlock? This is an epistemological formulation of the problem and for that reason I would rather call it the problem of "reidentification" or of "recognition." The metaphysical formulation of the problem of identity or sameness would in turn investigate the cause or principle of such identity. These problems are related to the problem of individuation but are not equivalent to it.

32. See G. E. M. Anscombe, "The Principle of Individuation" (1953), pp. 83–96.

33. The confusion between the two is rampant in the literature and helped, no doubt, by the modern and contemporary attempt to reduce metaphysics to epistemology. Anscombe in "The Principle of Individuation" (1953), pp. 92–93, provides us with a good example of this confusion. Among the alternatives to matter she seriously considers as "principles of individuation" are definite descriptions and pointing, and while she later rejects them, it is clear that she does so for reasons other than the fact that they are quite absurd as individuating principles. No one in his right mind would

want to say that pointing to X (and/or giving a definite description of X) is a necessary and sufficient condition of X's individuality, just as no one in his right mind would want to argue that pointing to X's hair (and/or giving a definite description of X's hair) is a necessary and sufficient condition of X's hair. They make some sense only in the context of discernibility, which is indeed what Anscombe is after, even if she talks about "individuation" rather than discernment.

34. See, for example, Douglas C. Long, "Particulars and Their Qualities" (1970), p. 275.

35. A. J. Ayer, for example, in "The Identity of Indiscernibles," *Philosophical Essays* (1954), pp. 26–35, although it should be kept in mind that for Ayer the principle, "in the forms in which it is usually stated, is at best contingently true." Interestingly enough, Leibniz is usually regarded as having formulated and adhered to the Principle of the Identity of Indiscernibles and yet he explicitly distinguishes between the principle of knowing an individual (what I have called "the problem of identifying criteria of individual discernibility") and the principle of the being of an individual (what I have called "the problem of individuation"). But he fails to distinguish between individuality and numerical difference. See *Metaphysical Disputation,* lines 15 ff.

36. It is also possible to refer to individuals with indefinite linguistic descriptions, but in such cases some mental or contextual element is supplied which determines just which individual is involved. John T. Kearns, *Using Language: The Structures of Speech Acts* (1984), p. 398.

37. Russell, *Human Knowledge* (1948), p. 84.

38. This is the sort of view that is usually associated with John Stuart Mill in *A System of Logic* (proper names denote but do not connote) (1872).

39. Another example commonly found in the literature is 'The Evening Star is the Morning Star'. But this example is problematic, for it is not clear that the terms 'Evening Star' and 'Morning Star' do not constitute definite descriptions. It has been argued by some, for example, John Searle in "Proper Names and Descriptions" (1967), that it is this example precisely that may have led Frege to think that proper names have sense.

40. See Gottlob Frege, "Sense and Reference" (1952).

41. Again, this view has been challenged by many. For example, W.V.O. Quine in *From a Logical Point of View* (1953), and elsewhere.

Chapter 1

1. The term 'noninstantiability' has not been widely used in the literature in connection with individuality, although the notions of instance and instantiability are frequent. D. J. O'Connor, for example, uses the notion of instance to define the

individual: "By an individual, I shall mean any entity that possesses qualities (including relational properties) and is not itself an instance of either a quality or a relation" (in "The Identity of Indiscernibles" [1954], p. 103). McTaggart defined substance in a similar way in *The Nature of Existence* according to O'Connor. See also M. J. Loux, "Kinds and the Dilemma of Individuation" (1974), pp. 773–84. D. M. Armstrong speaks of a "Principle of Instantiation" in connection with universals *(Nominalism and Realism 1* [1980], p. 113). And Strawson uses the notion of instantiability and its negation in "On Particular and General" (1976), pp. 59–86. See also G. F. Stout, "Are the Characteristics of Particular Things Universal or Particular?" (1923), p. 116. And Russell, as early as 1912 spoke of individuals as instances; see "On the Relations of Universals and Particulars," in *Logic and Knowledge: Essays 1901–1950* (1956).

2. Kearns, *Using Language* (1984), p. 87.

3. This sort of objection is found for the first time in the Middle Ages. See William of Ockham, *Ordinatio* I, dist. II, q. 6, in *Opera philosophica et theologica* (1967-); and the Introduction to Gracia, *Suárez on Individuation* (1982), pp. 10–15. The point of the objection is to indicate that if individuality is a feature of things, then it is not really *sui generis* to any one individual.

4. Gaos, *De la filosofia* (1982), pp. 133 ff.

5. See Gracia, *Introduction to Individuation* (1984), last chapter. Among the scholastics who adopt this view are Thomas Aquinas and Francisco Suárez.

6. Most continental philosophers follow this line of thought. But even in Latin America we find examples. See Francisco Romero, *Teoría del hombre* (1952), and Gracia, "Romero y la individualidad," *Francisco Romero: Maestro de la filosofia latinoamericana* (1983), pp. 85–102.

7. The uncritical nature of this position makes it difficult to find any true adherents to it, although there are many authors who point out why it is necessary to modify this view (see note about adherents to the relative indivisibility view). But occasionally one finds texts from the most uncritical authors of the medieval period (cf. John Eriugena's *Periphyseon*) and even from our contemporaries (cf. Antonio Caso, *La persona y el Estado totalitario* (1986), p. 43), that seem to take this position.

8. See the Introduction to Gracia, *Suárez on Individuation* (1982), pp. 2–6.

9. Goodman's view, that an individual is an entity such that no other entity breaks down into exactly the same entities as itself, has interesting similarities and differences with the Relative Indivisibility View. The similarities have to do with the fact that individuality involves indivisibility into entities; the differences hover around the comparison of the entities or parts of one individual with the entities or parts of another, rather than between the individual and the entities or parts into which it is divided. So, for example, for Goodman, Socrates and Aristotle would be individual because neither the entities or parts into which Socrates can be divided, nor those into which Aristotle can be divided, are the same (or are the same as the entities or parts of anything else). But for a traditional holder of the Relative Indivisibility View, Socrates

is an individual because he cannot be divided into other human beings, that is, into entities of the same type as the original. Incidentally, Goodman's view seems to have some serious difficulties. For one thing, it assumes that individuals must have parts or entities of which they are composed, ruling out the perfectly cogent notion of a simple individual. Moreover, it seems to conceive individuality as a kind of difference and, therefore, as relational. But that view, as shall become clear shortly, is subject to important objections. For Goodman's view, see "A World of Individuals," in Charles Landesman, ed., *The Problem of Universals* (1971), p. 296.

10. Cf. Francisco Suárez, *Disputationes metaphysicae*, Disp. V, sect. 1, par. 3 (1982).

11. Ibid.

12. I owe this example to Scott Roberts.

13. In fact, the controversy concerning the Principle of the Identity of Indiscernibles is in certain respects the result of the interpretation of individuality as distinction, as we shall see later. See, for example, Max Black "The Identity of Indiscernibles," in *Problems of Analysis* (1954); and in particular A. J. Ayer, "The Identity of Indiscernibles" (1954), pp. 26. ff. P. F. Strawson, in "On Particular and General," in Loux's *Universals and Particulars* (1976), p. 67, argues that the idea of an individual instance involves both distinction and recognition. And in *Individuals* (1959), chap. 3, s. 4, he argues that there is no principle of unity where there is no principle of differentiation. See also Moore, "Are the Characteristics of Particular Things Universal or Particular?" (1923), p. 101, and Hamlyn *Metaphysics* (1984), p. 69. Apart from contemporary figures, most modern and many medieval authors either explicitly interpret individuality as difference or fail to distinguish between the two. See, for example, Leibniz, *Metaphysical Disputation,* 1. 30 (1965) and elsewhere. But there are others who make the distinction. Among these is Suárez (*Metaphysical Disputation* V, s. 1 [1982]) and Peter of Auvergne (*Quodlibet* II, q. 5 [1934]). I have found two contemporary authors who seem to disagree with the tradition that interprets individuality as difference: Castañeda in "Individuation and Non-Identity" (1975), p. 131 ff., and K. R. Popper in "The Principle of Individuation" (1953), pp. 99 ff. Both authors seem to identify the problem of difference and distinction as epistemological (Castañeda, p. 131; Popper, p. 101).

14. According to Marc Cohen in "Aristotle and Individuation," (1984), p. 42 and elsewhere, the distinction between actual and possible individuals gives rise to two forms of the principle of individuation. But this is the case only when individuality is interpreted as distinction or difference.

15. Boethius, *De Trinitate* I, in *The Theological Tractates* (1968), p. 6.

16. For a contemporary interpretation of individuality as otherness and of the individual as other, see John Martine, *Individuals and Individuality* (1984), pp. 3–4, 63, 68, 75, 78.

17. I owe this point to William Rapaport.

18. Castañeda defends a similar thesis in "Individuation and Non-Identity: A New Look" (1975), pp. 131–40.

19. See Black, "The Identity of Indiscernibles" (1954).

20. See Ayer, "The Identity of Indiscernibles" (1954), p. 33.

21. See O'Connor, "The Identity of Indiscernibles" (1954), p. 103.

22. See Bertrand Russell, *The Principles of Mathematics*, cited by Ayer in "The Identity of Indiscernibles" (1954), p. 27.

23. Suárez gathers the standard arguments developed during the period in *Disputationes metaphysicae*, Disp. VI, s. 3, par. 2 (1861), p. 212.

24. *In "Isagogen" Porphyrii commentorum editio secunda* (1966), p. 228; in *Patrologia latina* 64, 111.

25. One thing that is clear, however, is that many scholastics were well aware of the distinction between "individuation" and "multiplication within the species." In fact they sometimes referred to species with single instantiation to underline the fact. Thus, for example, Peter of Auvergne speaks of the sun, the moon and the heaven, in *Quodlibet* II, q. 5 (1934), p. 373.

26. In modern times, those who interpret universals as sets and those who require multiple instantiability of universals belong to this group. There are texts from Russell and Sellars, as we shall see in Chapter 4, that may imply support for this position. In the Middle Ages, Ockham could be interpreted as a proponent of this position, even if a careful examination of his views would cast some doubts on this interpretation. And Castañeda explicitly accuses Bergmann of "mixing individuality and plurality" in "Individuality and Non-Identity" (1975), p. 132b. The Gustav Bergmann text to which he refers is found in *Logic and Reality* (1964), pp. 159 ff.

27. Thomas Aquinas in *On Spiritual Creatures* (1951).

28. The problem involved in the development of criteria for personal identity has been intensely debated in contemporary philosophical literature. See, for example, John Perry, *Personal Identity* (1975), but it is a derivative problem and one that need not be discussed here.

29. I am assuming, of course, that we are considering the same Socrates, not two different ones. Otherwise, there could be differences between the two. More on possible individuals later on.

30. See, for example, Suárez, *Disputationes metaphysicae*, Disp. XL, s. 8, par. 7 (1861), vol. 26, p. 579.

31. In a recent article ("Transtemporal Stability in Aristotelian Substances" (1978), Furth has introduced the distinction between "diachronic" and "synchronic" approaches to individuation. The first would involve questions about what individuates a thing at different times, while the second would involve questions about individuation at the same time. This terminology would be quite acceptable here were it not for

the fact that the issues with which I am concerned at this point are not of individuation at one time versus individuation at different times, but rather the issue of individuation versus individual continuity, or of individuality interpreted as some kind of identity through space and time and individuality interpreted in some other way.

32. For a criticism, see A. J. Ayer, "Individuals," *Philosophical Essays* (1954), p. 3.

33. Indeed, according to many Christian theologians, God is outside the realm of time and change.

34. The rest of the discussion in this section follows the points made in Jorge J. E. Gracia, "Numerical Continuity in Material Substances: The Principle of Identity in Thomistic Metaphysics" (1979), pp. 77-78.

35. Among those few who have clearly distinguished individuality from identity in contemporary literature is G. E. M. Anscombe, in "The Principle of Individuation" (1953). On the other hand, Henry Veatch leaves them undistinguished in "Essentialism and the Problem of Individuation" (1974).

36. The difference between proper names and universal terms is not universally accepted today. See W. V. O. Quine, *Word and Object* (1960).

37. They also used the expression 'not predicable of many'. The distinction between the 'is' of predication and the 'is' of identity does not seem to be explicitly formulated until the nineteenth century, with the development of quantification theory.

38. Aristotle, *De interpretatione*, chap. 7, 17a38 (1941), and Boethius, *Commentary on the "De interpretatione*," in *Patrologia latina* 64, 318–19.

39. Strawson, *Individuals* (1959), chap. v.

40. Ayer in "Individuals" (1954), p. 3.

41. This is the case of those medieval authors for whom predication was something more than a logical relation. For example, John of Salisbury in the twelfth century complains that there are many (e.g., Abailard) who deny that "things are predicable of other things," maintaining that only concepts or terms are predicable of other terms. See John of Salisbury's *Metalogicon*, bk. II, chap. 17 (1929), p. 92. More recently, Loux, in *Substance and Attribute* (1978), p. 90, has argued against a purely linguistic view of predication.

42. One may want to interpret the attitude of some disciples of Wittgenstein in this way. See, for example, R. Bambrough, "Universals and Family Resemblances" (1960-61).

43. This is a very widespread confusion, although its supporters would rather regard it as a "view." However, since most of the time it is assumed rather than explicitly defended, it is difficult to grant it the status of a "position." The view that particulars should be identified with substances was explicitly defended by Russell in "On the Relations of Universals and Particulars," in *Logic and Knowledge* (1956), next to the last paragraph. See also Loux, *Substance and Attributes* (1978), p. 107.

44. Chap. 5, 2a10.

45. Castañeda, "Individuation and Non-Identity" (1975), p. 132 b.

46. Mario Bunge, "¿Qué es un individuo?" (1985), p. 123. For Aristotle, see *Categories*, chap. 5, 4a10, but note that he distinguished substantiality from individuality (3b10).

47. For Castañeda, however, they have second-order properties.

48. *De interpretatione* in *Patrologia latina* 64, 462–64. In the first edition of his *Commentary on Porphyry's "Isagoge"* (1906, p. 81), written earlier he had introduced the notion of nontransferability. This is not picked up by others, but Milton Fisk in *Nature and Necessity: An Essay in Physical Ontology* (1973), p. 65, uses the notion of "transference" or "transferral" in connection with "similarity" among individuals.

49. It is found, for example, in Thomas Aquinas and later authors, including Francisco Suárez. For Suárez see *Disputationes metaphysicae*, Disp. V, s. 1 (1861), vol. 25, pp. 145 ff.

50. Boethius, *Commentary on Porphyry's "Isagoge,"* bk. I, chap. 10 (1906), pp. 160–61. The examples are mine.

51. In a recent book, Martine rejects the view that individuals can be described as instances. The reason he gives for this rejection is that this view "is ultimately reducible to the claim that individuals are nothing if not clusters of universals" (*Individuals and Individuality* [1984], p. 2). But this surely does not follow, for, as already stated, one can still hold on to the notion of noninstantiable instances and understand universals as instantiable. As we shall see later, I reject the cluster theory of the individual, while accepting the view that individuals are noninstantiable instances.

52. Some philosophers speak of "exemplification" rather than instantiation (Bergmann, *The Metaphysics of Logical Positivism* [1954], p. 52; Donagan, "Universals and Metaphysical Realism" [1970], pp. 135 ff.; Loux, *Substance and Attribute* [1978], p. 89), but this terminology is not quite felicitous. The main problem with it is that the models that become, as it were, "exemplified" in this scheme, can and are often individual. One can talk without awkwardness about Socrates being a model of virtue or about Aristotle being a model of philosophical acumen. But if models are exemplifiable then they should not be individual (i.e., nonexemplifiable). For the language of exemplification to work, one would have to restrict its meaning and usage arbitrarily, while there is no such need with the language of instantiation.

53. The first counterexample was suggested to me by Kenneth Barber and Zeno Swijtink.

54. I am presenting the counterexample in its strongest form, namely, when it assumes the exact identity of the clones with the cloned original. But, as we know, clones are not completely identical with the cloned original; they are only genetically identical.

55. Loux, in *Substance and Attribute* (1978), p. 5, gives the definition of particulars used by metaphysical realists as "entities that cannot be multiply examplified." Substitute 'exemplified' by 'instantiated' and we have the view opposite to the one I defend here.

56. Moore, for example, adopts the view that a universal need not be instantiated more than once in order to be universal in "Are the Characteristics of Particular Things Universal or Particular?" (1923), pp. 112-13. That is not sufficient, however, to establish that multiple instantiability is not a necessary condition of universality, since even if some universals are instantiated only once, this could be regarded as a contingent rather than as a necessary fact. For the view that universality does not imply multiple instantiability to work, it would have to be necessary that some universals be capable of being instantiated once and only once. Of course, this consequence is not inconsistent with Moore's definition of a universal as what "is either predicable of something or is a relation" (see ibid.), since there are predicates that if predicated at all can be predicated of only one thing. This is the case with many definite descriptions and the other examples given in the text below.

57. Ayer, "Individuals" and "The Identity of Indiscernibles" (1954), pp. 12, 20, 31.

58. The view that there are features which are subject only to single instantiation is not foreign to the contemporary literature. Alvin Plantinga, for example, has called such features "singular properties," in "The Boethian Compromise" (1978), p. 137.

59. Some scholastics, for example, tried to explain the relation between individuality and distinction by saying that distinction implies individuality, but not vice versa. See, for example, Suárez, *Disputatio metaphysica* V, s. 1 (1982).

60. Strawson, *Individuals* (1959), chap. 3, s. 4.

61. For the primitiveness of "person," see ibid.; for that of characterized particulars, see Douglas Long, "Particulars and Their Qualities" (1970).

62. Strawson, *Individuals* (1959), chap. 3.

63. That clarity is one of the conditions necessary for regarding a notion as primitive is accepted by many. See Dana Scott, "Advice on Modal Logic," (1970), p. 144.

64. Peter of Auvergne, *Quodlibet* II, q. 5 (1934), p. 371.

65. These are common scholastic doctrines. See Suárez, *Disputatio metaphysica* LIV, s. 5 (1861), vol. 26.

66. *Disputatio metaphysica* V, s. 1.

67. Popper, "The Principle of Individuation" (1953).

Chapter 2

1. Peter Damian (1007–1072) went so far as to claim that the devil had been the first teacher of grammar because he taught Adam to decline *deus* in the plural. E. Gilson, *History of Christian Philosophy in the Middle Ages* (1955), p. 616. Among other philosophers who have explicitly rejected God's individuality are Baruch Spinoza, *Epistolae* (1928), p. 50; and P. T. Geach, *Reason and Reality* (1972), p. 21.

2. Ayer, in "Individuals" (1954), pp. 1 ff, cites the case of the American Constitution rather than the Declaration of Independence, however. Moreover, in keeping with most contemporary discussions of these issues, he poses the problem in terms of the distinction between "individuals" and "properties" (p. 1), but later it becomes clear that he is speaking about "individuals" and "universals" as well (pp. 2 ff.).

3. But Ayer has also doubted it in the mentioned article.

4. Like many Aristotelian *formulae*, this one is recorded in the writings of Aristotle's followers, but not in his own.

5. The terms 'realism' and 'nominalism' have been used so differently in the history of philosophy that they will be of little help in sorting out anything unless their meaning is made clear. This is why I have made an effort to make explicit the conditions of their usage in this study. Moreover, I believe the way of understanding them presented here is the most consonant with the classical and medieval traditions, where the terms originate. Some contemporary definitions of these terms, such as that given by Bergmann in one of his works, would create considerable confusion if used to discuss classical and medieval views, for example. Bergmann's definition of a realistic ontology, in *Logic and Reason* (1964), p. 133, is as follows: "An ontology is realistic if and only if its individuals and its universals are both things and there are only two fundamental ontological differences between them; one, the obvious one; the other, that individuals are only numerically different (bare)." Other contemporaries, on the other hand, like Armstrong, have given definitions more concordant with traditional views. See Armstrong, *Nominalism and Realism* 1 (1980), p. 12.

6. I am quite aware, for example, that Plato did not use words whose meaning is equivalent to the terms 'instance', 'instantiable', and 'noninstantiable'; indeed, it is not clear he used the equivalent to the word 'universal'. Most of the terminology we use today is of Latin origin and came to us through translators who sometimes were inconsistent in their usage and often could not find exact Latin synonyms for Greek terms. In support of the view that Plato accorded the highest ontological status to what I have called here instantiables and the ontological status of appearance to noninstantiable instances, cf. *Republic*, bk. V, 507 ff. (1961). Supporting texts can also be found in the *Phaedo, Symposium, Parmenides* and elsewhere.

7. John M. Robinson, *An Introduction to Early Greek Philosophy* (1968), pp. 110–13.

8. It is considerations such as these that led Augustine to propose that knowledge would be impossible without divine illumination. Cf. *De magistro* (1968), a dialogue inspired in Plato's *Meno* (1961).

9. *Metaphysics* 990b1 ff. (1924).

10. There have been some exceptions to this. Russell, for example, defends a version of Transcendental Realism in *The Problems of Philosophy* (1912).

11. One of the most recent and thorough is given by Armstrong in *Nominalism and Realism* 1 (1980), pp. 66–76.

12. Even this example is not convincing, for it is not at all clear that what one sees is the universal white and not the individual white. If what I see when I see a white thing is "white" rather than "that white," then one could argue that the universal would have to be in space and time, and to have dimensions, and so on, for whenever I see white I always see it here and now, under these, or other, dimensions and not just as white, apart from time, space, and dimensions. But if the universal is subject to spatio-temporal location, then it can be in different places simultaneously, since many white things exist simultaneously. And this simultaneous multiple spatio-temporal location is not easy to explain. I bring these points up only to indicate that the example is controversial and does not constitute sufficient grounds to support the realist position. I shall have more to say about features later in the chapter.

13. For supporters of this view see the notes to the discussion of the Bundle View of Individuation in Chapter 4.

14. Armstrong, *Nominalism and Realism* 1 (1980), p. 76.

15. Since Transcendental Realism identifies the universal with something outside the individual, and the instance of the universal is only an appearance, whatever happens to that instance need not affect either the universal itself or other appearances.

16. For a different version of this argument and its answer, see Wolterstorff's "Qualities," in Loux, *Universals and Particulars* (1970), p. 94. The linguistic character of Wolterstorff's formulation and answer, however, detracts from its effectiveness.

17. Armstrong, in *Nominalism and Realism* 1 (1980), p. 112.

18. I owe this example and the objection to Kenneth Barber.

19. Of course, some of those who defend this view would deny this by resorting to differences implied by such features as place. But this move changes the view substantially as we shall see later.

20. See Plato's *Republic*, toward the end of Bk. V. This point has been repeated often enough in the history of philosophy.

21. This formula became popular in the Middle Ages and can also be found in some modern philosophers like Locke, although its interpretation varies considerably from author to author and in some cases is given more eclectic interpretations. This is in fact

the case with Locke. Many medievals referred to Aristotle to back up the formula, but Aristotle never stated it in quite the way we have. An approximation to it, however, is found in the *Categories* (later on in the *Metaphysics*, a much more realistic position seems to emerge), but even there (2b5) the position he adopts is that the existence of individual substances is a necessary condition for the existence of corresponding genera, species, and accidents, and not that only individuals exist. For the more realistic position of the *Metaphysics* see Owen, in I. Barnes et al., eds., *Articles on Aristotle* 1 (1979).

22. Some contemporary authors refer to universals also as "abstract particulars," "tropes," "aspects," and "cases." The first two are used by D. C. Williams in *Principles of Empirical Realism* (1953) and the last two by Wolterstorff in *On Universals* (1970), pp. 133 ff. For Ockham, see *Summa logicae*, chap. 15, and *Ordinatio*, d. 2, q. 7 (*prima redactio*) — in Boehner's ed. (1957), pp. 35 ff. Among other contemporary authors who seem to subscribe to a generally nominalist position are Quine, *From a Logical Point of View* (1961), p. 10, and Sellars, *Science and Metaphysics* (1967), p. 107.

23. Wolterstorff argues in favor of indecidability in "Qualities," see Loux, *Universals and Particulars* (1970). Others argue, however, that the onus of proof lies with Nominalism, since ordinary language and thought seem to support Realism (Armstrong, *Nominalism and Realism* 1 [1980], p. 19).

24. It should be pointed out that some philosophers classify some of these views as versions of Realism because they imply that the universal is more than a word. Thus, Abailard, for example, argued that what I have called here Collectionism is indeed a form of Realism. See *Logica ingredientibus* (1919), pp. 10 and 14.

25. The reporter is Anselm of Aosta in *Epistola de Incarnatione Verbi* (1952), chap. 2. But Anselm does not name Roscelin and, as Gilson has pointed out in *The History of Christian Philosophy* (1955), p. 625, Roscelin may have just been "restating in his own way what he had read in Priscian."

26. In an effort to explain how original sin affects all human beings, Odo of Tournai argued that all human beings are substantially one, for example. See Gracia, *Introduction to Individuation* (1984), pp. 135-36.

27. Whatever remains has been gathered in F. Picavet, *Roscelin philosophe et théologien d'après la légende et d'après l'histoire* (1911).

28. Abailard, *Logica nostrorum* (1919), p. 522.

29. Abailard, *Dialectica* (1956), pp. 69 and 112.

30. Cf. Armstrong, *Nominalism and Realism* 1 (1980), pp. 12–14, who refers to John Searle, *Speech Acts: Essay in the Philosophy of Language* (1969), pp. 105 and 120, as holding this view.

31. *De interpretatione*, chap. 7, 17a38 (1941).

32. Abailard, *Logica ingredientibus* (1919), pp. 19–20.

33. Cf. Armstrong, *Nominalism and Realism* 1 (1980), pp. 17–24.

34. Ibid., p. 25.

35. All these views were popular in the medieval period and some authors held several of them at various stages of their thought. A case in point is William of Ockham. See *Summa totius logicae* I, chaps. 14–16 (1967 ff.), and *Ordinatio*, d. 2, q. 8.

36. David Hume, *A Treatise of Human Nature* I, 1, (1975), pp. 1 ff. Of course, if these images are interpreted as resemblances or similarities, then Hume's position has much in common with what I later call "Similarism."

37. Rapaport brought to my attention the similarity between this view and that held in "procedural semantics," where the meaning of a term is conceived as a procedure (algorithm) used in processing sentences containing that term.

38. See Quine's "On What There Is," in Landesman, ed., *The Problem of Universals* (1971), p. 216.

39. The classical statement of the doctrine is discussed in Plato's *Parmenides*, but one can find a favorable recent discussion of it in H. H. Price, *Thinking and Experience* (1953), chap. 1. For other extensive discussions of the Resemblance Theory see P. K. Butchvarov, *Resemblance and Identity* (1966) and Armstrong, *Nominalism and Realism* 1 (1980), chap. 5.

40. Cf. A. E. Duncan-Jones, "Universals and Particulars" (1934), p. 85.

41. Armstrong, *Nominalism and Realism* 1 (1980), p. 51.

42. Armstrong goes as far as to say that "it is difficult to find a philosopher who explicitly defends" it, in ibid., p. 28. His name for this view is "Class Nominalism."

43. John of Salisbury ascribes this position, in *Metalogicon* (1929), bk. II, chap. 17, to Joscelin, Bishop of Soissons. And Abailard describes and argues against this view in *Logica ingredientibus* (1919), p. 14.

44. Among those who seem to support versions of this position are D. C. Williams in "The Elements of Being" (1953), and Wolterstorff, "Qualities," in Loux, *Universals and Particulars* (1970), pp. 99 ff. Wilfrid Sellars argues for a purely extensional theory of universals in *Science, Perception and Reality* (1963), pp. 282 ff. H. H. Price interpreted natural kinds as "groups of objects which have *many* . . features in common" in *Thinking and Experience* (1953), first page of chap. 1. Perhaps even Stout's notion of the universal as a distributive unity, in "The Nature of Universals and Propositions," *The Problem of Universals*, ed. by Landesman (1971), pp. 155 and 156, can be assimilated to this view.

45. *Parmenides* (1961), 131. Armstrong calls this position "Mereological Nominalism" in *Nominalism and Realism* 1 (1980), p. 34, and Bocheński refers to it as the "bit" view (individuals are bits of the whole) in "The Problem of Universals" (1956), p. 47.

46. As Boethius put it, the universal "is in the individuals wholly"; *Commentaria in Porphyrium* (1891), p. 83.

47. For a more detailed discussion of Class Nominalism, see Armstrong, *Nominalism and Realism* 1 (1980), pp. 29–34.

48. See Abailard's criticism in the text mentioned in no. 24 above.

49. For some attempts in this direction, see C. Lejewski, "On Lesniewski's Ontology" (1958).

50. Wolterstorff, *On Universals*, chap. 8 (1970).

51. Armstrong, *Nominalism and Realism* 1 (1980), p. 37.

52. The introduction of the notion of resemblance at this point as a way of answering some of these questions does not seem to be helpful. For one can always ask about the arbitrary or nonarbitrary character of resemblance itself. For a defense of Nominalism based on this notion, see Wolterstorff's "Qualities," in Loux, *Universals and Particulars* (1970), pp. 206–208.

53. Loux brings this up in *Substance and Attribute* (1978), p. 74.

54. D. C. Williams would probably take this road if pressed on this point. See *Principles of Empirical Realism* (1966), p. 239.

55. Cf. Kripke in *Naming and Necessity* (1980), pp. 24, 157–58, for some remarks to the contrary. In fact, I am told breeding of this kind has already happened and a controversy over whether such "genetically engineered" animals exhibited at a circus in New York were entitled to be advertised as unicorns has ensued. And Lucretius argued that there are some mythical beings that cannot exist, although this is so only if their parts are incompatible, as it happens with centaurs. See *De rerum natura* (1873), p. 878. Thus, Lucretius would agree with Kripke only if one could show an incompatibility of parts in unicorns.

56. Armstrong, *Nominalism and Realism* 1 (1980), p. 36.

57. Formulated thus, this view closely resembles that of Duns Scotus. See *Opus oxoniense* II, d. 3, q. 1. In *Opera Omnia* (1950 ff.).

58. Of course, not everyone agrees with this. Meinongians, like Castañeda and Rapaport, seem to hold that chairs, too, have a peculiar sort of being.

59. This view closely resembles that of Thomas Aquinas. See *On Being and Essence*, chap. 3 (1968).

60. Armstrong formulates this position in terms of predicates in *Nominalism and Realism* 1 (1980), p. 12.

61. This is the sort of view that P. F. Strawson holds in *Individuals* (1959), p. 2. Versions of it are widespread in contemporary circles. But there is a qualification that must be made. Many of those who accept this view nowadays regard it as being part of

what Strawson has called "descriptive metaphysics," that is, a description of the way we think about the world, not of the way the world is in itself. In that respect, the view of many contemporary philosophers differs drastically from that of most pre-Kantian philosophers. The latter, adapting Strawson's own words to our purposes, were "revisionists," since they were attempting to describe the way things are and consequently were engaged in many ways in changing the way we think about them. See Preface, above.

62. Gustav Bergmann, *Realism, A Critique of Brentano and Meinong* (1967), p. 24.

63. One word of caution: some supporters of this view go so far as to say that bare particulars "are not"; ibid: "Bare particulars neither are nor have natures." I am not sure what is meant by this, but I hope my use of the word 'existence' in the presentation of this view is taken in such a way that it does not contradict the thrust of the view.

64. The main proponent in contemporary circles of this position is Gustav Bergmann, but for a brief and clear exposition of the advantages of the view, see Edwin B. Allaire's "Bare Particulars" (1963).

65. See John Duns Scotus, *Opus oxoniense* II, d. 3, q. 6. In *Opera omnia* (1950ff.).

66. Aristotle, *Metaphysics* VII, 1029a23 (1941), p. 785.

67. Loux, *Substance and Attribute* (1978), pp. 112–13; and Armstrong, *Nominalism and Realism* 1 (1980), pp. 102–3.

68. Locke, *Essay* II, 23, 2 (1959).

69. There are others that have to do with other aspects of the theory. Some proponents of the view hold that bare particulars are not "continuants" and, therefore, that changes in things imply exchanges of bare particulars. See Bergmann, *Realism, A Critique of Brentano and Meinong* (1967), pp. 112 ff. This has given rise to questions regarding identity through time and change. However, since we have explicitly distinguished between individuality and identity through time and change, I shall not discuss this objection here. Moreover, Sellars has argued that the notion of bare particular is self-contradictory, since bare particulars are both supposed to be bare and also exemplify universals, in *Science, Perception and Reality* (1963), pp. 282–83. But I find this objection both superficial and inocuous. The proponent of bare particulars can easily answer that it is only bare particulars *qua* bare particulars that lack features and not bare particulars as individuators or as exemplifiers of features. See Robert Baker, "Particulars: Bare, Naked, and Nudes" (1967), p. 211. I am not impressed either by Loux's argument in *Substance and Attribute* (1978), pp. 147 ff., that the contradiction in the notion of bare particular lies in the fact that bare particulars are supposed to have no properties and yet that entails having the feature of "having no properties." Indeed, he also claims that they have transcendental properties such as "self-identity," "being human or nonhuman," and "being colored if green." But this is a verbal objection, for surely one can find categorical differences between such things as "white" and "being colored if white." And to say that having no properties is a property is very much like saying that having no color is a color. Interestingly

enough, Armstrong, in *Nominalism and Realism* 1 (1980), pp. 103–4, also rejects Loux's objection but actually seems to be convinced by a somewhat similar argument on p. 105. For Bergmann's view on some of these issues see *Logic and Reality* (1964), pp. 45–63.

70. I am using Allaire's formulation in "Bare Particulars" (1963), n. 2, but the Principle of Acquaintance is also adopted by others and formulated in various ways. See, for example, Herbert Hochberg, "Ontology and Acquaintance" (1966), p. 53.

71. Allaire, "Bare Particulars" (1963).

72. Ibid.

73. This point was made by V. C. Chappell, "Particulars Re-Clothed" (1964).

74. Edwin Allaire, "Another Look at Bare Particulars" (1965), p. 21.

75. See Bergmann, "Synthetic A Priori," in *Logic and Reality* (1964). This view resembles in many ways scholastic views in which place, understood as the innermost boundary of what contains a thing, was identified as the principle of individuation. See Gracia, *Introduction to Individuation* (1984), chap. 3.

76. Aristotle, *Categories*, chap. 5, 3a22 (1941).

77. D. C. Long, "Particulars and Their Qualities" (1970), pp. 280–81.

78. Loux, *Substance and Attribute* (1978), p. 163.

79. Ibid., pp. 158–63.

80. See Section on Immanent Realism above.

81. Boethius, *De Trinitate* II (1968), referred to spatio-temporal coordinates as "place."

82. Cf. Wolterstorff, "Qualities" (1960), in Loux, *Universals and Particulars* (1970), p. 93.

83. By this I do not mean to endorse the substance-feature distinction, since I have given no arguments for its support. For present purposes it is sufficient to refer to the ordinary distinction between a thing and its features.

84. The popularity of the view in the medieval period was partly due to the fact that the medievals understood Aristotle to adhere to it. See Aristotle, *Categories*, chap. 2, 1a22–23 (1941). For a dissenting voice see G. E. L. Owen, "Inherence" (1965).

85. In this century, G. F. Stout has been one of its main defenders; see "Are the Characteristics of Particular Things Universal or Particular?" (1923), and "The Nature of Universals and Propositions," in Landesman, *The Problem of Universals* (1971). Another more recent supporter is D. C. Williams in "The Elements of Being" (1953).

86. One of the most recent attacks of the view appears in Armstrong, *Nominalism and Realism* 1 (1980), pp. 77–87, although the view he attacks there is different in many respects from the view defended here.

87. The terminology varies widely. Williams, "The Elements of Being" (1953), calls them "tropes"; Wolterstorff, *On Universals* (1970), uses "cases"; and for Bergmann, *Realism* (1967), they are "perfect particulars."

88. Stout, "Are the Characteristics of Particular Things Universal or Particular?" (1923), p. 121.

89. Moore, "Are the Characteristics of Particular Things Universal or Particular?" (1923), p. 107.

90. Stout's example, in Landesman, *The Problem of Universals* (1971), p. 157.

91. Wolterstorff, "Qualities," in Loux, *Universals and Particulars* (1970), p. 104.

92. Armstrong saw this clearly in *Nominalism and Realism* 1 (1980), p. 79.

93. G. F. Stout, in Landesman, *The Problem of Universals* (1971), p. 157. Armstrong tries to assail the argument in *Nominalism and Realism* 1 (1980), pp. 81–82, by denying the assumption that a substance is nothing but the sum of its features (in his words: "an individual is nothing but the sum of its properties").

94. Gaos, *De la filosofía* (1982), p. 124.

95. This is what Armstrong does in *Nominalism and Realism* 1 (1980), pp. 79–81.

96. Ibid., p. 86; Section VIII of Suárez's Disputation V asks "Whether it is incompatible for two accidents, diverse only in number, to be simultaneously [present] in the same subject owing to their individuality"; in *Metaphysical Disputation* V (1982), pp. 145 ff.

97. Armstrong, *Nominalism and Realism* 1 (1980), p. 86.

98. Suárez, *Metaphysical Disputation* V (1982), p. 154.

99. Ibid., p. 121.

100. Ibid., pp. 146 ff.

101. Armstrong gives what he considers a decisive argument against this view in *Nominalism and Realism* 1 (1980), p. 86, which depends on individual properties (the yellowness of this lemon) having universal properties (being a certain shade of yellow). But this objection rests on the mistaken assumption that to hold this view is to hold that the individuality of features implies this consequence. Individual features *do not have* features; they *are instances* of those features, at least in my view.

102. Hamlyn, *Metaphysics* (1984), p. 93.

103. The similarity between the instances of thoughts is one of the reasons Averroes held that there was only one intellect for all beings capable of understanding. See *In "De anima"* (1953), pp. 401, 439, 452. But this, of course, is absurd, as it is absurd to conclude that similarity of color implies numerical identity of color. For the medieval controversy concerning the issue of the intellects, see Gracia, "The Doctrine of the Possible and Agent Intellects in Gonsalvus Hispanus' Question XIII" (1969).

104. A third way to establish existence which some philosophers favor is indirect or, as some would put it, "through transcendental proofs." But I see no reason to consider this a third category, since what is involved in these "proofs" is either a mixture of definition and experience or some kind of conceptual analysis. In the first case, we have a hybrid that need not be addressed separately, and in the second we have something very similar to a process not very different from that of formulating definitions.

105. See G. E. Moore, "Proof of the External World," in *Philosophical Papers* (1959), pp. 127 ff.

106. Barber in his comments to me.

107. Of course, Transcendental Realism tries to solve this problem by separating "man" and "men" and saying that necessary existence attaches only to the first, while contingent existence attaches to the second. But we saw already the difficulties created by this move.

108. The scholastics made this point by separating two issues concerning any thing: what it is from whether it is.

109. For a contrary position see Armstrong, *Nominalism and Realism* 1 (1980), p. 2.

110. Probably inspired by Aristotle, *Categories*, chap. 5, 2b5 (1941).

111. This seems to be the view defended by Dummett in *Frege* (1973). Abailard seems to think that "rose" is significant only as long as someone can think of it, in *Logica ingredientibus* (1919), pp. 29–30. Of course, for Abailard to signify means "to cause an understanding," so that it would really not make much sense to say that a universal was significant unless there were some minds that understood it.

112. Hamlyn, *Metaphysics* (1984), pp. 102–4.

113. Of course, that there is no distinction between "human being" and "centaur" *qua* universals does not entail that there is no distinction between "human being" and "square circle." The difference between the former and the latter is that the former is consistent, just as the notion of centaur is consistent, but the latter is contradictory.

114. For a recent reference to this classic objection, see Hamlyn, *Metaphysics* (1984), p. 102.

115. There are other senses of the word 'real' both in ordinary discourse and in philosophical discourse, but if clarified adequately, they should not militate against the point made here.

116. Thomas Aquinas, *On Being and Essence* (1968), pp. 46 ff. Veatch has defended this point of view in *Intentional Logic* (1952), pp. 111–13, and Owens has argued that it belonged to Aristotle in *The Doctrine of Being in the Aristotelian Metaphysics* (1957), pp. 242 ff.

Chapter 3

1. See, for example, Suárez, *Disputatio metaphysica* V, s. 2; in Gracia, *Suárez on Individuation* (1982), pp. 41 ff.

2. It must be remembered that, according to the scholastics, and as we saw earlier, there are two types of natures: substantial (generic or specific) and accidental. Moreover, a nature can be considered as a whole (for example, man), or as a part (for example, Peter's humanity). The status of all of these was discussed at length in the Middle Ages. Cf. Thomas Aquinas, *On Being and Essence*, chap. 2, par. 13 (1968), p. 44. However, since this concerns more universals than individuals, I shall not discuss these matters here.

3. For reasons of convenience, the examples used here are taken from Aristotelian primary substances, but it should be kept in mind that, according to what was said in the previous chapter, individuality extends to the features of things as well.

4. One of the few who did was perhaps Roscelin of Compiègne, to whom we have already referred earlier, and who said that a universal was a *flatus vocis*. No one has been able to make much sense of his reported statement, beyond what we suggested in Chapter 2, however.

5. William of Ockham seems to have maintained this point of view. See *Ordinatio* I, d. 2, q. 6 (1967 ff.).

6. Some held, however, that there is a real (roughly extensional) distinction between the individual and/or its individuality on the one hand, and the nature on the other, even if the nature is not real. For in order to have a real (roughly extensional) distinction, it is sufficient that one of the distinct entities (or distinguishing features) be real. This is Suárez's view in *Disputatio* V (1982), pp. 9 ff.

7. Suárez refers to this argument in *Disputatio metaphysica* V, s. 2, par. 2 (1982).

8. For Duns Scotus it is a formal distinction, for example, while for others it is real. See *Opus oxoniense* II, d. 3, q. 6 (1950 ff.).

9. The texts from Aristotle and Plato are too well known to need reference. For Hume, see *A Treatise of Human Nature* (1975), pp. 1 ff.

10. It should be kept in mind, however, that, as we shall see later, some ontologies hold that all individuals are complex. Most of these identify individuals with Aristotelian primary substances, but some hold that even things like "this yellow" are composites of the nature "yellow" and whatever turns the nature into "a this."

11. For a contemporary defense of the Substratum View, See Edwin B. Allaire's "Bare Particulars" (1963). In the Middle Ages, Duns Scotus seems to have held a version of this position; see *Opus oxoniense* II, d. 3, q. 6 (1950 ff.). There are other varieties of this view. For example, Hegel also seems to have interpreted the individual as a subject or substratum, but in his case it was not de-characterized. See *Logic* (1975), pp. 163 ff.

12. The formal distinction holds between things that, although conceptually (i.e., intensionally—they have different definitions) distinct, cannot even be thought to exist separately since they constitute one thing. *Opus oxoniense* II, d. 3, q. 6 (1950 ff.). There is a formal distinction among divine attributes and between animality and rationality in man (see Wolter, "The Realism of Scotus" [1969], p. 731). Suárez also accepts an intermediate distinction between the real and the conceptual, but he called it *"ex natura rei"* and also "modal." See *Disputatio metaphysica* VII (1861), vol. 25. More on this later.

13. See, for example, Thierry of Chartres and Gilbert of Poitiers, in Gracia, *Introduction to Individuation* (1984), chap. III. Among contemporary philosophers, Russell and Ayer, among others, have maintained versions of this position. See, for example, Ayer, "The Identity of Indiscernibles" (1954).

14. Among traditional authors who have interpreted the individual as a bundle of some kind are Berkeley (of ideas) and Mill (of sensations). In both of these cases, the bundles are "phenomenal," reflecting the general approach of their philosophies and giving rise to what Bunge has appropriately called a "phenomenist ontology"; see Bunge, "¿Qué es un individuo?" (1985), p. 121. For our purposes here, the issue of whether the individual is a phenomenal entity or something of a different kind is not pertinent. Such considerations involve a characterization of the ultimate nature of reality, not the ontological characterization of the individual. All the same, I must say that I am not in sympathy with phenomenalist metaphysics in general and that I find phenomenalist conceptions of the individual quite odd—to conceive of oneself as a phenomenal entity is very strange, for example—but I refer the reader to Bunge's previously mentioned publication for more specific arguments against this view.

15. Cf. James Van Cleve, "Three Versions of the Bundle Theory" (1985), p. 95.

16. Martine, in *Individuals and Individuality* (1984), pp. 4, 10, 72, 73, 75, explicitly speaks of individuality as a relation. For examples of those who speak of individuality as a tie, see n. 18 below.

17. I have discussed relations in "The Ontological Status of Value" (1976), pp. 393–96, and some of what will be said here originates there.

18. Cf. Kenneth Barber, "On Representing Numerical Difference" (1979) and Casteñeda, "Individuation and Non-Identity" (1975). I should mention, however, that Barber's remarks are cast in an epistemic mold. His article concerns the "representation" of individuality rather than its ontological status.

19. Peter Abailard describes this sort of position both in the *Logica ingredientibus* (1919), p. 14, and the *Logica nostrorum* (1919), p. 518. Its source is a text of Boethius from the *Commentary on Porphyry's "Isagoge,"* in *Patrologia latina* 64, 85 C. More recently, C. S. Peirce may have held a somewhat similar position, where the "phaneron" exhibits both individuality and universality. On the controversy of the place given to the individual by Peirce, see the articles published by Gresham Riley and Emily Michael in *Transactions of the C. S. Peirce Society* 10 (1974) and 12 (1976) respectively.

20. Of course, one could say that the "idea" in someone's mind is in reality distinct from the individual man. And this is only too true. But it does not really explain what distinguishes Socrates from "man," but only what distinguishes Socrates from the "idea of man."

21. There are some antecedents to this view. Descartes treated "number" as a mode, but for him it was a mode of thought (*Principles*, I, 55 [1951]), and Scotus refers sometimes to individuality as "a mode of existence" (see, *Opus oxoniense* II, d. 3, q. 1 [1950 ff.]). More recently, Martine has suggested that individuality is a mode of being in *Individuals and Individuality* (1984), pp. 4, 5, 75, 79, but he also says that it is a relation, pp. 4, 10, 73, 75, and he never explains how these two statements are to be reconciled. Moreover, he interprets "being" as "the phenomenal," thereby reducing it to that realm, and therefore takes away some of the advantages of the Mode View of individuality.

22. See, for example, *Summa theologiae* I-II, q. 49, a. 2, and q. 85, a. 4; also I, q. 5, a. 5 (1932).

23. See, for example, Durandus, *On I Sentences*, d. 30, q. 2 (1964).

24. Suárez, *Metaphysical Disputation* VII, s. 1, pars. 17–18 and elsewhere in the Disputation. See also Fonseca, *Commentary on the "Metaphysics"* V, chap. 6, s. 2; Descartes, *Principles* I, 55 (1951); Spinoza, *Ethics*, I, def. 5 (1963); and Locke, *Essay* II, 12, 4 (1959). For a discussion of Suárez's theory of modes, see Alcorta, *La teoría de los modos en Suárez* (1949).

25. In this century, American process metaphysicians have particularly been fond of modes. But even Paul Weiss, who devoted more than six hundred pages in *Modes of Being* (1958) to their study says very little about the nature of modes and modality themselves. The more recent replacement of talk about sense data ("red") by talk about modes of sensing ("sensing redly") by Chisholm, Sellars, and others, seems also a return to a philosophy in which modes and modality play important roles.

26. The definition given by Porphyry is: "Proper is what occurs in the entire [species], in one only, and always, as the capacity to laugh in man." In *Isagoge* (1966), p. 280.

27. See Aristotle's *Categories*, chap. 8; 8b25 ff. (1941)

28. Armstrong, *Nominalism and Realism* 1 (1980), pp. 108–11.

29. J. F. Boler, *Charles Peirce and Scholastic Realism* (1963); and A. B. Wolter, "The Realism of Scotus" (1962).

30. Armstrong, *Nominalism and Realism* 1 (1980), p. 110.

Chapter 4

1. Gracia, *Introduction to Individuation* (1984), last chapter.

2. For Ockham see *Ordinatio,* bk. I, d. II, q. 6 (1967 ff.). Hume's agenda is clear at the beginning of the *Treatise of Human Nature* where he is concerned with the origin of ideas.

3. For present purposes, the traditional distinction between property and accident is not important and, therefore, will be ignored. Properties, just like accidents, characterized substances and, consequently, should be individuated in the same way. I shall continue to refer to both of them generically as "features" for the moment, but I shall make further reference to the distinction below.

4. This understanding coincides with the Aristotelian notion of primary substance given in *Categories*, chap. 5, 2a11 (1941).

5. This view was very popular in the Early Middle Ages (see Gracia, *Introduction to Individuation* [1984], chap. 3), but was abandoned in the thirteenth century. It has become one of the dominant theories again in this century. Among those who have favored it are Russell and Ayer. See Russell, *An Inquiry into Meaning and Truth* (1940), p. 93 and *Human Knowledge* (1948), pp. 77 ff. and 292 ff.; Ayer "The Identity of Indiscernibles" (1954), pp. 26 ff. However, Russell had attacked the view in *The Problems of Philosophy* (1912).

6. The expression 'Principle of the Identity of Indiscernibles', is a misnomer because it suggests an epistemic principle, while the principle in question is frequently formulated metaphysically. I shall discuss this in more detail in Chapter 5.

7. Russell, *Human Knowledge* (1948), p. 295.

8. Arnauld seems to have used a version of this objection against Leibniz, in Leibniz, *Discourse on Metaphysics, Correspondence with Arnauld, and Monadology* (1973), pp. 90 ff. And Van Cleve echoes it in "Three Versions of the Bundle Theory" (1985), p. 96. For a defense against this objection, see Richard Sharvy, "Why a Class Can't Change Its Members" (1968).

9. Sometimes this is expressed by saying that change would be impossible. Van Cleve, "Three Versions of the Bundle Theory" (1985), p. 96.

10. This question could also be formulated epistemically thus: How do we know or tell that Socrates is the same individual at any two times of his life when at no two different times did he have the same bundle of features? In this way, the question raises the issue of the discernibility of identity, not of individuation or identity.

11. Loux, *Substance and Attribute* (1978), pp. 124–26.

12. Black, "The Identity of Indiscernibles" (1954); J.W. Meiland, "Do Relations Individuate?" (1966).

13. Hamlyn, *Metaphysics* (1984), p. 70.

14. Cf. David Wiggins, *Sameness and Substance* (1980), pp. 55 ff.

15. In *Naming and Necessity* (1981), p. 52, Kripke puts a similar criticism thus: "If a quality is an abstract object, a bundle of qualities is an object of an even higher degree of abstraction, not a particular." But, much earlier than Kripke, we find an echo of this objection in Peter of Auvergne, *Quodlibet* II q. 5, (1934), p. 371.

16. See, for example, D. C. Williams, "The Elements of Being" (1953), pp. 3–18 and 171–92.

17. Russell calls this relation "compresence" in *Human Knowledge* (1948), pp. 292 ff. and Goodman calls it "togetherness" in *The Structure of Appearance* (1951).

18. In "On Representing Numerical Difference" (1979), pp. 93–103, Kenneth Barber argues that "numerical difference is grounded in the instantiations of such [i.e., substance] kinds and that instantiation is handled by the tie . . ." The notion of operator is introduced in the discussion by Castañeda, "Individuation and Non-Identity" pp. 138-40.

19. In "Three Versions of the Bundle Theory" (1985), p. 97, Van Cleve identified this view with a different version of the Bundle Theory and argued as well, pp. 98–102, that it is subject to at least some of the same criticisms as the original one.

20. This is in fact what Barber seems to claim.

21. Russell, *Human Knowledge* (1948), p. 298.

22. The well known Porphyrian definition of property is "what occurs in the whole species, in it only, and always, as the capacity to laugh in man . . ." Of accident he gives two: (a) "what comes into being and passes away apart from the destruction of the substratum"; (b) "what can belong or not belong to the same thing." In *Isagoge* (1975), pp. 48 and 49.

23. This position goes back to Boethius' famous text in *De Trinitate*, where he says that "numerical difference is caused by variety of accidents; three men differ neither by genus nor species but by their accidents, for if we mentally remove from them all other accidents, still each one occupies a different place which cannot possibly be regarded as the same for each . . ." (1968), p. 6. This position became part in the Early Middle Ages of what I have called in *Introduction to Individuation* (1984) the "Standard Theory of Individuality". It lost favor in the later Middle Ages but became popular again in the modern period. Even Leibniz, who is credited with all sorts of other views, seems to defend it in *Confessio philosophi* (p. 104). See also Popper, "The Principle of Individuation" (1953), pp. 107–12.

24. Nevertheless, the version of the view that holds that spatio-temporal (external) location constitutes the primary individuator has had wide appeal among contemporary writers. See, for example, J. W. Meiland, "Do Relations Individuate?" (1966), pp. 65–69. V. C. Chappell has also defended a relational view of individuation

in "Particulars Re-Clothed" (1964), pp. 60–64. Herbert Hochberg, in "Moore and Russell on Particulars, Relations and Identity" (1969), propounds as well a relational theory, and more recently Armstrong, *Nominalism and Realism* 1 (1980), pp. 118–25. For a fairly recent and quite interesting criticism of this sort of position, see A. Quinton, *The Nature of Things* (1973), pp. 17 ff. Quinton's point, briefly stated, is that any description of an individual in terms of positional predicates includes singular terms and, therefore, is not fully determinate as it should be if position were to be the primary individuator. Other authors interpret individuality as dependent on identity through time and thus point to spatio-temporal location as a necessary condition of individuality if not as a sufficient condition of it. For an approach of this sort see Hans Reichenbach, *Space and Time* (1958), p. 142.

25. See Russell, "The World of Universals" (1970), p. 21. An obvious retort to this *reductio* would be that the objection relies on a confusion between accounting for individuality and accounting for identity, and the fact that this view may still have to resort to another principle to account for identity does not mean that it cannot account for individuality, that is, noninstantiability. Still there is something radically wrong with the notion that an intrinsic feature of a thing, like noninstantiability, can be accounted for by something completely extrinsic, like location.

26. *Physics* IV, chaps. 1 and 2, 208a28ff. (1941).

27. In *Human Knowledge* (1948), pp. 292–93, Russell gives an unusual type of argument against this view. He points out that it is reducible either to the Bare Particular View or to the Bundle View, but the way he goes about it shows not that the view is reducible to the ones in question, but rather that individuation is left unaccounted for unless one of the other views is adopted.

28. Russell considered a version of this objection in *The Principles of Mathematics* (1964), p. 452: "It is a sheer logical error to suppose that, if there were an ultimate distinction between subjects and predicates, subjects could be distinguished by differences of predicates. For before two subjects can differ as to predicates, they must already be two; and thus the immediate diversity is prior to that obtained from diversity of predicates." Of course, Russell did not hold that there is any fundamental distinction between subjects and predicates and so was not impressed by the argument. Note also that the argument has been cast in logical terms (subjects, predicates) and in the context of difference, not noninstantiability.

29. This is the case within an Aristotelian ontology. See n. 22 above for the definition of accident given by Porphyry. Aristotle gives two definitions of accident in *Metaphysics* V, chap. 29, 1025a13 and 1025a30 (1941): (1) "what attaches to something and can be truly asserted, but neither of necessity nor usually" and (2) "what attaches to each thing in virtue of itself but is not in its essence."

30. Very few contemporary philosophers voice this concern, probably because most of them reject the existence of purely spiritual entities. For an exception, see Hamlyn, *Metaphysics* (1984), p. 72.

31. Questions such as "What are you thinking about now?" and "Were you thinking about her yesterday?" are frequent. But we do not seem to talk about the place of thoughts. It would be odd to ask something like "Where is your thought?" or "Is your thought here?" Of course, one might want to argue that for every thought there might be an identifiable place in the brain, but that does not seem the same as "locating" the thought. Moreover, even when thought locational expressions as the ones just mentioned are used, they mean something quite different: 'Where is your thought?' means something like "What are you thinking about?" and 'Is your thought here' probably asks "Are you paying attention to what is going on here?"

32. This is the sort of problem that arises in Thomas Aquinas' philosophy. For him, the principle of individuation is designated matter (i.e., matter and quantity, where quantity is understood as dimensions). Therefore, spiritual beings who lack matter and quantity must be individuated in another way, even if they are differentiated from other beings in virtue of their species, for the specific difference, which is formal, cannot account for noninstantiability, let alone numerical distinction.

33. Kenneth Barber brought my attention to this objection.

34. Russell, *Human Knowledge* (1948), p. 310.

35. D. Sanford, "Locke, Leibniz and Wiggins on Being in the Same Place at the Same Time" (1970), pp. 75–82; J. M. Shorter, "On Coinciding in Space and Time" (1977), pp. 399–408.

36. Hamlyn, *Metaphysics* (1984), p. 74.

37. Russell, *Human Knowledge* (1948), p. 76.

38. Recently Hamlyn, in *Metaphysics* (1984), p. 75, has argued in favor of a theory of individuation of material substances based on spatio-temporal "history." The advantages of this view over the traditional Spatio-Temporal View are obvious: It would allow us to keep things different that do not share their entire spatio-temporal history. But the view is not convincing for many of the same reasons that have already been explained. Two of the most important ones have to do with the accidental character of spatio-temporal location and with the understanding of individuality as difference rather than noninstantiability assumed in this view.

39. This view is frequently attributed to Thomas Aquinas, although his supporters are quick to point out (1) that his view involves matter as well (I shall refer to that view as the Material View of Individuation); and (2) that quantity for Thomas does not function as principle of individuation, but rather as principle of distinction and/or multiplication. See Suárez, Disp. V, s. 3, in Gracia, *Suárez on Individuation* (1982), pp. 81, 95; and John Baconthorpe, *Questiones in Tertium et Quartum Librum Sententiarum* (1618), p. 73, cited by Wippel, in "Godfrey of Fontaines, Peter of Auvergne, John Baconthorpe, and the Principle of Individuation" (1985).

40. *Opus oxoniense*, bk. II, d. 3, q. 4 (1950 ff.).

Individuality

41. The point is well made in the Middle Ages by Peter of Auvergne, *Quodlibet* II, q. 5 (1934), p. 372.

42. This view is popular with contemporary interpreters of Aristotle. See, for example, Anscombe, in "The Principle of Individuation" (1953), and, more recently, A. C. Lloyd in "Aristotle's Principle of Individuation" (1970), pp. 519–29. W. Charlton has tried to cast doubt on the assignation of this view to Aristotle in "Aristotle and the Principle of Individuation" (1972), pp. 239-49. His approach, unfortunately, fails to distinguish clearly among the metaphysical, epistemic, and logical issues of the problem. S. Marc Cohen has offered a thorough criticism of Charlton's article in "Aristotle and Individuation" (1984). Anscombe's article has had a very wide circulation. It was reprinted recently in Barnes et al., eds., *Articles on Aristotle* 3 (1979). See also her "Aristotle: The Search for Substance," coauthored with P. T. Geach in *Three Philosophers* (1963), p. 55. In the Middle Ages the Material View was not held in a pure form by any major scholastic. Thomas Aquinas' view ("designated matter") is only a modified version of it. Scotus attacks the theory in *Opus oxoniense*, bk. 2, d. 3, q. 5 (1950 ff.). And Suárez rejects the Thomistic version in all its possible interpretations in Disp. V, s. 3 (1982). For one of the key texts of Aristotle used to support this view, see *Metaphysics* VII, chap. 8, 1034a5 (1941).

43. Scotus, *Opus oxoniense*, bk. II, d. 3, q. 5 (1950 ff.). Also Popper, "The Principle of Individuation" (1953), p. 99.

44. Thomas Aquinas seems to have held both versions of this view. In the *Commentary on Boethius' "De Trinitate,"* q. 4, a. 2 (1959), pp. 142–43, he held the dimensions to be indeterminate, but in *De ente et essentia*, chap. 2, he regarded the dimensions to be determinate ([1948], p. 11).

45. Disp. V, s. 3, in Gracia, *Suárez on Individuation* (1982), pp. 78.

46. Ibid., pp. 81 ff.

47. Cohen, "Aristotle and Individuation" (1984), p. 59.

48. This view was traditionally attributed by scholastics to Averroes. Some authors also hold it to be Aristotle's. See the articles by Charlton and Lloyd cited above. For the assignation of the view to Averroes, see Gracia, *Suárez on Individuation* (1982), p. 105. Others have argued that it is Thomas Aquinas' view, in spite of Thomas' repeated insistence that the principle of individuation is designated matter. Their claim is based on a text of Thomas' *De anima*, q. 1 a. 2, where he says that in all things being and individuation are due to the same. Now, since it is well known that he accepted that being comes to a thing through its form, the proponents of this interpretation argue that individuation must also come through form. See J. H. Robb's edition of *De anima* (1968), p. 61. Among scholastics who clearly adhered to it are Godfrey of Fontaines, Peter of Auvergne, and John Baconthorpe (see Wippel, "Godfrey of Fontaines" [1985]). Leibniz, who favors the view in *On Transubstantiation* (1969), p. 117, attributes it also to Angelus Mercenarius and Jacob Zabarella. More recently, it has been adopted, in a modified form, by David Wiggins, *Sameness and Substance* (1980), p. 92, and Lukasiewicz, "The Principle of Individuation" (1953), p. 81. But,

following the drift of modern philosophy in general, Wiggins' interpretation is "mentalistic," identifying form with concept, and Lukasiewicz gives it a logical bent. On Wiggins' interpretation, see my review of Wiggins' book in *Revista Latinoamericana de Filosofia* (1983).

49. See Thomas Aquinas, *On Being and Essence*, chap. 1 (1968); Suárez, Disp. XV, s. 5, par. 1 (1861), vol. 25; and Aristotle, *Physics*, chap. 3, 194b27 (1941).

50. See, for example, Alan Code, "What Is It to Be an Individual?" (1978).

51. It should be noted, however, that some interpreters of Aristotle consider his view of material individuation to be a bare particular view. See, for example, Lukasiewicz, "The Principle of Individuation" (1953), p. 71. And, indeed, there are some texts of Aristotle where he seems to conceive matter as devoid of all features, for example, *Metaphysics* VI, chap. 6, 1029a20 ff. (1924), a fact underlined by Ross's commentary. See Aristotle, *Metaphysics* 2 (1924), p. 165. But just below the mentioned text (1029a23), Aristotle makes clear that matter is not itself particular, and this makes his view quite different from that of those who hold a strictly bare principle of individuation.

52. As was suggested earlier, recently there has been an effort among proponents of this sort of view to find what might be characterized as empirical bases for bare particulars. Bergmann, for example, claims that one is acquainted and/or presented with these individuators. See *Logic and Reality* (1964), p. 288. More traditional views, such as that of Duns Scotus, did not have this empirical twist. See next note.

53. See Gustav Bergmann, *The Metaphysics of Logical Positivism* (1954), pp. 197 ff. and *passim*, and *Logic and Reality* (1964), pp. 133 and 318 ff., and E. B. Allaire, "Bare Particulars" (1963), pp. 1–8. In the later Middle Ages, the Scotist notion of *haecceitas* may have had a similar function to that of the bare particular; see *Opus oxoniense* II, d. 3, q. 6 (1950 ff.).

54. There have been several contemporary critics who follow this or a similar line of reasoning (see Loux, "Particulars and Their Individuation" [1970], p. 193; Lukasiewicz, "The Principle of Individuation" [1953], p. 72; and Russell, *Human Knowledge* [1948], p. 293). But the same approach is found among critics of Scotus' *haecceitas* in the Middle Ages as well. See Gracia, *Suárez on Individuation* (1982), pp. 45 and 139.

55. Allaire, "Bare Particulars" (1963).

56. This view seems to be restricted to a few medieval authors. To my knowledge no contemporary philosophers adhere to it. See Gracia, *Suárez on Individuation* (1982), p. 76.

57. This is not an exhaustive discussion of all the views on this issue. Many contemporaries, who use a logical and epistemological (the issue of discernibility discussed next) rather than a metaphysical approach to this issue have come up with other views, but insofar as their discussions are logical and epistemological in character their

discussion is out of place here. For an example, see N. L. Wilson, "Space, Time, and Individuals" (1955), pp. 589–98.

58. The best known among these is Stout. See the Bibliography at the back for his pertinent works.

59. This is the view favored by Thomas Aquinas. See *Summa theologiae* I, q. 50, a. 4 (1932), vol. 1, p. 342b. See also Suárez's discussion and criticism of this view in Disp. V, s. 7 (1982).

60. Versions of this view, also called the "Qualified Particular Theory," have been defended, among others, by D. C. Long in Loux's *Universals and Particulars* (1970), pp. 264–84, and by A. Quinton, *The Nature of Things* (1973), pp. 28 ff. The view should not be considered only as a view of the individuation of features; it is also a view about the individuation of substances. As such it may be considered a modified version of the Bundle View, as Quinton points out.

61. This is the sort of objection used by Suárez against this view. See Gracia, *Suárez on Individuation* (1982), pp. 140 and 142.

62. It is attributed to G. F. Stout in "The Nature of Universals and Propositions" (1971). See also his response to G. E. Moore's "Are the Characteristics of Particular Things Universal or Particular?" (1923), pp. 114–22. For a more recent criticism, see Bergmann, *Logic and Reality* (1964), p. 282.

63. Among the authors who made this distinction are Avicenna and Thomas Aquinas. Thomas presents his argument for what has come to be called "the doctrine of the real distinction between essence and existence" in *On Being and Essence* chap. 4, par. 6, (1968), p. 55.

64. This is the way Kant put it in his discussion of the impossibility of an ontological proof for the existence of God in *The Critique of Pure Reason* (1929).

65. Castañeda, "Individuation and Non-Identity" (1975), p. 136b.

66. An author who refers to existence as individuator is Locke in *An Essay Concerning Human Understanding* II, chap. 27 (1959), p. 441; he says: "the *principium indivi-duationis . . .* it is plain, is existence itself." But he quickly qualifies that by adding "which determines a being of any sort to a particular time and place, incommunicable to two beings of the same kind." And in other parts of the chapter, he seems to forget about existence and speaks mainly of space and time. This is why Popper, for example, in "The Principle of Individuation" (1953), p. 107, interprets his theory as spatio-temporal, although José Ferrater Mora, *Diccionario de Filosofía* (1980), vol. 2, p. 1663b, considers it existential. The matter is complicated because the chapter in which Locke discusses this issue is concerned with "identity" rather than individuality, so that he may be in fact holding an existential theory of identity—such as the one I have argued, in "Numerical Continuity in Material Substances" (1979), that Thomas must hold, while holding a spatio-temporal theory of individuation. There is one version of the Existential View, however, that has been quite popular. It interprets existence as "the whole entity of the thing." This is in fact identified by Suárez (Disp. V, s. 5

[1982]) and Leibniz (*Metaphysical Disputation*, lines 266—340) as their own view, but is reducible to the position that holds that each thing is its own principle of individuation. For this reason it cannot really be considered an existential theory of individuation. Indeed, it is rather a view quite akin to Essential Nominalism.

67. The scholastics usually attributed it to Avicenna. For discussions of the view, see the texts of Suárez and Leibniz mentioned in the previous note and also Duns Scotus, *Opus oxoniense*, bk. II, d.3 (1950 ff.), and Wiggins, *Sameness and Substance* (1980), p. 91. Finally, Ayer seems to argue against it in "Individuals" (1954), pp. 3–5.

68. Gracia, *Suárez on Individuation* (1982), p. 19, but I warned against a summary rejection in *Introduction to Individuation* (1984), p. 61 n. 60.

69. Alvin Plantinga, "World and Essence" (1970), pp. 355–56.

70. Suárez's objections along this line are contained in Disp. V, Sect. 7, in Gracia, *Suárez on Individuation* (1982), p. 141.

71. Cf. Thomas Aquinas, *On Being and Essence*, chap. 3, par. 1 (1968).

Chapter 5

1. Cf. Bertrand Russell, *Human Knowledge* (1948), pp. 292 ff.

2. Cf. P. F. Strawson, *Individuals* (1959), pp. 2 ff.

3. See, for example, Thomas Aquinas, *Summa theologiae* I, q. 85, a.1 (1932).

4. This is not a treatise on epistemology, and, therefore, a defense of a particular epistemological point of view is out of place here. A statement of the most general epistemic approach that has been adopted should be sufficient for present purposes.

5. Contrary to what some might think, this problem is not of interest exclusively to the theologian; for it raises an important philosophical issue, namely, the relation between spiritual and nonspiritual realities. The much debated mind-body problem is but an instance of this most vexing issue.

6. Even self-reflection implies some duality: the self as knower and the self as known. Plotinus understood this when he made the *Noûs* a hyposthasis different from the One. *Ennead* V, i (1950).

7. The fundamental error of most modern philosophy is to begin philosophizing with the question, "Can we know anything?," rather than the question, "How do we know?" It makes no sense to begin with the first question, since it is clear that we do know things—in this G. E. Moore was quite right—but once it is asked, it bogs down philosophy and stymies its development. The second question, of course, need not prevent philosophical development, for even if no answer to it is found, neither the search for knowledge nor the knowledge we have need be undermined.

8. This is the sort of view defended by Strawson in *Individuals* (1959), pp. 10 ff., but there are, of course, many others who have adopted this position. See, for example, the papers of J. W. Meiland and D. J. O'Connor listed in the Bibliography as well as the book by Hans Reichenbach. In the Middle Ages Gilbert of Poitiers (*De Trinitate* [1966], pp. 77–78; *Patrologia latina* 64, 1264) and Thomas Aquinas (*Expositio super librum Boethii "De Trinitate,"* q.4, a.4 (1959), p. 155) clearly adhered to this point of view. Other authors, like Duns Scotus, seem to have held a more general view, in which individual substance discernibility was accidental but not necessarily spatio-temporal. See Wolter, "The Realism of Scotus" (1962), p. 731.

9. See Max Black, "The Identity of Indiscernibles" (1954).

10. This is in fact what some medieval authors believed about God, whom they interpreted as an omnipotent being whose thought is reality.

11. I am using the terms 'relation' and 'relational feature' to mean the same thing in the present context.

12. I am not arguing at this point that two spheres could not have consciousness of their individuality under no circumstances, but only that they could not be conscious of that individuality *through* spatio-temporal considerations.

13. Ayer, "The Identity of Indiscernibles" (1954), p. 33.

14. Cf. Russell, "The World of Individuals," in Loux, *Universals and Particulars* (1970), p. 21.

15. Anscombe's mistake when she rejected the Spatio-Temporal Theory in "The Principle of Individuation" (1953), p. 93, was based on her view that "no individual is pre-eminent" and as a result cannot serve as an absolute point of reference. But we have seen that they do.

16. For references, see the texts mentioned in the pertinent section of Chapter 4.

17. For references, see the texts mentioned in the pertinent section of Chapter 4 under Bare Particular View. Among contemporary supporters of this view one may wish to count Bergmann and his followers, although it is not always clear that their view is aimed as a response to this problem or to the ontological problem discussed in Chapter 4.

18. See G. E. Moore, *Principia ethica*, chap. 1 (1968).

19. This point was made, although in a slightly different form and context, by Suárez in Disp. V, s. 2, par. 7 (1982).

20. This is the epistemic dimension of the ontological view concerning the individuation of features generally attributed, among others, to Thomas Aquinas and other Aristotelians.

21. For some classic contemporary discussions of this principle see the articles by Max Black, A. J. Ayer, and D. J. O'Connor listed in the Bibliography.

22. Leibniz, *Philosophical Papers and Letters* (1969), p. 506; *Metaphysical Disputation* 4 (1965), p. 514; and *Discourse on Metaphysics* (1973), pp. 14 and 252. I am just making a historical point about terminology here; I am not discussing the intensions of the terms or their relations. In the *Discourse* (1973), p. 14, his statement is as follows: "There follow from these considerations [namely, that the concept of an individual substance is sufficient for the understanding of it and for the deduction of all the predicates of which the substane is or may become the subject] several noticeable paradoxes; among others that it is not true that two substances may be exactly alike and differ only numerically, *solo numero.*"

23. Thierry of Chartres in *Lectiones* (1971), p. 152, says: "For if [different] accidents [by which he means also properties] were not [present] in them [i.e., substances or subjects] in any way, they could not differ in number nor would there be number in them, but everything would be reduced to unity." And Boethius, in the second edition of the *Commentary on the "Isagoge" (Patrologia latina* 64, p. 114), says: "[What is a property] of individuals is common to none. For [what was] a property of Socrates,— if he had been bald, snubnosed . . .—which formed his shape and figure, were found in no other . . . these whose property is not found in another are really called individuals." I have discussed what early medieval authors had to say about this matter in the last chapter of *Introduction to Individuation* (1984).

24. Leibniz's formulation is quite different, as is clear from n. 22.

25. The metaphysical understanding of the epistemic formulation is quite evident, for example, when Black says: "By 'indiscernible' I suppose you mean the same as 'having all properties in common'." (In "The Identity of Indiscernibles" [1954], p. 205).

26. Russell, *Logic and Knowledge* (1956), p. 118. Also Ludwig Wittgenstein, *Tractatus Logico-Philosophicus* (1961), 5.5302.

27. Russell, *Human Knowledge* (1948), pp. 295 ff. For a discussion of Russell's position on this issue see Loux, *Substance and Attribute* (1978), pp. 134–37.

28. Clearly, features such as identity serve this purpose but have the disadvantage of making the Principle of Identity trivial, and those who support it would rather give it teeth. Ayer, "The Identity of Indiscernibles" (1954), p. 19.

29. For a position that has some elements similar to my own, see D. C. Williams, "The Elements of Being" (1953). One could also argue that Hume exposed a similar view, but it must be kept in mind that when Hume talked about bundles and features he was talking about phenomena; I am talking about things.

30. The Principle of the Identity of Indiscernibles should not be confused with the Principle of the Indiscernibility of Identicals. The latter may be formulated as follows: If X is identical with Y, then X is indiscernible (or indistinguishable) from Y. Stated thus I do not see how it can be denied, although some philosophers have thought it can.

31. Castañeda, "Individuation and Non-Identity" (1975), p. 133b.

Chapter 6

1. Cf. Richard M. Gale, "Indexical Signs, Egocentric Particulars and Token-Reflexive Words" (1967), pp. 151 ff.

2. This understanding of referring was suggested to me by John Kearns.

3. Actually, what Kripke says, for example, is that "in the case of species terms . . . one should bear in mind the contrast between the *a priori* but perhaps contingent properties carried with a term, given by the way its reference was fixed, and the analytic (and hence necessary) properties a term may carry, given by its meaning. For a species, as for proper names, the way the reference of a term is fixed should not be regarded as a synonym for the term," *Naming and Necessity* (1981), p. 135.

4. For Mill, see *A System of Logic* (1872), p. 21; for Russell, *Logic and Knowledge* (1956), pp. 200–201; and for Wittgenstein, see the *Tractatus* (1961), 3.203. Although Plato is sometimes referred to as someone who held this view, I have not found any texts that unambiguously support this interpretation.

5. P. F. Strawson, "On Referring" (1950), pp. 320 ff.

6. Kearns, *Using Language* (1984), p. 396.

7. Russell, *Principia mathematica* (1962), 66: "Whenever the grammatical subject of a proposition can be supposed not to exist without rendering the proposition meaningless, it is plain that the grammatical subject is not a proper name, i.e., is not a name directly representing some object." In a recent book, D. P. Henry has claimed that the assumption "that a proposition is meaningful only if its subject-name stands for some appropriate object which is its meaning" is a corollary of Russell's view and responsible for a host of confusions in contemporary philosophy (*That Most Subtle Question* [1984], p. 7).

8. Russell, *Human Knowledge* (1948), p. 72.

9. For Frege, see "Sense and Reference" (1952).

10. For Frege see the paper to which reference has already been made. Russell's most famous text on this issue is "On Denoting," but see also *Human Knowledge* (1948), pp. 72–84. Searle has defended this view in a variety of texts; see the Bibliography for references.

11. This is not the only way in which philosophers have tried to deal with the difficulties raised. For example, Meinong tried to answer the puzzles concerning existential propositions with vacuous proper names as subjects by asserting that anything that can be named exists in some fashion. But this is an extreme position which seems to create more puzzles than it solves, for according to it not only Don Quijote would have to exist, but also square circles and the like. For Russell's criticism of this view see *Logic and Knowledge* (1956).

12. Russell, *Human Knowledge* (1948), p. 303. Searle seems to think that Russell did not hold such a view, but I find the text of Russell quite clear. For Searle, see *Intentionality: An Essay in the Philosophy of Mind* (1984), pp. 232–33. See also Quine's "On What There Is," in Landesman, ed., *The Problem of Universals* (1971), p. 223.

13. There are many varieties of this position. The strongest and most recent supporter of it is Searle. His view is that "proper names must in some way depend on Intentional content." Thus, he rejects the label "descriptivist" in favor of "intentionalist" or "internalist," in *Intentionality* (1984), p. 232. He also rejects Frege's view that descriptions give the definition of a name. Ibid, p. 244.

14. In these examples I am bracketing any sort of temporal modality for the sake of simplicity.

15. This position originates in the later Wittgenstein, *Philosophical Investigations* 79 (1965), pp. 36–37.

16. Searle, *Speech Acts* (1969), p. 170; see also p. 169 for the reference to a disjunction.

17. For other criticisms of the theory, see Kripke, *Naming and Necessity* (1981).

18. Some supporters of this view find fault with this label (see K. Donnellan, "Speaking of Nothing" [1977], pp. 3 ff.), but for lack of a better one I shall stick to it for the present.

19. For Donnellan, see ibid. and "Proper Names and Identifying Descriptions" (1970). Kripke's statement in *Naming and Necessity* (1981), p. 64, to the effect that he is not "proposing another theory" of names "because I'm sure it's wrong too if it is a theory" is quite puzzling. Having referred to his own view as a theory later on (p. 92), he tries to solve the inconsistency by explaining that he is not trying to provide "a real set of necessary and sufficient conditions for reference . . . ," but rather "to present just a *better picture*" than that presented by descriptivists (p. 93). But clearly, to present a picture and a better one at that, whether exact or not, involves precisely identifying conditions. As long as his view is not purely critical, he must be regarded as proposing a theory, which by his own reckoning must be false, even though, contrary to what he holds, it may not turn out to be so.

20. Kripke, *Naming and Necessity* (1981), pp. 96 and 59 n. 22.

21. Strictly speaking, the name that Cervantes received at baptism was a compound name (Miguel de Cervantes Saavedra) composed of his own name 'Miguel' and the last names of his father ('de Cervantes') and mother ('Saavedra'). For the sake of simplicity, I shall continue to use 'Cervantes' instead of the full name.

22. Whether this intention is conscious, of course, is a questionable matter. More on this later.

23. For discussion on this distinction, see Searle, "Referential and Attributive" (1979) and the Donnellan article mentioned in the next note.

24. Donnellan, "Reference and Definite Descriptions," in S. Schwartz, ed., *Naming, Necessity and Natural Kinds* (1977), pp. 46–48.

25. Kripke, *Naming and Necessity* (1981), p. 48.

26. Donnellan, "Speaking of Nothing," in Schwartz's *Naming, Necessity and Natural Kinds* (1977), p. 22.

27. Searle, chap. 9 of *Intentionality* (1984), p. 241 *et statim*.

28. Donnellan, "Speaking of Nothing" (1977).

29. Incidentally, the fact that 'Don Quijote' is also the name of a novel in addition to being the name of one of its characters is quite immaterial to the discussion, for the proposition we have in mind, 'Don Quijote was mad', certainly makes no sense if 'Don Quijote' refers to the novel and not the character.

30. Kripke, *Naming and Necessity* (1980), p. 109.

31. Plantinga presented this objection in "The Boethian Compromise" (1978), p. 131, although his example is Mark Twain and Samuel Clemens.

32. Kripke tries to defend himself, in *Naming and Necessity* (1981), p. 20, against this objection by pointing out that he does not hold that 'Cicero is Tully' is equivalent to 'Cicero is Cicero'. But this assertion cannot be taken to answer the objection by itself—an explanation of how the sentences differ while maintaining the Causal View is required.

33. Kripke, *Naming and Necessity* (1981), p. 59 n. 22, and p. 96.

34. Actually Kripke seems to leave open the door to these possibilities since he grants in ibid., p. 59 n. 22, that the fixing of the referent of a name through the causal chain occurs "for most speakers." And something similar is also granted in p. 106. Still, even after this, the criticism made holds, for he seems to think that the causal chain is at least sufficient in most cases to establish reference and the point I am making is that it is not.

35. Some supporters of this view may wish to argue (a) that for the new user the reference needs to be fixed in a sort of baptism and that that is why description or ostension comes in. But this seems confused, for baptism involves the giving of a name, while the case we are concerned with involves teaching and learning a name. Or alternatively, (b) they might grant certain exceptions to the theory. But if there are exceptions, perhaps the model is not as good as it was originally thought. Cf. Kripke, *Naming and Necessity* (1981), pp. 92–94.

36. The fact that proper names may also have meaning or sense and, therefore, be able to function as descriptions in some way does not conflict with the view that their *primary* and essential function is not descriptive, but referential.

37. For Kripke, ibid., p. 96, the reference at baptism may be fixed by ostension or by a description, for example. But presumably descriptions cannot be used to fix the reference on any other occasion (p. 5). At times other than baptism the reference is fixed by "a causal chain of communication" (p. 59).

276

38. Searle, *Intentionality* (1984), p. 241.

39. Ibid., p. 235.

40. Ibid., p. 241.

41. Geach, *Mental Acts* (1957), sect. 16.

42. Kripke, throughout *Naming and Necessity* (1981). For his reference to Geach's view, p. 115 n. 58.

43. Searle, "Proper Names" (1958).

44. Anscombe, *An Introduction to Wittgenstein's "Tractatus"* (1959), chap. 2.

45. Cf. Quine's "On What There Is," in Landesman, *The Problem of Universals* (1971), p. 217.

46. Searle has noticed the inconsistency of this aspect of the causalist account in *Intentionality* (1984), p. 235.

47. Gareth Evans, "The Causal Theory of Names" (1977), pp. 192–215.

48. Understood thus, a definite description is like a statement of what Plantinga, in "The Boethian Compromise" (1978), p. 137, has called a "singular property," that is, a property that cannot possibly be instantiated (his word is 'exemplified') by more than one thing.

49. This example may not be above question, since it might be my wife's intention after all to state something about the greenness of rye grass in general and not about the one on the back of our house in particular. But the fact that her intention could be *otherwise* is sufficient to make the point I am noting.

50. Russell, *Human Knowledge* (1948), p. 78; Searle, *Intentionality* (1984), pp. 257–58.

51. Kripke, *Naming and Necessity* (1981), p. 26; also in Saerle, *Speech Acts* (1969), p. 173.

52. But the reverse is also true; some proper names can become not just definite descriptions but indefinite ones as well. The term 'chesterfield' is used in Toronto to mean sofa, when in fact it is the proper name of a famous builder of sofas, whose product became so popular that his name displaced the specific term in the language. For the referential use of definite descriptions see Searle, *Speech Acts* (1979), pp. 137–61.

53. See n.1 above.

54. For Russell see *Human Knowledge* (1948); pp. 84 ff., and for Reichenbach see *Space and Time* (1958).

55. Russell, *Human Knowledge* (1948), p. 81.

56. Ibid., pp. 84–92.

57. Cf. Castañeda "'7 + 5 = 12' as a Synthetic Proposition" (1960), p. 157.

Bibliography

The list of books and articles that follows is not meant to be exhaustive. It consists primarily of materials I have consulted at one time or another while thinking about the issues discussed in this book.

Abailard, Peter. *Dialectica.* Edited by L. M. de Rijk. Assen: Van Gorcum, 1956.

Abailard, Peter. *Incipiunt Glossae secundum magistrum Petrum Abaelardum super Porphyrium,* in B. Geyer, ed. *Beiträge zur Geschichte der Philosophie des Mittelalters,* Band XXI, Heft 1-3, 1919. Known as *Logica ingredientibus.*

Abailard, Peter. *Logica nostrorum petitioni sociorum,* in B. Geyer, ed. *Beiträge zur Geschichte der Philosophie des Mittelalters,* Band XXI, Heft 4, 1919.

Adams, Robert M. "Primitive Thisness and Primitive Identity," *The Philosopher's Annual* 3 (1980).

Alcorta, J. I. *La teoría de los modos en Suárez.* Madrid, 1949.

Allaire, Edwin B. "Another Look at Bare Particulars," *Philosophical Studies* 16 (1965): 16–21.

Allaire, Edwin B. "Bare Particulars," *Philosophical Studies* 14 (1963): 1–7.

Allaire, Edwin B., et al., eds. *Essays in Ontology.* The Hague: M. Nijhoff, 1963.

Alston, W. P. "Ontological Commitments," *Philosophical Studies* 9 (1958): 8–17.

Alston, W. P. "Particulars—Bare and Qualified," *Philosophy and Phenomenological Research* 15 (1954): 257–58.

Angelelli, I. "Leibniz's Early Thesis on the Principle of Individuation," *Leibniz, Werk und Wirkung. IV Internationaler Leibniz-Kongress, Vorgrage.* Hannover: G. W. Leibniz Gesellschaft, 1983, pp. 863–69.

Anscombe, G. E. M. "Substance," *Proceedings of the Aristotelian Society.* Suppl. Vol. 38 (1964): 69–78.

Anscombe, G. E. M. and Geach, P. T. *Three Philosophers.* Oxford: Blackwell, 1963.

Anscombe, G. E. M. *An Introduction to Wittgenstein's "Tractatus."* London: Hutchinson and Co., 1959.

Anscombe, G. E. M. "The Principle of Individuation," *Berkeley and Modern Problems.* Suppl. Vol. 27. Aristotelian Society, (1953): 83–96.

Anselm. *Epistola de Incarnatione Verbi,* in *Obras completas.* Vol. I. Edited by P. Schmidt. Madrid: Biblioteca de Autores Cristianos, 1952.

Aquinas, Thomas. *On Being and Essence.* Translated by A. Maurer. Toronto: Pontifical Institute of Mediaeval Studies, 1968.

Aquinas, Thomas. *Expositio super librum Boethii "De Trinitate."* Edited by B. Decker. Leiden: E. J. Brill, 1959.

Aquinas, Thomas. *On Spiritual Creatures.* Translated by M. C. Fitzpatrick and J. J. Wellmuth. Milwaukee: Marquette University Press, 1951.

Aquinas, Thomas. *De ente et essentia.* Edited by M. D. Roland-Gosselin. Paris: J. Vrin, 1948.

Aquinas, Thomas. *Summa theologiae.* Edited by De Rubeis, et al. Turin: Marietti, 1932.

Aristotle. *Basic Works.* Edited by R. McKeon. New York: Random House, 1941.

Bibliography

Aristotle. *Metaphysics*. 2 vols. A revised text with Introduction and Commentary by W. D. Ross. Oxford: Clarendon Press, 1924.

Armstrong, D. M. *Nominalism and Realism*. 2 vols. Cambridge, England: Cambridge University Press, 1980.

Augustine. *The Teacher*. Translated by R. P. Russell. Washington, D.C.: Catholic University of America Press, 1968.

Austin, J. L. *Philosophical Papers*. Edited by J. O. Urmson and G. J. Warnock. Oxford: Clarendon, 1961. (Esp. I, II and VIII).

Austin, J. L. "The Meaning of a Word," *Philosophical Papers*. New York and Oxford: Oxford University Press, 1961.

Averroes. *In "De anima."* Edited by S. Crawford. Cambridge: University Press, 1953.

Ayer, A. J. "Individuals," *Philosophical Essays*. London: Macmillan and Co., Ltd., 1954, pp. 1–25.

Ayer, A. J. "The Identity of Indiscernibles," *Philosophical Essays*. London: Macmillan and Co., Ltd., 1954, pp. 26–35.

Ayer, A. J. "On What There Is," *Philosophical Essays*. London: Macmillan and Co., Ltd., 1954, pp. 215–30.

Ayer, A. J. "Universals and Particulars," *Proceedings of the Aristotelian Society* 34 (1933–34): 51–62.

Badereu, D. *L'individuel chez Aristote*. Paris: Bolvin, 1936.

Baker, Robert, "Particulars: Bare, Naked, and Nudes," *Nous* 1 (1967): 211–12.

Bambrough, R. "Universals and Family Resemblances," *Proceedings of the Aristotelian Society* 61 (1960–61): 207–22.

Barber, Kenneth. "On Representing Numerical Difference," *The Southwestern Journal of Philosophy* 10 (1979): 93–103.

Barnes, I. et al. eds. *Articles on Aristotle*. London: Duckworth, 1979.

Barnett, D. "A New Semantical Theory of Egocentric Particulars," *Synthese* 28 (1974): 533–47.

281

Basson, A. H. "The Problem of Substance," *Proceedings of the Aristotelian Society* 49 (1948–49): 65–72.

Baylis, C. A. "Logical Subjects and Physical Subjects," *Philosophy and Phenomenological Research* 17 (1957): 478–87.

Baylis, C. A. "Meanings and Their Exemplifications," *Journal of Philosophy* 27 (1930): 169–74.

Bergmann, Gustav. "Frege's Hidden Nominalism," in Charles Landesman, ed. *The Problem of Universals*. New York and London: Basic Books, 1971, pp. 67–83.

Bergmann, Gustav. *Meaning and Existence*. Madison, Wis.: The University of Wisconsin Press, 1968.

Bergmann, Gustav. *Realism, A Critique of Brentano and Meinong*. Madison, Wis.: University of Wisconsin Press, 1967.

Bergmann, Gustav. *Logic and Reality*. Madison, Wis.: University of Wisconsin Press, 1964.

Bergmann, Gustav. "Strawson's Ontology," *Journal of Philosophy* 68 (1961): 601–22.

Bergmann, Gustav. "Individuals," *Philosophical Studies* 9 (1958): 78–85.

Bergmann, Gustav. "Particularity and the New Nominalism," *Methodos* 6 (1954): 131–47.

Bergmann, Gustav. *The Metaphysics of Logical Positivism*. London: Longmans, Green and Co., 1954.

Bergmann, Gustav. "The Identity of Indiscernibles and the Formalist Definition of 'Identity'," *Mind* 62 (1933): 775–79. Reprinted in *The Metaphysics of Logical Positivism*, 1954, pp. 268–76.

Bérubé, Camille. *La connaissance de l'individual en moyen âge*. Montreal: University of Montreal, 1964.

Beuchot, Mauricio. *Filosofía analítica, filosofía tomista y metafísica*. Mexico: Universidad Iberoamericana, 1983.

Beuchot, Mauricio. *La filosofía del lenguaje en la Edad Media*. Mexico: UNAM, 1981.

Black, Max. "The Elusiveness of Sets," *The Review of Metaphysics* 24 (1971): 614–36.

Black, Max. "The Identity of Indiscernibles," *Mind* 61 (1952). Reprinted in *Problems of Analysis*. Ithaca, N.Y.: Cornell University Press, 1954.

Bobik, J. "A Note on a Problem about Individuality," *Australasian Journal of Psychology and Philosophy* 36 (1958): 210–15.

Bocheński, I. M. "The Problem of Universals," *The Problem of Universals*. Notre Dame, Ind.: University of Notre Dame Press, 1956.

Boethius, A. M. S. *In librum Aristotelis "Peri-Hermeneias."* Edited by C. Meiser. Leipzig: Teubner, 1977–80.

Boethius, A. M. S. *The Theological Tractates*. Edited and translated by H. F. Stewart and E. R. Rand. Loeb Classical Library Series. Cambridge, Mass.: Harvard University Press, 1968.

Boethius, A. M. S. *In "Isagogen" Porphyrii commentorum editio secunda*. Edited S. Brandt, in *Corpus scriptorum ecclesiasticorum latinorum*. Vol. 48. Vienna: Tempsky, 1906. Reprinted New York: Johnson, 1966.

Boethius, A. M. S. *Commentaria in Porphyrium a se translatum*, in *Patrologiae cursus completus; Series latina*. Vol. 64. Paris: 1891.

Boethius, A. M. S. *In librum Aristotelis "De interpretatione"*, editio secunda, in *Patrologiae cursus completus; Series latina*. Vol. 64. Paris: 1891.

Boethius, A. M. S. *In Categorias Aristotelis libri quatuor*. Edited by J. P. Migne, in *Patrologiae cursus completus; Series latina*. Vol. 64. Paris, 1891.

Boler, J. F. *Charles Peirce and Scholastic Realism*. Seattle: University of Washington Press, 1963.

Bosanquet, Bernard. *The Principle of Individuality and Value*. London: Macmillan and Co., 1927. (Esp. Lec. II).

Bradley, Michael C. "Russell and the Identity of Indiscernibles," *History of Philosophy Quarterly* 3 (1986): 325–33.

Braithwaite, R. B. "Universals and the 'Method of Analysis'," *Proceedings of the Aristotelian Society*. Suppl. Vol. 6 (1926): 27–38.

Brandt, R. B. "The Languages of Realism and Nominalism," *Philosophy and Phenomenological Research* 17 (1957): 516–36. Rep. in Charles Landesman, ed. *The Problem of Universals.* New York and London: Basic Books, 1971, pp. 243–60.

Brody, B. A. "Natural Kinds and Essences, *"Journal of Philosophy* 64 (1967): 431–46.

Bunge, Mario. "¿Qué es un individuo?" *Theoria.* Vol. 1, No. 1 (1985): 121–18.

Bunge, Mario. *Treatise on Basic Philosophy.* Vol. 3. *The Furniture of the World.* Dordrecht: Reidel, 1977.

Burke, M. B. "Cohabitation, Stuff and Intermittent Existence," *Mind* 89 (1980): 391–405.

Butchvarov, P. K. *Resemblance and Identity.* Bloomington, Ind.: Indiana University Press, 1966.

Butchvarov, P. K. "Concrete Entities and Concrete Relations," *Review of Metaphysics* 10 (1957): 412–22.

Campbell, Keith. "The Metaphysics of Abstract Particulars," *Midwest Studies in Philosophy* 6 (1981): 477–88.

Carmichael, P. "Professor Ayer on Individuals," *Analysis* 14 (1953): 37–42.

Carnap, Rudolph. "Empiricism, Semantics, and Ontology," in Charles Landesman, ed. *The Problem of Universals.* New York and London: Basic Books, 1971, pp. 228–42.

Carnap, R. *The Logical Structure of the World.* Translated R. A. George. London: Routledge and Kegan Paul, 1967.

Carnap, Rudolph. *Meaning and Necessity.* Chicago: University of Chicago Press, 1956.

Caso, Antonio. Selections from *La persona y el Estado totalitario,* in Jorge J. E. Gracia, ed. *Contemporary Latin American Philosophy: Man, Values and the Search for Philosophical Identity.* Buffalo: Prometheus, 1986.

Castañeda, Héctor-Neri. "The Semantics and the Causal Roles of Proper Names," *Philosophy and Phenomenological Research* 46 (1985): 91–113.

Castañeda, Héctor-Neri. "On the Philosophical Foundations of the Theory of Communication: Reference, *"Midwest Studies in Philosophy* 2 (1977): 165–86.

Castañeda, Héctor-Neri. "Individuation and Non-Identity," *American Philosophical Quarterly* 12 (1975): 131–40.

Castañeda, Héctor-Neri. "Rejoinder to Professor Michael Loux," *Crítica* 8 (1975): 109–16.

Castañeda, Héctor-Neri. "Thinking and the Structure of the World," *Philosophia* 4 (1974): 3–40.

Castañeda, Héctor-Neri. "Indicators and Quasi-Indicators," *American Philosophical Quarterly* 4 (1967): 85–100.

Castañeda, Héctor-Neri. "'7 + 5 = 12' as a Synthetic Proposition," *Philosophy and Phenomenological Research* 21 (1960): 141–58.

Chandler, Hugh S. "Essence and Accident," *Analysis* 26 (1966): 185–88.

Chappell, V. C. "Particulars Re-Clothed," *Philosophical Studies* 15 (1964): 60–64.

Charlton, W. "Aristotle and the Principle of Individuation," *Phronesis* 17 (1972): 239–49.

Chisholm, Roderick. *The First Person*. Minneapolis: University of Minnesota, 1981.

Code, Alan. "What Is It to Be an Individual?" *Journal of Philosophy* 75 (1978): 647–48.

Cohen, S. Marc. "Aristotle and Individuation," *New Essays on Aristotle*. Edited by F. J. Pelletier and J. King-Farlow. Guelph: Canadian Association for Publishing in Philosophy, 1984.

Copi, Irving M. *Introduction to Logic*. 6th ed. New York: Macmillan, 1982.

Copi, Irving M. and Beard, Robert, eds. *Essays on Wittgenstein's "Tractatus."* New York: Macmillan, 1966.

Copi, Irving M. "Essence and Accident," *The Journal of Philosophy* 51 (1954): 706–19.

285

Courtine, Jean-François. "Le principe d'individuation chez Suárez et chez Leibniz," *Leibniz et la Renaissance*. Wiesbaden: Franz Steiner Verlag, 1983.

Davies, Martin. "Individuation and the Semantics of Demonstratives," *Journal of Philosophical Logic* 11 (1982): 287–310.

Dawes-Hicks, G. "Are the Characteristics of Particular Things Universal or Particular?" *Proceedings of the Aristotelian Society.* Suppl. Vol. 3 (1923): 123–28.

Descartes, René. *A Discourse on Method and Selected Writings.* Translated by John Veitch. New York: E. P. Dutton and Co., 1951.

Donagan, Alan. "Universals and Metaphysical Realism," *Monist,* 1963. Reprinted in M. Loux, ed. *Universals and Particulars.* Garden City, N.Y.: Doubleday and Co., 1970, pp. 128–58.

Donnellan, K. "Speaking of Nothing," *The Philosophical Review* 83 (1974): pp. 3–32. Reprinted in S. P. Schwartz, ed. *Naming, Necessity and Natural Kinds.* Ithaca and London: Cornell University Press, 1977, pp. 216–44.

Donnellan, K. "Reference and Definite Descriptions," *Philosophical Review* 75 (1966): 281–304. Reprinted in S. Schwartz, ed. *Naming, Necessity and Natural Kinds.* Ithaca: Cornell University Press, 1977, pp. 42–65.

Donnellan, K. "Proper Names and Identifying Descriptions," *Synthese* 21 (1970): 335–58.

Ducasse, C. J. "Some Observations Concerning Particularity," *Philosophical Review* 58 (1949): 613–14.

Dummett, M. *Frege.* London: Duckworth, 1973.

Dummett, M. "Truth," *Proceedings of the Aristotelian Society* 59 (1958–59): 141–62.

Dummett, M. "Nominalism," *Philosophical Review* 65 (1956): 491–505.

Duncan-Jones, A. E. "Universals and Particulars," *Proceedings of the Aristotelian Society* 34 (1933–34): 63–86.

Duns Scotus, John. See John Duns Scotus.

Durandus of St. Pourçain. *Petri Lombardi sententias theologicas commentario-rium libri IIII.* Venice: Guerra, 1571. Reprinted Ridgewood, N.J.: Gregg, 1964.

Eriugena, John Scotus. See John Scotus Eriugena.

Evans, Gareth. "The Causal Theory of Names," in S. P. Schwartz, ed. *Naming, Necessity and Natural Kinds.* Ithaca: Cornell University Press, 1977, pp. 192–215.

Feibleman, J. K. "On Substance," *Review of Metaphysics* 8 (1955): 373–78.

Ferrater Mora, José. *Diccionario de Filosofía.* 4 vols. Madrid: Alianza Editorial, 1980.

Ferrater Mora, José. *El ser y la muerte. Bosquejo de filosofía integracionista.* Madrid: Aguilar, 1962.

Fisk, Milton. *Nature and Necessity: An Essay in Physical Ontology.* Bloomington and London: Indiana University Press, 1973.

Fonseca, Peter. *In libros metaphysicorum Aristotelis.* Cologne: Zetzner, 1615. Reprinted Hildesheim: Olms, 1964.

Frege, Gottlob. "On Concept and Object," in Charles Landesman, ed. *The Problem of Universals.* New York and London: Basic Books, 1971, pp. 56–66.

Frege, Gottlob. "Function and Concept," in P. Geach and M. Black, eds. and trans. *Translations from the Philosophic Writings of Gottlob Frege.* Oxford: Blackwell, 1952.

Frege, Gottlob. "Sense and Reference," in P. Geach and M. Black, eds. and trans. *Translations from the Philosophic Writings of Gottlob Frege.* Oxford: Blackwell, 1952.

Frege, Gottlob. *Translations from the Philosohical Writings of Gottlob Frege.* Translated and edited by P. T. Geach and M. Black. Oxford: Blackwell, 1952. Esp. II, III and IV.

Furth, Montgomery. "Transtemporal Stability in Aristotelian Substances," *Journal of Philosophy* 75 (1978): 624–46.

Gale, Richard M. "Indexical Signs, Egocentric Particulars and Token-Reflexive Words," in *Encyclopedia of Philosophy*. Vol. 4. Edited by Paul Edwards. New York and London: Macmillan Pub. Co. and The Free Press, 1967, pp. 151–55.

Gaos, José. *De la filosofía*. Vol. 12 of *Obras completas*. Mexico: Universidad Nacional Autónoma de México, 1982.

Gaskings, D. "Clusters," *Australasian Journal of Psychology and Philosophy* 38 (1960): 1–36.

Geach, P. T. *Reason and Reality*. New York: Macmillan, 1972.

Geach, P. T. "What Actually Exists," *Proceedings of the Aristotelian Society*. Suppl. Vol. 42 (1968): 7–16.

Geach, P. T. *Reference and Generality*. Ithaca, N. Y.: Cornell Univesity Press, 1962.

Geach, P. T. *Mental Acts*. London: Routledge and Kegan Paul, 1957.

Geach, P. T. "On What There Is," *Proceedings of the Aristotelian Society*. Suppl. Vol. 25 (1951): 125–36.

Gilbert of Poitiers. *The Commentaries on Boethius*. Edited N. Häring. Toronto: Pontifical Institute of Mediaeval Studies, 1966.

Gilson, E. *History of Christian Philosophy in the Middle Ages*. New York: Random House, 1955.

Godfrey of Fontaines. *Les Quodlibets Cinq, Six, et Sept de Godfroid de Fontaines*, Edited by M. De Wulf and J. Hoffmans, in *Les Philosophes Belges*. Vol. 3. Louvain, 1914.

Goodman, Nelson. *The Structure of Appearance*. Cambridge, Mass.: Harvard University Press, 1951.

Goddman, Nelson. "A World of Individuals," in Charles Landesman, ed. *The Problem of Universals*. Notre Dame, Ind.: University of Notre Dame Press, 1956.

Gracia, Jorge J. E. "Los problemas filosóficos de la individualidad," *Revista Latinoamericana de Filosofía* 11 (1985): 3–26.

Gracia, Jorge J. E. *Introduction to the Problem of Individuation in the Early Middle Ages*. München and Washington, D.C.: Philosophia Verlag and The Catholic University of America Press, 1984.

Bibliography

Gracia, Jorge J. E. "Individuals as Instances," *Review of Metaphysics* 37 (1983): 39–59.

Gracia, Jorge J. E. "Suárez y la individualidad," *Cuadernos Salmantinos* 10 (1983): 157–82.

Gracia, Jorge J. E. "Romero y la individualidad," in *Francisco Romero: Maestro de la filosofía latinoamericana*. Edited E. Mayz Vallenilla, et al. Caracas: Sociedad Interamericana de Filosofía, 1983, pp. 85–102.

Gracia, Jorge J. E. Review of D. Wiggins' *Sameness and Substance*, *Revista Latinoamericana de Filosofía* 9 (1983).

Gracia, Jorge J. E. *Suárez on Individuation*. Milwaukee: Marquette University Press, 1982.

Gracia, Jorge J. E. "Numerical Continuity in Material Substances: The Principle of Identity in Thomistic Metaphysics," *The Southwestern Journal of Philosophy* 10 (1979): 72–93.

Gracia, Jorge J. E. "Suárez's Criticism of the Thomistic Principle of Individuation," *Atti del Congresso di S. Tommaso d'Aquino nel suo VII Centenario*. Rome, 1977, pp. 563–68.

Gracia, Jorge J. E. "The Ontological Status of Value," *The Modern Schoolman* 53 (1976): 393–97.

Gracia, Jorge J. E. "The Doctrine of the Possible and Agent Intellects in Gonsalvus Hispanus' Question XIII," *Franciscan Studies* 20 (1969): 5–36.

Gregory, J. C. "Leibniz, the Identity of Indiscernibles and Probability," *Philosophy and Phenomenological Research* 14 (1954): 365–69.

Grossmann, R. *Ontological Reduction*. Bloomington, Ind.: Indiana University Press, 1973.

Grossmann, R. *Reflections on Frege's Philosophy*. Evanston, Ill.: Northwestern University, 1969.

Grossmann, R. "Conceptualism," *Review of Metaphysics* 14 (1960): 243–54.

Hall, E. W. "Logical Subjects and Physical Objects," *Philosophy and Phenomenological Research* 17 (1957): 478–82.

Hamlyn, D. W. *Metaphysics.* Cambridge: University Press, 1984.

Hampshire, Stuart. *Thought and Action.* London: Chatto and Windus, 1959.

Hartman, Edwin. *Substance, Body and Soul.* Princeton: University Press, 1977.

Hegel. *Logic.* Translated William Wallace. Oxford: Clarendon Press, 1975.

Henry, Desmond Paul. *That Most Subtle Question (Quaestio Subtilissima): The Metaphysical Bearing of Medieval and Contemporary Linguistic Disciplines.* Manchester: University Press, 1984.

Hickman, Larry. *Modern Theories of Level Predicates. Second Intentions in the Neuzeit.* Munich: Philosophia Verlag, 1980.

Hicks, G. Danes. "Are the Characteristics of Particular Things Universal or Particular?" *Proceedings of the Aristotelian Society.* Suppl. Vol. 3 (1923): 123–28.

Hobbes, Thomas. *Leviathan.* New York: Collier Books, 1971.

Hochberg, H. "Moore and Russell on Particulars, Relations and Identity," in *Studies in the Philosophy of G. E. Moore.* Edited by E. D. Klemke. Chicago: Quadrangle Books, 1969; and in *Logic, Ontology and Language.* München: Philosophia Verlag, 1984

Hochberg, H. "Ontology and Acquaintance," *Philosophical Studies* 17 (1966): 49–55.

Hume, David. *A Treatise of Human Nature.* Edited by L. A. Selby-Bigge. Oxford: Clarendon Press, 1975.

Hummel, C. *Nicolaus Cusanus. Der Individualitätsprinzip in seiner Philosophie,* 1961.

John Baconthorpe. *Quaestiones in Tertium et Quartum Librum Sententiarum et Quodlibetales.* Cremona, 1618.

John Duns Scotus. *Ordinatio.* Edited by Carolo Balić, in *Opera omnia.* Vatican, 1950 ff.

John of Salisbury. *Metalogicon.* Edited by Clemens C. Webb. Oxford, 1929.

John Scotus Eriugena. *Periphyseon (De divisione naturae)*. Bks. I, II and III. Edited by I. P. Sheldon-Williams. Dublin: IAS, 1968–81.

Jones, J. R. "Characters and Resemblances," *Philosophical Review* 60 (1951): 551–62.

Jones, J. R. "Simple Particulars," *Philosophical Studies* 1 (1950): 65–74.

Jones, J. R. "What Do We Mean by an 'Instance'?" *Analysis* 11 (1950): 11–18.

Jones, J. R. "Are the Qualities of Particular Things Universal or Particular?" *Philosophical Review* 58 (1949): 152–70.

Joske, W. D. *Material Objects*. London: Macmillan, 1967.

Kant, Immanuel. *Critique of Pure Reason*. Translated Norman Kemp Smith. New York: St. Martin's Press, 1929.

Kearns, John T. *Using Language: The Structures of Speech Acts*. Albany: SUNY Press, 1984.

Kearns, John T. "Sameness or Similarity?" *Philosophy and Phenomenological Research* 29 (1968): 105–15.

Keene, G. B. "A Note on the Identity of Indiscernibles," *Mind* 65 (1956): 252–54.

Kiefer, Howard E. and Milton K. Munitz, eds. *Language, Belief and Metaphysics*. Albany: State University of New York, 1970.

Klemke, E. D., ed. *Essays on Frege*. Urbana: University of Illinois Press, 1968.

Klemke, E. D. "Universals and Particulars in a Phenomenalist Ontology," *Philosophy of Science* 27 (1960): 254–61.

Kneale, W. "Modality, De Dicto and De Re," in Ernest Nagel, Patrick Suppes, and Alfred Tarski, eds. *Logic, Methodology and the Philosophy of Science: Proceedings of the 1960 International Congress*. Stanford: University Press, 1962, pp. 622–33.

Kneale, W. "The Notion of Substance," *Proceedings of the Aristotelian Society* 40 (1939–40): 103–34.

Korner, S. "Substance," *Proceedings of the Aristotelian Society.* Suppl. Vol. 38 (1964): 79–90.

Kripke, Saul A. *Naming and Necessity.* Cambridge Mass.: Harvard University Press, 1981. Reprint of 1980 edition. First published in 1972.

Kung, Guido. *Ontology and the Logistic Analysis of Language.* Dordrecht: D. Reidel Publishing Company, 1967.

Landesman, Charles, ed. *The Problem of Universals.* New York and London: Basic Books, 1971.

Landgrebe, Ludwig. *Faktizität und Individuation: Studien zu den Grundfragen der Phänomenologie.* Hamburg: Felix Meiner Verlag, 1982.

Lazerowitz, M. "Substratum," *Philosophical Analysis.* Ed. M. Black. Englewood Cliffs, N. J.: Prentice-Hall, 1963.

Leblanc, H. and Hailperin, T. "Nondesignating Singular Terms," *Philosophical Review* 58 (1959): 239–43.

Leibniz, G. W. *Discourse on Metaphysics, Correspondence with Arnauld, and Monadology.* Translated G. R. Montgomery. LaSalle, Ill.: Open Court, 1973.

Leibniz, G. W. *Philosophical Papers and Letters.* Edited by L. E. Loemker. Dordrecht, 1969.

Leibniz, G. W. *Metaphysical Disputation on the Principle of an Individual,* in C. J. Gerhardt, *Die Philosophischen Schriften von Gottfried Wilhelm Leibniz.* Edited by C. I. Gerhardt. Hildesheim, 1965, pp. 17–26.

Leibniz, G. W. *Correspondence with Clarke.* Edited by H. G. Alexander. Manchester, 1956.

Lejewski, C. "On Lesniewski's Ontology," *Ratio* 1 (1958).

Lejewski, C. "Proper Names," *Proceedings of the Aristotelian Society.* Suppl. Vol. 31 (1957): 229–56.

Leonard, H. S. and Goodman, N. "The Calculus of Individuals and Its Use," *The Journal of Symbolic Logic* 5 (1940): 45–55.

Linsky, L. *Names and Descriptions*. Chicago: University of Chicago Press, 1977.

Linsky, L. "Referring," in P. Edwards, ed. *Encyclopedia of Philosophy*. Vol. 7. New York: Macmillan and The Free Press, 1967, pp. 95–99.

Linsky, L. "Reference and Referents," in Caton, ed. *Philosophy and Ordinary Language*. Urbana: University of Illinois Press, 1963.

Lloyd, A. C. "Aristotle's Principle of Individuation," *Mind* 79 (1970): 519–29.

Locke, John. *An Essay Concerning Human Understanding*. 2 vols. Edited by Alexander Campbell Fraser. New York: Dover, 1959.

Long, Douglas C. "Particulars and Their Qualities," *Philosophical Quarterly* 18 (1968): 193–206. Reprinted in M. Loux, ed. *Universals and Particulars*. New York: Anchor Books, 1970.

Loux, Michael J., ed. *The Possible and the Actual*. Ithaca, N.Y.: Cornell University Press, 1979.

Loux, Michael J. *Substance and Attribute: A Study in Ontology*. Dordrecht and Boston: Reidel, 1978.

Loux, Michael J. "Comments on 'Individuation and Non-Identity'; A Reply to Héctor-Neri Castañeda," *Crítica* 8 (1975): 105–8.

Loux, Michael J. "Kinds and the Dilemma of Individuation," *The Review of Metaphysics* 26 (1974): 773–84.

Loux, Michael J. "Particulars and Their Individuation," *Universals and Particulars*. Edited by Michael J. Loux. New York: Anchor Books, 1970, pp. 189–204.

Loux, Michael J., ed. *Universals and Particulars; Readings in Ontology*. New York: Anchor Books, 1970.

Lowe, V. "The Concept of the Individual," *Methodos* 5 (1953): 155–74.

Lucca, A. *I rapporti fra l'individuo e l'universo*, 1937.

Lucretius. *De rerum natura* V. Edited by H. A. J. Munro. Cambridge, 1873.

Lukasiewicz, J. "The Principle of Individuation," *Proceedings of the Aristotelian Society*. Suppl. Vol. 27 (1953): 69–82.

Mahnke, Dietrich. "Leibnizens Synthese von Universalmathematik und Individualmetaphysik," *Jahrbuch für Philosophie und phänomenologische Forschung* 7. Reprinted (1962).

McTaggart, John. *The Nature of Existence*. 2 vols. Cambridge: The University Press, 1921–22.

Marcus, Ruth Barcan. "Modalities and Intensional Languages," in *Boston Studies in the Philosophy of Science*. Vol. I. Dordrecht: Reidel, 1963, pp. 77–116.

Martine, Brian John. *Individuals and Individuality*. Albany: State University of New York Press, 1984.

Matthews, G. B. and Cohen, S. M. "The One and the Many," *Review of Metaphysics* 21 (1967): 630–55.

Meiland, J. W. "Do Relations Individuate?" *Philosophical Studies* 17 (1966): 65–69.

Michael, Emily. "Peirce on Individuals," *Transactions of the Charles S. Peirce Society* 12 (1976): 321–29.

Mill, John Stuart. *A System of Logic*. London: Longmans, 1872.

Millas, Jorge. *Idea de la individualidad*, 1943.

Moore, G. E. "Proof of the External World," Hertz Annual Philosophical Lecture. Reprinted in *Philosophical Papers*. London: Allen and Unwin Ltd., 1959.

Moore, G. E. "Are the Characteristics of Particular Things Universal or Particular?" *Proceedings of the Aristotelian Society*. Suppl Vol. 3 (1923): 95–113. Reprinted in *Philosophical Papers*. London: Allen and Unwin, 1959.

Moore, G. E. *The Philosophy of G. E. Moore*. Edited by Paul A. Schilpp. Chicago: Northwestern University Press, 1942.

Moore, G. E. *Principia ethica*. Cambridge: University Press, 1968.

Müller, A. *Das Individualitäts-problem und die Subordination der Teile*, 1930.

Müller-Freienfels, R. *Philosophie der Individualität*, 1921.

Munitz, Milton K., ed. *Identity and Individuation*. New York: New York University Press, 1971.

Nelson, James A. "Abortion and the Causal Theory of Names." State University of New York at Buffalo Unpublished Doctoral Dissertation, 1980.

Nerlich, G. C. "Evidence for Identity," *Australasian Journal of Philosophy* 37 (1959): 201 ff.

Ockham, William of. *Opera Philosophica et theologica,* Edited by G. Gál, et al. St. Bonaventure: Franciscan Institute, 1967-.

Ockham, William of. *Philosophical Writings.* Edited by P. Boehner. London: Nelson, 1957.

O'Connor, D. J. "The Identity of Indiscernibles," *Analysis* 14 (1954): 103–10.

Odegard, D. "Indiscernibles," *Philosophical Quarterly* 14 (1964): 204–13.

Odo of Tournai. *De peccato originali. Libri tres.* Edited by J. P. Migne, in *Patrologiae cursus completus; Series latina.* Vol. 160. Paris, 1880.

Owen, G. E. L. "Inherence," *Phronesis* 10 (1965): 97–105.

Owens, Joseph. *The Doctrine of Being in the Aristotelian Metaphysics.* Toronto: PIMS, 1957.

Pap, Arthur. "Are Individual Concepts Necessary?" *Philosophical Studies* 1 (1950): 17–24.

Pears, D. F. "A Critical Study of P. F. Strawson's *Individuals,*" *Philosophical Quarterly* 11 (1961): 172–85 and 262–77.

Pears, D. F. "The Identity of Indiscernibles," *Mind* 64 (1955): 522–27.

Pears, D. F. "Universals," *Philosophical Quarterly* 1 (1951). Rep. in *Universals and Particulars.* Edited by Michael J. Loux. New York: Doubleday, 1970, pp. 35–49.

Peirce, C. S. *Collected Papers.* Edited by Charles Hartshorne, Paul Weiss, et al. Cambridge, Mass.: Harvard University Press, 1931–58.

Perry, John. *Personal Identity.* Berkeley: University of California Press, 1975.

Perry, Thomas D. *Professional Philosophy: What It Is and Why It Matters.* Dordrecht: Reidel, 1985.

Peter Abailard. See Abailard, Peter.

Peter of Auvergne. *Quodlibet* II, q. 5, and *Quaestiones metaphysicae* L, VIII, in E. Hocedez. "Une Question inedite de Pierre d'Auvergne sur l'individuation," *Revue Neoscholastique de Philosophie* 36 (1934): 355–86.

Picavet, F. *Roscelin philosophe et théologien d'après la légende et d'après l'histoire; sa place dans l'histoire générale et comparée des philosophes médiévales.* Paris: Felix Alcan 1911.

Pichler, Hans. "Zur Lehre von Gattung und Individuum," *Beiträge zur Philosophie des deutsches Idealismus* 1 (1918).

Pitcher, George, ed. *Wittgenstein. The Philosophical Investigations.* New York: Doubleday and Co., 1966.

Plantinga, Alvin. "The Boethian Compromise," *American Philosophical Quarterly* 15 (1978): 129–38.

Plantinga, Alvin. "World and Essence," *Philosophical Review* 79 (1970). Reprinted in M. Loux, ed. *Universals and Particulars.* Notre Dame, Ind.: University of Notre Dame Press, 1976.

Plato. *The Collected Dialogues of Plato, Including the Letters.* Edited by E. Hamilton and H. Cairns. New York: Pantheon Books, 1961.

Plotinus. *Enneads,* in *The Philosophy of Plotinus; Representative Books from the "Enneads."* Edited by J. Katz. New York: Appleton-Century-Crofts, Inc., 1950.

Popper, K. R. "The Principle of Individuation," *Proceedings of the Aristotelian Society* 27 (1953): 97–120.

Porphyry. *Isagoge.* Translated Edward W. Warren. Toronto: Pontifical Institute of Mediaeval Studies, 1975.

Price, H. H. *Thinking and Experience.* London: Hutchinson, 1953.

Putnam, Hilary. "Language and Reality," *Mind, Language and Reality: Collected Papers.* Vol. 2. London: Cambridge University Press, 1975.

Putnam, Hilary. "It Ain't Necessarily So," *Journal of Philosophy* 59 (1962): 658–71.

Quine, W. V. O. *From a Logical Point of View.* Cambridge: Harvard University Press, 1953. 2nd ed. rev., 1961.

Quine, W. V. O. *Word and Object.* Cambridge: The M.I.T. Press, 1960.

Quine, W. V. O. "On What There Is," *Review of Metaphysics* 2 (1948). Reprinted in Charles Landesman, ed. *The Problem of Universals.* New York: Basic Books, 1971, pp. 216–27.

Quinton, A. *The Nature of Things.* London: Routledge and Kegan Paul, 1973.

Raju, P. J. "The Nature of the Individual," *Review of Metaphysics* 17 (1963): 33–58.

Ramsey, F. P. *The Foundations of Mathematics.* London: Routledge and Kegan Paul Ltd. and New York: Humanities Press, Inc., 1950.

Reichenbach, Hans. *Space and Time.* Translated M. Reichenbach and J. Freund. New York: Dover, 1958.

Rescher, Nicholas. *Leibniz: An Introduction to His Philosophy.* Oxford: Blackwell, 1979.

Rescher, Nicholas. "The Identity of Indiscernibles. A Re-Interpretation," *Journal of Philosophy* 52 (1955): 152–55.

Riley, Gresham. "Peirce's Theory of Individuals," *Transactions of the Charles S. Peirce Society* 10 (1974): 135–65.

Robinson, John Mansley. *An Introduction to Early Greek Philosophy.* Boston: Houghton Mifflin Co., 1968.

Robles, José Antonio, ed. *El problema de los universales: El realismo y sus críticos.* Mexico: Universidad Nacional Autónoma de México. 1980.

Romero, Francisco. *Teoría del hombre.* Buenos Aires: Losada, 1952.

Rorty, Amelie O., ed. *The Identities of Persons.* Berkeley, Los Angeles, London: University of California Press, 1976.

Ross, M. A. "A Note on Hume's Principle of Individuation," *Gnosis* 1 (1973): 19–22.

Rossi, Alejandro. "Nombres propios," *Diánoia*. Vol. 3, No. 15 (1969): 180–92.

Russell, Bertrand. *A Critical Exposition of the Philosophy of Leibniz*. London: Allen and Unwin, 1971.

Russell, Bertrand. "The World of Universals," in *The Problems of Philosophy*. Reprinted in M. Loux, ed. *Universals and Particulars*. New York: Doubleday, 1970.

Russell, Bertrand. *The Principles of Mathematics*. New York: Norton, 1964.

Russell, Bertrand and Whitehead, A. N. *Principia mathematica*. Cambridge: University Press Rep., 1962.

Russell, Bertrand. *Logic and Knowledge, Essays 1901-1950*. Edited by R. C. Marsh. London: Allen and Unwin, 1956.

Russell, Bertrand. "Reply to My Critics," in P. A. Schilpp, ed. *The Philosophy of Bertrand Russell*. New York: Tudor Publishing Co., 1951.

Russell, Bertrand. *Human Knowledge: Its Scope and Limits*. New York: Simon and Schuster, 1948.

Russell, Bertrand. *An Inquiry into Meaning and Truth*. London: Allen and Unwin, 1940, Chap. 6.

Russell, Bertrand. *The Problems of Philosophy*. Oxford: Clarendon Press, 1912.

Salisbury, John of. See John of Salisbury.

Sanford, D. "Locke, Leibniz and Wiggins on Being in the Same Place at the Same Time," *Philosophical Review* 79 (1970): 75–82.

Savery, B. "Identity and Difference," *Philosophical Review* 51 (1942): 205–12.

Saw, R. L. "Our Knowledge of Individuals," *Proceedings of the Aristotelian Society* 52 (1951–52): 167–88.

Scott, Dana. "Advice on Modal Logic," in K. Lambert, ed. *Philosophical Problems in Logic*. Dordrecht: Reidel, 1970.

Scotus, John Duns. See John Duns Scotus.

Scotus Eriugena, John. See John Scotus Eriugena.

Searle, John R. *Intentionality: An Essay in the Philosophy of Mind.* Cambridge: Cambridge University Press, 1984.

Searle, John R. "Referential and Attributive," in *Expression and Meaning.* Cambridge, England: Cambridge University Press, 1979, pp. 137–61.

Searle, John R. *Speech Acts: An Essay in the Philosophy of Language.* Cambridge, England: Cambridge University Press, 1969.

Searle, J. "Proper Names and Descriptions," in *The Encyclopedia of Philosophy.* Vol. 6. London: Macmillan, 1967.

Searle, John R. "Proper Names," *Mind* 67 (1958): 166–73.

Sellars, Wilfrid. "Grammar and Existence: A Preface to Ontology," in Charles Landesman, ed. *The Problem of Universals.* New York and London: Basic Books, 1971, pp. 261–92.

Sellars, Wilfrid. *Philosophical Perspectives.* Springfield, Ill.: Charles C. Thomas, 1967.

Sellars, Wilfrid. *Science and Metaphysics.* London: Routledge and Kegan Paul, 1967.

Sellars, Wilfrid. *Science, Perception and Reality.* London: Routledge and Kegan Paul, 1963.

Sellars, Wilfrid. "Particulars," *Philosophy and Phenomenological Research* 13 (1952): 184–99.

Sellars, Wilfrid. "On the Logic of Complex Particulars," *Mind* 58 (1949): 306–38.

Sharvy, Richard. "Why a Class Can't Change Its Members," *Nous* 2 (1968): 303–14.

Shorter, J. M. "On Coinciding in Space and Time," *Philosophy* 52 (1977): 399–408.

Simondon, Gilbert. *L'individu et sa genère physico-biologique,* 1964.

Smith, Barry, ed. *Parts and Moments: Studies in Logic and Formal Ontology.* Munich: Philosophia Verlag, 1982.

Spinoza, Baruch. *Ethics,* in *Spinoza's "Ethics" and "On the Correction of the Understanding."* Translated Andrew Boyle. London and New York: Everyman's Library, 1963.

Spinoza, Baruch. *Epistolae*. Translated by A. Wolf. London, 1928.

Sprigge, Timothy L. S. *Facts, Words and Beliefs*. London: Routledge and Kegan Paul, 1970.

Stout, G. F. "The Nature of Universals and Propositions," *Proceedings of the British Academy* 10 (1921). Reprinted in *Studies in Philosophy and Psychology*. London: Macmillan, 1930, pp. 384–403, and in Charles Landesman, ed. *The Problem of Universals*. New York and London: Basic Books, 1971, pp. 153–66.

Stout, G. F. "Things, Predicates and Relations," *Australasian Journal of Psychology and Philosophy* 18 (1940): 117–30.

Stout, G. F. "Are the Characteristics of Particular Things Universal or Particular?" *Proceedings of the Aristotelian Society*. Suppl. Vol. 3 (1923): 114–22.

Stove, D. C. "Two Problems about Individuality," *Australasian Journal of Psychology and Philosophy* 23 (1955): 183–88.

Strawson, P. F. "On Particular and General," *Proceedings of the Aristotelian Society* 54 (1953-54): 233–61. Reprinted in Charles Landesman, ed. *The Problem of Universals*. New York and London: Basic Books, 1971, pp. 131–52; also in *Universals and Particulars*. Edited by M. J. Loux. Notre Dame, Ind.: University of Notre Dame Press, 1976, pp. 59–86.

Strawson, P. F. "Singular Terms and Predication," *Journal of Philosophy* 58 (1961): 393–412.

Strawson, P. F. *Individuals*. London: Methuen and Co., 1959.

Strawson, P. F. "Logical Subjects and Physical Objects," *Philosophy and Phenomenological Research* 17 (1957): 441–57 and 473–77.

Strawson, P. F. "Singular Terms, Ontology and Identity," *Mind* 65 (1956): 433–54.

Strawson, P. F. "On Referring," *Mind* 59 (1950): 320–44.

Suárez, Francisco. "Metaphysical Disputation V: Individual Unity and Its Principle." Trans. Jorge J. E. Gracia, in *Suárez on Individuation*. Milwaukee: Marquette University Press, 1982.

Suárez, Francisco. *On the Various Kinds of Distinctions (Disputationes Metaphysicae, Disputatio VII, De variis distinctionum generibus)*. Translated

Cyril Vollert. Milwaukee: Marquette University Press, 1947. Reprinted, 1976.

Suárez, Francisco. *On Formal and Universal Unity (De unitate formali et universali)*. Trans. J. F. Ross. Milwaukee: Marquette University Press, 1964.

Suárez, Francisco, *Disputationes metaphysicae*, in *Opera omnia*. Vols. 25 and 26. Edited by C. Berton. Paris: Vivès, 1861.

Tertullian. *De monogamia*. Vol. 76 of *Corpus scriptorum ecclesiasticorum latinorum*. Vienna: Tempsky, 1957.

Thierry of Chartres. *Commentaries on Boethius*. Edited by N. M. Häring. Toronto: Pontifical Institute of Mediaeval Studies, 1971.

Thomas Aquinas. See Aquinas, Thomas.

Thompson, M. H. "On the Distinction Between Thing and Property." *The Return to Reason*. Edited by J. D. Wild. Chicago: Henry Regnery, 1953.

Van Cleve, James. "Three Versions of the Bundle Theory," *Philosophical Studies* 47 (1985): 95–107.

Vaught, C. G. "The Identity of Indiscernibles and the Concept of Substance," *Southern Journal of Philosophy* 6 (1968): 152–58.

Veatch, Henry B. "Essentialism and the Problem of Individuation," *Proceedings of the American Catholic Philosophical Association* 47 (1974): 64–73.

Veatch, Henry B. *Realism and Nominalism Revisited*. Milwaukee: Marquette University Press, 1954.

Veatch, Henry B. *Intentional Logic*. New Haven: Yale University Press, 1952.

Volkelt, Johannes. *Das Problem der Individualität*, 1928.

Webb, C. W. "The Antinomy of Individuals," *Journal of Philosophy* 55 (1958): 735–39.

Weiss, Paul. *Modes of Being*. Carbondale: Southern Illinois University Press, 1958.

Whiting, Jennifer E. "Form and Individuation in Aristotle," *History of Philosophy Quarterly* 3 (1986), 359-77.

Wiggins, David. "On Singling out an Object Determinately," in Philip Pettit and John McDowell, eds. *Subject, Thought and Context*. Oxford: Clarendon Press, 1986.

Wiggins, David. *Sameness and Substance*. Oxford: Blackwell, 1980.

Wiggins, David. "The Individuation of Things and Places," in Michael J. Loux, ed. *Universals and Particulars*. New York: Anchor Books, 1970, pp. 307–35.

Wiggins, David. *Identity of Spatio-Temporal Continuity*. London: Blackwell, 1967.

Wiggins, David. "Identity Statements," *Analytical Philosophy*. Edited by R. J. Butler. Oxford: Blackwell, 1965.

William of Ockham. See Ockham, William of.

Williams, B. A. O. "Mr. Strawson on Individuals," *Philosophy* 36 (1961): 309–32.

Williams, B. A. O. "Bodily Continuity and Personal Identity," *Analysis* 21 (1960): 43 ff.

Williams, B. A. O. "Personal Identity and Individuation," *Proceedings of the Aristotelian Society*, New Series 57 (1956–57): 229–52.

Williams. D. C. *Principles of Empirical Realism*. Springfield, Ill.: Charles Thomas, 1966.

Williams, D. C. "The Elements of Being," *Review of Metaphysics* 7 (1953): 3–18 and 171–92.

Wilson, N. L. "Substances without Substrata," *Review of Metaphysics* 12 (1959): 521–39.

Wilson, N. L. "Space, Time, and Individuals," *Journal of Philosophy* 52 (1955): 589–98.

Wilson, N. L. "The Identity of Indiscernibles and the Symmetrical Universe," *Mind* 62 (1953): 506–11.

Wittgenstein, Ludwig. *Philosophical Investigations.* Translated by G. E. M. Anscombe. New York: Macmillan, 1965.

Wittgenstein, Ludwig. *Tractatus Logico-Philosophicus.* Translated by D. F. Pears and B. F. McGuiness. London: Routledge and Kegan Paul, 1961.

Wippel, John F. *The Metaphysical Thought of Godfrey of Fontaines.* Washington, D.C.: Catholic University of America Press, 1981.

Wippel, John F. "Godfrey of Fontaines, Peter of Auvergne, John Baconthorpe, and the Principle of Individuation," in *Essays Honoring Allan B. Wolter.* Edited by William A. Frank and Girard J. Etzkorn. St. Bonaventure: The Franciscan Institute, 1985, pp. 309–49.

Wolter, A. B. "The Realism of Scotus," *Journal of Philosophy* 59 (1962): 725–36.

Wolterstorff, Nicholas. *On Universals.* Chicago: University Press, 1970.

Wolterstorff, Nicholas. "Qualities," *Philosophical Review* 69 (1960). Reprinted in M. Loux, ed. *Universals and Particulars.* Garden City, N.Y.: Doubleday and Co., 1970.

Woods, M. J. "Identity and Individuation," *Analytical Philosophy.* Edited by R. J. Butler. Oxford: Blackwell, 1965.

Woods, M. J. "The Individuation of Things and Places," *Proceedings of the Aristotelian Society.* Suppl. Vol. 38 (1963): 203–16.

Ziff, P. *Semantic Analysis.* Ithaca: Cornell University Press, 1960.

Zink, S. "The Meaning of Proper Names," *Mind* 71 (1963): 401–99.

Zubiri, Xavier. *Sobre la esencia.* 1962. English translation by A. Robert Caponigri. *On Essence.* Washington, D.C.: Catholic University of America Press, 1968.

Index of Authors

307

Index of Subjects